The CHALLENGE of the CULTS

and New Religions

The
CHALLENGE
of the
CULTS
and New Religions

The **Essential** Guide to Their History, Their Doctrine, and Our Response

Ron Rhodes

Foreword by Lee Strobel
Author of *The Case for Christ*

GRAND RAPIDS, MICHIGAN 49530

ZONDERVAN™

The Challenge of the Cults and New Religions
Copyright © 2001 by Ron Rhodes

Requests for information should be addressed to:

Zondervan, *Grand Rapids, Michigan 49530*

Library of Congress Cataloging-in-Publication Data

Rhodes, Ron.
    The challenge of the cults and new religions : the essential guide to their history, their doctrine, and our response / Ron Rhodes.
        p. cm.
    Includes bibliographical references and index.
    ISBN 0-310-23217-1
    1. Apologetics. 2. Cults. I. Title.
BT1240.R48 2001
239'.9—dc21   2001026583

This edition printed on acid-free paper.

Interior design by Todd Sprague

Printed in the United States of America

---

07 08 /❖ DC/ 10 9 8 7 6

To the students and faculty of
Southern Evangelical Seminary
Charlotte, North Carolina

CONTENTS

FOREWORD

On January 20, 1980, God cracked my wall of atheism. After hearing the message of Jesus Christ explained in a way I could understand, I began to ask a question that once had been unthinkable to me: Could Jesus really be the Son of God? I decided to use my legal training and journalism experience to investigate whether there was any credibility to Christianity—or any other world religion, for that matter.

At first the process was pretty easy. The more I would look at various other faith systems, the more I would see their internal contradictions and lack of evidentiary support. One by one their credibility collapsed under the weight of scrutiny.

However, as I narrowed down my investigation to the Christian faith, matters became increasingly murky.

While the contrast between Christianity and other world religions was stark and clear-cut—for instance, there was no confusing the Koran and the Bible—investigating Christianity was maddeningly confusing. Is Mormonism just another species of Christianity? What about Oneness Pentecostalism? How about the Jehovah's Witnesses or Unitarian Universalism? Is Freemasonry Christian-based? And what should I think of the claim of Reverend Moon of the Unification Church that he had been chosen to complete Jesus' mission in the world?

It soon became clear that many groups claim they fit under the Christian umbrella. But do they really? As I delved into Mormonism, for example, I quickly encountered beliefs that run contrary to historic Christian theology. Not only that, but archaeology fails to corroborate the Book of Mormon in the same way that it substantiates the Bible. It took me a lot of time and effort to evaluate each one of these pseudo-Christian faith systems one by one.

Ultimately, I found that Christianity—and Christianity alone—withstood my scrutiny. Moreover, I discovered there are many counterfeit gospels that claim to be consistent with Christianity when they really aren't.

I wish I had had Ron Rhodes's excellent new book *The Challenge of Cults and New Religions* back then. If you would like to separate the truth of Christianity from the fiction of cults and new religions, you will find this book an invaluable resource. Ron has used his impressive theological skill to carefully analyze a dozen different faith systems, providing a concise and well-documented assessment of how they differ from Christianity. He focuses on the most important issues so readers don't get bogged down in extraneous details. And his tone is authoritative without being derogatory or inflammatory, which is consistent with the Bible's admonition to defend the truth "with gentleness and respect" (1 Peter 3:15).

I heartily recommend this balanced and helpful volume to all sincere seekers and Christians who are determined to "test everything" so that they can "hold on to the good," as 1 Thessalonians 5:21 encourages us to do.

Lee Strobel
Author, *The Case for Christ* and
The Case for Faith

ACKNOWLEDGMENTS

I want to express deep appreciation for my wife, Kerri, and our two children, David and Kylie, for their sacrificial commitment to my work. As well, I want to give thanks in a general way to all the cult and world religion specialists, apologists, theologians, and researchers I have had the pleasure of interacting with over the years. This interaction has sharpened my thinking considerably in many areas related to cultic studies. I also want to give thanks to the thousands of individuals who have contacted me for information on cults and cult apologetics over the past decade. This continued, heavy demand for reliable information has caused me to stay current on the ever-emerging "kingdom of the cults." Finally, Kurt Goedelman and Jack Roper deserve special mention for the wonderful photographs they have made available for this book.

INTRODUCTION

Lighting a Candle

Every American is guaranteed the free exercise of religion. This is one of the things that makes America so great. The First Amendment, ratified in 1791, affirmed that "Congress shall make no law respecting an establishment of religion or prohibiting the free exercise thereof."[1]

In keeping with this, James Madison, who became the fourth president of the United States (1809–17), wrote, "The religion . . . of every man must be left to the conviction and conscience of every man. . . . We maintain, therefore, that in matters of religion no man's right is [to be] abridged by the institution of civil society."[2] Such religious freedom is cherished by every American.

Yet to say that every man and woman is free to choose his or her religion is not the same as saying that every religion is *equally true* or *equally healthy* or *equally beneficial* for people. Nor is it the same as saying that every religion yields *equal eternal results*—that is, living eternally with the one true God in heaven. One of my life passions is to help educate people on cults and new religious movements so they can use their cherished religious freedom to *choose rightly* and avoid belief systems that will damage them—temporally *or* eternally.

An obvious natural consequence of the First Amendment is that there never has been, nor will there ever be, a Theological Federal Communications Commission, or a Spiritual Pure Food and Drug Administration.[3] Today, in the midst of such freedom, America has become a vast melting pot of religious ideas, including *cultic* ideas, and many Americans are drinking richly from this pot. The religious scene has changed considerably since the time of America's founding fathers.

Prior to 1850, cultists were practically unheard of in America. Today there are well over 20 million Americans involved in the cults and the occult. Some research suggests that among the cults and religious movements founded in the last 150 years, membership has escalated by up to 3,000 percent.[4] A perusal of the contemporary religious scene makes it clear that the cults have truly taken advantage of the great American heritage of freedom of speech and religion to spread their unorthodox and, in some cases, *dangerous* doctrines.

Especially over the past three decades, it seems that the winds of change have swept across America's religious landscape with hurricane force, and therefore the landscape has been radically altered. If we were to travel across America today, I think we would witness, at the very least, some of the following on this landscape:

- Rapidly eroding spiritual foundations, with a huge percentage of the public rejecting any concept of absolute truth
- A majority of people holding to moral relativism
- A Christianity that is only one choice in a vast and ever-growing smorgasbord of religious options
- A significant number of impotent and lifeless Christian churches that have produced indifference, lack of commitment, spiritual dryness, doctrinal immaturity, and bib-

lical illiteracy among members, thus rendering them open to seeking out other religious options
- A deluge of cultic and occultic groups vying for the American mainstream
- An incredible increase in Eastern religions
- A cultic *and* occultic penetration of America's businesses, health facilities, and public schools via the New Age movement
- A pervasive disillusionment and lack of direction among many of America's youth, rendering them vulnerable to cultic leaders who promise black-and-white answers to today's toughest dilemmas
- A shifted family structure, with many children growing up in single-parent households—many of which provide little or no religious foundation for the children

To be sure, not all is bleak. Many great churches are seeking to equip members to reach out to those oppressed in cultic bondage. Some outstanding seminaries are beginning to take the cultic challenge seriously.[5] For all this I am thankful. Nevertheless, at present the harvest is plentiful and the workers seem so very few.

This book is written with a view to training those who seek to understand and perhaps dialogue with some of the people in these cults and new religious movements. I want to say right up front that this book is not written merely to "curse the darkness"; rather, it seeks to light a candle in the midst of the darkness. In other words, the book not only points to the *problem* of the cults and new religious movements, but also seeks to provide helpful information for theologically interacting with them with a view to motivating them to use their religious freedom to *choose to leave* the cult and transfer allegiance to the one true God of whom Scripture speaks (John 17:3). Hence, there is an apologetic dimension to the book. Let us not forget that Jesus has called each of us as Christians to be salt and light in our world (Matt. 5:13–16).

Of course, the very process of being salt and light in a pluralistic culture is a risky business today. After all, we live in an age of tolerance. We risk being accused of *intolerance* if we should say anything negative about someone else's religious beliefs. The apostle Paul once asked, "Have I now become your enemy by telling you the truth?" (Gal. 4:16). Likewise, many within cultic movements ask, "Why are you attacking us?" when Christians share the true gospel with them. However, the motive never has been and never will be to attack. The motive is nothing less than *love*.

It is because Christians *care about others* that they "tell the truth," as the apostle Paul did. An "enemy" would withhold truth that could save another person. To have in one's possession vital information that another needs to know in order to be saved and then to withhold it is not something any loving person would do. To "tolerate" something that can severely damage another person, whether in this life or in eternity, is evil, plain and simple.

The damage one can suffer in a cult has been well documented in various news publications over the past few decades. I am sure that many reading this book can recall news reports about Jehovah's Witnesses who have tragically and meaninglessly died as a result of seeking to be faithful to the Watchtower Society's strict prohibition against receiving blood transfusions. Likewise, little children have died painful deaths for the reason that medical treatment was avoided because their parents were Christian Scientists who believe sin, sickness, and death are mere illusions. There are little children who have been sexually abused within the Children of God (now known as "The Family"), a cult that is well known for using "flirty fishing" (sexual enticement involving prostitution) to lure people into their circle.

And who can forget the hundreds of people who died in the Jonestown tragedy? One father and mother who sought to get their five-year-old son, John Victor, out of Jonestown can tell you firsthand how damaging cults can be. In a letter to *Newsweek* magazine, the father lamented,

> When I tried to get him out, Jones refused. Grace and I spent months filing lawsuits and traveling to Guyana to free our boy. In November 1978, we accompanied Rep. Leo Ryan on his mission to Guyana to investigate alleged human-rights abuses. When Jones heard we were with Ryan, he specifically forbade us to travel to the compound. That's why I'm alive today. While waiting in our hotel, we heard that Ryan and his four companions had been killed on the Jonestown airstrip. We realized immediately there would be a collective suicide. We knew our son, along with the other 918 people in the compound,

would die. We couldn't do a d**n thing. It was the most horrible night of my life.[6]

These people at Jonestown paid the ultimate price: their lives. Countless others suffer spiritual, emotional, and psychological damage. Dr. Paul Martin, the director of the Wellspring Retreat and Resource Center (that provides counseling and help for ex-cultists), has heard countless tales of woe related by thousands of former cult members.[7] Martin tells us that "the most conservative estimates based on a number of surveys are that 185,000 Americans alone join a destructive cult each year. Of those 185,000 at least 25% will suffer enduring irreversible harm that will affect their ability to function adequately in the emotional, social, family, and occupational domains."[8]

As horrible as these physical and emotional consequences are, an even worse result of the cults is that every single day people affiliated with them are dying without the true gospel. They are going into eternity believing in a *counterfeit Jesus* who preaches a *counterfeit gospel*, and hence they are in possession of a *counterfeit salvation* (which is no salvation at all). The eternal consequences of the cult problem are ultimately far worse than the temporal ones. And yet the clarion call today is "be tolerant." Certainly if tolerance means "be kind, considerate, and loving to people," then Christians can and should agree without hesitation. But if tolerance means "be silent in the midst of the temporal and eternal carnage," that is something that *loving* Christians cannot go along with.

What all this means on a practical level is that Christians involved in cult apologetics must have a hardy measure of holy boldness in being willing to stand up to accusations of intolerance and, without flinching, *tell the truth*. That is Christ's mandate, and we are called to obey it (Matt. 28:19–20; Jude 3). Those who truly love their fellow human beings will voluntarily stand against the cold, harsh winds of political correctness and be the truth-telling witnesses that Christ calls them to be.

Never forget that while there will be accusations of intolerance, the truth of the matter is that more often than not, *those making the accusations are the truly intolerant ones in our midst*. They claim to be tolerant of the beliefs of all people but are unbendingly *intolerant* of Christians who love Jesus. As one thinker recently put it, "The fundamentalism of tolerance is just as dogmatic as any other fundamentalism, only it is deceptive in its profession of tolerance.... It may actually prove to be less tolerant, since it does not seem to recognize the right of others to reject its relativistic view."[9]

CHARTING OUR COURSE

Let me offer some brief notes regarding my guiding perspectives in this book. First, no single-volume book can provide *comprehensive* information on *every* cult. (There are thousands of cults in the world.) Hence I have chosen to focus my entire attention on 12 of the most significant cults and new religious movements we are likely to encounter in the world today. (Training in the major cults will more than adequately equip us to deal with the lesser ones.)

Second, it has been my experience in more than 15 years of cult studies that most people are interested in three primary issues regarding the cults: *history, doctrine,* and *apologetic response.* Therefore, this book will focus chiefly on these issues in regard to each respective cult or religious movement. Even then, primary attention will be devoted to the *major* currents in history, doctrine, and apologetic response. In other words, I will not bury the reader in unnecessary detail or secondary issues. I will focus primarily on the "big picture." (Those interested in minutiae can consult the bibliography.)

Third, it is not my goal to continually draw attention to the more sensational factors of each respective cult, thereby arousing the emotions of the reader against them. My desire is not to make fun of adherents of cultic belief systems, for I have consistently found that they are typically *sincere though misled.* So I focus primarily on the *facts* of history, doctrine, and apologetic response.

Fourth, I have sought in every chapter to use authoritative resources produced by the cult or new religious movement that are most representative of their beliefs. This provides us with an accurate grasp of their beliefs.

Finally, this book stresses the authority of Scripture—the Bible—as a "barometer of truth" for measuring doctrinal claims. I say this with caution, for I recognize that many cults also claim to use the Bible as their authority. Throughout the book I will demonstrate how such cults engage in "Scripture twisting" to support their unique theological positions.

DEFINING CULTS

It is for good reason that every book in the New Testament except Philemon has something to say about false teachers, false prophets, false gospels, or heresies. Jesus Himself sternly warned His followers to watch out for false prophets (Matt. 7:15–23) and false Christs (Matt. 24:5). The apostle Paul warned of a different Jesus, a different spirit (2 Cor. 11:4), false apostles (2 Cor. 11:13–15), and those who preach "another gospel" (Gal. 1:8; cf. 2 Cor. 11:4). First John 4:1 understandably urges believers to "test the spirits." The concern is obvious: *Counterfeit prophets who speak of a counterfeit Christ who preaches a counterfeit gospel can yield only a counterfeit salvation.* Because there are eternal consequences to false teachings, Scripture bears numerous warnings.

With that in mind, we can see that a study of the various cults in our midst should be a high priority for us all. But before we can focus attention on specific cults, we must be clear on what a "cult" is. This is a seemingly formidable task. Talk to 10 different cult "experts" and you may well be given 10 different definitions. Sociologists have their opinions (authoritarianism and exclusivism play big roles in their thinking), psychologists have their opinions (mind-control is a big issue with them), and theologians have their opinions (heretical doctrines are the main issue of concern). Still others, like journalists and reporters, often focus on the more sensational elements of the cults, such as mass suicides and bizarre rituals and practices.

Some people today say we shouldn't even use the term *cult* because it carries such negative connotations. Instead, they prefer terms like "new religions" or "alternative religions."[1] While I understand this viewpoint, I think it is legitimate to use the term *cult*. I want to emphasize, though, that when I use the term in this book I do not intend it as a pejorative, inflammatory, or injurious word.[2] As it will become clear below, I use the term simply as a means of categorizing certain religious or semi-religious groups in the world.

Our English word *cult* comes from the Latin word *cultus*, which means "worship."[3] Linguistically a cultic action is one that involves external rites and ceremonies with a worshipful attitude on the part of the devotee. A "cult" in this sense refers to a system of worship distinguishable from others.[4] Of course, the modern usage of the word is much more specific than this linguistic definition.

In modern times, the term *cult* has primarily been defined from both sociological and theological perspectives.[5] Those who opt for the sociological definition say that a cult is a religious or semi-religious sect or group whose members are controlled or dominated almost entirely by a single individual or organization. This definition generally includes (but is not limited to) the authoritarian, manipulative, and sometimes communal features of cults.[6] Cults that fall into this category include the Hare Krishnas, the Children of God (The Family), and the Unification Church.

While I believe we gain some very important insights on the cultic mentality from sociology (which I will discuss later in the chapter), my long experience in dealing with cultists has convinced me that it is more accurate to define a cult from a theological perspective. As one cult observer put it, "Sociological, psychological, and journalistic observations sometimes show us the human dynamics that frequently result from a cult belief system, but they are not sufficient Christian foundations for determining a group's status *as* a cult."[7] Therefore, I believe the best policy is to define a cult theologically, but we can then gain some key insights into the cultic mentality from sociology and psychology.

The problem is how to word a theological definition of a cult. What specific components should make up this definition? Different cult experts have offered different opinions.

Gordon Lewis, in his book *Confronting the Cults*, suggests that the term *cult* "designates a religious group which claims authorization by Christ and the Bible, but neglects or distorts the gospel— the central message of the Savior and the Scripture."[8] James Sire, author of *Scripture Twisting*, suggests that a cult is "any religious movement that is organizationally distinct and has doctrines and/or practices that contradict those of the Scriptures as interpreted by traditional Christianity as represented by the major Catholic and Protestant denominations, and as expressed in such statements as the Apostles' Creed."[9]

My late colleague Walter Martin defined a cult this way:

> By "cult," we mean a group, religious in nature, which surrounds a leader or a group of teachings which either denies or misinterprets essential biblical doctrine. Most cults have a single leader, or a succession of leaders, who claim to represent God's voice on earth and who claim authority greater than that of the Bible. The cultic teaching claims to be in harmony with the Bible but denies one or more of the cardinal doctrines presented therein.[10]

Orville Swenson, in his book *The Perilous Path of Cultism*, suggests that a cult is "a religious group whose doctrines involve a distortion of biblical truth; whose dedication and subservience to their domineering leaders is frequently excessive and blind; and whose attitudes, aims, practices, and teachings are divisive, creating an exclusive body of deviates from historic biblical Christianity."[11]

While all these definitions are helpful and are also accurate to a degree, I think a key point they fail to include is that cults always derive from a "parent" or "host" religion. As Alan Gomes put it, "cults grow out of and deviate from a previously established religion."[12] Seen in this light, a cult *of Christianity*, according to Gomes, would be "a group of people, which claiming to be Christian, embraces a particular doctrinal system taught by an individual leader, group of leaders, or organization, which [system] denies (either explicitly or implicitly) one or more of the central doctrines of the Christian faith as taught in the sixty-six books of the Bible."[13] Likewise, a cult *of Islam* would be, for example, the Nation of Islam, and a cult *of Hinduism* would be the Hare Krishnas. The Nation of Islam and the Hare Krishnas both derive from parent or host religions, yet both deviate from the doctrinal beliefs of these hosts. Hence they are "cults."

Gomes's definition is accurate, I believe, because it rightly recognizes that

1. Not every cult is a cult related to Christianity
2. Cults typically deviate from a host religion (whether Christianity, Islam, Hinduism, or some other religion)
3. Such cults can be headed by *individual leaders* (as is the case with the Unification Church, led by Reverend Moon) or by *an organization* (as is the case with the Jehovah's Witnesses, led by the Watchtower Society's Governing Body)
4. The point of deviation involves essential doctrines (for example, the deity of Christ) as opposed to mere peripheral doctrines (for example, the mode of baptism or style of church government)
5. Such deviations can be *explicit* (such as the Jehovah's Witnesses' flat denial of the Trinity) or *implicit* (for example, Mormons believe in the "heavenly Father" but redefine Him to be an exalted man)[14]

If the above definition of a cult is correct, then we must also be clear concerning what constitutes the "major" or "essential" doctrines of Christianity. I believe there are five basic doctrines that are particularly pertinent for cultic studies:

1. *God*—including the biblical facts that there is *one* God who is *triune* in nature and is infinite and eternal
2. *Jesus Christ*—including the biblical facts that He is the second person of the Trinity and is therefore eternal God,

was virgin born, died for humanity's sins, and was physically resurrected from the dead

3. *Mankind*—including the biblical facts that man was created in God's image, is forever distinct from God, is morally responsible to God, and is destined to live forever with God in heaven or to suffer eternally in hell, depending on whether he has been saved

4. *Sin and salvation*—including the biblical facts that all people are born into the world in a state of sin, that people can do nothing to merit their own salvation or earn favor with God, and that salvation is by grace alone through faith alone, based on the atonement wrought by Christ

5. *Scripture*—including the biblical facts that both the Old and New Testaments are inspired by God, are inerrant, and are therefore authoritative

A cult of Christianity, then, is a group that claims to be Christian but in fact is not Christian because it explicitly or implicitly denies one or more of these central doctrines of the historic Christian faith.[15]

WARNINGS FROM SCRIPTURE		
Passage	**Warning**	**Illustration**
Matthew 7:15–23	False Prophets	Joseph Smith of the Mormon church
Matthew 24:5	False Christs	Reverend Moon of the Unification Church
Galatians 1:8	False Gospels	The works gospel of the Jehovah's Witnesses
Exodus 20:3	False Gods	New Age pantheism

DOCTRINAL CHARACTERISTICS OF CULTS

Because the largest and most influential major cults we encounter are cults of Christianity, it is important to understand some of the primary doctrinal characteristics of cults, some obviously being more important than others. Note that these characteristics are quite common, even though not every cult manifests every characteristic or does so to the same degree.[16] I will touch on two or three representative cults that illustrate each characteristic.

New Revelation from God

Many cult leaders claim to have a direct pipeline to God. Mormon leader Brigham Young, for example, claimed, "I have had many revelations; I have seen and heard for myself; and know these things are true, and nobody on earth can disprove them."[17] Reverend Moon of the Unification Church claimed to have received a revelation from Christ on Easter morning in 1936. Baha'is claim that the latest and greatest revelation from God has come through the prophet Baha'u'llah. Christian Scientists believe Mary Baker Eddy received revelations that are necessary to understand previous revelations in the Bible.

It is interesting that the teachings of cults often change and that the groups need new "revelations" to justify such changes. Mormons once excluded African Americans from the priesthood. When social pressure was exerted on the Mormon church because of this racist practice, the Mormon president received a "new revelation" reversing the previous decree.

New revelations are certainly common within the New Age movement. New Age channelers claim to receive revelations from Ascended Masters. New Age psychics claim to be able to read the Akashic Record (an alleged cosmic energy field surrounding the earth that records all historic events). New Age astrologers derive their "revelations" from planetary alignments. Other New Agers engage in "automatic writing," wherein a person writes down information (including whole books) under the control of a spirit entity. (An example of this is *A Course in Miracles*, penned by Jewish psychologist Helen Schucman, who says a spirit named "Jesus" was the actual source of her words.)

In cults, greater credence is generally given to new revelations than past revelations (such as those found in the Bible). If there is ever a conflict between the new revelation and past revelations, the new revelation is always viewed as being authoritative.

Denial of the Sole Authority of the Bible

In keeping with the above, many cults deny the sole authority of the Bible. Christian Scientists, for example, elevate Mary Baker Eddy's book *Science and Health with Key to the Scriptures* to supreme authority. The Mormons say there are translational errors in the Bible and contend that *The Book of Mormon, Doctrine and*

Covenants, and *The Pearl of Great Price* are more reliable than the Bible. New Agers place faith in such "holy books" as *The Aquarian Gospel of Jesus the Christ* and *A Course in Miracles*. Members of the Unification Church elevate Reverend Moon's *Divine Principle* to supreme authority. Scientologists believe the writings of L. Ron Hubbard are "Scripture." The Jehovah's Witnesses' *Studies in the Scriptures* goes so far as to claim:

> If anyone lays the *Scripture Studies* aside, even after he has used them, after he has become familiar with them, after he has read them for 10 years—if he then lays them aside and ignores them and goes to the Bible alone, though he has understood his Bible for 10 years, our experience shows that within two years he goes into darkness. On the other hand, if he had merely read the *Scripture Studies* with their references, and had not read a page of the Bible, as such, he would be in the light at the end of the two years, because he would have the light of the Scriptures.[18]

Cult expert Anthony Hoekema has cogently pointed out that when cults raise their own books or sets of books to the level of Scripture, "God is no longer allowed to speak as He does in the Bible; He may now speak only as the sect deems proper. Thus the Word of God is brought under the yoke of man."[19] This is certainly the case with the Mormons, Jehovah's Witnesses, Christian Scientists, and some of the other cults discussed in this book.

Denial of the Trinity

Many cults deny the doctrine of the Trinity. The Jehovah's Witnesses say it is a doctrine rooted in paganism and inspired by the Devil. They point out that the word *Trinity* is not found in the Bible, and they believe that although the Father is God Almighty, Jesus is just a lesser god. Likewise, The Way International says the "false doctrine of the Trinity" is rooted in ancient pagan religions. The Mormons speak of the "Trinity," but they define it in terms of Tritheism (belief in three separate gods). The Unitarian Universalists quite obviously deny the doctrine of the Trinity (they are *Unitarians*), using reason to point out how illogical the doctrine is. The Baha'is argue against the Trinity and suggest that Christian leaders do not rightly understand their own Scriptures.

Oneness Pentecostals also deny the Trinity, but in a different way. Most cults deny the Trinity primarily by first denying the deity of Christ. Oneness Pentecostals, by contrast, argue for the *full* deity of Jesus Christ, yet argue that Jesus Himself *is* the "Father," "Son," and "Holy Spirit" (viewed as different modes of manifestation of the one true God, who is Jesus). Like some other cults, Oneness Pentecostals say the Trinity doctrine is rooted in ancient paganism.

Denial of the Full Deity of Christ

Another common mark of the cults is that they deny the full deity of Jesus Christ. The Jehovah's Witnesses hold that Jesus was created by the Father billions of years ago as the archangel Michael and is hence a lesser god than the Father, who is "God Almighty." The Mormons argue that Jesus was born as the first and greatest spirit child of the Heavenly Father and Heavenly Mother and was the spirit-brother of Lucifer. He attained deity during the so-called preexistence, of which I will say more later. The Baha'is say Jesus was just one of many prophets of God and is lesser than the most recent prophet Baha'u'llah. Unitarian Universalists deny that Jesus is God and argue that he was basically a good moral teacher. The Jesus of the Masonic Lodge is one of many ways to God. The Jesus of the spiritists is just an advanced medium. The Jesus of psychic Edgar Cayce is a being who in his first incarnation was Adam and in his thirtieth reincarnation became "the Christ" (the sinner and the Savior are found in the same person). Oneness Pentecostals hold that Jesus alone is the Father, Son, and Holy Spirit. The Jesus of the UFO (New Age) cults is said to be half human and half alien, thereby accounting for his seemingly supernatural powers. Cultists have come up with many strange ideas about Jesus, as we will see.

Devaluation of the Work of Christ

Cultists not only deny the full deity of Christ, but also invariably devalue and redefine His salvific work on the cross. The Mormons, for example, say the work of Christ on the cross provided for the ultimate resurrection of all people but did not provide individual salvation from sin's guilt and condemnation. Mormon leader Brigham Young taught that some sins are so serious that the sinner must shed his own blood for atonement.

Jehovah's Witnesses say that Jesus, as a mere man (not an incarnation of God), died at the stake. The human life Jesus laid down in sacrifice was exactly equal to the human life Adam fell with. If Jesus had been God-incarnate, the "ransom payment" would have been way too much. Jesus' sacrifice is viewed as taking care of the sin we inherited from Adam, but we are on our own after that. We must "work out" our own salvation.

Reverend Moon of the Unification Church teaches that Jesus was not able to complete the work of redemption. He was able to provide spiritual redemption for humankind at the cross, but not physical redemption. Why not? Because He was crucified by the Jews before He was able to meet His perfect mate, get married, and establish the Kingdom of Heaven on earth.[20] Reverend Moon is here to complete what Jesus allegedly failed to accomplish.

Many New Agers believe Jesus did not die for the sins of man but died in order to "balance the planetary karma." Others say that at the crucifixion, Jesus' etheric (spiritual) blood flowed into the etheric (spiritual) earth, whence the resurrection and ascension of Christ consciousness has "up-flowed" out of the bowels of the earth so that all humanity is now recognizing its Christhood.

Denial of the Personality and Deity of the Holy Spirit

Cults often deny either the personality or the deity of the Holy Spirit, or both. The Jehovah's Witnesses, for instance, deny the Holy Spirit's personality and deity and argue that the Spirit is simply God's impersonal "active force" for accomplishing His will and purpose in the world. This denial of the Spirit's personality and deity is in keeping with the Watchtower denial of the doctrine of the Trinity. The Way International and the Christadelphians are other cults that view the Holy Spirit as an impersonal force of God.

Other cults offer strange ideas about the Holy Spirit. "Moonies," for example, argue that the Holy Spirit is a female spirit and that together Jesus and the Holy Spirit took the roles of "Second Adam" and "Second Eve." Oneness Pentecostals argue that the Holy Spirit is simply one of the modes of manifestation of Jesus Christ. In the Mind Sciences, the Holy Spirit is interpreted not to be the third person of the Trinity, but rather is Divine Science itself. Some New Agers try to equate the Holy Spirit with the "chi" force or "prana" energy of Eastern religions.

Denial of Salvation by Grace

Without exception, cults deny salvation by grace, thus distorting the purity of the Gospel. Works are typically viewed as being necessary in attaining salvation. The Mormons emphasize the need to become increasingly perfect in this life; "justification by faith alone" is said to be a "pernicious doctrine." In Mormon theology one cannot become eligible for the highest degree of salvation without keeping the commandments of the Lord in all things.

The Jehovah's Witnesses emphasize the importance of distributing Watchtower literature door-to-door as a part of "working out" their salvation. They must dedicate their lives to Jehovah and remain faithful to Him to the end for fear of losing salvation.

In Oneness Pentecostalism, salvation comes very hard. In their theology, faith, repentance, water baptism (by immersion only) in the name of Jesus only, and baptism in the Holy Spirit (as evidenced by speaking in tongues) are *all* necessary for the new birth to be achieved.

It is true that some cults pay lip service to salvation "by grace" (such as the Mormons and the Jehovah's Witnesses). But by this they mean that because of God's great favor, humans now have the wonderful *opportunity* to "work out" or earn salvation. Others describe this grace as being more of a *reward* for those who are faithful to the conditions and requirements laid down by the cult. This is not true biblical grace at all. Biblical grace involves God giving the unworthy sinner the gift of salvation based on faith in Christ.

Denial of the Priesthood of the Believer

Cults often deny or at least compromise the idea of the priesthood of the believer. Alan Gomes notes, "Most cultic groups insist that in order for people to understand God's truth, they must submit to the teaching of the cult leader or organization, thus denying the priesthood of all believers."[21] A prime example is the Jehovah's Witnesses, who must submit their understanding (and their minds) to the Watchtower Society—God's alleged channel of truth today. Likewise, members of the Unification Church are expected to submit to the teachings of Reverend Moon. By contrast, 1 Peter 2:4–10 indicates that all believers are priests before God and thus have direct access to Him without a need for intermediaries (see Heb. 4:16).

Redefinition of Christian Terms

As has already become clear from this survey of beliefs, cults typically use Christian doctrinal words—such as *God, Jesus, Christ, atonement,* and *salvation*—but pour their own cultic meanings into them. As an illustration, consider the statement: "Jesus Christ is God, was crucified and died, and was resurrected from the dead."

Jehovah's Witnesses would interpret this statement as meaning that

- Jesus is a "mighty god" (lesser than the Father),
- was crucified on a stake (not a cross),
- and then was resurrected spiritually (not physically).

New Agers, by contrast, would interpret this statement as meaning that

- Jesus was both "Christ" and God (as all of us can become "Christ" and God, since *all is* God),
- was crucified in the sense that His spiritual blood poured into the spiritual earth (thereby infusing Christ consciousness into the earth),
- and then was "resurrected" in the sense of Christ consciousness rising up out of the spiritual dimension of the earth and coming upon all humankind.

Such cultic redefinitions should not surprise us, for Scripture itself cautions us in this regard. Second Corinthians 11:4 warns of a different Jesus, a different spirit, and a different gospel (see also Matt. 24:24; Acts 20:28–31; Gal. 1:6–9; 2 Peter 2:1–3).

The importance of recognizing the "terminology" block cannot be overstated. As Walter Martin once put it, "Unless terms are defined when one is either speaking or reading cult theology, the semantic jungle that the cults have created will envelop him, making difficult, if not impossible, a proper contrast between the teachings of the cults and those of orthodox Christianity."[22]

Compartmentalizing Conflicting Facts

"Compartmentalization" refers to the process in which cults "selectively ignore facts that obviously contradict their claims."[23] Martin notes that this process suggests "the ability of the human mind to live in two 'worlds' at once with a state of peaceful(?) coex-istence between them. Logically, they are incompatible, involving a logical contradiction."[24] In *1984*, novelist George Orwell describes this phenomenon as "double think."

An example is the Mormon claim that the Book of Mormon is inspired and is "the most perfect book on earth"—despite the fact that Mormons have introduced over 3,913 corrections into the text over the years. Another example relates to the Christian Science denial of the reality of sickness, pain, and death—despite the fact that in her declining years, founder Mary Baker Eddy was under a physician's care, received morphine injections to ease her pain, wore eyeglasses, had teeth extractions, and eventually died, thus giving the lie to all she professed to believe and teach.[25] Yet another example relates to the faith of Jehovah's Witnesses that the Watchtower Society speaks God's prophetic truth—despite the fact that the Society has uttered one false prophecy after another, including those relating to the years 1914, 1925, and 1975.

A Central Role in Fulfilling Prophecy

A number of cults see themselves as playing a central role in fulfilling biblical prophecy and thus view themselves as an important part of the unfolding of God's plan on earth. Baha'is claim that Jesus' prophecy of "the Spirit of truth" in the Upper Room Discourse (John 14–16) was a prophecy of its leader, Baha'u'llah, and that references to the Second Coming in the New Testament are fulfilled in Baha'u'llah.

The Mormon *Inspired Version* of the Bible (personally edited by Joseph Smith) contains a prophecy of Smith in Genesis 50. Mormons also claim to be the "restored church" with a "restored priesthood" and a "restored gospel" and view themselves as God's "latter-day saints," proclaiming God's last word to the people of the earth.

Jehovah's Witnesses have often portrayed themselves as God's witnesses on earth prior to the unleashing of Armageddon, and they consider themselves the only ones who will survive this worldwide catastrophe. Yet, as noted above, the Watchtower Society has set forth many false prophecies regarding the end times.

Unificationists often cite Revelation 7:2–4, which prophesies that an angel will come *from the East* with a seal of God, as evidence that the second messiah will be born somewhere in the Far

East. They contend that Korea is the only logical country that could possibly be referred to, because Japan worships pagan gods and China is a communist country. Korea is viewed as a suitable birthplace for the messiah because people there have a strong faith in God. (Note that Reverend Moon was born in Korea.)

A Tendency to Revise the History of the Cult

The cults often revise the histories of their movements, leaving out damning details from the lives of its founders or early leaders. Such revisionist histories often serve to cover up embarrassments that might dissuade people from joining the cult.[26] Jehovah's Witness leaders are not forthright about the marital failure (with all its very ugly details) of their founder, Charles Taze Russell. Mormon histories are not forthright about how, following the prohibition of polygamy in the United States, some Mormon leaders and presidents continued to live in polygamy and, after being caught, were fined by the government. Historic accounts produced by new religions and cults are generally "kinder and gentler" than the reality.

SOCIOLOGICAL CHARACTERISTICS OF CULTS

I noted previously that even though cults should be defined from a theological point of view, we can nevertheless gain valuable insights into certain aspects of the cultic mentality from sociology.[27] Sociological characteristics of cults include such things as authoritarianism, exclusivism, dogmatism, isolationism, and threats of satanic attack.[28] Let us briefly consider these.

Authoritarian Leadership

Authoritarianism involves the acceptance of an authority figure who exercises excessive control on cult members. As prophet or founder, this leader's word is considered ultimate and final.[29] The late David Koresh of the Branch Davidian cult in Waco, Texas, is a tragic example, as 71 members of this cult followed him to a fiery death in 1993. Another example is Jim Jones of the People's Temple, who brought about the mass suicide of 911 followers in Jonestown, Guyana, in 1978. A more recent authoritarian group is the Boston Church of Christ, which practices an excessive and stringent form of discipleship by which the personal life of every believer is controlled by a discipler. Jim Bjornstad notes, "There is a discipler over every discipler, a hierarchy of disciplers working its way up to the top. Through this the church maintains control of each person."[30]

Ron Enroth has noted that the authoritarian nature of cult leaders is often evident in their titles. Examples include "Guru Ma" (Elizabeth Clare Prophet of the Church Universal Triumphant), "Perfect Master" (Guru Maharaj Ji), "Father David" (late leader of the Children of God), and "True Parent" (Reverend Moon, who heads the Unification Church).[31]

Often this authoritarianism involves legalistic submission to the rules and regulations of the group as established by the cult leader (or, as in the case of the Jehovah's Witnesses, submission to the Watchtower Society). Cult members are fully expected to submit, even if they do not agree with the requirements. Unquestioning obedience is compulsory.

Exclusivism

Cults often believe that they alone have the truth. The cult views itself as the single means of salvation on earth; to leave the group is to endanger one's soul. The Mormons believe they are the exclusive community of the saved on earth and that all other churches are "an abomination in God's sight." Mormons believe they possess the "restored gospel" and have the only legitimate priesthood on earth. Without affiliation with this priesthood, one cannot be saved.

The Jehovah's Witnesses, likewise, believe they are the exclusive community of Jehovah on earth. Christendom, by contrast, is viewed as apostate—the adulterous woman of Revelation 17, and a part of Satan's kingdom. The Watchtower is viewed as the sole channel through which Jehovah communicates today as "the faithful and wise servant" of which Jesus spoke in Matthew 24:45.

Isolationism

The more extreme cults sometimes create fortified boundaries, often precipitating tragic endings (we have already mentioned the tragedies in Waco and Jonestown). Some cults require members to renounce and break off associations with parents and siblings. Sometimes cult members are told that Satan may try to work through parents or other relatives (or friends) to get them out of the group. Such family members or friends may actually be "the Devil in disguise." Breaking off such relations is then viewed as justified and necessary. Among the cults engaging in this kind of practice are the Children of God, the Unification Church, the Branch Davidians, the Way International, and Hare Krishna.

Opposition to Independent Thinking

Some cultic groups discourage members from thinking independently. The "thinking," as it were, has already been done for them by the cult leadership; the proper response is merely to submit. The Jehovah's Witnesses are a prime example of this. In various Watchtower publications we read the following:

- "God has not arranged for [His] Word to speak independently or to shine forth life-giving truths by itself. It is through his organization God provides this light."[32]
- "Avoid independent thinking . . . questioning the counsel that is provided by God's visible organization."[33]
- "Fight against independent thinking."[34]
- "We should seek for dependent Bible study, rather than for independent Bible study."[35]
- "If we have love for Jehovah and for the organization of his people we shall not be suspicious, but shall, as the Bible says, 'believe all things,' all the things that *The Watchtower* brings out."[36]

Because they fellowship with one another, a Witness may feel great trepidation about sharing doubts with others for fear of reprisal. Thus there may be numerous Jehovah's Witnesses suffering emotional difficulty at not being able to express some of their intellectual struggles in regard to the Watchtower Society.

Fear of Being "Disfellowshiped"

It is not uncommon in cults that people are urged to remain faithful to avoid being "disfellowshiped," or disbarred, from the group. Again, the Jehovah's Witnesses are a prime example, for a person can be disfellowshiped merely for questioning a Watchtower doctrine. The reason is that because the Watchtower Society considers itself God's prophet and voice of truth for today, to question its authority is tantamount to questioning Jehovah's authority. So challenging the Watchtower is considered an intolerable offense.

Jehovah's Witnesses are also warned that if they leave the Watchtower organization or are disfellowshiped, they will be shunned by family members and friends who remain in the group.[37] Fear of shunning makes it very difficult to leave the Jehovah's Witnesses, for it involves great sacrifice.

Chuck Love and his wife experienced this after leaving the Jehovah's Witnesses and becoming Christians. Chuck recalls, "My family disowned me. My wife—who also became a Christian—received similar treatment from her family. Her parents won't even talk to her. Our brothers and sisters cut us off. And all of my close friends—those whom I thought were close friends—shut us out of their lives. When we trusted in Christ, it wasn't just a matter of changing churches; it was a matter of changing *lives*."[38] The same thing often happens in the Mormon church. As cult apologists David Reed and John Farkas observe,

> Mormons who contemplate leaving the organization know that they risk losing their LDS spouse, their children, their parents, and any other relatives or close friends in the faith. A man who leaves the church faces the possibility that his Mormon wife will listen to encouragement from others in the sect to divorce him, since women are taught that achieving their heavenly goal in the afterlife depends on their being married in the temple to a Mormon man. From the point of view of these individuals, a religious organization is, in effect, holding their relatives hostage.[39]

Threats of Satanic Attack

Finally, some cults use fear and intimidation to keep members in line. Members may be told that something awful will happen to them should they choose to leave the group.[40] Others may be told that Satan will attack them and may even kill them, for they will have committed the unpardonable sin. Such fear tactics are designed to induce submission. Even when people do muster enough courage to leave the group, they may endure psychological consequences and emotional baggage for years to come.

A LOOK AHEAD

Having defined what a cult is and described its primary characteristics, I will in the next chapter examine the important question, Why are cults growing so rapidly in American society? The remaining chapters focus detailed attention on 12 of the most influential cults or new religious movements of our time. The characteristics we have discussed here will resurface repeatedly as we examine each group.

2

UNDERSTANDING CULTIC GROWTH

Estimates vary as to how many cults exist on the religious landscape in America today. The best estimate is that there are at least 20 million people, and perhaps as many as 30 million, actively participating in a cult or some form of the occult in the United States.[1] Worldwide, it is estimated that there may be as many as 5,000 cults, with perhaps as many as 150 million people involved. The two largest—the Mormons and the Jehovah's Witnesses—account for at least 14 million.[2]

The growth of cults in the United States is attributable to a number of factors, including the failure of the Christian church (in certain regards), an increase in biblical illiteracy, the growth in relativism, and the emphasis on selfhood. I will briefly summarize these and other important factors that have contributed to cultic growth.

I. THE FAILURE OF THE CHURCH

There is little doubt that one reason that counterfeit religions are flourishing in America is what many perceive to be an impotent and lifeless Christian church. Statistically speaking, a significant percentage of cultists formerly attended a Christian church.[3] Dr. Paul R. Martin is the director of the Wellspring Retreat and Resource Center, an organization devoted to helping former cultists overcome the harmful effects of their experience. It is highly revealing that of the thousands of cultists Martin has personally worked with at Wellspring, some 25 percent formerly attended evangelical or fundamentalist churches, and more than 40 percent had backgrounds in the large, more liberal Protestant denominations.[4] Chris Elkins, a former member of the Unification Church, agrees, noting that "in most cults, a majority of the members left a mainline, denominational church."[5]

This fact has led cult watcher Ruth Tucker to conclude that "the increase in cult membership is a direct result of a failure on the part of the church."[6] Cult expert J. K. Van Baalen likewise says that the cults are "the unpaid bills of the church."[7]

The widespread failure of churches in America is multifaceted. The evidence points to a broad failure (1) to make a real moral difference in the lives of church members, (2) to provide a sense of belonging among members, (3) to meet people's deepest needs, and (4) to make Bible doctrine a high priority.*

The Failure to Make a Real Moral Difference

A study conducted by the Roper organization tested the behavior of "born-again" Christians before and after their conversion experiences. The disturbing result was that conversion in many cases seems to have had little effect on moral behavior.[8] This suggests that genuine discipleship and training are simply not occurring as they need to in local churches.

Chuck Colson cites a similar poll (conducted by Gallup) that found there is little difference in the ethical behavior of people who go to church and people who don't. "One has to conclude—painful though it is—that over the past decade in American life, churches have made *very little* difference in the lives of people. As a matter

---

*My comments here should not be taken to mean that *virtually all* churches fail in these areas. I am speaking in general terms about a broad problem.

of fact, polls taken among pastors show that pastors themselves acknowledge that they aren't doing the job they're supposed to do."[9]

Recognizing this lack in Christian churches, many people turn elsewhere to religious groups they feel *can* make a difference in their lives. People want something that "works" in day-to-day living.

The Failure to Provide a Sense of Belonging

Cult expert Ken Boa suggests that many people join cults because of loneliness, alienation, and lack of personal identity. "By submitting to the teachings and requirements of the cult, they hope to find the love, acceptance, and fellowship they long for."[10] The sad reality is that many Christian churches fail to meet this basic human need.

Cult researcher J. Gordon Melton is right when he says that many of the large, impersonal churches fail to give many people a sense of belonging.[11] But it is not just the large churches that have this problem; smaller churches have failed in this as well.

By contrast, many cults often provide a genuine sense of belonging to members. People are welcomed and made to feel an important part of the group. In fact, laypeople are typically given an important role, which makes them feel as if they are making a contribution. Mormon young people, for example, engage in door-to-door missionary service, and male members can hold either the Aaronic or the Melchizedek priesthood. Such activities foster a sense of belonging among members. Until the Christian church deals with this problem, the cults will continue to draw people from church pews.

The Failure to Meet People's Deepest Needs

People today are seeking answers to life's most perplexing questions: "Who am I?" "Where did I come from?" "What is life all about?" "Why am I here?" "Where am I going when this life on earth is over?" When answers to these basic questions are not provided by church leaders, people turn elsewhere for answers.[12] Sociologist Ron Enroth notes that "people join cults because they hope such groups will fulfill very real, perceived needs. These needs are generated in large part by the changing and confusing society that is America today."[13]

People with inner emotional struggles are particularly susceptible and vulnerable to the cults. Robert and Gretchen Passantino aptly observe that "a person does not usually join a cult because he has done an exhaustive analysis of world religions and has decided that a particular cult presents the best theology available. Instead, a person generally joins a cult because he has problems that he is having trouble solving, and the cult promises to solve these problems."[14] The church needs to reclaim lost ground in genuinely helping people with life issues.

The Failure to Make Doctrine a High Priority

Numerous cult authorities have noted that a key factor giving rise to the cult explosion in the United States is that churches have failed to make Bible doctrine and Bible knowledge a high priority. My late colleague Walter Martin once said that the rise of the cults is "directly proportional to the fluctuating emphasis which the Christian church has placed on the teaching of biblical doctrine to Christian laymen."[15]

Tragically, many people who attend church have not been given biblical discernment skills, and they end up joining a particular cult without realizing that its teachings go against the Bible. Such people are unable to distinguish cultic doctrine from biblical doctrine.[16]

Among the many real-life examples that illustrate this, the one that stands out in my mind relates to David Koresh and the Branch Davidian cult that met a fiery end in Waco, Texas. One news publication indicated that two of the girls who died there had formerly attended a Christian church. If these girls had become biblically literate in their former church, enough to detect the Scripture-twisting antics of David Koresh, perhaps they would be alive today. The consequences of biblical illiteracy can be deadly in certain contexts.

We must not forget that cults are *counterfeit* religious systems. The problem is that the counterfeits are often taken for the real thing. Such groups might look so good and seem so right that a person might not suspect anything is amiss. It is only when the counterfeit religious system is measured against Scripture, properly interpreted, that problems appear. So, for example, it is only when one measures the messianic claims of David Koresh against the biblical portrayal of the divine Messiah that a notable discrepancy emerges. Likewise, it is only when one examines Jehovah's Witness theology against the Bible that one sees they have an entirely different God (not a Trinity), a different Jesus (a lesser god created by Jehovah billions of years ago), a different Holy Spirit (not a person and not God), and a different salvation (involving the necessity of works).

The apostle Paul made reference to "God's household, which is the church of the living God, the pillar and foundation of the truth" (1 Tim. 3:15). If the church fails to set forth and defend doctrinal truth, it fails to fulfill its God-appointed role.

2. FAMILIES IN TROUBLE

One may not realize that there is a connection between troubled families and the growth of the cults, but the evidence suggests there is. I draw four factors to your attention in this regard: (1) many of today's youth have become disillusioned with their parents' values, (2) there is a pervasive lack of direction among many youth, (3) cults often function as surrogate families, and (4) young people may be especially vulnerable to joining a cult following a personal crisis.

Disillusionment with Parental Values

It would seem that many young people today have become disillusioned with the values of their parents. In many cases this disillusionment is rooted in the disparity that young people observe between their parents' claims regarding values and the way their parents actually live. That is, the young people see hypocrisy.

Further, because of the current attitude that each individual is the ultimate judge of what is right and wrong, young people have reexamined their inherited values and have rejected them as irrelevant to the way *they* want to live. Therefore, for many American youth, truth and morality have become completely subjective.

Instead of deriving values from their parents, many youth are constructing their own values, through vehicles such as the New Age program for public education called Values Clarification. The idea in Values Clarification is that values are not to be imposed from *without* (such as from Scripture or from parents) but must be subjectively discovered from *within*. The underlying assumption is that there are no absolute truths or values.[17] "Whatever works for you" is considered right. This relativism proves to be fertile soil in which the weed of cultism can grow unhindered.

Lack of Direction among Young People

Many young people today seem to have a pervasive lack of direction in their lives—a reality some sociologists feel may be due in part to a lack of genuine interaction with their parents day by day. Although this in itself does not cause a person to want to join a cult, a case can be made that it at least makes one more susceptible to the lure of cults. The reality is that young people who lack direction sometimes choose to latch on to authority figures around which they can govern their lives.[18] Such people seem to thrive on external authority figures to give a framework to their lack of direction and provide structure for their lives. Cult leaders often manifest absolute conviction and certainty and provide black-and-white answers to young people who are unsure about what path to take in life.

Cults as Surrogate Families

Cult observers have long noted that many cults provide the sense of belonging that is lacking in many biological families. Indeed, many cults and religious movements actually function as surrogate families for their members. Such cults virtually replace biological families for some members and meet all the needs that the biological families failed to meet.

It is noteworthy that many cult members address the leaders of the cult in parental terms.[19] Cult leaders are sometimes spoken of as "spiritual parents" or "parents in the Lord."[20] New Ager Elizabeth Clare Prophet, who heads the Church Universal and Triumphant, is affectionately known among her followers as "Guru Ma."[21] David "Moses" Berg, founder of the Children of God, was often called "Father David" by cult members. Likewise, Reverend Moon is often called "Father Moon" by members of the Unification Church.

Vulnerability Following a Personal Crisis

In evaluating the available data, I want to emphasize that just because a person comes from a less than ideal home does not mean that he or she will join a cult. Although a number of cult members do come from disturbed or dysfunctional homes, there are also many people from such homes who do not end up in cults. Sometimes young people from seemingly normal families end up in cults. What, then, should we make of this?

THE CHALLENGE OF THE CULTS

A key factor in answering this question seems to be that recruitment into a cult is much more likely to occur in association with a severe crisis in a young person's life. The fact is, many young people are in the midst of a personal crisis at the time they join a cult. These people may feel confused and depressed and not know what to do. One study involving 237 members of the Unification Church indicates that two-thirds of them were facing some kind of crisis at the time they joined the group.[22] Paul Martin likewise warns that "research shows that young people are more vulnerable to cultic affiliation during or immediately after suffering a severe crisis."[23]

It stands to reason that a young person in a disturbed or dysfunctional home who encounters a severe crisis will be more *susceptible* to a cult (if a cult should come along at an opportune moment) than one from a healthy home. Why? Simply because he or she will likely not find loving support and sympathy from other family members. A young person in a healthy home, by contrast, will very likely have a much higher level of emotional support and psychological nurturing during times of trouble.

3. REACTION AGAINST SECULAR HUMANISM

Humanist Manifesto II—signed by such luminaries as author Isaac Asimov, psychologist B. F. Skinner, and ethicist Joseph Fletcher—states, "We find insufficient evidence for belief in the existence of a supernatural; it is either meaningless or irrelevant to the question of the survival and fulfillment of the human race. As nontheists, we begin with humans not God, nature not deity."[24] Humanists promote a way of life that systematically excludes God and all religion in the traditional sense. Man is on his own in this great big universe.[25]

Humanists assert that there is no divine purpose for humanity. *Humanist Manifesto II* states, "We can discover no divine purpose or providence for the human species. While there is much that we do not know, humans are responsible for what we are or will become. No deity will save us; we must save ourselves."[26] Likewise, in his book *Forbidden Fruit: The Ethics of Humanism*, humanist leader Paul Kurtz said that "the theist's world is only a dream world; it is a feeble escape into a future that will never come."[27]

How does all this relate to the growth of the cults? Whether humanists admit it or not, their philosophy robs humankind of ultimate purpose, meaning, and value. How could there be ultimate purpose, meaning, and value when human beings are viewed simply as products of chance evolutionary forces? Secular humanism all too easily leads to nihilism—the belief that everything is meaningless and absurd.[28]

For many years secular humanism focused so much on the all-sufficiency of humanity that God was left entirely out of the picture. As a result, man lacked a sense of the *transcendent*—something he yearned for in the deepest part of his being. Indeed, the inadequacy of secular humanism has made man crave for something more—something divine, something sacred. As Mircea Eliade put it, secular man "killed a God in whom he could not believe but whose absence he could not bear."[29] Philosopher Douglas Groothuis observes that while secular humanism appeals to humanity's quest for autonomy and crowns man *the measure of all things*, "we find ourselves the lords of nothing—nothing but a meaningless universe with no direction, destiny, or purpose."[30]

It is a fact that when people lack a sense of fulfillment and meaning—when they feel despair in the deepest part of their being—it is much easier for a cult leader to victimize them, promising a solution to that emptiness. Orville Swenson has aptly noted, "The prevailing feeling of despair that permeates American society fosters the climate in which a leader with 'charisma' can bring some sense of hope, no matter how false it may be."[31]

Tragically, many have turned to one or another of the many cults in America to find fulfillment for the God-shaped vacuum that is in every human heart. The cults "are filling a need in people for stability and meaning in life. They are filling a spiritual vacuum created by the inability of materialism, hedonism, and existentialism to supply lasting purpose to one's existence."[32]

4. THE TURN EAST

The 1960s brought a massive Eastern invasion into the West. Os Guinness described it this way: "The East is still the East, but the West is no longer the West. Western answers no longer seem to fit the questions. With Christian culture disintegrating and humanism failing to provide an alternative, many are searching the ancient East."[33]

The counterculture of the 1960s played a key role in the explosive growth of Eastern religions in the West. One of the most influential gurus on the scene during that decade was Maharishi Mahesh Yogi, who taught his followers all about Transcendental Meditation (TM). The Maharishi's rise to fame was partly due to the fact that his early disciples included the Beatles, one of the most popular rock groups of all time. This gave TM more than a little media attention in America.

More than a million Americans have been initiated into TM. Indeed, one observer said that "what McDonald's has done for the hamburger, Transcendental Meditation has done for Eastern mysticism."[34] Transcendental Meditation has succeeded in making Eastern mysticism acceptable, fashionable, and desirable to the American public.

James Sire, author of *The Universe Next Door*, believes that the openness to Eastern ideas among the Western youth of the 1960s was largely a reaction against traditional Western values. These values include high technology, reason and rationalism, materialism, economics, and the like.[35] Sire observes that "with its antirationalism, its syncretism, its quietism, its lack of technology, its uncomplicated lifestyle, and its radically different religious framework, the East is extremely attractive."[36] Many Americans have concluded that the East—that quiet land of meditating gurus and simple life—has the answer to our longing for meaning and significance.

As a result of the Eastern explosion in the 1960s and beyond, American soil is now saturated with Eastern ideas. Although Americans in A.D. 2000 may no longer be fascinated with the world of Eastern gurus, the *teachings* of these gurus remain. As Groothuis says, the age of exotic, Eastern "guruism" may be waning, but the gurus' teachings are not: "What was once on the esoteric periphery has moved into the spotlight. Much of what used to be underground is seeping—if not rushing—into the mainstream, as a plethora of New Age teachers, practices, and events contend for our souls."[37]

5. INCREASE IN RELATIVISM

The New Age movement has given relativism probably its greatest boost in modern times. According to one critic, New Agers believe "it is the height of presumption to think that one knows the key truth for all people. On the other hand, it is the apex of love to 'allow' others to have their own 'truth.' 'Thou shalt not interfere with another's reality' might be called the First Commandment of New Age revelation."[38]

The New Age doctrines of pantheism (all is God) and monism (all is one) relate very closely to relativism. Obviously, if pantheism is true, this means that man himself is God. And if man is God, then man is a law unto himself and need not obey the laws of any deity external to himself. If monism is true, then the distinction between good and evil—between right and wrong, true and false—disappears. *All is relative.* Amazingly, polls indicate that 66 percent of Americans deny there is such a thing as absolute truth.[39] And, as noted earlier, relativism has even entered the public schools through the Values Clarification curriculum.

Obviously, if all truth is relative, then one person's "truth" is just as good as another person's "truth." This ultimately means that any religion's "truth"—and any cult's "truth"—is as good as Christianity's truth.

6. EMPHASIS ON SELF

Certainly today's "do your own thing" mentality contributes to the growth of the cults. This is especially true among those with affinities toward New Age thinking. New Agers David Gershon and Gail Straub illustrate this in their blockbuster book, *Empowerment: The Art of Creating Your Life As You Want It.* They assure readers that "empowerment" gives us the ability to create our own reality by the power of the mind. What "manifests" in life will be a direct result of the thoughts we affirm, whether on a conscious or an unconscious level. Gershon and Straub's central idea is that empowerment "will free you from boundaries that have limited you in the past and show you your power to shape your own destiny. On this journey you will learn the art of creating your life as you want it."[40] Self rules!

This New Age team also provides a list of "limiting beliefs" with the injunction that we can dispose of these unhealthy beliefs by mentally affirming the accompanying "turnarounds." Here are a few examples:

Limiting Belief	Turnaround
God is a male figure with a lot of power who will punish me if I don't do the right thing.	I create God as a loving, kind, playful, wise, powerful friend. We play together co-creating the universe.
Spirituality means giving over control of my life to some higher power that's outside of me.	God's will is my own highest consciousness in this moment.
To be spiritual I must follow a code of conduct laid out by a religion/guru/writer of a spiritual book.	My spirituality grows out of my own self-knowledge. I trust it and found my actions upon it.[41]

By using positive affirmations such as these, combined with visualizations, thoughts supposedly can begin to change the reality around us. By using our minds we have true power. We can create whatever kind of reality we desire. We can even create self-styled religions if we wish.

7. EMPHASIS ON FEELINGS AND EXPERIENCE

We live in experiential times. People put a lot of stock in feelings: "If it feels good, do it." Orville Swenson says that "rather than embracing a factually-based faith, resting on divine authority, many are seeking mystical and emotional experience, the very kind offered by contemporary cults."[42]

Mormons, for example, will often speak of a "burning in the bosom" that testifies to the "truth" of the Book of Mormon. Rajneesh, a pop-guru, taught his disciples to follow their feelings.[43] The Unification Church in past decades has used a "love-bombing" technique to draw people into the cult.

The desire for a "feel-good" religion is at times a reaction against religions that make a moral requirement on one's life— which is what Christianity does. This is illustrated in the New Age angel spirituality that emerged in the mid 1990s. As *Time* magazine put it, "For those who choke too easily on God and his rules . . . angels are the handy compromise, all fluff and meringue, kind, nonjudgmental. And they are available to everyone, like aspirin."[44] *Christianity Today* magazine suggested that "angels too easily provide a temptation for those who want a 'fix' of spirituality without bothering with God himself."[45]

8. PENETRATION OF BUSINESS, EDUCATION, AND HEALTH FIELDS

The fields of education, business, and health altogether embrace a huge segment of Americans. Education encompasses children, parents, and teachers; business embraces the entire work force, both employers and employees; health includes virtually all of us, because each of us gets sick at one time or another. The cults have penetrated these three fields, with the greatest influence coming from the New Age movement. Millions of people have been introduced to a New Age worldview at school, at work, or at the doctor's office.

The Business Community

The human potential movement blossomed in the 1970s. Since that time, numerous companies have drawn on various New Age human potential seminars. One reason so many Fortune 500 companies have been eager to use such seminars is that they promise increased productivity, better employee relations, more creativity among workers, and—bottom line—more sales.

These New Age seminars typically teach that (1) you are your own God, (2) you can create your own reality, and (3) you have unlimited potential. Seminar leaders usually begin by tearing down or undermining the learners' worldview. Then they attempt, via some kind of esoteric exercise, to trigger an altered state of consciousness in hopes of inducing a mystical experience so potent that it will cause the participants to question or doubt their previous understanding of reality. The participants are then exposed to a New Age explanation that makes sense of the mystical experience. They are introduced to a new worldview that says you are your own God and you can create your own reality. Many businesspeople have been drawn into the New Age movement through such seminars.[46]

Penetration of Public Schools

In his book *Censorship: Evidence of Bias in Our Children's Textbooks*, Paul Vitz provides decisive evidence that Christianity and Christian values have been systematically stripped from children's school curricula.[47] While children's textbooks are silent on Christianity, many of them continue to contain ideas or statements about Buddhism, Hinduism, Eastern meditation, magic, Indian spirituality, and yoga.[48]

Aside from textbooks, New Agers have conceded that they have a definite agenda for what they see as important in public school curricula. A key emphasis is on "right-brain learning techniques"—what educators call man's creative and intuitive abilities in contrast to the "left brain's" more static and analytical abilities. While this right-brain/left-brain distinction is not New Age *per se*, New Agers have made much use of it. Their right-brain learning techniques include practices such as yoga, meditation, chanting, and visualization. Through these practices children are led into mystical experiences and are introduced to a New Age worldview.

Penetration of Health Services

The New Age "holistic" approach to health is said to be a "multidimensional phenomenon involving interdependent physical, psychological, and social aspects."[49] The holistic approach seeks to treat the whole person—body, mind, and spirit—and also considers the social aspects of the patient's life to be a factor in health. Holistic health claims to be person-centered, not disease-centered.

Certainly some aspects of holistic health sound reasonable enough and can be accepted by Christians. However, many New Age health therapies betray an unchristian worldview. Indeed, the New Age model of holistic health is based primarily on their conception of *energy*, not matter. This energy is not a visible, measurable, scientifically explainable entity. Rather, New Agers speak of a "cosmic" or "universal" energy based on their monistic and pantheistic worldview. To enhance the flow of "healing energy" in the body, one must allegedly *attune* to it and realize one's unity with all things. Through such therapies, more than 30 percent of Americans have been exposed to the New Age worldview.[50]

9. EFFECTIVE USE OF THE MEDIA

Television journalist Bill Moyers once asked whether television could be "a force in the central issue of our time, the search to signify and affirm meaning, open our souls to others," and be a channel for the "biggest story of the century, the struggle to define what it means to be spiritual." That "little screen," Moyers said, is "the largest classroom, perhaps the largest chapel, God has given us in a long, long time."[51]

Moyers has sized up the power of television very well. As powerful as television is, however, it is not the only effective medium of communication. Print and radio are also powerful. These three outlets combined exercise tremendous influence on the minds of Americans, as evidenced in the following statistics:

- Some 97 percent of Americans own television sets. About 98 percent of these watch television regularly.[52]
- Americans average about four hours of television viewing per day. This means that over the past year, the typical American adult spent an equivalent of two full months (24 hours a day for 61 days) watching television.[53]
- Scholarly studies reveal that "kids draw most of their information from television, spending an average of more than 10,000 hours watching it by the time they reach age 18. (That is the equivalent of one entire year absorbing the messages broadcast by television producers.) The typical child in preschool through sixth grade watches more than 30 hours of television programming per week."[54]
- There are 350 million radios in America—more radios than people.[55]
- Some 124 million Americans read a newspaper every day.[56]

In view of these staggering numbers, can anyone doubt why some cults seek to purchase, manage, and influence the media in America? The media represent the single most effective means of reaching large numbers of people in a quick, efficient way. Consider the Mormons, who own a $300-million-a-year media conglomerate and spend roughly $550 million per year on media for their worldwide missionary efforts.[57] Another example is the Unity School of Christianity (a mind science group), which broadcasts its doctrines on more than a thousand radio and TV stations.

Yet another highly influential media of our day is the Internet, a worldwide network of computers and smaller networks that emerged in the mid-1980s. Conservative estimates are that over 35 million people are presently connected to the Internet, and that figure is growing rapidly. Most of the major cults have their own official web sites where one can access and download massive amounts of data related to their history and doctrine.[58]

10. MORAL REBELLION

Romans 1:18 affirms that human beings are in moral rebellion against God. One manifestation of this rebellion is seeking out and participating in false religions. (The Old Testament is full of examples—see 1 Kings 16:34; 18:25–26; 19:18.) Another manifestation relates to the practices that take place within these false religions.

This moral rebellion is more than evident in some of the practices of the cults. For example, the Children of God has long been known for its practice of "flirty fishing"—using sex to lure new people into the cult. Followers of the Hindu guru Rajneesh regularly engaged in sexual orgies. There have been a number of allegations, including one from a former daughter-in-law,[60] that Reverend Moon of the Unification Church engaged in a "purification rite" known as *p'i kareun,* in which he, as a messianic figure, "cleansed" female members of the church by having sexual intercourse with them. The Mormon church in its early history promoted and practiced polygamy. New Age leader Matthew Fox has said that both heterosexuality and homosexuality are equally acceptable to the "cosmic Christ" (that spirit that has allegedly manifested itself through the leaders of all world religions).[61] Moral rebellion is at the very heart of false religious systems.

PUTTING IT ALL TOGETHER

It is clear that the growth of the cults in America does not hinge on any single factor but rather is rooted in a convergence of factors. Taken together, these factors have provided a rich and fertile soil for the rapid growth and proliferation of cultic ideas in America.

Now that we understand *what* a cult is and *why* the cults are growing so fast, we will turn our attention to one of the most successful cults in world history—the Church of Jesus Christ of Latter-day Saints. They are more popularly known as the Mormons.

3

The Church of Jesus Christ of Latter-day Saints

The Mormon church is one of the wealthiest cults in the world. The church has between $25 and $30 billion in assets[1] and controls at least a hundred companies or businesses, including a $300-million-a-year media conglomerate. The church's investments in stocks, bonds, and church-controlled businesses were worth $6 billion in 1997. The church also owns $5 billion in agriculture and commercial real estate. A great deal of this wealth comes from the $3 million a day generated by church tithes. (Members are required to contribute 10 percent of their gross income.)

The church at present has more than 11 million members and is growing at the rate of more than 1,500 people per day. Mormon baptisms occur at a rate of one every 1 minute and 55 seconds. John Heinerman and

Anson Shupe point out in their book *The Mormon Corporate Empire* that "Mormon membership on the average has doubled every 15 years since World War II, but from 1970 to 1985, it nearly tripled in size."[2] During the past quarter-century the Mormon church has moved up to seventh place among America's church bodies, bypassing the Presbyterians, the Episcopalians, and the Lutheran Church—Missouri Synod.[3] Part of this growth is due to the effective use of media—running TV ads on TNT, CNN, and Headline News and print ads in *Reader's Digest* and *TV Guide*.

Brigham Young University president, Merrill Bateman, predicted in early 2000 that "by 2025, the number of missionaries converting people to the Mormon faith will more than double, rising from about 60,000 to 125,000."[4] Mormon missionaries now proselytize in more than 150 countries. It is possible that by the year 2025 there could be a thousand or more Mormon temples in the world. This requires constructing 36 new temples each year, which is feasible given the fact that 35 temples were dedicated in 2000.

MORMON ROOTS

Mormonism's founder, Joseph Smith Jr., was born in Sharon, Vermont, on December 23, 1805. Eleven years later, Smith and his large family moved to Palmyra, New York, where, just a few years later, a series of events unfolded that would lead to the founding of the Mormon church.

Beginning around 1819, there were religious revivals in the area where Smith lived. In 1820, at age 15, he became troubled about the conflict he saw among the people and clergy of the Methodist, Presbyterian, and Baptist churches. His mother, sister, and two brothers joined the Presbyterian church while Joseph later claimed he felt drawn toward the Methodists.

Because of the strife between the denominations—and because he was not sure who was right and who was wrong—Smith did not know what to do about joining a church. But he was soon to receive what he claimed was divine direction on the issue.

Joseph Smith Has a Vision

One day in the spring of 1820 as Joseph Smith was reading the Bible at James 1:5—"If any of you lacks wisdom, he should ask God, who gives generously to all without finding fault, and it will be given to him"—that verse suddenly came alive to him. He determined to ask God which church to join and went into the woods to pray. There he received a vision in which he encountered two personages: the Father and the Son. Smith recounts how "the Son" instructed him not to join any of the churches, for they were all wrong: "The Personage who addressed me said that all their creeds were an abomination in his sight."[5]

Accordingly, Smith did not join any of the churches. But neither did he attempt to "draw near" to the Lord and live a virtuous life. Instead, he later confessed, during the next three years, he frequently "fell into many foolish errors, and displayed the weakness of youth, and the foibles of human nature."[6] (Some of Smith's contemporaries would later list treasure-hunting using divining rods, ritual magic, and other occultic practices as among the "errors" of his youth.)[7]

Discrepancies in the "First Vision" Accounts

There are rather significant discrepancies in the existing accounts of Joseph Smith's "First Vision." (There are at least six visions.) They are significant because, as one Mormon prophet put it, "The appearing of the Father and the Son to Joseph Smith is the *foundation* of the church."[8] The chart below highlights just a few of the problems in two major First Vision accounts—the 1832 version by Smith himself, and the church's 1838 version, which is the basis for the story as told officially by the church today.

An Angel Appears to Joseph Smith

Smith claimed that when he went to bed on September 21, 1823, he prayed to God asking for forgiveness for all his sins and

FIRST VISION ACCOUNTS		
	1832 Version	**1838–39 Version**
Personage(s)	Smith claimed *only* a vision of Christ.	Smith claimed a vision of both the Father *and* the Son.
Seeking God	Bible reading stirred Smith to seek God.	A revival motivated Smith to seek God.
Churches Wrong	Smith already knew all the churches were wrong.	The "two personages" informed Smith the churches were wrong.

also for a manifestation. An angel named Moroni soon appeared and informed him "there was a book deposited, written on gold plates, giving an account of the former inhabitants of this continent [America], and the source from whence they sprang."[9] He also said the fullness of the everlasting Gospel was contained in it, as delivered by the Savior to the ancient inhabitants. Moroni further informed Smith that the "Urim and Thummim"—a translation device ("seer stone")—was buried with the plates.

Moroni appeared again to Smith—three times in the same night, once the following day, and annually for the next four years. The angel had warned him that he was not yet spiritually mature enough to take custody of the gold plates but one day would be. Smith was told that when he was finally permitted to retrieve the plates, he must not reveal them to anyone except to those to whom he would be commanded to show them lest he be destroyed.

In 1827, nine months after Smith married Emma Hale, Moroni allowed him to retrieve the plates with the charge to keep them safe until the angel "should call for them." Smith then translated the sacred records from "Reformed Egyptian" into English. After the translation was complete, the golden plates were removed by Moroni and are to this day unavailable for inspection. This means there is no concrete evidence the plates ever, in fact, existed. In any event, the original Book of Mormon was published in 1830.

"Joseph Smith would put the seer stone into a hat, and put his face in the hat, drawing it closely around his face to exclude the light; and in the darkness the spiritual light would shine. A piece of something resembling parchment would appear, and on that appeared the writing. One character at a time would appear, and under it was the interpretation in English. Brother Joseph would read off the English to Oliver Cowdery, who was his principal scribe, and when it was written down and repeated to Brother Joseph to see if it was correct, then it would disappear, and another character with the interpretation would appear. Thus the Book of Mormon was translated by the gift and power of God, and not by any power of man" (David Whitmer, *An Address to All Believers in Christ,* 12).

Before the plates were taken from the earth, three witnesses—David Whitmer, Martin Harris, and Oliver Cowdery—prayed with Smith that they might see them. According to Mormon accounts, an unnamed angel appeared in June 1829 and displayed the plates so that each could see the engravings himself. Harris later testified that he saw the plates with his "spiritual eye" or "eye of faith" rather than his naked eyes. Conflicting reports state that he and the other witnesses never saw the actual engraved plates, only something covered with a cloth.[10]

Just a few weeks earlier, in May, Smith and Cowdery had gone out in the woods to pray about baptism for the remission of sins. While they were praying, John the Baptist reportedly appeared and conferred the Aaronic Priesthood upon them and gave them instructions regarding how to baptize each other. Later Peter, James, and John appeared and conferred the Melchizedek Priesthood upon them.

(Whitmer, Harris, and Cowdery all ended up leaving the church. Harris did return to the church late in life, although in the interim he had said that several other churches were true.)

The "One True Church" Is Born

Since Joseph Smith had been told by Jesus that all the existing churches and creeds and those who professed them were false and abominable, the "one true church" was organized on April 6, 1830, by Smith and five others in Fayette, New York. At the founding meeting, Smith received a revelation from God that he was to be "a seer, a translator, a prophet, and an apostle."[11]

As the church grew, so did public opposition, forcing the Mormons to move on to other areas. According to Smith, he was instructed by the Lord to move the church to Ohio, so in February 1831 he moved to the town of Kirtland, Ohio, and established the church there. Within months, however, it became evident that the church would soon need to move again. Public opposition seemed to arise wherever Smith and his followers went.

In the middle of July 1831, Smith and a few of the "Saints" arrived in Independence, Missouri. At once he received a revelation indicating that "Zion" would be established at this place, a temple would be built, and the Saints should purchase land in that vicinity and "in the regions round about."[12] Smith left some of his followers there to buy land and establish the church while he and others went back to Kirtland.

While Smith remained in Kirtland, the church published many of his early revelations under the title "Book of Commandments" in Missouri in mid 1833. But public opposition to Mormon teachings grew swiftly in Missouri. The Mormons' rapid growth and unconventional beliefs caused great alarm in Jackson County, and in July, non-Mormons issued a manifesto stating their charges against the Mormons and their intent to remove them.

When the Mormons refused to leave, Missourians began a violent campaign against the church, destroying the church's printing office in the process. Smith, still in Kirtland, learned of the trouble and raised a large group of men to ride to Missouri to defend the Saints.

In the fall of 1835 Smith published the Doctrine and Covenants, a dramatic reworking of the then-suppressed Book of Commandments. Many changes were made—deletions and additions—to those original "revelations." Earlier that same year, Smith also acquired assorted Egyptian artifacts, including papyrus fragments taken from the cavities of some mummies. He attempted to translate portions of them and thus produced the Book of Abraham. This book and "Joseph Smith—History," an extract of his own "translations" of Matthew and the Book of Moses (allegedly lost from the Old Testament and restored to Smith through revelation) and the Articles of Faith were all combined into a single volume entitled The Pearl of Great Price—the third book of Mormon scriptures.

Although the Mormons continued to move from one Missouri county to another in the attempt to find a permanent place to live, Smith continued to give revelations that caused the Saints further trouble. The Mormons and non-Mormons were virtually at war, with atrocities being committed by both sides. Governor Lilburn Boggs of Missouri tried to quiet the problems, but trouble continued to escalate. Finally, in October 1838 he issued an order to the militia stating that because of "the attitude of open and avowed defiance of the laws, and of having made open war upon the people of this state, ... the Mormons must be treated as enemies and exterminated or driven from this state."[13]

The Mormons scattered, and some were killed, others jailed. But many made it out of Missouri to Illinois, where they built an attractive city called Nauvoo (which, Joseph Smith asserted, was

Hebrew for "beautiful place," and was briefly the second-largest city in Illinois). While there, Smith was the mayor of the city, the general of his own army, a candidate for the U.S. presidency, and the Prophet, Seer, and Revelator of the Mormon church.

Joseph Smith Dies in a Shootout

One thing that caused great concern for many people—Mormons and non-Mormons alike—were the sordid rumors regarding polygamy. Smith was definitely a polygamist. The actual number of his wives is not known for certain, but estimates range from 28 to 84. The most likely count is 33, most of whom were younger than Smith—one being a mere 14 years of age.[14] His first (and true) wife Emma was deeply hurt and angered about it all. Joseph, however, had a word from the Lord for Emma to the effect that the Lord would kill her if she did not submit and cleave to Joseph.[15]

By 1842 rumors were widespread regarding these immoralities. On June 7, 1844, a group of dissident Mormons—angry about the gross immoralities being practiced among church members—published a newspaper detailing their grievances against Smith. It was the first and last issue of the *Nauvoo Expositor*. Smith knew that the charges of polygamy and of mishandling church funds would cause trouble for him. Days later, he and his city council decided to destroy the printing office. This act resulted in Smith's arrest for treason, and he, his brother Hyrum, and two other Mormon leaders were jailed in Carthage, Illinois.

On June 27 a mob stormed the jail, killing Joseph and Hyrum Smith and wounding the other men. Before Smith died, however, he used a six-shooter to wound a few of the men in the mob during a blazing gun battle. Smith's role as God's "Prophet, Seer, and Revelator" came to an abrupt end in bloody violence.

Brigham Young Takes Over

Brigham Young, the senior Mormon apostle at the time of Smith's death, quickly assumed leadership of the church. There was initial resistance to Young's taking over, not the least of which came from Emma Smith.[16] But Young prevailed.

A powerful and organized leader, Young led a company of Latter-day Saints across the treacherous Great Plains, reaching the valley of the Great Salt Lake in Utah in July 1847. There they built their new

Zion, namely, Salt Lake City. Young ruled the people with an iron hand and both practiced and encouraged polygamy for the rest of his life. He himself had some 20 wives by the time he died, and he fathered 57 children by 16 of these wives.[17]

The practice of polygamy would "officially" end, however. On September 24, 1890, a "manifesto" was issued by Wilford Woodruff, fourth president of the Mormon church, declaring his advice that Mormons give up the practice. Among the obvious reasons were that the church's top leaders were in jail or in hiding as a consequence of polygamy, that the United States government threatened to confiscate the church's temples and other property, and that Utah had no chance of gaining statehood otherwise.

It is estimated that there are still some 30,000 polygamists living clandestinely in Utah. The church of the Latter-day Saints (LDS) says that any member caught practicing polygamy will be excommunicated. It is revealing to note, however, that even after the 1890 manifesto a number of Mormon leaders were tried and convicted of unlawful cohabitation with plural wives.[18]

Since it began, the church has had 15 presidents. Among the most notable are Joseph Fielding Smith (1876–1972), Spencer W. Kimball (1895–1994), Ezra Taft Benson (1899–1994), and Howard W. Hunter (1907–95). All the presidents are viewed as prophets who serve as God's mouthpiece.

The church is led by a First Presidency (a "collective trio" made up of the president of the church and a first and second counselor), the Council of Twelve Apostles (who hold lifetime positions), and the "First Quorum of the Seventy" and the "Second Quorum of the Seventy" (stemming from Moses' calling of 70 elders to assist him). The 15 men at the top—the First Presidency and the Council of Twelve Apostles—rule with unchallenged authority in the church.

Structurally the church is divided into branches, wards, stakes, and areas. A branch is a local congregation with usually fewer than 200 members and is headed by a branch president. A ward is a local congregation of 200 to 800 members and is led by a bishop. A stake is a collection of 5 to 12 wards in an area, governed by a stake president. An area is a large geographical district encompassing stakes, wards, and branches. The headquarters for the Mormon church is in Salt Lake City.

Gordon B. Hinckley became president in 1995 and maintains a high profile partly because of television interviews with Mike Wallace, Larry King, and other TV hosts. Under Hinckley's leadership there has been a strong missionary advance, the building of an unprecedented number of Mormon temples and meeting houses, increased administrative efficiency, and good public relations. He has been an effective leader.

MORMON BELIEFS

The "Restored" Church

According to Smith's First Vision, all the churches were corrupt in God's sight, and therefore the "one true church" needed to be restored (cf. Acts 3:20–21; 20:29–31; 2 Thess. 2:3). Mormons claim that proper church organization with its respective offices had been lost along with continual revelation through God's appointed representatives. The true gospel in its completeness had also been lost from the Bible due to "designing priests" removing its "plain and precious" truths. Further, the Melchizedek Priesthood had been lost from the earth after the death of the last apostle (cf. Acts 3:20–21). But the church teaches that all these lost elements had been restored by Joseph Smith.[19] Mormons believe that the presence or absence of this eternal priesthood determines the divinity or falsity of a professing church. Because the Mormon church exclusively has this "restored" priesthood, it alone is the one true church.

Downplaying Its Exclusivist Doctrines

In recent years the church has become increasingly involved with the Interfaith movement. Mormons recognize that it would be difficult to pursue working relationships with Protestants, Catholics, and others with their historical claim that theirs is the only true church; therefore, they have recently softened their stance on this claim.[20]

To make this plausible, however, Mormon scholars have had to adopt strained interpretations of Smith's statements that all other churches are an abomination. One conciliatory Mormon leader suggested, "By reading the [First Vision] passage carefully, we find that the Lord Jesus Christ was referring only to that particular group of ministers in the Prophet Joseph Smith's community who were quarreling about which church was true."[21] This revisionist line of reasoning fails because, if this were so, all Smith had to do was move to a neighboring community and seek out a minister who was not corrupt. It would not have been necessary to completely "restore" the church of Jesus Christ on earth by founding the Mormon church.

New Scriptures for a New Church

The Mormon church has three standard works besides the Bible that it views as authoritative and inspired scripture. These are the Book of Mormon, Doctrine and Covenants, and the Pearl of Great Price, the first being the most widely known outside the church.

The Book of Mormon: "Another Testament" of Jesus Christ

Joseph Smith once said the Book of Mormon is "the most correct of any book on earth, and the keystone of our religion, and a man would get nearer to God by abiding by its precepts, than any other book."[22] This book is an abridged account of God's dealings with the original inhabitants of the American continent from about 2247 B.C. to A.D. 421. It is alleged that it was originally engraved on gold plates by ancient prophets, deposited in a stone box, and buried in the Hill Cumorah in New York State. It is said to be God's uncorrupted revelation to humankind, the "fullness of the everlasting gospel," and "another Testament of Jesus Christ."

Mormons believe the Bible prophesies about the Book of Mormon. Isaiah 29:1–4, for example, purportedly tells how the Book of Mormon would be taken out of the ground (Hill Cumorah). The two sticks mentioned in Ezekiel 37:16–17 are said to refer to the Bible and the Book of Mormon, thus affirming the authority of the latter.

Corruptions in the Bible

The Mormons' eighth Article of Faith affirms, "We believe the Bible to be the Word of God, as far as it is translated correctly."[23] Mormons believe that because of poor transmission, large portions of the Bible have been lost down through the centuries. The portions of the Bible that have survived have become corrupted because of faulty transmission. While Mormons acknowledge that the original manuscripts penned by biblical authors were the Word of God, they believe that what passes as "the Bible" today is corrupt. It can only be trusted insofar as "it is translated correctly." Mormon apostle Orson Pratt once went so far as to ask, "Who, in his right mind, could, for one moment, suppose the Bible in its present form to be a perfect guide? Who knows that even one verse of the Bible has escaped pollution?"[24]

Joseph Smith's "Inspired Version" of the Bible

Joseph Smith is credited with the "translation" of the Inspired Version of the Bible. Actually, it is not a new translation; instead, Smith added to and subtracted from the King James Version (KJV)—not by examining Bible manuscripts, but by "divine inspiration." Smith "corrected, revised, altered, added to, and deleted from" the KJV.[25] Virtually thousands of changes were introduced. While it took nearly 50 of the world's greatest Bible scholars, with a knowledge of Hebrew and Greek, seven years to finish their work on the KJV, it took Smith a mere three years to complete his work—despite the fact that he had virtually no knowledge of the biblical languages. Smith even added a passage in Genesis 50 that predicted his own coming: "That seer will I bless . . . and his name shall be called Joseph."[26]

God Is an Exalted Man

Mormon prophets and apostles teach that God the Father was once a mortal man who continually progressed to become a God (an *exalted man*)—and that the rest of mankind can become gods like him by adopting and faithfully adhering to Mormonism. As Mormon general authority Milton R. Hunter put it, "God the Eternal Father was once a mortal man who passed through a school of earth life similar to that through which we are now passing. He became God—an exalted being—through obedience to the same eternal Gospel truths that we are given opportunity today to obey."[27] Today, then, "God the Eternal Father, our Father in Heaven, is an exalted, perfected, and glorified Personage having a tangible body of flesh and bones."[28]

Mormons often cite verses from the Bible to show that God is a physical being. It is suggested that since Adam was created in the image of God (Gen. 1:26–27), God must have a physical body. This physicality is also evident in that Moses spoke with God "face to face" (Ex. 33:11). Further, since Jesus said, "Anyone who has seen me has seen the Father" (John 14:9), the Father must have a physical body as does Jesus.

There Are Innumerable Gods

Mormonism teaches that the Trinity is not three persons in one Being, as historic Christianity has always taught, but rather three separate beings. In other words, the Father, Son, and Holy Spirit are separate Gods. They are "one" only in their common purpose and their attributes of perfection. Other gods exist.

Spencer W. Kimball, former president of the church, made the following remarks in a priesthood meeting: "Brethren, 225,000 of you are here tonight. I suppose 225,000 of you may become gods. There seems to be plenty of space out there in the universe. And the Lord has proved that he knows how to do it. I think he could make, or probably have us help make, worlds for all of us, for every one of us 225,000."[29]

In Mormon theology, just as Jesus has a Father, so the Father has a Father, and the Father of Jesus' Father has a Father. This endless succession of Fathers goes on and on, up the hierarchy of exalted beings in the universe. There is a Father of the Father of the Father of the Father ad infinitum.

There are not only numerous Father-gods but also a heavenly wife (or wives) for each. In 1853, Orson Pratt explained,

> Each God, through his wife or wives, raises up a numerous family of sons and daughters; ... As soon as each God has begotten many millions of male and female spirits, ... he, in connection with his sons, organizes a new world, after a similar order to the one which we now inhabit, where he sends both the male and female spirits to inhabit tabernacles of flesh and bones.... The inhabitants of each world are required to reverence, adore, and worship their own personal father who dwells in the Heaven which they formerly inhabited.[30]

Not unexpectedly, Mormons feel the Bible supports their belief in many gods. For example, Jesus told some Jews, "You are gods" (John 10:34–35). The apostle Paul in 1 Corinthians 8:5 made reference to "gods" in heaven and on earth. The Mormons contend that if Jesus and the chief among the Apostles taught a plurality of gods, the doctrine must be true.

Jesus Christ Is the Father's Greatest Spirit-Son

According to official Mormon teaching, Jesus was "begotten" as the first spirit child of the Father (Elohim) and one of his unnamed wives ("Heavenly Mother"—see Ps. 2:7). Because the Heavenly Father and Mother had many spirit children, Jesus is often referred to by Mormons as "our elder brother." (Lucifer, too, is the spirit brother of Jesus.) Jesus, as a spirit son, then progressed by obedience and devotion to the truth in the spirit world until he became a God. Prior to his incarnation Jesus was the Jehovah of the Old Testament.

When it came time for his birth on earth, Jesus in his mortal state was "begotten" through sexual relations between a flesh-and-bone Heavenly Father and Mary. There is nothing figurative in the word *begotten*.

Such a doctrine naturally raises questions about the virginity of Mary. Mormon theologians maintain that even though the Father had sexual relations with Mary, she remained a virgin. Bruce McConkie fancifully argues that a "virgin" is a woman who has had no sexual relations with a *mortal* man. Because God the Father was an *immortal* man, Mary remained a virgin after having relations with him.[31]

It is noteworthy that even though Mormons believe in innumerable gods, they try to argue they are not polytheists because

	TWO VIEWS OF JESUS CHRIST	
	Evangelical Christian View	**Mormon View**
Relation to Time	Eternally God	Preexistent, not eternally God
Identity	Unique Son of God	Spirit-brother of Lucifer
Divine Names	Jehovah and Elohim	Jehovah, but not Elohim
Human Conception	Holy Spirit overshadowed Mary	The Father and Mary procreated
Trinity	Father, Son, and Holy Spirit; one in nature, distinct in personhood	Three distinct Gods

they worship and pray to only one God, the Father. They do not worship or pray to Jesus.

Humans as Preexistent Beings

In Mormonism, all the people who have ever inhabited the earth were first born in spirit form in heaven. "Preexistence" is the term commonly used to describe the premortal existence of the spirit children of the Father (see Jer. 1:5; John 17:5; Acts 17:28–29). This preexistence was allegedly a time of *probation*.

One of the most repellent aspects of the Mormon doctrine of *preexistence* is the racist concept that black people are dark-skinned as God's punishment for wrong choices they supposedly made before they were born. The 1966 edition of *Mormon Doctrine* states that those who were "less valiant" in the preexistence "are known to us as Negroes."[32] For many years the "curse" of dark skin prevented black people from entering the Mormon priesthood.

With such blatant racism at the heart of Mormonism, it is not surprising that the church came under criticism in the 1960s and 1970s. Pressure was brought to bear by people inside and outside the church, including people involved in the civil rights movement. On June 9, 1978, President Kimball received a "revelation" from God that said all worthy male church members could be eligible for the priesthood *regardless of race.*

The Mormon Teaching on Sin and Salvation

In Mormon theology, Adam and Eve were not yet "mortal" prior to the "fall." Mormons interpret "mortal" not in the sense of death and dying, but primarily in the sense of having the capacity to bear children. Before the "fall," Adam and Eve did not have the ability to bear children; when they became mortal at the point they "sinned," they acquired that ability. Thus, in a way, the "fall" of Adam and Eve was a good thing. Spirit children need bodies to "progress" toward godhood, and what Adam did made this possible. If Adam and Eve fell, then, it was a "fall upward."[33]

Mormons typically define *sin* as a wrong judgment, a mistake, an imperfection, or an inadequacy. The moral sting is thereby taken out of sin. Moreover, instead of holding to original sin, Mormons say children are "innocent" until they reach accountability at the age of eight. Children are born innately good and have no propensity toward evil.

With this weak view of sin, it is not surprising that Jesus' role in the salvation process is much reduced. In Mormonism, Jesus' atonement basically means that He was able to overcome physical death for the human race. He paid the price for us to rise from the grave. Because of what He accomplished, we will all be resurrected. Thus, when Mormons talk about salvation (or *"general salvation"*), they essentially mean *resurrection*. Jesus is the "Savior" because He saved the human race from permanent physical death. Mormons say that what Jesus did was very important because, obviously, without a resurrected body one cannot become a God and give birth to spirit children. Jesus' accomplishment, however, did not do away with the need for good works. Indeed, Jesus did his part, and now it is up to us to do our part and prove ourselves worthy of *exaltation*.[34]

Grace in terms of Mormon salvation is simply God's enabling power that allows people to "lay hold on eternal life and exaltation after they have expended their own best efforts."[35] Grace aids people as they seek (by personal effort) to attain perfection (see Matt. 5:48). But God's grace alone does not save. Spencer W. Kimball made the point that "one of the most fallacious doctrines originated by Satan and propounded by man is that man is saved alone by the grace of God; that belief in Jesus Christ alone is all that is needed for salvation."[36]

Although Jesus provided "general salvation" (resurrection) for all people, "individual salvation" refers to that which people merit through their own acts throughout life by obedience to the laws of the gospel. Salvation in its fullest sense is synonymous with exaltation (as a God) and consists of gaining an inheritance in the highest of the three heavens (see below).[37]

Understanding Eternal Progression

Fundamental to understanding the Mormon concept of exaltation is the doctrine of *eternal progression*. Mormons say we do not seek perfection only in this life. Rather, it begins before birth and continues beyond the grave. Salvation does not come all at once. Exaltation to godhood ultimately involves not just what we do in this earthly life (mortality), but what we have already done in *premortality* (one's "preexistence" as a spirit child) and in *postmortality* (one's return to the spirit world following physical death).

A key concept related to this process is *agency*, which describes each human being's right to choose between good and evil. Agency is very important, Mormons say, for without it humanity cannot "progress." People progress toward godhood by making "wise use" of their agency in premortality, mortality, and postmortality.

In premortality, spirit children begin progressing toward godhood. This is a probationary period. Mormons believe that the very fact that they have been born on earth is an indication that they used their agency wisely in the preexistence. It proves that they did not follow Lucifer when he rebelled against God.[38]

Mortality—our earthly life, or "Second Estate"—is a time of testing for Mormons. To become gods they must face (and overcome) physical temptations and trials. As spirit children they cannot be physically tempted because they do not have physical bodies. Hence, spirit children take on human bodies, and during this time of mortality they face physical temptations and make progress toward godhood.

Once they enter mortality, they are faced with an unbelievable list of requirements to progress toward godhood. This list includes repentance, baptism (which renders them "born again"—Acts 2:38; John 3:1–5), membership in the LDS church, innumerable good works (James 2:17, 26), keeping the Mormon "Word of Wisdom" (which prohibits the use of coffee, tea, alcohol, or tobacco), eternal marriage (so that as gods in the future, they can procreate and give birth to spirit children), and a variety of temple rituals. These temple rituals include the *endowment ritual* (in which one is given a new name, learns secret handshakes, and is given protective sacred undergarments) and *baptism for the dead* (whereby one can be baptized on behalf of a dead relative [1 Corinthians 15:29] who believes the gospel in the spirit world following death [1 Peter 3:18–19]). They must also progressively become more "perfect" and "worthy" by living a perpetually clean life—a requirement for being granted entrance into the temple. Each of these plays a critical role and is necessary in the Mormon system of salvation.

In terms of postmortality, Mormons say that at the moment of death the spirit enters the spirit world. Mormons go to a place called "paradise," where they continue in their efforts to work toward godhood. Non-Mormons go to a spirit prison, where Mormon spirits "evangelize" them in missionary activities. If spirits in prison accept Mormonism, they can leave the prison and enter into paradise as long as someone (a living relative) has been baptized on their behalf. Otherwise, they remain in spirit prison indefinitely. After entering paradise, the spirits are free to work toward their own progression.[39]

Three Kingdoms of Glory

At the end of the world, people are said to end up in one of "three kingdoms of glory": the celestial kingdom, the terrestrial kingdom, and the telestial kingdom. Their level of worthiness determines which kingdom. Mormons believe there is support in the Bible for these three kingdoms in 1 Corinthians 15:40–44.

The celestial kingdom is the highest degree of glory and is inhabited by faithful Mormons—the "righteous, those who have been faithful in keeping the commandments of the Lord, and have been cleansed of all their sins"[40]—and children who die before the age of eight. This is the kingdom where people will live with the Heavenly Father and Jesus Christ. On this level they can attain exaltation to godhood.

The second of the three degrees is the terrestrial kingdom, which is reserved for non-Mormons who live moral lives (they are "morally clean") and for "less than valiant" Mormons. "Less than valiant" Mormons are those who did not live up to their church's expectations or requirements.

The lowest degree is the telestial kingdom, which is where the great majority of people go. It is reserved for those who have been carnal and sinful throughout life. People must temporarily suffer through hell ("outer darkness") before entering. After people "suffer in full" for their sins, they are permitted to enter into the telestial kingdom.

CHALLENGING MORMON BELIEFS

The Problem with the "Restored Church" Claim

The history of the Christian church shows clearly that the Mormon claim of a "restoration" is pure fiction. In church history we have an accurate picture not only regarding the teachings of the early church, but also of the deviations from orthodoxy that took place—including Gnosticism, Arianism, and Sabellianism. If it were true that Mormonism is the "restored" church, we would expect to find evidence elsewhere for such unique doctrines as the plurality of gods, men becoming gods, and God the Father having once been a man. But we do not find even a hint of any of these in ancient church history.

Further, the whole idea that the priesthoods are restored in the Mormon church is plagued with problems. There is not a single example anywhere in the New Testament of a believer ever being ordained to the Melchizedek Priesthood. It is noteworthy that in Hebrews 7:24 Jesus' priesthood is said to be "permanent" (NIV) or "unchangeable" (KJV). The *Theological Dictionary of the New Testament* tells us, "In the New Testament Hebrews 7:24 says that Christ has an eternal and imperishable priesthood, not just in the sense that it cannot be transferred to anyone else, but in the sense of 'unchangeable.'"[41] This, combined with the fact that Scripture asserts that the Aaronic Priesthood has permanently passed away (Heb. 7:11–12), renders the Mormon claim of a "restored priesthood" false.

Changes in the Book of Mormon

History proves there have been more than 3,913 changes between the original edition of the Book of Mormon published in 1830 and the ones printed and issued through the mid 1970s. The 1981 edition introduced between 100 and 200 additional word changes.[42] Though many of the changes relate to spelling and grammar, some are quite substantial. For example, in 1 Nephi 11:21 the phrase "Behold the Lamb of God, yea, even *the eternal Father*" is changed to "Behold the Lamb of God, yea even *the son of the eternal Father*" (emphasis added).

The problem is that the Mormon account of how Smith went about translating the Book of Mormon disallows any possibility of errors, even relating to misspellings and grammar. The translation process involved Smith's using a "seer stone." This entailed Smith's seeing one character at a time through the seer stone and reading it aloud to Oliver Cowdery, after which Cowdery would repeat the character to ensure accuracy, and then that character would disappear and another would appear in its place. Hence, every letter and word was allegedly given by the power of God.[43]

Plagiarisms in the Book of Mormon

Besides thousands of changes being made in the Book of Mormon, the book is also undermined by the many plagiarisms it contains from the King James Version of the Bible. Whole chapters have been lifted from the book of Isaiah. The problem is this: If the Book of Mormon was first penned between 600 B.C. and A.D. 421, as claimed, how could it contain such extensive quotations from the KJV, which was published in A.D. 1611 and which uses the archaic English of the Elizabethan era?[44]

Even the italicized words from the KJV were plagiarized. This is relevant because, as noted in the preface of the KJV, these words were not in the original languages but were added by the KJV translators to provide clarity. How could the Book of Mormon be written far in advance of the KJV but contain the King James translators' "inserted clarifying words"?

There have also been charges through the years that Smith may have borrowed from other extant sources of his day. Some believe he plagiarized from Solomon Spaulding, a retired minister who wrote two fictional narratives about the early inhabitants of America. The problem is that the particular book from which the Book of Mormon was allegedly plagiarized is missing. As Ruth Tucker explains, "This missing volume, known as *Manuscript Found*, was, as the theory goes, left in a print shop where it was stolen by Sidney Rigdon, a close associate of Smith in the early days of Mormonism. Spaulding died in 1816, fourteen years before the Book of Mormon was published, but his stories had not been forgotten."[45] Spaulding had apparently told stories of Nephi and Lehi to customers in his tavern, and this material allegedly later found its way into the Book of Mormon. Mormons have made great efforts to discredit all this. Without more evidence, the issue is still open to debate.

Others have suggested Smith may have borrowed from a book by Ethan Smith entitled *View of the Hebrews*, which held that the American Indians held Hebraic origins. Critic Fawn Brodie notes that "it may never be proved that Joseph [Smith] saw *View of the Hebrews* before writing the Book of Mormon, but the striking parallelisms between the books hardly leave a case for mere coincidence."[46]

No Archaeological Support for the Book of Mormon

According to Mormon Scriptures, the Nephite and Lamanite nations had huge populations that lived in large, fortified cities. They allegedly waged large-scale wars with each other for hundreds of years, culminating in a conflict in which hundreds of thousands of people were killed in A.D. 385 near Hill Cumorah in present-day New York State (see the Book of Mormon 6:9–15). One would think that if all this really happened, there would be archaeological evidence to support it. But there is none. While there is massive archaeological evidence to support the people and places mentioned in the Bible, evidence is completely missing with regard to the Book of Mormon and other Mormon scriptures.

Archaeological institutions have found no support for Mormon claims. The National Museum of Natural History at the Smithsonian Institution in Washington, D.C., affirmed, "Smithsonian archaeologists see no direct connection between the archaeology of the New World and the subject matter of the book [of Mormon]."[47] Similarly, the Bureau of American Ethnology asserted, "There is no evidence whatever of any migration from Israel to America, and likewise no evidence that pre-Colombian Indians had any knowledge of Christianity or the Bible."[48] In a letter dated February 4, 1982, the National Geographic Society stated, "Although many Mormon sources claim that the Book of Mormon has been substantiated by archaeological findings, this claim has not been verified scientifically."[49]

Many Mormon scholars try hard to find Book of Mormon lands somewhere in Central America. These scholars, however, disagree among themselves as to where in Central America the Book of Mormon lands may be; that is, some say the Costa Rica area, others say the Yucatan Peninsula, and still others say the Tehuantepec area. The fact remains that there is virtually no solid archaeological support for any of this.

The Book of Mormon *Not* Prophesied in the Bible

Mormons are practicing fanciful *eisogesis* (reading a meaning into the text of Scripture) instead of *exegesis* (drawing the meaning from the text of Scripture) in claiming that the Bible prophesies the Book of Mormon. Isaiah 29:1–4 refers not to the Book of Mormon coming out of the ground, as claimed, but to Jerusalem being judged by God so harshly that the inhabitants are brought down to the ground, as if buried. (This was fulfilled during Sennacherib's siege of the city in 701 B.C.) The two sticks in Ezekiel 37:16–17 refer not to the Bible and the Book of Mormon, but to the unification of the southern kingdom

(Judah) and the northern kingdom (Israel) into a single nation. There is no reference in the Bible to the Book of Mormon.

God Is an Eternal Spirit, Not an Exalted Man

The verses Mormons cite for the idea that God has a physical body are being misinterpreted. While it is true that Adam was created in the image of God (Gen. 1:26–27), the image cannot be physical because God is spirit (John 4:24) and a spirit does not have flesh and bones (Luke 24:39). Adam was created in the image of God in the sense that he finitely reflected God's communicable attributes (life, personality, truth, wisdom, love, holiness, and justice). When Exodus 33:11 says Moses spoke to God "face to face," that is simply an anthropomorphic way of indicating "personally," "directly," or "intimately"—not physically. When Jesus said, "Anyone who has seen me has seen the Father" (John 14:9), He was simply saying that He was the ultimate revelation of the Father (see John 1:18; 12:45; 13:20), not that the Father has a body. Mormons often misinterpret key verses this way.

Many passages in Scripture assert that God is not a man or an exalted man. In Hosea 11:9 we find God Himself affirming, "I am God, and not man." Numbers 23:19 tells us that "God is not a man, that he should lie, nor a son of man, that he should change his mind." Romans 1:22–23 says, "Although they claimed to be wise, they became fools and exchanged the glory of the immortal God for images made to look like mortal man and birds and animals and reptiles." Further, Scripture portrays God as being invisible, which would not be possible if God had a body of flesh and bones (see John 1:18; Col. 1:15; 1 Tim. 1:17).

We must also make note of the immutability of God. God does not change in His nature, which means He did not progress from a mortal man into an exalted man. Malachi 3:6 quotes the living God as saying, "I the LORD do not change." James 1:17 says that God "does not change like shifting shadows." Psalm 90:2 affirms that "from everlasting to everlasting you are God." There has never been a time when God was not God.

There Is Only *One* God

Mormons often cite Bible verses in affirming that there are many gods, but they are all taken out of context. Jesus' statement "You are gods" in John 10:34 must be understood in light of Psalm 82, the passage Jesus was quoting. Jesus was essentially telling the Jewish leaders this: If the unjust judges mentioned in Psalm 82 can be called "gods" (with a small g) because of their acts of rendering life and death decisions over the people, then how much more appropriate it is that I (Jesus) be called "God" (with a capital G) in view of the fact that I am truly the Son of God—which is something that My acts (miracles, or "signs") bear witness to. (Significantly, Psalm 82:7 affirms that these unjust judges would die like the men they really were—thereby "giving the lie" to their so-called godhood.)

Likewise, 1 Corinthians 8:5 does not provide the support for the plurality of gods that Mormons hope for. Indeed, in the preceding verse Paul flatly asserts that there is only one God. In the next verse he asserts there is only one true God. In verse 5, Paul was speaking only about *false* gods or idols.

Scripture emphatically declares there is only one God. In Isaiah 44:8 God Himself asks, "Is there any God besides me? No, there is no other Rock; I know not one." If this is true, then God could not have had a Father and a Grandfather who were gods in their own right. Similarly, Isaiah 43:10 portrays God as saying, "Before me there was no God formed, nor will there be one after me." Since there were no gods before the God of the Bible, this means that God had no Father-gods or Grandfather-gods before Him. Since no gods will come after God, this means that none of His children will become gods after Him. That there is only one God is the consistent testimony of Scripture (John 5:44; 17:3; Rom. 3:29–30; 16:27; 1 Cor. 8:4; Gal. 3:20; Eph. 4:6; 1 Thess. 1:9; 1 Tim. 1:17; 2:5; James 2:19; 1 John 5:20–21; Jude 25).

Philosophically, of course, an infinite number of gods prior to God the Father is impossible. Such a view sets into motion an "infinite regress" of gods in eternity past. It is impossible that every Heavenly Father has a "Father" before him, for this view cannot account for a *first* Father that got it all started.

Humans Can Never Become Gods

The fact that humans cannot become gods is illustrated repeatedly throughout Scripture. One example is Acts 14, where Paul demonstrated he was an uncompromising monotheist. After Paul healed a man in Lystra, the people there started to worship him and

Barnabas as gods. When Paul and Barnabas understood what was going on, "they tore their clothes and rushed out into the crowd, shouting: 'Men, why are you doing this? *We too are only men, human like you.* We are bringing you good news, telling you to turn from these worthless things to *the living God,* who made heaven and earth and sea and everything in them'" (vv. 14–15, emphasis added). Paul and Barnabas not only emphatically denied they were gods, but spoke of the only true God, who created the universe.

Paul and Barnabas's attitude is in clear contrast to the folly of Herod related in Acts 12:21–23. After Herod had given a public address, the people shouted, "'This is the voice of a god, not of a man.' Immediately, because Herod did not give praise to God, an angel of the Lord struck him down, and he was eaten by worms and died." Clearly, God does not look kindly on human pretenders to the divine throne.

Although Mormons think they have it in themselves to attain perfection and achieve exaltation as gods, Jesus' view of human sin more than quashes any such hope. Jesus taught that man is evil (Matt. 12:34) and capable of great wickedness (Mark 7:20–23). He said that man is utterly lost (Luke 19:10), is a sinner (Luke 15:10), is in need of repentance before a holy God (Mark 1:15), and needs to be "born again" (John 3:3, 5, 7). Jesus described sin as blindness (Matt. 23:16–26), sickness (Matt. 9:12), being enslaved (John 8:34), and living in darkness (John 8:12; 12:35–36). Moreover, Jesus taught that sin is a universal condition and that all people are guilty (Luke 7:37-48). Jesus also taught that both inner thoughts and external acts render a person guilty (Matt. 5:28). And He affirmed that God is fully aware of every person's sins; nothing escapes His notice (Matt. 22:18; Luke 6:8).

Obviously, sin is not just a "mistake" or "bad judgment," as Mormons maintain. There is no hope for the Mormons who are seeking to attain perfection and exaltation to godhood in their own efforts. By trusting in Christ, however, they can be redeemed and live forever with the one true God (Heb. 10:14; John 3:16). (See further evidence against man's alleged divinity in the chapter on the mind sciences.)

Jesus Is Eternal Deity

Jesus was not a procreated being. It is true, as Mormons note, that Psalm 2:7 cites the Father as saying to Jesus, "This day I have begotten thee" (KJV). However, Acts 13:33–34 informs us that Psalm 2:7 is expressly fulfilled in Jesus' resurrection. The verse has nothing to do with procreation. Further, the idea that Jesus was born on earth as a result of sexual relations between the Father and Mary is not only profane, but contradicts the scriptural fact that the Holy Spirit overshadowed Mary and produced a human nature for the eternal Son of God (Luke 1:34–35).

Mormons fail to recognize the scriptural teaching on the eternality of Christ. John 1:1, as one example, plainly affirms, "In the beginning was the Word, and the Word was with God, and the Word was God." "In the beginning" is a translation of the Greek words *en arche*. These are the same two words that begin the book of Genesis in the Septuagint (the Greek translation of the Hebrew Old Testament). The obvious conclusion we must draw is that John's "beginning" is identical to the Genesis "beginning." When the time-space universe came into being, Christ the divine Word already existed. Jesus did not come into being at a specific point in eternity past, but at that point at which all else began to be, He already was. No matter how far back we go in eternity past, we will never come to a point at which we could say of Christ the Word that "there was a time when He was not."

The Mormon view that Elohim (the Father) and Jehovah (Jesus) are two different gods in the Old Testament is fallacious. Numerous verses in the Bible demonstrate that Elohim and Yahweh are the same God. In Genesis 27:20 Isaac's son said, "The LORD [Yahweh] your God [Elohim] gave me success" (inserts added). Likewise, in Jeremiah 32:18 we find reference to the "great and powerful God [Elohim], whose name is the LORD [Yahweh] Almighty."

Scripture is also clear that Jesus was not the spirit brother of Lucifer. Colossians 1:16 informs us that the entire angelic realm—including the angel Lucifer—was personally created by Jesus Christ. Apparently there was a heresy flourishing in Colossae (to whom Paul wrote the book of Colossians) that involved the worship of angels, an act that degraded Christ. To correct this grave error, Paul emphasized that Christ is the One who created all things—including all the angels. Therefore, He is supreme and is alone worthy to be worshiped. Lucifer and Christ are of two entirely different classes: the created and the Creator.

Finally, the Mormon rendition of Christ's atonement bears little resemblance to the pages of Scripture. Jesus' mission was to provide a substitutionary atonement on the cross, and this atonement covered the sins of all humanity (Isa. 53:6; 1 John 2:2). By so doing, Jesus provided a total salvation (not just resurrection from the dead) for human beings that they had no hope of procuring for themselves (Matt. 26:26–28; John 12:27). It is by believing in Him alone—with no works involved, no personal perfection, no eternal progression—that we appropriate the gift of salvation He made possible (John 3:16–17).

Only Two Possible Destinies in the Afterlife

While Mormons cite 1 Corinthians 15:40–42 in favor of "three kingdoms of glory," they read something into the passage that simply is not there. The verse reads as follows in the KJV:

> There are also celestial bodies, and bodies terrestrial: but the glory of the celestial is one, and the glory of the terrestrial is another.
> There is one glory of the sun, and another glory of the moon, and another glory of the stars: for one star differeth from another star in glory.
> So also is the resurrection of the dead. It is sown in corruption; it is raised in incorruption.

These verses do not even mention "telestial" and are therefore disqualified as a support for the idea that there is a telestial kingdom. The context for this passage is set in verse 35, where Paul raises questions about the heavenly (celestial) resurrection body and how it differs from an earthly (terrestrial) body. He indicates that the earthly body is fallen, temporal, and weak while the heavenly body is eternal, perfect, and powerful. Three kingdoms are nowhere in view.

The Scriptures consistently categorize people into one of two classes (saved and unsaved, or believers and unbelievers) and portray the final destiny of every person as being one of two realities (heaven or hell). In a parable in Matthew 13:30, for example, Jesus speaks of believers and unbelievers as wheat and tares that will be separated at the end of the age. The Bible does not speak of three categories of wheat, each going to a different "barn." All the wheat

THE CHALLENGE OF THE CULTS

is gathered into Christ's one barn, as it were (see also Matt. 13:49; 25:32–46; Luke 16:19–31).

Jesus consistently affirmed that all the saved will be with Him in a single location. He promised, "Whoever serves me must follow me; and where I am, my servant also will be" (John 12:26). All who believe in Christ are heirs of the eternal kingdom (Gal. 3:29; 4:28–31; Titus 3:7). Romans 3:21 states that the righteousness of God that leads to life in heaven is available "unto all and upon all them that believe." Furthermore, in John 10:16 Jesus affirms that all who believe in Him will be in one "sheep pen" under "one shepherd." There will not be three separate sheep pens or "kingdoms." One sheep pen, one shepherd. One kingdom, one King.

4

THE JEHOVAH'S WITNESSES

The Jehovah's Witnesses today are growing at a phenomenal pace, due largely to the astonishing amount of literature they distribute. During the late 1980s, the Jehovah's Witnesses published their 10-billionth piece of literature, representing about a hundred years of publishing. The next 10 billion pieces took only about a decade.[1] In 1999 the Jehovah's Witnesses devoted more than 1.1 billion man-hours distributing Watchtower literature and spreading Watchtower doctrines.

With a twice-monthly printing in excess of 16 million copies per issue, *The Watchtower* magazine currently approaches the circulation of *Reader's Digest* and *TV Guide* and easily surpasses the combined total of *Time, Newsweek,* and *U.S. News & World Report.*[2] *The Watchtower* is now published simultaneously in 121 languages.[3]

The Watchtower's main "Bethel" plant in Brooklyn prints on almost 1,000 miles of paper—or 61 million pages—per day and turns out more than 3 million copies of the New World Translation Bible per month.[4] More than 100 million copies of this translation have now been distributed in whole or in part in 34 languages. With such impressive literature distribution, it is no wonder that some 50 new Jehovah's Witness congregations emerge each week world-wide, and more than 4.5 million Bible studies are conducted each month with prospective converts.[5] All of this started with a single man named Charles Taze Russell.

WATCHTOWER ROOTS

Charles Taze Russell (1852–1916)

Charles Taze Russell was born in Pittsburgh, Pennsylvania, on February 16, 1852. His parents were committed Presbyterians, and young Charles received a religious upbringing. His mother, who died when Charles was only nine, encouraged Charles to consider the Christian ministry as a vocation. As it happened, however, Charles got involved in his father's clothing business at age 11, working part-time while attending school.

In his teenage years Russell abandoned the Presbyterian church because he did not like their doctrines of predestination and eternal punishment. He became a Congregationalist for a while, but by the time he was 17 he was an avowed skeptic, discarding the Bible and the church creeds.

During this time, Russell became interested in studying different religions, including Eastern religions, but did not find what he was looking for. Yet he became excited when he came into contact with some Adventists. In particular, he was impressed with the prophetic millenarian views they held. This would begin his life-long interest in prophetic speculation. Russell also appreciated the Adventist rejection of eternal punishment, teaching instead that *hell* was just another word for the grave and that death involves annihilation.

In 1870 Russell began to meet with some friends and associates in a Bible study in Pittsburgh. His companions there became known simply as "the Bible Students."[6] As a result of this study, Russell and his friends came to reject the Trinity and garnered further arguments against the immortality of the soul and hell. They came to believe that immortality is a gift to be attained. Since the wicked do not have immortality, there is no eternal torment in hell.

The Bible Students also investigated prophecy and came to believe that Christ would be *invisibly present* on earth before Armageddon broke out. There would not be a visible Second Coming. This belief was based largely on their translation of Matthew 24:3: "What will be the sign of thy presence, and of the consummation of the age?" It was argued that the Greek word in question, *parousia*, should be translated "presence" instead of "coming." (Most translations render the verse, "What will be the sign of your coming...?")

Not long after this, 23-year-old Russell came into possession of a magazine published by Adventist preacher Nelson H. Barbour of Rochester, New York, entitled *The Herald of the Morning*.[7] Barbour held that the Lord's invisible presence had begun in 1874 and that the "harvest" work of gathering "the wheat" (true Christians) was already due. Barbour persuaded Russell that his date-setting scheme was correct—including not just the idea that the Lord had been spiritually present since 1874 but also that 1914 would mark the year when Christ's kingdom would be fully established on earth.[8]

Convinced of Christ's invisible presence, Russell was determined to proclaim it to others. He curtailed his business interests and devoted both his time and his money to "the great harvest work." He sent Dr. Barbour home with money and instructions for preparing a book on "the good tidings so far as then understood."[9]

Russell also revived a journal, called the *Herald*, that Barbour had published earlier but then suspended for lack of subscriptions. But Russell soon split with Barbour over differences regarding the nature of the atonement, and he discontinued financial support to the *Herald*.[10]

In 1879 Russell founded a new magazine entitled *Zion's Watch Tower and Herald of Christ's Presence*, which would eventually become today's *Watchtower* magazine. In this periodical Russell promoted the idea that Christ had returned invisibly to earth in 1874 and that God's kingdom would be established on earth in 1914. It was not long before congregations that were committed to Russell's interpretation began to crop up in various cities.

Then in Pittsburgh in 1881 Russell established Zion's Watch Tower Tract Society, known today as the Watchtower Bible and Tract Society of Pennsylvania, the legal agency that acts on behalf of Jehovah's Witnesses. Realizing that 1914 was rapidly approaching, Russell put out a call from this headquarters and recruited hundreds of evangelists who would go door-to-door to distribute the magazines, books, and tracts that Russell and his associates published. This work was done with great religious fervor.

By 1904 "Pastor" Russell, as he was called, had written six volumes that came to be known as *Studies in the Scriptures*. This series would be foundational to all future Watchtower theology. Russell proclaimed that anyone who read these volumes alone, even without consulting the Bible, would nevertheless have "the light of the Scriptures." Reading the Bible without these studies, however, would cause one to end up in darkness.[11]

One reason Russell's writings were revered by Jehovah's Witnesses is that he was viewed as the "faithful and wise servant" of Matthew 24:45. The fact is, from 1879 to 1895 Russell held that the servant was the 144,000-member church. Later Russell's followers proclaimed *him* as the servant. Russell's wife affirmed that also—until, after their marriage developed irreconcilable difficulties (and ultimately ended in divorce), she changed her mind and said he was the "evil servant" mentioned a few verses later in Matthew 24. By 1927 Christ's "anointed" followers in the Society were viewed as God's collective chosen servant.[12]

Toward the end of Russell's ministry it was decided that the Society needed to move out of Pittsburgh. If the Society was going to influence the world, it needed to be strategically located in a city that enabled utmost efficiency in shipping and communication. It was decided that Brooklyn, New York, would be the ideal center for the "harvest work" during the few years remaining until 1914.[13]

When 1914 came and went, many Jehovah's Witnesses were extremely disappointed because God's kingdom had not been set up as promised. They had worked hard spreading the word all over the world, and they were bitterly disillusioned when nothing happened.

Judge Joseph Franklin Rutherford (1869–1942)

Following Russell's death in 1916, Judge Joseph Franklin Rutherford became the second president of the Watchtower Society. Rutherford was born in 1869 in Morgan County, Missouri, to hardworking Baptist parents. During his childhood he got into arguments with his parents regarding hell—a factor that would become important later in life as he embraced Jehovah's Witness teachings.

Rutherford pursued a law career and was granted a license to practice law in Missouri in 1892. He did not hold a permanent position as "judge," though he did fill in as a judge from time to time in the Eighth Judicial Circuit Court of Missouri.

Having been an encyclopedia salesman prior to becoming a lawyer, Rutherford vowed that if someone ever visited him and tried to sell him books, he would try to help out the salesman by making a purchase. Rutherford ended up becoming a convert to the Jehovah's Witnesses when a member visited his office and sold him some Watchtower books.

Soon after Rutherford joined the movement in 1906, he became the Watchtower's legal counselor and represented Russell in numerous law cases. He became highly visible in the organization, and as soon as Russell died, Rutherford solidified his position as the new president. It was anything but a smooth transition. Apparently Russell had left instructions that after he died, the organization was to be run by a president who would share power with an editorial committee and the Watchtower's board of directors (whom Russell had appointed for life). Rutherford, however, wanted power, and he wanted to run things by himself.

The board of directors was not willing to bend, and the conflict soon escalated. Rutherford was set on being Jehovah's mouthpiece for this age.[14] He saw himself as inheriting all the authority Russell had held. But the board saw him as a usurper and worked to restrain him. Headquarters staff began choosing sides.

Things came to a head when Rutherford announced the publication of *The Finished Mystery*, presented as the seventh volume of Russell's series *Studies in the Scriptures*. Rutherford published the book without consulting the board, and they saw this as further evidence of his trying to usurp authority.

Rutherford then dropped another bombshell. He announced that four directors on the board had been removed and replaced by his supporters. Although the directors had been appointed for life, Rutherford obtained an outside attorney's opinion and discovered a loophole whereby their appointments could be invalidated by an oversight: routine reelection by shareholders had been neglected. A five-hour shouting match took place that day, and the conflict grew. A week later Rutherford had the disrupters removed from the building. Several splinter sects resulted from the disruption that rocked Watchtower headquarters that day, including the Layman's Home Missionary Movement and the Dawn Bible Students Association.

Rutherford soon developed the Watchtower Society into a hierarchical organization. He was overbearing and took an authoritarian approach. History reveals that he used vulgar language on occasion and also had an alcohol problem.[15] He also enjoyed opulent living at Watchtower expense (see below).

During the 1920s and 1930s, house-to-house witnessing became a heavy emphasis. Also during this time, Rutherford wrote relentlessly. Before it was all over, Rutherford had penned more than a hundred books and pamphlets.

Rutherford also tried his hand at Bible prophecy, focusing attention on the year 1925.[16] Not only was the old order of things to pass away that year, but the Old Testament patriarchs were also to be resurrected and usher in the righteous government of Jehovah. In expectation of this event, a magnificent residence called Beth Sarim was constructed in San Diego.[17]

The Old Testament patriarchs never showed up in 1925, and this led to bitter disappointment for many Jehovah's Witnesses. Rutherford himself ended up spending winters at Beth Sarim with a staff of servants until his death in 1942.[18]

At a convention in 1931, Rutherford deemed that those affiliated with the Watchtower would now be called "Jehovah's Witnesses." His goal was to distinguish followers of the Watchtower Society from individuals and groups that had broken away from the Watchtower but still referred to themselves as Bible Students.

The name of the society's magazine was soon changed from *Zion's Watch Tower and Herald of Christ's Presence* to *The Watchtower Announcing Jehovah's Kingdom.* This change reflects the Watchtower's abandonment of Russell's chronology—that is, they abandoned the idea that Christ's presence had become a reality in 1874 and now began teaching that Christ's presence was a period of time beginning, rather than ending, in 1914.

One distinctive of the Rutherford presidency was the use of portable phonographs in door-to-door witnessing. The Witness on the doorstep would play a recording from Rutherford that concluded with an appeal to buy a Watchtower book. Moreover, cars with loudspeakers affixed on top would cruise through neighborhoods to blare Rutherford's messages.

Rutherford died of bowel cancer at Beth Sarim in 1942.

Nathan Knorr (1905–77)

When Rutherford died, Nathan Knorr became the new president. Knorr was born in 1905 in Bethlehem, Pennsylvania, and was raised in the Reformed Church. He became associated with the Jehovah's Witnesses in 1922. He joined the Watchtower staff, worked in the shipping department for a time, and later in the printing factory, rising to the position of plant manager. Just 20 years after becoming affiliated with the organization, Knorr became its president.

Knorr did not have the charisma of his predecessors, nor was he a prolific writer, but he was an energetic businessman and a good administrator. More quiet and shy than Russell and Rutherford, Knorr avoided public appearances and worked behind the scenes, leaving doctrinal matters in the hands of the up-and-coming Frederick W. Franz. During Knorr's presidency, the Watchtower began publishing its books without listing authors' names.

The greatest distinctive of Knorr's presidency was that he instituted a program to train Jehovah's Witnesses in how to give presentations on the doorstep, including how to answer common objections. Jehovah's Witnesses going door-to-door no longer had to play phonograph records but instead were able to articulate Watchtower beliefs on their own.

A new Bible translation was also produced under Knorr's leadership. The New World Translation "restored" the divine name of Jehovah 237 times in the biblical text from Matthew to Revelation. It was claimed to be the best translation available.

Unfortunately, the society still had not learned enough lessons from its past prophetic failures. The society's followers were told that 6,000 years of human history (from the time of Adam and Eve) would come to an end in 1975. Armageddon was to occur that year, and Christ was to set up the Millennial Kingdom of earthly paradise. This prophecy led many Jehovah's Witnesses to sell their homes and quit their jobs in order to devote all their energy to witnessing to others. And, as with the earlier false predictions by the Watchtower, many Jehovah's Witnesses were greatly disappointed when 1975 came and went without anything happening. From 1976 to 1978, 390,000 Witnesses left the Watchtower organization.[19]

A change in leadership protocol took place in 1975. Until that time, the organization had been run by a president with the Governing Body playing only a supportive role. In 1975, however, the Governing Body sought more control in the day-to-day running of the organization. Starting January 1, 1976, the activities of the Watchtower Society and its congregations fell under the supervision of six administrative committees of the Governing Body. Knorr, then age 71, reluctantly accepted this change, but he died only 18 months later from an inoperable brain tumor. To the present, the Governing Body rules over Jehovah's Witnesses with unchallenged authority.

Frederick W. Franz (1893–1992)

Frederick W. Franz was born in Covington, Kentucky, in 1893. He grew up as a Presbyterian and aimed to become a Presbyterian minister one day. However, as a result of reading a booklet his brother sent him from the Bible Students, Franz left the Presbyterians and was baptized as a Jehovah's Witness.

Franz moved up through the ranks of the Watchtower for 35 years and became the premier theologian of the movement. On June 22, 1977, two weeks after Knorr's death, 83-year-old Franz was elected president of the society. He was not professionally trained in biblical studies, but he is regarded now as having been more knowledgeable than previous Watchtower presidents.

Toward the end of Franz's reign a crisis developed within the Watchtower Society as many Witnesses began to examine the history of the society independently.[20] Some of those raising questions were prominent leaders, and they were forced out of the organization for their "disloyalty." One of these was Raymond Franz, former Governing Body member and nephew of the president, and his dismissal was an event newsworthy enough that *Time* magazine ran a full-page article on it.[21] After being disfellowshiped, Raymond later affirmed that service on the Governing Body was disillusioning—something he documented in a book called *Crisis of Conscience*. He demonstrated in this book that the society is not biblical, has uttered false prophecies, has altered key teachings and policies, and has participated in lying and cover-ups.[22]

Milton G. Henschel (1920–)

Following Frederick Franz's death in 1992, Milton G. Henschel was elected society president. Henschel was born as a third-generation Jehovah's Witness in Pomona, New Jersey, in 1920. He served in various positions at the Watchtower, including personal secretary to Knorr and eventually a member of the Governing Body.

Henschel's significance is rooted in solving a major dilemma for the Jehovah's Witnesses. The dilemma relates to the Watchtower's earlier prophecy that some of the people alive in 1914 would still be alive when Jehovah's kingdom would finally be established. The problem is, almost everyone alive during 1914 was dead by 1992.

Through the years the Watchtower continually revised its understanding of the 1914 "generation." In 1968 the society taught that Jehovah's Witnesses who were 15 years of age in 1914 would be alive to see the consummation of all things.[23] However, a 15-year-old in 1914 would be 81 in 1980. This generation was quickly dying off.

A 1980 issue of *The Watchtower* gave a revised understanding and said this "generation" referred to Witnesses 10 years old in 1914.[24] This solution did not alleviate the problem, however. Another step had to be taken, so a 1984 issue of *The Watchtower* said the prophecy referred to Witnesses who were babies in 1914.[25] But this, too, failed to solve the problem.

Enter Milton Henschel. In the November 1, 1995, issue of *The Watchtower* magazine, Henschel discarded the entire generation prophecy. On the basis of "new light," he redefined the "generation" Jesus speaks of in Matthew 24 to mean "wicked mankind in general"—more specifically, any and all people of the earth in *any* generation who "see the sign of Christ's appearance but fail to mend their ways."[26] This "generation" could be people today or 100 years from now or anytime thereafter. Problem solved.

Watchtower Organizational Shakeup

In late 2000, a radical restructuring of leadership took place at the Watchtower Society. Eighty-year-old Milton Henschel resigned as president, and Don Adams, a 50-year veteran of the Watchtower, became the new president. Six other directors also resigned, although they (along with Henschel) remained members of the Governing Body, which up till this time had exercised unchallenged control over the Society.

In the organizational shakeup, religious and administrative duties passed from the Governing Body to be divided among three new nonprofit corporations. Kingdom Support Services, Inc., focuses on everyday needs in individual congregations. The Religious Order of Jehovah's Witnesses works with Witnesses involved in full-time ministry. The Christian Congregation of Jehovah's Witnesses oversees religious matters. The Governing Body, relieved of administrative tasks, now focuses on the "ministry of the word."

Today Jehovah's Witnesses meet in Kingdom Halls around the world. Most of these are constructed with volunteer labor, and 300 volunteers can erect a building in about 48 hours. On the average, four to six new Kingdom Halls are built each month in the United States.

There are no full-time ministers. All Jehovah's Witnesses are viewed as "ministers," and the laymen, called elders, who lead the Kingdom Halls are chosen because of their faithfulness and knowledge. Services involve a lecture, a few songs, and a study hour involving questions and answers.

Above the elders are district and circuit overseers. ("Circuits" are associations of about 20 congregations.) These overseers visit congregations twice a year, instruct the elders, and accompany Witnesses door-to-door to help them perfect their proselytizing techniques.

THE AUTHORITY OF THE WATCHTOWER SOCIETY

The Jehovah's Witnesses are described in Watchtower literature today as the "worldwide Christian society of people who actively bear witness regarding Jehovah God and his purposes affecting mankind."[27] They say that no other group may lay claim to being the witnesses of Jehovah, that it is through this organization and no other that God teaches the Bible to humankind today.

Jehovah's Witnesses believe the teachings of the Watchtower are all-encompassing and should affect every aspect of life. One issue of The Watchtower refers to the society as "an organization to direct the minds of God's people."[28] Watchtower literature is also replete with admonitions to "dependent" Bible interpretation: "Avoid independent thinking . . . questioning the counsel that is provided by God's visible organization [the Watchtower]."[29] "We should seek for dependent Bible study, rather than for independent Bible study."[30] Following are some of the doctrines Jehovah's Witnesses are expected not to question.

WATCHTOWER BELIEFS

Jehovah Is the One True God

Jehovah's Witnesses believe superstitious Jewish scribes long ago removed the sacred name "Jehovah" from the Bible. The New World Translation "restores" the name in the Old Testament where the Hebrew consonants "YHWH" appear and inserts the name in the New Testament where the text speaks of "the Father." This was done even though it blatantly goes against the thousands of Greek manuscripts of the New Testament available today. Jehovah's Witnesses believe that because they are the only group that refers to God by His "true" name, they are the only true followers of God.

The Trinity Is a Pagan Lie

Jehovah's Witnesses believe that if people were to read the Bible from cover to cover without any preconceived ideas, they would never arrive at a belief in the Trinity. Bible students would consistently find "monotheism" set forth—the belief that God is one.

It is argued that because God is not a God of disorder (1 Cor. 14:33), it is impossible that Scripture would speak of a God impossible to understand by human reason. The concept of the Trinity is incomprehensible and hence cannot be correct. Moreover, the word *Trinity* is not in the Bible.

Throughout its history the Watchtower Society has misrepresented the doctrine of the Trinity in order to make its denial more plausible to "reasonable" people. The doctrine is described as "three Gods in one God" or "three Gods in one person."[31] (Trinitarians, by contrast, believe that there is one God and that within the unity of the Godhead there are three coequal and coeternal persons—the Father, the Son, and the Holy Spirit.)

Satan is viewed as the true originator of the doctrine of the Trinity.[32] The doctrine is said to be rooted in paganism. It is argued that many centuries before the time of Christ, there were trinities of gods in ancient Babylonia, Egypt, and Assyria. Therefore God cannot be the author of this doctrine.

Jesus Is a Lesser God

Jehovah's Witnesses say that Jesus and the archangel Michael are the same being. Michael was allegedly created first and then was used by God to create all other things in the universe (see Col. 1:16).

Witnesses concede that Jesus is a "mighty god," but they deny he is God Almighty as Jehovah is. To support this claim, they often point to passages that seem to indicate that Jesus is inferior to the Father. For example, Jesus said that "the Father is greater than I" (John 14:28) and referred to the Father as "my God" (John 20:17). First Corinthians 11:3 states that "the head of Christ is God." Jesus is called God's "only begotten son" (John 3:16 KJV), the "firstborn over all creation" (Col. 1:15), and the "beginning" of God's creation (Rev. 3:14 KJV). Jehovah's Witnesses thus reason that Jesus is not God in the same sense Jehovah is. In keeping with this, the Watchtower teaches that Jesus should not be worshiped as Jehovah is.

Although Michael (Jesus) existed in his prehuman state for billions of years, at the appointed time he was born on earth as a human being—*ceasing his existence as an angel.* In order to "ransom" humankind from sin, Michael gave up his existence as a spirit creature (angel) when his life force was transferred into Mary's womb by Jehovah. This was no incarnation (God in the flesh). Rather, Jesus became a perfect human being. He died as a mere human.

Witnesses allege that Jesus was crucified, not on a cross but on a stake. The cross is said to be a pagan religious symbol the church adopted when Satan took control of ecclesiastical authority in the early centuries of Christianity.[33]

When Jesus died, He became nonexistent and was raised (*re-created*) three days later as a spirit creature (that is, as Michael the archangel). A physical resurrection did not occur. Jesus gave up his human life as a ransom sacrifice for the benefit of humankind. "Having given up his flesh for the life of the world, Christ could never take it again and become a man once more."[34] As for what happened to his body, Jehovah's Witnesses suggest that perhaps it was dissolved into gases, or perhaps it is still preserved somewhere as a grand memorial of God's love. Or it may be that the body was simply disposed of by Jehovah.[35]

In terms of how Jesus *proved* his "resurrection" to the disciples, Witnesses say Jesus "appeared to his disciples on different occasions in various fleshly bodies, just as angels had appeared to men of ancient times. Like those angels, he had the power to construct and to disintegrate those fleshly bodies at will, for the purpose of proving visibly that he had been resurrected."[36]

Consistent with Jesus' alleged spiritual resurrection is the teaching that a spiritual "second coming" of Christ occurred in 1914. Since then he has been ruling as King on earth through the Watchtower Society.

The Holy Spirit Is God's Active Force

In Watchtower theology the Holy Spirit is neither a person nor God. Rather, the Holy Spirit is God's impersonal "active force" for accomplishing His will in the world. Watchtower literature likens the Holy Spirit to electricity—"a force that can be adapted to perform a great variety of operations."[37]

In proof of the Watchtower position, it is argued that Scripture portrays people being "filled" by the Holy Spirit and "anointed" by the Spirit. These expressions would be appropriate only if the Spirit were a force and not a person. After all, how can one person "fill" thousands of people at one and the same time? Besides, if the Holy Spirit were a person, it would have a name just as the Father and the Son do.[38]

Man Is a "Living Soul"

Jehovah's Witnesses do not believe man's soul or spirit is distinct from the physical body. Rather, man is a combination of body

"Jesus never claimed to be God. Everything he said about himself indicates that he did not consider himself equal to God in any way—not in power, not in knowledge, not in age.... In every period of his existence, whether in heaven or on earth, his speech and conduct reflect subordination to God. God is always the superior, Jesus the lesser one who was created by God" (*Should You Believe in the Trinity?* online ed.).

and "breath" that together form a "living soul." In other words, the "soul" refers not to an immaterial part of man that survives death, but to the very life a person has. Every person is a "soul"—not because he or she possesses an immaterial nature but because he or she is a living being (see Gen. 9:5; Josh. 11:11; 1 Peter 3:20).

The doctrine of the soul closely relates to the question of what happens at death. Because of the inheritance of sin from Adam, human beings die and return to the dust, just as animals do. They do not possess a spirit that goes on living as an intelligent personality after death. Man's "spirit" is interpreted as the "life-force" within him, and at death that life-force wanes.

Since at death man has no immaterial nature that survives, he is obviously not conscious of anything after death. Even the righteous dead remain unconscious and inactive in the grave until the time of the future resurrection. Nor do people consciously suffer in hell. Satan, the father of lies, is said to be behind this concept. Hell is viewed as the common grave of all humankind. "Yes, good people go to the Bible hell. . . . Sheol and Hades refer not to a place of torment but to the common grave of all mankind."[39]

Salvation Must Be Earned

Although Jehovah's Witnesses often speak of salvation by grace through faith in Christ, in reality they believe in a works-oriented salvation. Salvation is impossible apart from total obedience to the Watchtower and vigorous participation in its various programs (Phil. 2:12). Good works are critically important. *The Watchtower* says that "to get one's name written in that Book of Life will depend upon one's works."[40] Witnesses are to continually be "working hard for the reward of eternal life."[41]

Part of "working out" one's salvation depends on faithfulness in distributing Watchtower literature door-to-door. Full-time "pioneer ministers" can be required to spend 100 hours each month preaching from house to house and conducting home Bible studies.

Jehovah's Witnesses cannot know for sure if they have salvation during this life. Only an unbending stance against sin and total obedience to the Watchtower gives Witnesses any hope of salvation. Even then, Witnesses are told that if they should fail during the future millennium, they will be annihilated. However, if they faithfully serve God throughout this 1,000-year period, eternal life may finally be granted.

Such a view obviously downplays the significance of Christ's sacrificial death. The Watchtower teaches that the human life Jesus laid down in sacrifice was exactly equal to the human life of Adam. "Since one man's sin (that of Adam) had been responsible for causing the entire human family to be sinners, the shed blood of another perfect human (in effect, a second Adam), being of corresponding value, could balance the scales of justice."[42] According to the Watchtower, if Jesus had been God, the ransom payment would have been way too much.

Jehovah's Witnesses do speak of the need for grace and faith in Christ to be saved, and they speak of salvation as a "free gift." But grace and faith are not enough. Nor is salvation really a "free gift." Former Jehovah's Witness Duane Magnani explains it this way:

> What the Watchtower means by "free gift" is that Christ's death only wiped away the sin inherited from Adam. They teach that without this work of atonement, men could not work their way toward salvation. But the "gift" of Christ's ransom sacrifice is freely made available to all who desire it. In other words, without Christ's sacrifice, the individual wouldn't have a chance to get saved. But in view of His work, the free gift which removed the sin inherited from Adam, the individual now has a chance.[43]

Jehovah Has Two Peoples

In Watchtower theology there are two classes of saved people, with very different destinies and sets of privileges involved.

The Anointed Class

Jehovah's Witnesses believe only 144,000 Jehovah's Witnesses go to heaven—and these make up the "Anointed Class" (Rev. 7:4; cf. 14:1–3): "God has purposed to associate a limited number of faithful humans with Jesus Christ in the heavenly Kingdom."[44] Only those who become "born again"—thereby becoming "sons" of God—can share in this heavenly kingdom (John 1:12–13; Rom. 8:16–17; 1 Peter 3–4). These individuals look forward not to physical existence but to spiritual existence in heaven.

Only a relative "few" find entrance into this spiritual kingdom—and they are a "little flock" when compared with earth's population. This "little flock" of true believers (Luke 12:32) allegedly began with the 12 apostles and other Christians of the first century and was completely filled by the year 1935 (according to a "revelation" Rutherford received). Less than 5,000 of these "anointed" believers are still alive today.

The primary activity of the Anointed Class in heaven will be to rule with Christ. "They will be priests of God and of the Christ, and will rule as kings with him for the thousand years" (Rev. 20:6 NWT). And if the Anointed Class is made up of "kings," there must be others over whom the Anointed Class will rule.[45] These are the "other sheep" who have an earthly destiny.

The Other Sheep

Jehovah's Witnesses who are not members of the Anointed Class look forward, not to a heavenly destiny, but to living eternally in an earthly paradise. Since the required number of 144,000 members for the Anointed Class was attained in 1935, all Jehovah's Witnesses since that year have looked forward to an earthly destiny.

These people make up what Revelation 7:9 calls the "great multitude," or what John 10:16 calls the "other sheep." These are followers of Jesus Christ but are not in the "New Covenant sheepfold" with a hope of heavenly life. These people hope to survive the approaching Great Tribulation and Armageddon and then enjoy perfect human life on earth under the rule of Christ. Those among the "other sheep" who have died will experience a "resurrection of life" and will fully enjoy earthly blessings.

Jehovah Prohibits Contamination by the World System

Blood Transfusions Forbidden

Jehovah's Witnesses must refuse transfusions of "whole blood" in all circumstances—even when doctors say death is inevitable without it (although some blood components such as albumin and immunoglobulin are allowed). Parents are required to see to it that their children never receive blood transfusions.[46] Witnesses believe that references to "eating blood" in the Bible prohibit such transfusions (Gen. 9:4; Lev. 7:26–27; 17:11–12; Acts 15:28–29). For this reason many Witnesses carry a signed card stating that they are not to receive a blood transfusion in the event that they are found unconscious.

The Society has recently softened its stance somewhat in the sense that if Jehovah's Witnesses are *repentant* following a whole blood transfusion, they can be forgiven. (Blood transfusions are still viewed as a violation of God's law, so repentance is a necessity.) But if they "willfully" and "without regret" receive a blood transfusion, they are showing through that action that they no longer wish to be Jehovah's Witnesses.

Celebrating Birthdays Forbidden

The Watchtower Society strictly forbids Jehovah's Witnesses to celebrate birthdays. There are only two references in the Bible to birthday celebrations—Genesis 40:20–22 and Matthew 14:6–10—and in both cases they are presented in a very negative light. Both persons (Pharaoh and Herod) were pagans, and both had someone put to death on their birthdays. In view of this, no follower of Jehovah should ever celebrate a birthday. To do so would be an affront against God Himself.

Wearing a Cross Forbidden

Jehovah's Witnesses teach that the cross is a pagan religious symbol adopted by the church when Satan took control of it in the early centuries of Christianity. Christ was crucified not on a cross but on a stake. Hence, for people to wear crosses today dishonors God and constitutes a form of idolatry.

WATCHTOWER DOCTRINES DISTINGUISHED FROM CHRISTIANITY

	Watchtower View	Christian View
Authority	Watchtower Society	Bible alone
God	No Trinity	Trinity
Jesus' Identity	A lesser god	God Almighty
Jesus' Death	Died as a man	Died as the God-Man
Jesus' Resurrection	Spiritual	Physical
Second Coming	Spiritual and invisible, in 1914	Physical, yet future
Salvation	By works	By grace
People of God	Two peoples—heavenly and earthly	One people
Hell	The grave (No eternal punishment)	Place of eternal punishment

More Prohibitions

Witnesses are also prohibited from participating in major holiday events such as Christmas, Easter, President's Day, Memorial Day, Thanksgiving, New Year's Day, and Mother's Day. They are prohibited from participating in voting, holding government office, saluting a flag, and participating in war in any capacity on the grounds that these prohibitions are Jehovah's will.

CHALLENGING WATCHTOWER BELIEFS

The New World Translation Cannot Be Trusted

Dr. Julius Mantey, author of *A Manual Grammar of the Greek New Testament*, calls the New World Translation "a shocking mistranslation."[47] Dr. Bruce M. Metzger, professor of New Testament at Princeton University, calls it "a frightful mistranslation," "erroneous," "pernicious," and "reprehensible."[48] Dr. William Barclay concluded that "the deliberate distortion of truth by this sect is seen in their New Testament translation. . . . It is abundantly clear that a sect which can translate the New Testament like that is intellectually dishonest."[49]

In view of the broad censure this translation has received from renowned biblical linguistic scholars, it is not surprising that the Watchtower has always resisted efforts to identify members of the translation committee. The claim was that they preferred to remain anonymous and humble, giving God the glory. However, such anonymity also prevented scholars from checking their credentials.

When defector Raymond Franz finally revealed the identity of the translators (Nathan Knorr, Frederick Franz, Albert Schroeder, George Gangas, and Milton Henschel),[50] it quickly became apparent that the committee was completely unqualified for the task. Four of the five men in the committee had no Hebrew or Greek training whatever and, in fact, had only a high school education. The fifth—Frederick Franz—claimed to know Hebrew and Greek, but upon examination under oath in a court of law in Edinburgh, Scotland, was found to fail a simple Hebrew test.[51]

The One True God Is a Trinity

Even though the word *Trinity* is not in the Bible, as Jehovah's Witnesses correctly assert, the concept of the Trinity is clearly derived from the Bible. One might point out to a Jehovah's Witness that while the word *Jehovah* may be considered by some to be an acceptable way to render references to YHWH in the Old Testament (as does the American Standard Version of 1901), strictly speaking *Jehovah* does not appear in any Hebrew or Greek manuscripts of the Bible.[52] "Jehovah" is a manmade word.* If it is going to be argued that the doctrine of the Trinity is unbiblical because the word *Trinity* does not appear in the Bible, then by that same logic the doctrine of Jehovah must be considered false.

As for the claim that the Trinity is a pagan concept, it is crucial to recognize that the Babylonians and Assyrians believed in *triads* of gods who headed up a pantheon of many other gods. But these triads comprised three separate gods (polytheism), in contrast to the doctrine of the Trinity, which maintains that there is only one *God* (monotheism) with three persons within the one Godhead. In view of this, the suggestion that Christianity borrowed the Trinitarian concept from pagans is quite infeasible.

Further, the Watchtower interpretation of 1 Corinthians 14:33 (that the Trinity cannot be true because "God is not a God of confusion") is a woeful violation of the context. The church in Corinth was plagued by disorder as a result of too many people speaking in tongues and giving prophecies, apparently simultaneously. To restore order, Paul gave the church specific instructions on the proper use of spiritual gifts in the church (1 Cor. 14:27–30) and then stated the underlying principle of his instructions: God is not a God of confusion but of peace (v. 33). Paul was thus not dealing with the Trinity but with disorder in the church! Since God is not a God of confusion, His church should not be a church of confusion.

There is more than ample biblical support for the doctrine of the Trinity through three lines of biblical evidence:

1. Evidence for One God

The consistent testimony of Scripture from Genesis to Revelation is that there is only one true God (see Isa. 44:6; 46:9; John 5:44; 17:3; Rom. 3:29–30; 16:27; 1 Cor. 8:4; Gal. 3:20; Eph. 4:6; James 2:19).

---

*The ancient Jews inserted the vowels from Adonai (a-o-a) among the consonants YHWH, resulting in *Yahowah*, or *Jehovah*. They came up with this term as a substitute for God's name so they would not inadvertently break the Third Commandment.

2. Evidence for Three Persons Who Are Called God

The Father is called God (1 Peter 1:2), Jesus is called God (John 20:28; Heb. 1:8) and the Holy Spirit is recognized as God (Acts 5:3-4). Moreover, each of the three persons on different occasions is seen to possess the attributes of deity. All three, for example, are said to be *omnipresent:* the Father (Matt. 19:26), the Son (Matt. 28:18), and the Holy Spirit (Ps. 139:7). All three are *omniscient:* the Father (Rom. 11:33), the Son (Matt. 9:4), and the Holy Spirit (1 Cor. 2:10). All three are *omnipotent:* the Father (1 Peter 1:5), the Son (Matt. 28:18), and the Holy Spirit (Rom. 15:19).

Further, each of the three is called *Lord* (Rom. 10:12; Luke 2:11; 2 Cor. 3:17), *everlasting* (Rom. 16:26; Rev. 22:13; Heb. 9:14), *almighty* (Gen. 17:1; Rev. 1:8; Rom. 15:19), and *powerful* (Jer. 32:17; Heb. 1:3; Luke 1:35). Still further, each of the three persons were involved in doing the *works* of deity. For example, all three were involved in the creation of the world: the Father (Gen. 2:7; Ps. 102:25), the Son (John 1:3; Col. 1:16; Heb. 1:2), and the Holy Spirit (Gen. 1:2; Job 33:4; Ps. 104:30).

3. Three-in-Oneness in the Godhead

Matthew 28:19 states, "Therefore go and make disciples of all the nations, baptizing them in the name of the Father and the Son and the Holy Spirit." Notice that the distinctness of each of the three persons is emphasized by the use of the definite article *the.* Yet the word *name* is singular in the Greek. Such linguistic factors indicate that there is one God, but three distinct persons within the Godhead. This three-in-oneness is also evident in Paul's benediction (2 Cor. 13:14).

The Watchtower Jesus Is a Different Jesus

Jesus Is Not Michael the Archangel

Michael is specifically called "one of the chief princes" in Daniel 10:13. The fact that he is "one of" them indicates he is one among a group and is not unique. By contrast, Jesus is the unique "KING OF KINGS AND LORD OF LORDS" (Rev. 19:16). Moreover, the New Testament portrays Christ as the *Creator* of the angels (Col. 1:16), not as one of them.

Further, we note that Christ, as God, is immutable—that is, unchangeable in nature. Christ's immutability is affirmed in

Hebrews 13:8: "Jesus Christ is the same yesterday and today and forever." This contrasts with the Watchtower teaching that Christ was created as an angel, later became a human being, and then (at the "resurrection") became an angel again.

Jesus Is Not a Lesser God Than the Father

Jehovah's Witnesses often cite a series of Bible verses to "prove" that Jesus is a lesser god than the Father, but in each case they misinterpret the passage in question:

Isaiah 9:6. Because this messianic verse refers to Jesus as "mighty God," Jehovah's Witnesses reason that Jesus is a lesser God than God the Father, since the Father is God Almighty. However, in the next chapter of Isaiah, Yahweh Himself is called "Mighty God" (10:16, using the same Hebrew word, *Elohim*). This obliterates any suggestion that the expression must refer to a lesser deity. The Father and Jesus are equally divine.

Mark 13:32. Jehovah's Witnesses reason that since Jesus does not know the hour of His return, He must be lesser than God the Father, who is omniscient. This allegation is easily answered. Christ as God *is* omniscient (see Matt. 11:27; 17:27; Luke 5:4, 6; John 7:29; 8:55; 10:15; 16:30; 17:25; 21:17; 21:6–11), but in the incarnation He took on a human nature, which *is not* omniscient. It was only from His humanity that Christ could say He did not know the day or hour of His return. Philippians 2:5–11 indicates that Christ, to fulfill His messianic role on earth, voluntarily chose not to use some of His divine attributes (such as omniscience) on some occasions. Mark 13:32 is an example of this.

John 1:1. The New World Translation renders this verse, "The Word [Christ] was *a* god," making it appear that Jesus is a mighty God, but not God Almighty as the Father is. However, the absolute deity of Christ is supported by numerous references in John (for example, 8:58; 10:30; 20:28) as well as the rest of the New Testament (Col. 1:15–16; 2:9; Titus 2:13; Heb. 1:8). Further, it is not necessary to translate Greek nouns that have no definite article with an indefinite article (there is no indefinite article in Greek). In other words, *theos* ("God") without the definite article *ho* ("the")—as is the case in John 1:1—does not need to be translated as "a God" as the Jehovah's Witnesses have done in reference to Christ. The presence or absence of the definite article does not alter the fundamental meaning of *theos* (God). Properly understood, John 1:1 is telling us that in the beginning the second person of the eternal Godhead (Jesus) was "with" the first person of the eternal Godhead (the Father), and that the second person of the Godhead (Jesus) "was" God by nature, just as the Father is God by nature.

John 3:16. Jehovah's Witnesses reason that because Jesus is called God's "only begotten Son," He must not be God in the same sense as the Father. However, the phrase "only begotten" (Greek *monogenes*) does not mean Christ was created, but rather means "unique" or "one of a kind." Jesus is the one-of-a-kind "Son of God" in the sense that He has the same nature as the Father—a *divine* nature (see John 5:18).

John 14:28. Jehovah's Witnesses reason that since the Father is "greater" than Jesus, then Jesus must be a lesser God than the Father. However, in this verse Jesus is not speaking about His nature (Christ had earlier said, "I and the Father are one" in this regard—John 10:30), but is speaking of His lowly position in the incarnation. The Father was seated upon the throne of highest majesty in heaven. It was far different with His incarnate Son: despised and rejected by all kinds of people, surrounded by implacable enemies, and soon to be nailed to a criminal's cross.

First Corinthians 11:3. Because 1 Corinthians 11:3 says that "the head of Christ is God," Jehovah's Witnesses reason that Jesus must be a lesser deity than the Father. But Paul says in the same verse that the man is the head of the woman, even though men and women are equal in their essential nature (*human*—Gen. 1:26–28). This indicates that *equality of being* and *functional subordination* are not mutually exclusive. Christ and the Father are equal in nature (John 10:30), though Jesus is functionally under the Father's headship (1 Cor. 11:3).

Colossians 1:15. Jehovah's Witnesses reason that because Jesus is called "firstborn," He must have come into being at a point in time and is therefore a lesser God than the Father. However, "firstborn" (Greek *prototokos*) does not mean "first created," but rather "first in rank, preeminent one, heir."[53] Christ is the "firstborn of creation" in the sense that He is positionally preeminent over creation and is supreme over all things. If Paul here had wanted to identify Christ as first created, he would have used a different Greek word (*protoktisis*), a term that is never used of Christ in the

New Testament. It is logical that Christ is preeminent over creation (Col. 1:15), since He is the Creator of it (see verse 16).

Jesus Was and Is Yahweh

A comparison of the Old and New Testaments provides powerful testimony to Jesus' identity as Yahweh. In Isaiah 43:11, for example, Yahweh asserts, "I, even I, am the LORD, and apart from me there is no savior." This verse indicates, first, that a claim to be Savior is in itself a claim to deity, and second, there is only one Savior—God (Yahweh). Against this backdrop it is truly revealing of Christ's divine nature that the New Testament refers to Him as the Savior (Luke 2:11; John 4:42).

Similarly, Yahweh asserts in Isaiah 44:24: "I, the LORD [Yahweh], am the maker of all things, stretching out the heavens by Myself, and spreading out the earth all alone." The fact that Yahweh is the "maker of all things" who stretched out the heavens "by myself" and spread out the earth "all alone" (Isa. 44:24)—and the accompanying fact that Christ Himself is the Creator of "all things" (John 1:3; Col. 1:16)—proves the absolute deity of Christ.

Another illustration is Isaiah 6:1–5, where the prophet recounts his vision of Yahweh "seated on a throne, high and exalted" (v. 1). The seraphs proclaim, "Holy, holy, holy is the LORD [Yahweh] Almighty; the whole earth is full of his glory" (v. 3). Isaiah also quotes Yahweh as saying, "I am the LORD; that is my name! I will not give my glory to another" (42:8). Later, the apostle John under the inspiration of the Holy Spirit wrote that Isaiah "saw Jesus' glory" (John 12:41). Jesus' glory is equated with Yahweh's glory.

Further support is found in Jesus' crucifixion. In Zechariah 12:10, Yahweh is speaking prophetically: "They will look on me, the one they have pierced." Although Yahweh is speaking, this is obviously a reference to Jesus' future crucifixion. We know that "the one they have pierced" is Jesus, for He is described this same way by the apostle John in Revelation 1:7.

Moreover, contrary to Jehovah's Witnesses, Christ *was* worshiped (Greek *proskuneo*) as God many times, according to the gospel accounts. He accepted worship from Thomas (John 20:28), the angels (Heb. 1:6), some wise men (Matt. 2:11), a leper (Matt. 8:2), a ruler (Matt. 9:18), a blind man (John 9:38), Mary Magdalene

(Matt. 28:9), and the disciples (Matt. 28:17). The fact that Jesus willingly received worship on various occasions says much about His true identity, for it is the testimony of Scripture that only God is to be worshiped (Ex. 34:14).

The Incarnate Christ Was God in Human Flesh

Contrary to the Watchtower view that Jesus during the incarnate state was *just* a man and nothing more, we must ask, "Why send Jesus at all?"[54] If all that was required was "a perfect human," God could easily have created one from scratch if He wanted. There was certainly no need for God to send His first and greatest creature: Jesus (the archangel Michael).

Further, the reality is that Jesus was a perfect mediator between God and man precisely because He is both God *and* man. If Christ the Redeemer had been only God, He could not have died, because God by His very nature cannot die. It was only as a man that Christ could represent humanity and die as a man. As God, however, Christ's death had infinite value sufficient to provide redemption for the sins of all humankind. Clearly, then, Christ had to be both God and man to secure man's salvation (1 Tim. 2:5; see also Heb. 2:14–16; 9:11–28).

This wonderful salvific work of Christ is appropriated by faith alone—with no works in sight (see Eph. 2:8–9; Titus 3:5). John 3:15 states that "everyone who believes in him may have eternal life." In John 5:24 Jesus says, "I tell you the truth, whoever hears my word and believes him who sent me has eternal life and will not be condemned; he has crossed over from death to life." In John 11:25 Jesus says, "I am the resurrection and the life. He who believes in me will live, even though he dies."

Jesus Was Physically Resurrected

The resurrected Jesus flatly asserted that He was not a spirit but had a body of flesh and bones (Luke 24:39; see also John 2:19–21, where Jesus indicated His physical body would be raised). Further, the resurrected Jesus ate physical food on four different occasions, which proved that He had a real physical body (Luke 24:30; 24:42–43; John 21:12–13; Acts 1:4). His physically resurrected body was also touched and handled by different people (Matt. 28:9; John 20:17). It would have been deception on Jesus' part to have offered such proofs of a bodily resurrection if He had not truly been resurrected in a physical body.

The Second Coming Will Be Bodily and Visible

Scripture indicates that the Second Coming will be a physical, visible event (Acts 1:9–11). One Greek word used of Christ's second coming is *epiphaneia*, which carries the basic meaning of "to appear." Christ's first coming, which was both bodily and visible, was called an *epiphaneia* (2 Tim. 1:10). The Second Coming is also an *epiphaneia* (Titus 2:13). Matthew 24:29–30 declares that this visible event will be accompanied by visible cosmic disturbances. Revelation 1:7 indicates that *every* eye will see Him.

The Holy Spirit Is God and Is a Person

The Watchtower contention that the Holy Spirit is not a person because He does not have a name is mistaken because spiritual beings are not always named in Scripture. For example, evil spirits are rarely named in Scripture, but are rather identified by their particular character (such as "unclean" or "wicked"—see Matt. 12:45). In the same way, the Holy Spirit is identified by His primary character—which is holiness. Moreover, the Holy Spirit is related to the "name" of the other persons of the Trinity mentioned in Matthew 28:19.

The Watchtower argument that the Holy Spirit cannot be a person because He fills so many people at the same time cannot be correct because Ephesians 3:19 speaks of God Himself filling all the Ephesian believers. Likewise, Ephesians 4:10 speaks of Christ filling all things, and Ephesians 1:23 speaks of Christ as the one who "fills everything in every way." The Holy Spirit is a person just as the Father and Son are persons.

It has long been recognized that the three primary attributes of personality are mind, emotions, and will.[55] Scripture indicates that the Holy Spirit has a mind (Rom. 8:27), emotions (Eph. 4:30), and a will (1 Cor. 12:11). Moreover, the Spirit is seen doing many things that only a person can do—including teaching (John 14:26), testifying (John 15:26), guiding (Rom. 8:14), commissioning (Acts 13:4), issuing commands (Acts 8:29), interceding (Rom. 8:26), and speaking (John 15:26; 2 Peter 1:21).

Contrary to the Watchtower view that the Holy Spirit is not God, the Bible indicates that the Holy Spirit *is* God (see Acts 5:3).

He has all the attributes of deity, such as omnipresence (Ps. 139:7), omniscience (1 Cor. 2:10), omnipotence (Rom. 15:19), holiness (John 16:7–14), and eternity (Heb. 9:14). The Holy Spirit also performs works that only God can do, such as creating (Gen. 1:2; Ps. 104:30), begetting Christ (Matt. 1:20), inspiring Scripture (2 Peter 1:21), and causing the new birth by regeneration (Titus 3:5). Further, the titles of deity are ascribed to the Holy Spirit—such as "Lord" (2 Cor. 3:18).

There Is Conscious Existence in the Afterlife

In contrast with the Watchtower view, Scripture indicates that man has an immaterial nature that consciously survives death. Revelation 6:9–10 speaks of "the souls of those who had been slain," and they are portrayed as speaking to God—which requires consciousness. In Philippians 1:23 the apostle Paul speaks of his "desire to depart and be with Christ." In 2 Corinthians 5:6–8 Paul says that "to be away from the body" is to be "at home with the Lord." (Note that the Greek word for "with" [pros] suggests very close [face-to-face] fellowship.) The Scriptures state clearly that the souls of both believers and unbelievers are fully conscious between death and the future day of resurrection. Unbelievers are in conscious woe and "torment" (see Luke 16:22–23; Mark 9:43–48; Rev. 19:20), while believers are consciously with the Lord (Phil. 1:23).

Scripture also assures us that hell is a real place of suffering and not merely a "grave," as Jehovah's Witnesses assert (see Matt. 5:22; 18:8; 25:41; Jude 7; Rev. 20:14). Scripture consistently emphasizes the eternal nature of suffering in hell. Jesus affirmed that the wicked "will go away to *eternal* punishment, but the righteous to *eternal* life" (Matt. 25:46, italics added). Notice that the punishment of the wicked and the eternal life of the righteous both have eternality. Those conditions never cease. The fire of hell is called unquenchable (Mark 9:43 KJV); the "smoke of their [sinners'] torment rises for ever and ever" (Rev. 14:11).

Against the Watchtower view is the fact that there are no *degrees* of annihilation. One is either annihilated or one is not. The Scriptures, by contrast, teach that there will be degrees of punishment in hell following the day of judgment (Matt. 10:15; 11:21–24; 16:27; Luke 12:47–48; John 15:22; Heb. 10:29; Rev. 20:11–15; 22:12).

There Is One People of God

Never once did Jesus restrict the kingdom of God to a mere 144,000 people, as Jehovah's Witnesses do. (Contextually the 144,000 are Jews [12,000 from each tribe] who live in the end times—Revelation 14:1–3.) Jesus taught that *all* people should seek the kingdom, and He said that whoever seeks it will find it (for example, Matt. 9:35–38; Mark 1:14–15; Luke 12:22–34). It is the clear testimony of Scripture that a heavenly destiny awaits all who believe in Christ, not just a select group of 144,000 (Eph. 2:19; Phil. 3:20; Col. 3:1; Heb. 3:1; 12:22; 2 Peter 1:10–11). All who believe in Christ are "heirs" of the eternal kingdom (Gal. 3:29; 4:28–31; Titus 3:7; James 2:5). The righteousness of God that leads to life in heaven is available "through faith in Jesus Christ to all those who believe. There is no difference" (Rom. 3:22). Jesus promised, "Whoever serves me must follow me; and where I am, my servant also will be" (John 12:26). Jesus clearly affirmed that all believers will be together in "one flock" under "one shepherd" (John 10:16).

In view of all the above, it is clear that the Jehovah's Witnesses set forth a different God, a different Jesus, and a different gospel. The challenge for evangelicals is to communicate what Scripture states about the true God, the true Jesus, and the true gospel.

5

THE MIND SCIENCES

Phineas Parkhurst Quimby was born in New Lebanon, New Hampshire, in 1802. As a boy he was trained as a clock maker and had a skill for mechanics. As an adult he developed a knack for metaphysics. Ultimately he is the father of all the mind sciences.

Quimby would often use his metaphysical techniques to heal people, whether or not they could pay for it. He eventually committed his theories to writing, producing some 10 volumes of manuscripts in which he discussed religion, disease, spiritualism, clairvoyance, science, error, and truth. As a whole, his writings have never been formally published.

In his writings he espoused the metaphysical idea that physical diseases are caused by wrong thinking or false beliefs. Disease is merely an "error" created "not by God, but by man."[1] Eliminate false beliefs, and the chief culprit for disease is thereby removed, yielding a healthy body. These false beliefs are remedied, Quimby believed, by "the Christ."

The human Jesus and the Christ are distinguished in Quimby's theology. Jesus was a mere human who discovered the "Truth" of how to correct the error of sickness. This Truth, or "higher Wisdom," was an impersonal mind-principle Quimby called "the Christ." This Christ is something all people may discover and embody.

Quimby's metaphysics spawned several important movements. He did not create an organization himself, but people he helped adopted his ideas and passed them on to others, adding to or modifying them along the way. The term "New Thought" surfaced as a way of describing some of the metaphysical groups that emerged from his thinking.

THE NEW THOUGHT MOVEMENT

The New Thought movement gradually developed after Quimby's death in 1866. The primary reason the "New Thought" label stuck as a description of the movement was its optimistic ring. New Thought author Horatio Dresser commented, "The 'old thought' was undeniably pessimistic; it dwelt on sin, emphasized the darkness and misery of the world, the distress and the suffering. The new dwelt on life and light, pointing the way to the mastery of all sorrow and suffering."[2] This optimism has remained one of the most characteristic features of New Thought.

According to New Thought, human beings can experience health, success, and abundant life by using their thoughts to define the condition of their lives. New Thought proponents subscribe to the "law of attraction." This law states that just as like attracts like, so our thoughts can attract the things they want or expect. Negative thoughts attract dismal circumstances; positive thoughts attract more desirable circumstances. Our thoughts can be either creative or destructive. New Thought sets out to teach people how to use their thoughts creatively.

Truth in All Religions

New Thought proponents espouse a unity of religions. One advocate, Emma Hopkins, writes, "The remarkable analogies of the Christian Bible, and Hindu Sacred Books, Egyptian Ancient Teachings,

Persian Bible, Chinese Great Learning, Oriental Yohar, Saga, and many others, show that the whole world has had life teachings so wonderfully identical as to make them all subjects for respectful attention and investigation by the thoughtful of our age."[3]

All Is God—Including Man

In New Thought circles, God is called "Universal Wisdom and Intelligence," "Presence," "Infinite Idea," "Loving Principle," "One Mind," and "Universal Life Force." Such terms communicate an impersonal, nebulous concept of God.

New Thought essentially espouses a pantheistic God. Proponent Ralph Waldo Trine asserted that the great central fact of the universe is the "Spirit of Infinite Life and Power that is back of all, that animates all, that manifests itself in and through all; that self-existent principle of life from which all has come, and not only from which all has come, but from which all is continually coming."[4] Trine believed that all is one and all is God.

With this understanding of God, it is no surprise that man is viewed as divine. Trine said that "in essence, the life of God and the life of man are identically the same, and so are one. They differ not in essence, in quality; they differ in degree."[5] Therefore man has unlimited potential. By using the principles of New Thought, this unlimited potential becomes readily attainable.

There is no real sin in New Thought theology. Sin is viewed as a succumbing to the illusory world of matter, which is the source of all sickness and death. Sin against God in the moral sense does not exist. Right thinking is the cure for the New Thought version of sin. Salvation entails a release from ignorance concerning oneness with God. Being "born again" refers to being born anew in one's consciousness. "You are constantly being born again as you develop in your awareness of the Christ within."[6]

In New Thought theology there is no death. "So-called death is an entry into the fourth dimension of life, and our journey is from glory to glory, from wisdom to wisdom, ever onward upward and Godward for there is no end to the glory which is man."[7]

Jesus Is Distinct from the Christ

The Christ of New Thought—an outgrowth of Quimby's metaphysics—is considered not a person but an impersonal Divine Nature. Jesus is believed to have embodied or appropriated the

Christ-principle as no human had before. "The Christ represents the universal and eternal divine sonship—the highest possible inner consciousness. In most men it is latent or but feebly developed. It was locally and historically expressed in full degree through the personality of Jesus, but by no means limited to him."[8] Jesus was not a savior to mankind; he was merely a "way-shower." All humanity can embody the Christ-principle by following Jesus' example.

The New Thought concept of an impersonal Christ-principle is reflected in the three major movements it spawned: Christian Science, the United Church of Religious Science, and the Unity School of Christianity. These movements are collectively known as the "mind sciences." The word *mind* communicates the idea that God is a Divine Mind that is all in all. The word *science* refers not to medical science but rather to metaphysical (or mental) science. Mind science groups advocate that Divine Mind fills all reality and that we should seek to harmonize our mind with it so we become one with it.

CHRISTIAN SCIENCE

Mary Baker Eddy, born on a farm in New Hampshire in 1821, was raised by her parents as a Congregationalist. She joined the Congregational Church as a teenager, though she did not like their teachings on predestination or hell.

As a young girl Mary Baker was delicately formed and had extremely small hands and feet. During her childhood she endured a great deal of illness, including spasmodic seizures. "She was subject from infancy to convulsive attacks of a hysterical nature" and had many nervous fits.[9] Such illnesses made her highly neurotic. These attacks continued until late in life.

As an adult Mary Eddy* developed clairvoyant powers and dabbled in spiritualism and the occult. She would fall into trances, and people sought advice from her while she was in such states. Eddy would sometimes hear mysterious rappings at night, and "she saw 'spirits' of the departed standing by her bedside, and she received messages in writing from the dead."[10]

Eddy derived most of her theology from Quimby. She had become interested in him because of his growing fame as a healer.

---

*She is most often referred to by the surname of her third husband, Asa G. Eddy.

As noted previously, Quimby believed that sin, sickness, and disease exist only in the mind. By following his New Thought techniques, people could correct their wrong thinking and eradicate these undesirable things from their lives. Quimby referred to his metaphysical belief system by various terms, including "Science of Health" and even "Christian Science."[11] Eddy was not an original thinker, but took what Quimby developed and popularized it in a new movement she called "Christian Science."

Eddy first came into contact with Quimby in 1862 when she sought treatment for spinal inflammation. She claims she became healed as a result of Quimby's care. This motivated her to study and even begin teaching Quimby's metaphysical system of thought. Historically, her "cure" was short-lived as the pain soon returned, but she remained convinced that the answer to her suffering was the metaphysical teachings of Quimby.

In 1875, nine years after Quimby died, Eddy published her book *Science and Health with Key to the Scriptures*. In this book, which only mentions Quimby in passing, Eddy set forth the metaphysical principles she learned from Quimby. She spoke of her ideas as new revelation, even though it was derived "revelation."[12] This plagiarism later became public. While Eddy denied stealing her ideas from Quimby, a *New York Times* article published in 1904 thoroughly documented it.[13] Eddy rebutted that she herself had discovered miraculous metaphysical healing techniques three days after a fall on icy pavement. She claims she had only been given three days to live by medical authorities but was restored to health through metaphysical healing techniques *she* discovered. The doctor who treated her, Dr. Alvin M. Cushing, contradicted her claim, stating in an affidavit that she had not been in critical condition or near death, and he knew of no such miracle of which Eddy spoke.[14]

In the years that followed, Eddy continued to promote her metaphysical ideas. After relocating in Boston, she eventually established the Massachusetts Metaphysical College and taught more than 4,000 students over an eight-year period. In 1879 she founded the Church of Christ, Scientist.

The Christian Science movement mushroomed within just a few decades. By 1896 there were more than 400 Christian Science churches and societies. By the time Eddy died in 1910, about one million people were attending Christian Science churches.

Before she died, Eddy arranged for a board of directors to continue the work she began in such a way that no one would be put in a place of absolute authority (as she had been). Some groups within the church challenged this, but their effort soon faded. Today the board exercises authority over thousands of Christian Science branches and practitioners.

The church maintained impressive membership figures through the mid 1950s, but a decline began in the 1960s. One estimate placed membership at 400,000 in the mid 1960s, and today there are probably fewer than 250,000 members worldwide.[15]

Along with this decline in membership came significant losses in revenue. In 1992 *Time* magazine reported a financial loss of $235 million suffered by the Christian Science Monitor television channel. Further, over a four-year period from 1987 to 1991, church funds dropped from $208 million to $117 million while at the same time operating expenses went from $54 million to $115 million. During that same general period, the *Christian Science Monitor* newspaper lost some $138 million. As a result of such losses, the church was forced in 1993 to sell off or close some of its media network.[16]

Understandably, many church members were distressed with these conditions. In 1976 some longtime members accused church leaders of gross mismanagement. There were accusations of a lack of financial accountability and moral failures among church leaders.[17]

To make matters worse, the church in the 1990s received a tremendous amount of negative press upon disclosure that 18 children had suffered preventable deaths since 1980 as a result of parents choosing Christian Science's metaphysical healing techniques instead of taking their children to a doctor. Several Christian Science couples were eventually tried and convicted in court for child endangerment and some for manslaughter.

Another controversy erupted in the 1990s as a result of the publishing of Bliss Knapp's book *Destiny of the Mother Church*, which declared Mary Baker Eddy to be equal to and a successor of Jesus Christ. The book essentially deified Eddy. This is something that even many within the Christian Science movement considered heresy. However, the Knapps had stipulated that $90 million would be left to the church on the condition that this book be published and then prominently displayed in Christian Science reading rooms across the country. As it turns out, the church never collected the full $90 million. About half the money had to be split with other beneficiaries—Stanford University and the Los Angeles County Art Museum, which filed a suit alleging that the church had not fulfilled the terms of the will. The church ended up with only $53 million. Many church members resigned over the affair.

Today church headquarters are located on a 14-acre complex in Boston. At present there are 2,300 branch churches in more than 60 countries, 1,600 of which are in the United States. Church by-laws forbid releasing membership statistics, but as noted previously, it is estimated that the church currently has fewer than 250,000 members.

The Bible Should Be Interpreted Esoterically

Christian Science teaches that the Bible is to be interpreted esoterically. One must seek the *spiritual* interpretation.[18] The only way to ascertain the proper spiritual interpretation of the Bible is to use Eddy's *Science and Health with Key to the Scriptures* as a guide. This book alone can unlock the mysteries of the Bible and help the seeker understand the metaphysical meanings that lie beneath the literal text. Hence, instead of judging Eddy's book according to what the Bible teaches, the Bible is to be judged according to what Mary Baker Eddy teaches. Eddy boasted, "The works I have written on Christian Science contain absolute Truth."[19]

Sin, Sickness, and Death Are Illusions

True to its roots in the New Thought movement, Christian Science holds that sin, evil, sickness, and death are mere illusions that can be conquered by denying them. Evil, sickness, and death are but "states of false belief."[20] The only reality that truly exists is God, or Divine Mind. Nothing "nonspiritual" can exist except in one's mind or thoughts. Since matter does not truly exist, neither can sickness, pain, or death. "The cause of all so-called disease is mental, a mortal fear, a mistaken belief or conviction of the necessity and power of ill-health."[21]

In the *New York Sun* of December 19, 1898, Mary Baker Eddy "challenged the world to disprove" that she had healed a variety of serious illnesses, including cancer. Dr. Charles A. Reed, who would later become the president of the American Medical Association, offered to present Eddy similar cases for her to heal. He affirmed,

"If she, by her Christian Science, shall cure any one of them, I shall proclaim her omnipotence from the housetops; and, if she shall cure all, or even half of them, I shall cheerfully crawl upon my hands and knees that I may but touch the hem of her walking-dress."[22] Eddy refused Dr. Reed's offer.

All Is God

Borrowing heavily from Quimby, Eddy argued that God is not a person but is rather Divine Mind or Divine Principle. Divine Mind is said to be devoid of personality. Therefore we are not to approach God in a personal way. "All is God, and there is naught beside Him."[23] Because God is all, and because God is Spirit, this means that Spirit is the real and the eternal, while matter is unreal and temporal. God is viewed as the only true reality; everything else is an illusion. Nothing possesses true reality except Divine Mind. In keeping with this, the Trinity is not interpreted in terms of three persons within the one God, but rather (confusingly) in terms of a triple Divine Principle: Life, Truth, and Love.[24]

Jesus Demonstrated the Christ

With obvious dependence on Quimby, Christian Science interprets Jesus as a mere human who demonstrated the divine Christ. The Christ was the divinity of the man Jesus. Jesus was not himself the Christ but merely embodied the Christ. The significance of Jesus' ministry was that he came as a way-shower. He came to rescue us "from the illusion which calls sin real, and man a sinner, needing a Savior; the illusion which calls sickness real, and man an invalid needing a physician; the illusion that death is as real as Life. From such thoughts—mortal inventions, one and all—Christ Jesus came to save men."[25]

Eddy taught that the idea that God's wrath was poured out on his beloved Son at the cross is a manmade theory. She argued that the blood of Jesus did not and could not cleanse anyone from sin. It is not Jesus himself who saves anyone, but rather it is the metaphysical principles he taught that can bring salvation. We save *ourselves* through the metaphysical principles he taught.

Man Is Divine

The Christian Science view of man is an outgrowth of its view of God. Because God is all in all, man himself is a part of the divine.

Man does not have a separate existence apart from God. Just as a drop of water is one with the ocean, so every human being is one in nature with the Divine Mind.

Since God is good and man is a part of the divine, man does not sin. Indeed, sin is an illusion and unreal. Like God, or Divine Mind, man is good and perfect and is therefore incapable of sin, sickness, and death. "There is in reality no evil, no disease, no death."[26]

There Was No Real Crucifixion or Resurrection

In Eddy's view, there was no sacrifice on Calvary. Because death is ultimately an illusion, Jesus did not and could not truly die on the cross. And since there is no such thing as death, there could never be such a thing as a literal resurrection from the dead. Eddy writes, "His disciples believed Jesus to be dead while he was hiding in the sepulcher, whereas he was alive, demonstrating within the narrow tomb the power of Spirit to overrule mortal, material sense."[27]

What, then, did the disciples perceive? Jesus reappeared to his followers—that is, "to their *apprehension* he rose from the grave, on the third day of his ascending thought."[28] We are told, "In his final demonstration, called the ascension, which closed the earthly record of Jesus, he rose above the physical knowledge of his disciples, and the material sense saw him no more."[29] The absurdity of this explanation is exceeded only by its ambiguity.

Salvation Involves Denying the Illusion of Sin

Since sin, evil, disease, and death are viewed as illusions and as being unreal, "salvation" in Christian Science refers to a person's ceasing to believe in the illusion of sin, sickness, and death. Our problem is rooted not in sin, but in the errors of mortal mind. Through Christian Science, the errors of mortal mind can be cast out. In the end all people will be "saved," because ultimately nothing exists except God or Divine Mind.

According to Christian Science, there is no literal hell. People make their own hell in the present by thinking wrongly; their hell is the "fire of a guilty conscience."[30] Likewise, heaven is reinterpreted in terms of the good circumstances that result from right thinking.

In Christian Science thought, man continues to live following what is called "death." "Man is not annihilated, nor does he lose his identity, by passing through the belief called death. After the momentary belief of dying passes from mortal mind, this mind is still in a conscious state of existence."[31] Following this so-called death, there is a probation during which we continue to fight and overcome the "errors" regarding matter, sickness, and death. "As death findeth mortal man, so shall he be after death, until probation and growth shall effect the needed change."[32] In the end, all such illusions will be dispelled and all will be saved.

THE UNITED CHURCH OF RELIGIOUS SCIENCE

Religious Science was founded by "Dr." Ernest S. Holmes (1887–1960). In his early years Holmes was influenced by various metaphysical teachers (including Quimby). He also had an interest in occultism and attended séances on many occasions.

In 1912 Ernest and his brother Fenwicke traveled to California, and in the years that followed he continued on a quest for spiritual knowledge and studied metaphysics, religion, and philosophy as related to the power of the mind to change one's circumstances. In 1917 the brothers founded the Metaphysical Institute in Los Angeles. Almost a decade after that, Ernest published his 667-page book, *The Science of Mind*, which has become the standard textbook for all followers of Religious Science. In this book Ernest states that "Religious Science is a correlation of the laws of science, the opinions of philosophy, and the revelations of religion applied to human needs and the aspirations of man."[33]

In 1927 Holmes officially founded his new religion and incorporated the Institute of Religious Science and School of Philosophy. Holmes said, "I didn't like any of the religions I was acquainted with, and so I made up one that I did like."[34] The movement grew through speaking engagements, radio programs, the magazine *Science of Mind*, and endorsements from the likes of Norman Vincent Peale (author of numerous books on positive thinking), Robert Young (actor best known for the television series *Father Knows Best*), Norman Cousins (editor of the *Saturday Review*), and Maurice Stans (former U.S. secretary of commerce). Holmes changed the name of the institute to the United Church of Religious Science in 1967. Today there are more than 180 churches of Religious Science in the United States.

There Are Many Holy Books

Proponents of Religious Science do not believe Christianity has a corner on the truth, and therefore the Bible is not viewed as

God's only revelation. Holmes believed that many other holy books are just as legitimate as the Christian Bible, including the Muslim Koran, the Jewish Talmud, and Eastern writings such as the Bhagavad-Gita, the Vedas, and the Upanishads.

Even though the different holy books of the various religions may seem to contain different ideas, in reality they are speaking of the same ultimate truth. Holmes stated, "It has been well said that 'religions are many'; but Religion is one. . . . There is One Reality at the heart of all religions, whether their name be Hindu, Mohammedan, Christian or Jewish."[35] By taking an esoteric approach to interpreting the various holy books, Holmes claims to have synthesized the truth found in all religions.

God Is in All Things

Holmes espoused a God that is impersonal ("The Thing Itself," "Principle," and "Neutral Force") and permeates all things. God is viewed as an infinite divine presence that becomes personified in human beings. Each of us has the God Principle within us, just as Jesus did.

Religious Science views the universe as the body of God, a view known in theological circles as panentheism. "The physical universe is the Body of God—the Invisible Principle of all life. The entire manifestation of Spirit, both visible and invisible, is the Body of God."[36] God is viewed as being *in* everything, but he is also seen as *greater than* everything.

Using esoteric methodology, Holmes reinterpreted the Trinity in metaphysical terms. He said that "the Father [is] the supreme creative Principle . . . and means Absolute Being."[37] The Son is "the entire manifestation of the infinite in any and all planes, levels, states of consciousness, or manifestations."[38] Moreover, "the Holy Ghost signifies the feminine aspect of the Divine Trinity. It represents the divine activity of the higher mental plane."[39]

"It is unreasonable to suppose that any one person, or race, encompasses all truth, and alone can reveal the way of life to others. Taking the best from all sources, Religous Science has access to the highest enlightenment of the ages. Religious Science reads every man's Bible and gleans the truths therein contained" (Ernest Holmes, *What Religious Science Teaches*, 9–10).

Jesus Was a Way-Shower

Like the other mind sciences, Religious Science regards Jesus as just a human being who had the same divinity other people can attain. He was essentially a "way-shower," and what he accomplished, all people can accomplish. "Mental science does not deny the divinity of Jesus, but it does affirm the divinity of all people. It does not deny that Jesus was the Son of God, but it affirms that all men are sons of God."[40]

Jesus allegedly taught that "every man is a potential Christ."[41] The term *Christ* is here used in the sense of *higher divine self*. "Christ is God in the soul of man. To practice the Presence of God, is to awaken within us the Christ consciousness."[42] Jesus was the embodiment of the Christ just as we can be the embodiment of the Christ.

Jesus did not have to die for any so-called sins. "Jesus made no claim that he had paid Man's debt to God, nor must God's wrath be stayed nor be appeased by a sacrifice of blood."[43] Moreover, since death is viewed as an illusion, Jesus did not really die on the cross. Hence there could be no true bodily resurrection from the dead.[44]

Man Is an Incarnation of God

The Religious Science teaching that God is *in* all things means God is *in man*, and therefore man is divine. Man is a *personification* of the infinite. "There is that within us which partakes of the nature of the Divine Being, and since we partake of the nature of the Divine Being, we are divine."[45] "Every man is an incarnation of God."[46]

But if we are divine beings, Holmes asks, why do we appear to be so limited, so forlorn, so miserable and sick? The answer, Holmes says, is that "we are ignorant of our own nature, and also ignorant of the Law of God which governs all things."[47] The only "sin" is ignorance of one's divinity. Through Religious Science, this ignorance can be rectified, and humans—as divine beings—can become the masters of their own destiny. When individuals, through Religious Science, recognize their union with the Infinite, they automatically become the Christ.

Salvation Is a Matter of the Mind

Like other mind science metaphysicians, Holmes rejects any idea of a literal hell: "I do not believe in hell, the devil, damnation, or in any future state of punishment; or any other of the fantastic ideas which have been conceived in the minds of those who are either morbid, or who have felt the need of a future state of damnation to which to consign the immortal souls of those who have not agreed with their absurd doctrines. God does not punish people."[48] Nor is there a literal heaven. Jesus "did not say there is a heaven which God has provided for us in life after this life; he said that heaven is present with us."[49] Heaven and hell are "states of consciousness in which we now live according to our own state of understanding."[50]

Salvation in Religious Science is a matter of the mind. Everyone is *already* saved if they will only realize it. "There is no need to seek unity with God and the Universe. We already have it. It is something we must become *aware* of."[51] "There must come a new impulse to the mind, a new way of looking at things. This is what Jesus called the new birth."[52] Understanding alone constitutes true salvation. Holmes is sure that full and complete salvation will come alike to all. "Even the lowest and most hopeless savage will sometime attain to Christ consciousness."[53]

THE UNITY SCHOOL OF CHRISTIANITY

The Unity School of Christianity was founded in 1891 by Charles and Myrtle Fillmore. Their individual backgrounds provided fertile soil for the emergence of Unity's theology. Myrtle developed tuberculosis, which caused her health to decline in 1886, at which time she began to seek answers. During that year, she attended a lecture by Dr. Eugene B. Weeks, an advocate of Quimby's New Thought, who focused attention on the power of the mind to bring healing to the body. Myrtle was so tired of suffering that she was open to just about anything.

This lecture turned out to be a life-changing experience for Myrtle. In fact, one particular comment made by Dr. Weeks changed the entire course of her life: "I am a child of God and therefore I do not inherit sickness."[54] Myrtle repeated this revolutionary statement over and over again for a period of two years, during which time she claims she became completely healed.

It was not long before Myrtle wanted to share this wonderful metaphysical healing discovery with the whole world. She saturated her mind with all of the metaphysical literature she could find, including that from New Thought, Christian Science, and Divine Science.

Meanwhile Charles, now her husband, arrived at a commitment to metaphysics by a different path. He was initially an agnostic and was very skeptical about the claims his wife made. Nevertheless, he hungered for knowledge and began to study not just metaphysics, but also occultism, Eastern religions, and various philosophies. Before it was over, Charles's worldview was molded by Hinduism, Theosophy, Rosicrucianism, Spiritualism, Christian Science, New Thought, and other metaphysical schools of thought.

Charles and Myrtle began to hold meetings to share their eclectic theological hodgepodge with other people. In 1889 Charles began to publish his metaphysical ideas in a magazine called *Modern Thought*. The magazine soon went through several name changes—including *Christian Science Thought* (which Mary Baker Eddy objected to) and then finally *Thought*. The magazine featured articles by a variety of metaphysical writers on such topics as Buddhism, Hinduism, Theosophy, Rosicrucianism, and the occult.

The movement started by the Fillmores eventually became the Unity School of Christianity in 1890 as a result of a mystical revelation Charles claimed he received. Just as Paul heard the voice of Jesus on the road to Damascus (Acts 9:4), so Charles heard a voice from the etheric realm that said, "UNITY."[55] Charles felt the term was appropriate, for the Fillmores "borrowed the best from all religions." Indeed, "Unity is the Truth that is taught in all religions, simplified and systematized so that anyone can understand and apply it."[56]

From the 1890s forward, the group experienced steady growth. This was due to the distribution of Unity literature (including books and magazines), educational outreaches, radio, television, and small Unity "societies" that met across the nation involving tens of thousands of followers. Unity seems to have touched a nerve with many people because it claims that by following its principles people can have happier, healthier, and more productive lives. As well, people can achieve their divine potential by following Unity principles.

Today Unity has an estimated 110,000 members, though an additional 35,000 persons attend some of its weekly study groups. There are over 300 Unity churches, involving 930 licensed ministers and 680 licensed teachers, making it one of the largest metaphysical groups in the United States. The Unity School of Christianity has been called the largest mail-order religion in the world (they send out more than 33 million pieces of mail annually, promoting their many books).[57] Unity programs presently air on more than 1,000 radio and television stations. The group's magazines—the most popular being *Daily Word*—have millions of readers.

The Bible Should Be Interpreted Metaphysically

Unity does not render exclusive devotion to the Christian Bible, but rather believes revelations have come to humankind through the sacred writings of *all* the world religions. Unity utilizes a metaphysical or esoteric method of interpreting Scripture, seeking to get beneath the text of Scripture and unveil hidden metaphysical meanings. To aid in the process of interpreting the Bible in an esoteric way, Unity publishes the *Metaphysical Bible Dictionary*.

Unity also emphasizes that one can obtain spiritual insights without having to consult holy books. Each of us can receive revelations and find truth *within* ourselves. "Truth is in every person, and it is only through the awakening of this inner Spirit that anyone can come to know Truth. . . . In the final analysis each individual has to find Truth for himself, within himself."[58]

This concept is in keeping with Unity's open-ended approach to divine truth. While one can start with Unity principles, one is encouraged to *evolve beyond* this starting point to the ascertaining of *new* spiritual truths that are discovered within oneself. There is no finalized creed, but rather one's belief system is to continually emerge.[59]

God Is in All Things

God is viewed by Unity not as a person but as impersonal Divine Mind or Principle. The God of Unity is more of a cosmic, impersonal "It" than a personal "He." The Trinity is likewise described in impersonal terms: "The Father is Principle, the Son is that Principle revealed in creative plan, the Holy Spirit is the executive power of both Father and Son carrying out the creative plan."[60]

Similar to Religious Science, the Unity view of God can best be categorized as a form of panentheism, which involves the idea that God *is in* all and all *is in* God. "Each rock, tree, animal, everything visible, is a manifestation of the one spirit—God—differing only in degree of manifestation; and each of the numberless modes of manifestation, or individualities, however insignificant, contains the whole."[61] God is the "real thing standing under every visible form of life."[62] God "lives within every created thing at very center as the life."[63]

Jesus Embodied the Christ

Like other metaphysicians, Holmes separated the human Jesus from the impersonal Christ. He believed that "Jesus was a man, a human being,"[64] while the Christ is "the embodiment of all divine ideas, such as intelligence, life, love, substance, and strength."[65] At some point in Jesus' earthly life, this impersonal "Christ"—or divine idea—came upon him. "As Jesus, the man, gave way to the Divine Idea, the human took on the Christ Spirit and became the voice of God to humanity."[66]

Man, Too, Is Divine

Unity's panentheistic view of God leads to the view that man himself is divine. "This divine nature is in us all, waiting to be brought into expression to our recognition of the power and might of I AM."[67] Each individual has within himself or herself the Christ potential, the Christ presence, the Christ reality. "There is no absence or separation in God. His omnipresence is your omnipresence."[68] "God is man and man is God and there is no separation."[69]

Since all is in God and God is in all, this leaves no room for sin. In Unity, man is viewed as perfect and sin is viewed as unreal. Unity writer Emilie Cady said, "There is no evil (or Devil). . . . Pain, sickness, poverty, old age, and death are not real, and they have no power over me. There is nothing in the universe for me to fear."[70] Because man is one with God, there can be no sin, ignorance, or limitations.

Crucifixion and Resurrection Relate Only to Human Consciousness

Obviously, since sin is unreal, there could be no sin for Jesus to die for on the cross. And since death is unreal, Jesus could not really die. Since Jesus did not really die, this means he could not be literally raised from the dead.

In keeping with its esoteric methodology, Unity interprets crucifixion and resurrection metaphysically. *Crucifixion* refers to the perishing of unenlightened consciousness while *resurrection* refers to the raising of a spiritual consciousness. Indeed, "the resurrection is the lifting up of the whole man into the Christ-consciousness."[71] This "resurrection" is an ongoing experience for the enlightened.

Salvation Comes by At-one-ment with God

Salvation in Unity is attained by "at-one-ment" with God—a reuniting of human consciousness with God-consciousness. The goal is perfect union with the mind of God. Jesus attained this at-one-ment with the Divine Mind; indeed, all humanity can. The difference between Jesus and other humans is not one of inherent spiritual capacity, but in difference of manifestation. Jesus was potentially perfect, and He expressed that perfection; other humans are potentially perfect, but they have not yet expressed it. Jesus attained a divine awareness without parallel in world history. Unity literature assures us that we can bring forth the Christ within us. When that happens, we are "born again."[72]

Reincarnation Restores Man to a Deathless State

Unity is distinguished from other New Thought groups by its doctrine of reincarnation. The Unity Statement of Faith tells us, "We believe that dissolution of spirit, soul and body, caused by death, is annulled by rebirth of the same spirit and soul in another body here on earth. We believe the repeated incarnations of man to be a merciful provision of our loving Father to the end that all may have opportunity to attain immortality through regeneration, as did Jesus."[73]

Unity's concept of reincarnation is different, however, from that of traditional Hinduism. This becomes evident in Unity's rejection of the Hindu "law of karma." (Karma refers to the "debt" a soul accumulates as a result of good or bad actions committed during one's life [or past lives]. If one accumulates good karma, he or she will allegedly be reincarnated in a desirable state. If one accumulates bad karma, he or she will allegedly be reincarnated in a less desirable state.) According to Unity, "Christ" has set humanity free from the wheel of karma. Charles Fillmore argued that "the regenerative work of Christ released man from the karmic wheel and prepared him for new life, a series of new lives, in fact, which might be looked upon as vehicles for the attainment of the perfect, deathless body."[74] Unity teaches that reincarnation is God's means of restoring humankind to a deathless state.

God does not wrathfully condemn anyone to an eternity in hell but rather, through reincarnation, lovingly helps all his children find eternal life. Through numerous reincarnations, one becomes increasingly like Jesus (becoming a vehicle for "the Christ" and overcoming ignorance by rejecting the ideas of sin, sickness, and death) and eventually does not need reincarnation any longer. In the end, all people will be saved.

CHALLENGING MIND SCIENCE BELIEFS

Esotericism Is an Unreliable Hermeneutic

As a method of interpreting Scripture, mind science esotericism proves to be utterly unreliable as a means of ascertaining the biblical author's intended meaning (the only *legitimate* meaning):

1. *Esotericism violates the scriptural injunction to rightly handle the Word of God and not distort its meaning.* Some people distort Scripture "to their own destruction" (2 Peter 3:16). Contrary to this, we should avoid distorting God's Word and should set forth God's truth *plainly* (2 Cor. 4:2). Paul writes, "Do your best to present yourself to God as one approved, a workman who does not need to be ashamed and who *correctly handles the word of truth*" (2 Tim. 2:15, emphasis added).

2. *Esotericism fails to recognize that each verse of Scripture has only one true meaning.* The International Council on Biblical Inerrancy (ICBI) published a small book in 1983 entitled *Explaining Hermeneutics: A Commentary*, in which Article VII states, "We affirm that the meaning in each biblical text is single, definite and fixed."[75] The commentary for this article tells us that the affirmation here is directed at those who claim a double or deeper meaning of Scripture than that expressed by the authors. It stresses the unity and fixity of meaning as opposed to multiple and pliable meanings.

This is an important point, for mind science proponents try to make a case for hidden or inner meanings of Bible verses. We agree that everyone is entitled to his or her own interpretation of the Bible, but we insist that *not all interpretations are equally correct.*

An illustration often used by Christian apologists to make this point is that of following a recipe to bake a cake. To make a good cake, one must observe how the recipe instructs one to follow certain steps, such as using particular ingredients, mixing them in a precise order, and placing the batter in the oven at a precise temperature and for a precise length of time. *Only one interpretation of the recipe is correct*, and that interpretation is the one that accurately reflects the intentions of the person who wrote the recipe. The same is true of Scripture. The correct interpretation is the one that accurately reflects the intentions of the biblical author.

3. *In esotericism the basic authority in interpretation ceases to be Scripture and instead becomes the mind of the interpreter.* Because of this, esoteric interpreters come up with radically different (and contradictory) meanings of specific Bible verses. Such contradictions are inevitable when the mind of the interpreter is made the authority instead of Scripture.

4. *Esotericists rely on their own inner illumination to determine what Scripture means, whereas Christians rely on the Holy Spirit for illumination.* Scripture indicates that full comprehension of the *Word of God* is impossible without prayerful dependence on the *Spirit of God* (1 Cor. 2:9–11), for He who inspired the Word (2 Peter 1:21) is also its supreme interpreter (John 16:12–15). It is crucial to recognize that the Holy Spirit's ministry of illumination operates within the sphere of man's rational capacity, which God Himself gave man (cf. Gen. 2–3). James Sire comments that illumination "comes to the minds of God's people—not to some nonrational faculty like our emotions or our feelings. To know God's revelation means to use our minds. This makes knowledge something we can share with others, something we can talk about. God's Word is in words with ordinary rational content."[76]

5. *Esotericism superimposes mystical meanings on Bible verses instead of objectively seeking the biblical authors' intended meaning.* In approaching the Scriptures we ought to put nothing into them, but rather draw everything from them. What a passage means is fixed by the author and is not subject to alteration by readers. "Meaning is *determined* by the author; it is *discovered* by readers."[77]

Article XIX of ICBI's *Explaining Hermeneutics: A Commentary* addresses this issue: "We affirm that any preunderstandings which the interpreter brings to Scripture should be in harmony with scriptural teaching and subject to correction by it. We deny that Scripture should be required to fit alien preunderstandings, inconsistent with itself. . . ." The point of this article is to guard against interpreting Scripture through an alien grid or filter that obscures or negates its true message. It acknowledges that one's preunderstanding will affect his or her understanding of a text. Hence, to avoid misinterpreting Scripture, one must be careful to examine one's own presuppositions in the light of Scripture.[78]

6. *Esotericism ignores the context of Bible verses.* Every word in the Bible is part of a verse, and every verse is part of a paragraph, and every paragraph is part of a book. No verse of Scripture is independent from the verses around it. Interpreting a verse apart from its context is like trying to analyze a Rembrandt painting by looking at a single square inch of the painting, or like trying to analyze Handel's *Messiah* by listening to a few short notes. The overall context is critical to properly interpreting Bible verses.

7. *Esotericism ignores grammar, history, and culture.* If we ignore grammar, history, and culture, how can we possibly hope to ascertain the authors' *intended* meaning? Gordon Lewis asserts, "When we claim Biblical authority for an idea, we must be prepared to show from the grammar, the history, the culture and the context that the writer in fact taught that idea. Otherwise the Bible is not *used* but *abused*."[79]

8. *Esotericism goes against the example set by Jesus Christ in how to properly interpret Scripture.* Jesus *never* interpreted the Old Testament Scriptures esoterically. On the contrary, He interpreted events in the Old Testament quite literally, including the creation account of Adam and Eve (Matt. 13:35; 25:34; Mark 10:6), Noah's ark and the flood (Matt. 24:38–39; Luke 17:26–27), Jonah and the whale (Matt. 12:39–41), Sodom and Gomorrah (Matt. 10:15), and the account of Lot and his wife (Luke 17:28–29). Jesus' interpretation of Scripture was always in accord with the grammatical and historical meaning. Would mind science proponents say Jesus was wrong in this? If so, then why do they call Him enlightened? If Jesus was not wrong, then why don't mind science proponents follow His enlightened example?

There Is a Distinction Between God and His Creation

Whether one holds to the pantheistic ("God is all") view of Christian Science or the panentheistic ("God is *in* all") view of Religious

MIND SCIENCES VERSUS CHRISTIANITY

	Mind Science View	Christian View
God	God is all, or God is *in* all	God is distinct from the creation
Jesus Christ	Jesus = human, Christ = Divine Idea	One person, the human-divine Messiah
Sin	Illusion, ignorance of divinity	Real rebellion against God
Salvation	Involves denial of the illusion of sin	Based on faith in Christ the Savior
Death	An error of mortal mind	A real consequence of sin

Science and the Unity School of Christianity, both positions are unbiblical. Such views entail a number of critical problems. First, all distinctions between creation (which is finite) and the Creator (who is infinite) are ultimately destroyed. As Norman L. Geisler put it, "all alleged I-thou or I-I relations reduce to I."[80] From a biblical perspective, God is eternally distinct from what He created. God, who is infinite and eternal, created all things out of absolute nothingness (Heb. 11:3; see also Gen. 1:1; Neh. 9:6; Ps. 33:8–9; 148:5). While God is omnipresent (Ps. 139:7–9), He most certainly is not pantheistically "one with" the universe or panentheistically "in" the universe; He remains eternally distinct from creation and from humankind (cf. Num. 23:19; Eccl. 5:2; Heb. 11:3).

Further, the mind science view of God fails to adequately deal with the existence of real evil in the world. If evil is real and not just an illusion, as the mind sciences contend, then what? If God is the essence of *all* life forms in creation (Holmes, a panentheist, said, "I do not believe there is a single fact in human history, or a single manifestation in the universe, which is or could possibly be *anything other than* a manifestation of the One Divine Mind . . ."),[81] then one must conclude that both good and evil stem from one and the same essence (God). Contrary to this, the God of the Bible is light, and "in him is no darkness at all" (1 John 1:5; cf. Hab. 1:13; Matt. 5:48). First John 1:5 is particularly cogent in the Greek, which translates literally: "And darkness there is not in Him, not in any way." John could not have said it more forcefully.

Related to this is a warning from Isaiah: "Woe to those who call evil good and good evil" (Isa. 5:20). Saying that good and evil stem from the same essence of God is the same as calling evil "good" and calling good "evil."

Finally, contrary to the mind science view that God is an impersonal force and not a personal Being with whom relationships can be established, the biblical concept of God involves a loving Father unto whom believers may cry, "Abba" (Mark 14:36; Rom. 8:15; Gal. 4:6). Walter Martin sheds some light on the personal nature of God:

> This Almighty Person performs acts that only a personality is capable of: God hears (Exodus 2:24); God sees (Genesis 1:4); God creates (Genesis 1:1); God knows (2 Timothy 2:19; Jeremiah 29:11); God has a will (1 John 2:17); God is a cognizant reflectable ego, i.e., a personal being—"I AM that I AM" (Exodus 3:14; Genesis 17:1). This is the God of Christianity, an omnipotent, omniscient, and omnipresent Personality, who manifests every attribute of personality.[82]

Man Is Not Divine

If the essence of human beings is God, and if God is an infinite, changeless being, then how is it possible for man (if man is a manifestation of divinity) to go through a changing process of enlightenment by which he discovers his divinity? The fact that a man comes to realize he is God proves that he *is not* God. For if he were God, he never would have passed from a state of ignorance to a state of awareness as to his divinity.[83]

The perverted desire for godhood has a long history in the universe. If it is correct that Isaiah 14:12–14 and Ezekiel 28:12–19 refer to the fall of Lucifer (and there is good reason to believe this), then it seems that this was the beginning of the desire for godhood in the universe. Lucifer was originally created as the most magnificent of angels. But then an unholy desire entered his heart. His sinful yearning is summed up in the statement, "I will make myself like the Most High" (Isa. 14:14). Lucifer wanted to take God's place. But the only true God cast the self-inflated Lucifer from His holy presence.

In the Garden of Eden, this fallen angel sought to tempt Eve to eat the forbidden fruit. He enticed her by saying, "God knows that in the day you eat from it your eyes will be opened, and you will be like God, knowing good and evil" (Gen. 3:5). The fall of man was the result of this encounter. But man—to the present day—continues yearning to be "like God."

This leads me to make an observation about human nature. If it were true that all people possess a part of the divine essence and that they are all manifestations of God, then one would expect them to display qualities similar to those known to be true of God. This seems only logical. However, when one compares the attributes of humankind with those of God (as set forth in Scripture), we find more than ample testimony for the truth of Paul's statement in Romans 3:23 that human beings "fall short of the glory of God." God is all-knowing (1 John 3:20), but man is limited in knowledge (Job 38:4); God is all-powerful (Rev. 19:6), but man is weak (Heb. 4:15); God is present everywhere (Ps. 139:7–12), but man is confined to a single space at a time (for example, John 1:50); God is holy (1 John 1:5), but even man's "righteous" deeds are as filthy garments before God (Isa. 64:6); God is eternal (Ps. 90:2), but man was created at a point in time (Gen. 1:1, 27); God is truth (John 14:6), but fallen man's heart is deceitful above all else (Jer. 17:9); God is characterized by justice (Acts 17:31), but fallen man is lawless (1 John 3:4; cf. Rom. 3:23); God is love (Eph. 2:4–5), but fallen man is plagued with numerous vices like jealousy and strife (1 Cor. 3:3). If man is a god, one could never tell it by his attributes!

In total antithesis to the idea that man is a god (or that he possesses a part of the divine essence), the biblical view is that no one on earth comes even remotely close to God's greatness and majesty. Recall the message God instructed Moses to pass on to Pharaoh regarding the 10 plagues: "I will send the full force of my plagues against you and against your officials and your people, so you may know that there is no one like me in all the earth" (Ex. 9:14). When it is realized that these words were spoken to a man who was himself considered a god (that is, the Pharaoh was thought to be the incarnation of the Egyptian sun god, Ra (or Re), and was hence considered a "god" in his own right), these words of Yahweh become extremely relevant to the current mind science claim that human beings are divine. Yahweh's response to such claims is that "there is no one like me in all the earth." *Yahweh is incomparable.*

Inasmuch as God is the Incomparable One, it is highly revealing to observe the responses of human beings when they come face to face with Him. When Isaiah found himself in the presence of God, he cried out, "Woe to me! . . . I am ruined! For I am a man of unclean lips, . . . and my eyes have seen the King, the LORD

Almighty" (Isa. 6:5). Similarly, when John had a vision on the Isle of Patmos and beheld the glorified Christ, he said, "When I saw him, I fell at his feet as though dead" (Rev. 1:17). Something about seeing God *as He really is* has an indescribable effect on human beings. In view of passages like this, it is the height of human arrogance to even toy with the idea that man is divine.

Jesus Alone Is the Christ

The Scriptural testimony is that Jesus *alone* is the Christ. When the angel announced the birth of Jesus to the shepherds, he identified Jesus this way: "Today in the town of David a Savior has been born to you; he is Christ the Lord" (Luke 2:11). Jesus did not become the Christ as an adult, but rather was the one and only Christ from the very beginning. John's first epistle thus warns us, "Who is the liar? It is the man who denies that Jesus is the Christ. Such a man is the antichrist—he denies the Father and the Son" (1 John 2:22).

It is also noteworthy that the Old Testament presents hundreds of prophecies regarding the coming of a single Messiah (for example, Isa. 7:14; 53:3–5; Mic. 5:2; Zech. 12:10). The New Testament counterpart of the Old Testament word for "Messiah" is *Christ* (see John 1:41). Jesus alone fulfilled these hundreds of prophecies, and thus *He alone* is the Christ. There is no other.

Significantly, when Jesus was acknowledged as the Christ by people in the New Testament, He never said, "*You too* have the Christ within." Instead, He warned that others would come falsely claiming to be the Christ (Matt. 24:5).

(*Note:* In chapter 8, "Hindu-Based Cults," I deal with the claim that Jesus taught the doctrine of reincarnation. See page 185.)

Matter, Sin, Sickness, and Death Are Real

The biblical account indicates that after God created the universe *(which included matter)*, He declared that it was very good (Gen. 1:31). The world of matter is not an illusion, nor is it evil. It is real and a part of God's good creation.

Simply denying that sin, sickness, and death are real does not make it so. During Mary Baker Eddy's declining years, she was under a doctor's care and received regular morphine injections to ease her pain. She wore eyeglasses, had teeth extractions, and eventually died, thus "giving the lie" to all she professed to believe and teach.[84] Her act of denying sin, sickness, and death was itself denied by her own life and death.

The reality is that the Christian Science worldview (like the worldview of the other mind sciences) is unlivable. When one faces genuine pain in life—whether physical (like cancer eating away at the body), emotional (such as the grief one feels when a spouse dies), or mental (negative thoughts)—simply saying that all is rooted in errors of the mortal mind is no comfort. Denying that evil is real is itself evil, because doing so causes evil consequences in people's lives.

Likewise, the very claim that sin does not exist is itself a prime manifestation of sin and fallenness. Because sin is real, a real Savior is needed. Jesus did not just come as a way-shower; He came to die as a substitutionary atonement for the sins of man (1 John 2:2). One must emphasize to mind science enthusiasts that it is only by trusting in Jesus that one can receive a real salvation made possible by a real Savior (John 3:16).

• Mind Sciences •

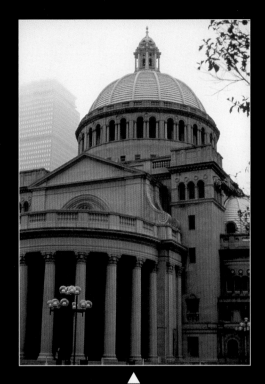

▲

The Mother Church of the Christian Science
movement in Boston. *Courtesy George Mather*

▲

Founder's Church of Religious Science in Los Angeles

· Mormonism ·

▲
The Mormon Temple in Salt Lake City.
Courtesy Jim McKeever

▲
Hill Cumorah, the place where Joseph Smith is said to have dug up the golden plates containing the Book of Mormon text (allegedly written in Reformed Egyptian). *Courtesy Personal Freedom Outreach*

▲
A painting depicting Joseph Smith and Oliver Cowdery being bestowed with the priesthood by John the Baptist.
Courtesy Personal Freedom Outreach

· Mormonism ·

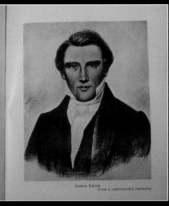

Joseph Smith, founder of the Mormo[n] church. *Copyright © 2001 Jack Roper*

Brigham Young, who became leader of the Mormon church following the death of Joseph Smith. *Copyright © 2001 Jack Roper*

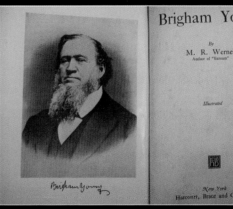

A facsimile of the golden plates discovered by Joseph Smith. *Courtesy Personal Freedom Outreach*

· Jehovah's Witnesses ·

One of numerous Watchtower Bethel headquarters buildings in Brooklyn, New York. *Courtesy Personal Freedom Outreach*

A Jehovah's Witness Kingdom Hall (place of worship) being built in 24 hours. *Courtesy Personal Freedom Outreach*

Awake, a magazine that is distributed to millions of people semimonthly. *Courtesy Personal Freedom Outreach*

• Jehovah's Witnesses •

The "Trust in Jehovah" District Convention, the 1987 annual district convention of the Jehovah's Witnesses. *Courtesy Personal Freedom Outreach*

Charles Taze Russell's pyramid grave marker in Pittsburgh. Russell believed the Egyptian pyramids held prophetic significance. *Courtesy Personal Freedom Outreach*

Beth Sarim—a San Diego mansion built for the Old Testament patriarchs, who were prophesied by Jehovah's Witnesses to be resurrected unto life in 1925. *Courtesy Personal Freedom Outreach*

• New Age Movement •

An occult shop, frequently visited
by New Agers. *Courtesy George Mather*

An astrologer at a psychic fair.
Copyright © 2001 Jack Roper

Tarot cards, often used by New Agers for divination.
Copyright © 2001 Jack Roper

· New Age Movement ·

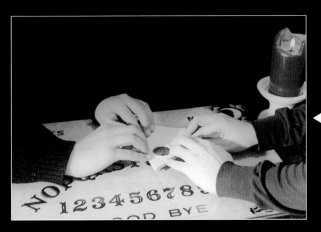

◄ A Ouija board, used for divination.
Courtesy Personal Freedom Outreach

A horoscope vending machine, where New Agers can pick up astrology readings. *Courtesy Personal Freedom Outreach* ►

◄ More New Age vending machines, where people can obtain astrology or bio-rhythm readings. *Courtesy Personal Freedom Outreach*

· New Age Movement ·

Astrology and Tarot card shop in Greenwich Village, New York City, a popular venue for New Agers. *Copyright © 2001 Jack Roper*

New Age occult literature.
Courtesy George Mather

A New Age psychic shop in New Orleans. *Copyright © 2001 Jack Roper*

Crystal balls. *Copyright © 2001 Jack Roper*

6

THE NEW AGE MOVEMENT

The New Age movement has been called the fastest-growing alternative belief system in the country. Sociologists at the University of California–Santa Barbara estimate that as many as 12 million Americans could be considered active participants in the movement, and another 30 million are avidly interested. New Ager Marilyn Ferguson asserts that "if all these people were brought together in a church-like organization, it would be the third-largest religious denomination in America."[1]

Certainly a large percentage of Americans are involved in some form of New Age occultism or another. Some 42 percent of American adults presently believe they have personally been in contact with someone who has died. Fourteen percent of Americans endorse the work of spirit mediums or channelers.

About 67 percent of American adults claim to have had a psychic experience such as extrasensory perception. Approximately 30 million Americans believe in reincarnation. Some 67 percent of American adults read astrology columns. One out of three Americans believe that fortunetellers can actually foretell the future. There are presently 2,500 occult bookstores in the United States and over 3,000 publishers of occult and New Age books, journals, and magazines. The New Age tome *A Course in Miracles* has now sold a million copies and has spawned more than 1,000 study groups in the United States alone.[2] Such statistics point to the broad penetration of New Age ideas in Western culture.

One difficulty in discussing the New Age movement is defining it, for it is not a single monolithic organization. It is best understood as a loosely structured network of individuals and organizations who share a common vision of a new age of enlightenment and harmony (the "Age of Aquarius"), and who subscribe to a common set of religious and philosophical beliefs ("worldview"). This common set of beliefs is based on *monism* (all is one), *pantheism* (all is God), and *mysticism* (the experience of oneness with the divine).[3]

Because it is so broad and organizationally diffuse, the New Age movement cannot be categorized as a cult by any accepted definition of "cult." *Cults* are exclusivistic groups made up of individuals who subscribe to uniform beliefs and operate according to a rigidly defined organizational structure. *Movements*, while having an element of unity, are multifaceted—involving a variety of individuals and groups (including cults) whose beliefs, practices, and emphases are distinctive and diverse. This is the case with the New Age movement. To be a New Ager, one need not join a certain organization or confess a certain creed.

There is diversity and unity within the movement. Its diversity is evident in that it is made up of many different individuals and organizations who have a variety of interests and are committed to different causes. The movement embraces holistic health professionals, ecologists, political activists, educators, human potential advocates, Goddess worshipers, reincarnationists, astrologers, and much more. In terms of unity, all these diverse individuals associate comfortably under the common umbrella of the New Age movement. The vision and worldview they share in common enables them to "network" together to accomplish common ends.

CHARACTERISTICS OF THE NEW AGE MOVEMENT

One of the best ways to understand the New Age movement is to examine its primary characteristics. Of course, not every New Ager would hold to every characteristic below. But most New Agers would hold to most of them.

Eclecticism

New Agers are eclectic, meaning they draw from various sources of "truth." They feel equally at home with the Christian Bible, Levi Dowling's *The Aquarian Gospel of Jesus the Christ*, the readings of "sleeping prophet" Edgar Cayce, and advice from "Ramtha" (an alleged 35,000-year-old Lemurian warrior-king as channeled through J. Z. Knight).

Religious Syncretism

The New Age movement is syncretistic, meaning that it attempts to combine and synthesize different (and sometimes contradictory) religious and philosophical teachings. Like a huge cosmic sponge, the New Age movement absorbs the teachings of all the world religions and syncretizes these into its mystical worldview. New Agers do not render exclusive devotion to any one teacher or teaching. They agree that God revealed himself in Jesus. However, they say he also revealed himself in Buddha, Krishna, and a host of others. The Bible can therefore make no claim to be God's only revelation.

Monism

Monism—from the Greek word *monos* (meaning "one")—is a theory that sees all reality as a unified whole. Everything in the universe is viewed as composed of the same substance. As New Ager George Trevelyan put it, "Life is a Divine Oneness."[4] In monism, man, God, and the world of nature are likened to "waves" in a single cosmic "ocean." Perceived differences are apparent, not real. Therefore, all of reality is interrelated and interdependent.

> "The New Age is fundamentally a spiritual event, the birth of a new consciousness, a new awareness and experience of life.... It is a deepening into the sacramental nature of everyday life, an awakening of the consciousness that can celebrate divinity within the ordinary and, in this celebration, bring to life a sacred civilization" (David Spangler, *Emergence: The Rebirth of the Sacred*, 80–81).

Pantheism

Pantheism—from the Greek words *pan* ("all") and *theos* ("God")—is the view that God is all. All reality is viewed as being infused with divinity.[5] The pantheistic God is an impersonal, amoral "It" as opposed to the personal, moral "He" of Christianity. The distinction between the Creator and the creation is completely obliterated in pantheism.

Deification of Humanity

The belief in human divinity follows from the New Age worldview: if all is one (monism) and all is God (pantheism), then humans too are God. New Ager Beverly Galyean asserts, "Once we begin to see that we are all God, that we all have the attributes of God, then I think the whole purpose of life is to reown the God-likeness within us."[6]

Transformation

There are two aspects of transformation within the New Age movement—personal transformation and planetary transformation. Personal transformation hinges on one's personal recognition of oneness with God, humanity, and the universe. This "recognition" is described variously as "enlightenment," "attunement," "self-realization," "God-realization," and "self-actualization." We need such enlightenment because we have succumbed to the illusion of human limitation and finitude. We have forgotten our true divine identity. Only by a transformation of consciousness can we escape this lie and realize our true potential. Planetary transformation is brought about as a "critical mass" of personally transformed individuals take sociopolitical responsibility for the world of humankind.

Networking

Networking is how New Agers loosely coordinate their efforts. Though New Agers are diverse—having a wide variety of interests and being committed to different causes (such as health, psychology, politics, science, education, and the like)—they unite through networking to accomplish common goals.[7] One way New Agers network is by use of various media (computers, tapes, newsletters, and so on).

Ecological Orientation

If it is true that all is one (monism), it is obvious that human beings are intimately interrelated with the world of nature. To damage nature is ultimately to damage ourselves. Many New Agers also view the earth as a living organism, and hence it must be treated as such and be cared for ecologically.[8]

Belief in a Coming Utopia

New Agers believe a new world is coming. This utopian world is often described as involving a one-world government, global socialism, and a New Age religion.[9]

Not a Conspiracy

Contrary to the sensational claim of some Christian critics of the New Age movement, New Agers are not following the lead of a single human being or group in the unfolding of some sinister New Age master plan. Though New Agers share a common world-view and a common vision for the future and they network to attain common goals, no human conspiracy exists.

UNDERSTANDING NEW AGE SPIRITUALITY

New Age spirituality is multifaceted—involving such things as Eastern meditation, reincarnation, Spiritism (channeling), and altered states of consciousness (a mental state other than normal waking consciousness that ranges from a mild sense of the tran-scendent to a deep trance induced by spiritual exercises such as meditation or guided imagery). New Age spirituality is a hybrid spirituality, drawing from many different sources.

New Age spirituality is life- and world-affirming in that New Agers value other people, worldly pleasures, culture, and the entire universe. This is in contrast to classic Hinduism, which is world- and self-denying. The importance of this is seen in the fact that some Christian analysts have said that the New Age movement is nothing more than Hinduism repackaged. While many New Age ideas about God, man, salvation, and the world are rooted in Hindu-ism, New Age spirituality departs from Hinduism in its world-affirming emphasis.

New Age spirituality also involves a revival of paganism—called neopaganism. Neopagans reject such allegedly Western dis-tinctives as organized religion; male-dominated society; "patriar-chal," male-exalting religion (evidenced by such phrases as "God the Father"); and man's abuse of the world of nature. Instead, neopagans share a feminist perspective and seek to reharmonize themselves with "the One," which is called the *Goddess*. Goddess worshipers equate the Goddess with the world, which they say is manifest in each of us.

FACTORS GIVING RISE TO THE NEW AGE MOVEMENT

No single person or school of thought gave rise to the New Age movement. Rather, a number of historical factors converged to provide fertile soil for the eventual emergence and growth of the New Age movement in Western society.

Ancient Gnosticism

Many modern New Agers draw heavily from ancient Gnosticism. Gnosticism (from the Greek *gnosis*, "knowledge") was a heresy that briefly flourished in the second century A.D., purporting to offer knowledge of otherwise hidden "truth" as the indispensable key to man's salvation. Gnostic speculation begins with a single eternal principle (that is, God) from which multiple aeons (that is, intermediate beings or manifestations) spring in a declining hierarchy. Due to an error of one of the lower aeons (a subordinate god called the "Demiurge," usually considered to be Yahweh of the Old Testament), the material world was produced. This gave birth to a dualism between matter and spirit, or between the earthly and the heavenly.

In this world of matter created by the "Demiurge," there is to be found a remnant of the spiritual world; namely, the soul of man—a spark of divinity from the upper world (though ignorant of its celestial origins). In some inexplicable way, man's soul became entangled in the world of matter, an unfortunate turn of events that required intervention by the *good* God (that is, that single eternal principle from which all aeons spring). Deliverance was provided by the sending of a special emissary from the kingdom of light into the world of darkness. This emissary is most often identified with Christ. He is variously represented, either as a celestial being appearing in a phantom-like body (a view labeled "Docetism") or as a higher power or spirit (Christ) who temporarily associated himself with an earthly being (Jesus). This Gnostic Christ allegedly came to earth to provide a "Gnostic redemption" for humanity. For the Gnostics, "Christ came into the world, not in order to suffer and die, but in order to release the divine spark of light imprisoned in matter. The Gnostic Jesus was not a savior; he was a revealer. He came for the express purpose of communicating his secret gnosis."[10]

Many New Age ideas are noticeably similar to ancient Gnostic doctrines, including: (1) man has the spark of the divine within; (2) man is ignorant of his divinity; (3) Jesus came as a way-shower to bring enlightenment.

Nineteenth-Century Transcendentalism

Ralph Waldo Emerson (1803–82) and the Transcendentalists helped lay the foundation for the emergence of the New Age movement. Emerson elevated intuition over the senses as the means of finding "truth." He said God could reveal himself through man's intuitions. He claimed that the goal of religion is the conscious union of man with God, and he believed God had given revelation in all the religions. New Age critic Russell Chandler suggests that the Transcendentalists "eclectically borrowed from the Eastern scriptures, molding them to fit American standards of autonomy and individual determination, and set the stage for New Age luminaries to take the spotlight 130 years later."[11]

A Revival of the Occult

A revival of the occult in groups like the Theosophical Society (1875), Anthroposophy (1912), the Arcane School (1923), and the I AM movement (early 1930s), laid a strong foundation for the emergence of the New Age movement.

The Theosophical Society

Theosophy comes from the Greek word *theosophia*, which means "divine wisdom." The Theosophical Society was founded in New York in 1875 by Madame Helena Petrovna Blavatsky and Henry Olcott, and teaches that the "Ascended Masters" guide humans' spiritual evolution. "Ascended Masters" are believed to be formerly historical persons who have finished their earthly evolutions via reincarnation. Now, even as these Ascended Masters continue in their own evolution toward the godhead, they voluntarily help lesser-evolved humans to reach the Masters' present level. These Masters give revelations to spiritually attuned human beings. Blavatsky believed that her own personal revelations from these Ascended Masters marked the beginning of the Aquarian Age.

Theosophy teaches that God is a "Universal Divine Principle."[12] Jesus is viewed as a mere human who became a "vehicle" for "the Christ." This "Christ"—or "World Teacher," as he is sometimes called—is a spirit that periodically incarnates into humans to help guide their spiritual evolution. Past incarnations include Buddha, Hermes, Zoroaster, and Orpheus. Not surprisingly, Theosophy holds that there is a "central truth" common to all religions. Many New Agers have borrowed quite heavily from such Theosophical teachings, particularly from the writings of Madame Blavatsky and Annie Besant, who took over when Blavatsky died.

Anthroposophy

Rudolf Steiner was an active member of Theosophy but parted company over doctrinal issues in 1912, at which time he founded Anthroposophy. Instead of holding to a Christ who periodically incarnates into individuals, Steiner's emphasis was on what the Christ accomplished through his decisive "incarnation" in the human Jesus. In Steiner's theology, the Christ's descent on Jesus became necessary because humanity's consciousness had progressively become too focused on the material realm and had completely lost touch with the spiritual nature behind physical reality. The danger was that this situation could become permanent. To prevent this, the Christ's initial goal was to "incarnate" into a human being (Jesus) so he could accomplish his greater goal of "incarnating" from Jesus into the "etheric earth" (a spiritual earth that lies behind the physical earth that has a cause-and-effect relationship to the physical earth—that is, all things on the physical earth have their ultimate source in the etheric realm). The Christ desired to enter this etheric earth so he could bring about spiritual changes among people living on the physical earth. To transfer from his spiritual realm to the etheric realm, he needed a human instrument to work through—and this was Jesus.

The Christ thus "incarnated" into Jesus at His baptism and three years later was crucified. At the crucifixion the Christ left Jesus and "incarnated" into the etheric earth. Having mystically entered the etheric earth via Jesus' "etherized" blood, the Christ now seeks to "mass incarnate" into all humanity. This is redemption. This, says Steiner, is the true "Second Coming." Modern New Agers who are disciples of Rudolf Steiner include David Spangler and George Trevelyan.

The Arcane School

Alice Bailey had been an active member of Theosophy but became critical of the organization's policy that one could not become a mouthpiece for an Ascended Master (which Bailey believed she already was) unless one was notified by Annie Besant. This led to Bailey's eventual dismissal, and she promptly founded the Arcane School with her husband Foster in 1923. Like Theosophy and Anthroposophy, Bailey believed that Jesus was a medium who allowed the Christ to use his body. But Bailey distinguished her beliefs from Anthroposophy by arguing that the "Second Coming" referred to the Christ coming in a single Avatar (Maitreya), not in all humanity. Benjamin Creme is a modern New Ager who has drawn most of his ideas from the Arcane School.

The I AM Movement

Guy and Edna Ballard were Theosophists until Guy was contacted by Saint Germain, an Ascended Master who allegedly appeared to him in a physical body. Saint Germain informed him he lived on Mount Teton with 98 other Ascended Masters. Saint Germain appointed Guy, Edna, and their son Donald as the only "accredited" spokespeople for the Ascended Masters. Saint Germain also taught Guy about the "Great Creative Word" (I AM). The "I AM Presence" is said to be in each person and represents a point of contact with divine reality. One can attune to the I AM Presence by chanting I AM decrees. Elizabeth Clare Prophet is a modern New Ager who has drawn most of her beliefs from the I AM movement.

Spiritism

Spiritism may be defined as "the practice of attempting communication with departed human or extra-human intelligences (usually nonphysical) through the agency of a human medium, with the intent of receiving paranormal information and/or having direct experience of metaphysical realities."[13] The "Spiritualist movement" (involving Spiritism) emerged in 1848 at the home of farmer John Fox in Hydesville, New York. Not quite three decades later, Spiritism received a shot in the arm from spiritualist Helena Petrova Blavatsky (founder of Theosophy). Spiritism continued to be promoted in the Arcane School in 1923 and the I AM movement in the early 1930s.

Today Spiritism is renamed "channeling." Jane Roberts (d. 1983), who channeled an entity named Seth, wrote books that attracted millions of readers. Channeling generally takes place while the channel is in a trance. Wouter Hanegraaff writes, "The trance in such cases may vary from a state of complete or almost complete dissociation, during which the medium has no conscious knowledge of what happens, to a very light trance in which part of the medium's consciousness remains able to witness the channeling process as an outside observer."[14]

Astrology

Astrologers believe that man evolves through progressive cycles corresponding to the signs of the zodiac. Each of these cycles reportedly lasts between 2,000 and 2,400 years. According to astrologers, man is now moving from the Piscean Age (the age of intellectual man) into the Aquarian Age (the age of spiritual man). The Aquarian Age is the New Age.

The Inadequacy of Secular Humanism

Another contributing factor that led to the emergence of the New Age movement is secular humanism. For decades secular humanism focused so much on the all-sufficiency of humanity (and human reason) that the divine was left entirely out of the picture. This led to a dilemma: human reason failed to solve all of humanity's problems. Worse, with God out of the picture, there came a time when people sensed they were all alone in a vast universe. Humans discovered what it was like to be without ultimate purpose; life was lacking true meaning and value. The inadequacy of secular humanism made people crave for something more—something divine, something sacred. The New Age movement rushed in to fill the void.

The Counterculture of the 1960s

The counterculture of the 1960s also prepared the groundwork for the emergence of the New Age movement. The counterculture *countered* Western culture's traditional way of doing things and was open to trying new options—in religious beliefs, worldviews, and much more. The counterculture quickly became a hotbed for fringe ideas. Key similarities between the New Age movement and the counterculture of the 1960s include utopianism, an ecological outlook, a rejection of traditional morality, and an interest in the occult.[15]

An Influx of Eastern Ideas

Finally, the flood of Eastern ideas into the West in the 1960s helped pave the way for the emergence of the New Age movement. Hindu monism and pantheism—especially as set forth in the *Upanishads*, the *Bhagavad-Gita*, and the *Vishnu Purana* from India—all helped set aside the idea of a personal Creator-God. Significantly, Hindus and New Agers hold a number of similar views about God, the world, man, and salvation.

NEW AGE BELIEFS

The Bible Must Be Interpreted Esoterically

New Agers believe all religious books have been written with symbolism that can be understood only by "initiates." David Spangler calls this symbolic language the "language of esotericism" and says it is "a new way of talking about a new way of being."[16] Since the Bible uses the language of esotericism, we must approach the Bible with a view to discovering its hidden, secret meanings.

New Agers claim that Jesus established this method in Matthew 13, where Jesus is portrayed as speaking to a mixed multitude of believers and unbelievers. He did not attempt to separate the believers from the unbelievers and then instruct only the believers. Rather, he constructed his teaching so that believers would understand what he said but unbelievers would not—and he did this by using parables. After teaching one such parable, Jesus was asked by a disciple, "Why do you speak to the people in parables?" (Matt. 13:10). He answered, "The knowledge of *the secrets* of the kingdom of heaven has been given to you [believers], but not to them [unbelievers]" (v. 11, inserts mine, emphasis added). This verse clearly indicates that that there are *secrets* in the words of Jesus that only true "believers" can discern. Therefore, we must approach the Bible with a view to uncovering secret meanings.

An example relates to Jesus' words in Matthew 11:29. Elizabeth Clare Prophet tells us that when Jesus said, "Take my yoke upon you and learn from me" (Matt. 11:29), he was teaching his disciples to "take my yoke, *yoga*, upon you and learn of me [take my consciousness of my sacred labor, my Christhood bearing the burden of world karma ... and learn of my Guru, the Ancient of Days]; for I am meek and lowly in heart, and ye shall find rest unto your souls. For my yoke, *yoga,* is easy and my burden in heaven and on earth is truly Light."[17]

There Are Many Sources of Revelation

New Agers argue that revelation has come through Jesus *and* through the leaders of all the other world religions. If all is one (monism) and all is God (pantheism), then it should come as no surprise that the leaders of the various world religions taught the same ultimate truth.

Jesus himself allegedly taught that the world religions worship the same God with different names. According to Levi Dowling, author of *The Aquarian Gospel of Jesus the Christ,* Jesus said, "The nations of the earth see God from different points of view, and so he does not *seem* the same to everyone. ... You Brahmans call him Parabrahm; in Egypt he is Thoth; and Zeus is his name in Greece; Jehovah is his Hebrew name."[18] Each of the world religions is said to teach the same core truth, which is that all is one, all is God, and man is God.

Revelation is not a thing of the past, according to New Agers. Many "revelations" are received today though channelers. A channeler is a person who yields control of his or her perceptual and cognitive capacities to a spiritual entity or force with the intent of receiving paranormal information. Channelers can receive "revelations" from spirit entities or "read" from the so-called Akashic Records.

Spirit Channeling

Kevin Ryerson, one of today's best-known New Age channelers (he is Shirley MacLaine's channeler), wrote a book entitled *Spirit Communication,* in which he compares channeling to a radio broadcast. If two stations are competing for the same frequency, by slightly adjusting the dial, we can tune one down, and the other will come in more clearly. "Kevin Ryerson," he tells us, is the channel that gets tuned down; this allows the other frequency (spirit entities) to come through. The "spirit entities" who speak through Ryerson bear testimony to basic New Age "truths": you are God, you have unlimited potential, you create your own reality, and there is no death.[19]

The Akashic Records

Other channelers receive so-called revelations, not from spirit entities, but from the Akashic Records. The physical earth is said to be surrounded by an immense spiritual field known as Akasha, in which is impressed—like a celestial tape recording—every impulse of human thought, will, and emotion. These records therefore constitute a complete record of human history. Some New Age seers claim the ability to "read" the Akashic Records. Levi Dowling, for example, claimed to have transcribed *The Aquarian Gospel of Jesus the Christ* (1911) from the Akashic Records.

God Is All There Is

New Agers are pantheists, and they argue that there is nothing anywhere in the universe that is not God. As Benjamin Creme put it, "God is the sum total of all that exists in the whole of the manifested and unmanifested universe—everything we know and see and hear and touch and everything we don't know or hear or see or touch, everywhere, in the totality of the cosmos. Every manifested phenomenon is part of God."[20]

New Agers claim Jesus himself taught both pantheism and monism. *The Aquarian Gospel of Jesus the Christ* quotes Jesus as follows: "With much delight I speak to you concerning life—the brotherhood of life. The universal God is one, yet he is more than one; *all things are God; all things are one.*"[21]

Jesus Attained Christhood

In New Age theology, *Jesus* and *the Christ* are to be distinguished (as in the mind sciences). Jesus refers to the mere human vessel, while the Christ—variously defined—is divine. While not all New Agers give the same explanation for *how* the human Jesus became the Christ, they are unanimous *that* he became the Christ.

David Spangler says that the human Jesus merely "attuned" to the cosmic Christ and that the Christ descended upon the human Jesus at his baptism.[22] Those who follow psychic Edgar Cayce's lead believe Jesus became the Christ in his thirtieth reincarnation, after shedding his bad karma.[23] Levi Dowling said Jesus underwent seven degrees of initiation (an occultic ceremony) in Egypt, the seventh degree being THE CHRIST.[24] Benjamin Creme interprets the word *Christ* as being an office that was held by Jesus in his day and is today held by Maitreya. Elizabeth Clare Prophet says Jesus traveled to India as a child and underwent a learning process under Hindu gurus that led to his eventual Christhood.[25]

This idea that Jesus received spiritual training in the East is particularly widespread in New Age circles. Kevin Ryerson wrote, "A lot of people think that those eighteen missing years were spent traveling in and around India. . . . There are all kinds of legends and stories about a man who sounds just like Christ. . . . They say he became an adept yogi and mastered complete control over his body and the physical world around him."[26]

The "legends and stories" he refers to are rooted in a manuscript reportedly discovered in 1887 by Nicolas Notovitch (a Russian war correspondent) in a Buddhist monastery in Northern India along the Tibetan border. Notovitch, while at the monastery, had a monk read the manuscript to him, had it translated by an interpreter (since he did not understand Tibetan), and edited it into publishable form.[27] *The Life of Saint Issa* was first published in 1894.

This book chronicled the life of a monk named Issa (Tibetan for "Jesus") who allegedly preached the same doctrines in India as he later did in Israel. Issa left home when he was 13 and studied for six years among the Brahmins in Indian holy cities. The priests allegedly "taught him to read and understand the Vedas [scriptures], to cure by aid of prayer, to teach, to explain the holy scriptures to the people, and to drive out evil spirits from the bodies of men, restoring unto them their sanity."[28] This Jesus is viewed as an enlightened "way-shower" for humanity.

Man Is Divine

New Agers believe man has a spark of the divine within. Ramtha (a 35,000-year-old Lemurian knight), as channeled through New Ager J. Z. Knight, said, "You be unequivocally God! You say you are tired of hearing the word? Never tire of hearing the word; you cannot say it nearly enough."[29] New Ager Theodore Roszak said that a goal of the New Age movement is "to awaken to the god who sleeps at the root of the human being."[30]

New Agers believe Jesus himself taught that human beings are God. In John 8:58, for example, Jesus said to some of his Jewish critics, "I tell you the truth, before Abraham was born, I am!" Mark and Elizabeth Clare Prophet are sure Jesus said this "in the full awareness that the 'I AM' of him had always been the Christ. And he also knew that the permanent part of each one of you was and is that same Christ."[31] The Prophets tell us that "Jesus' I AM Presence looks just like yours.... He created you equal in the sense that he gave you an I AM Presence—he gave you a Divine Self."[32]

In view of man's alleged deity, human beings are viewed as having unlimited potential. George Trevelyan said that each human being is "an eternal droplet of the Divine Ocean, and that potentially it can evolve into a being who can be a *co-creator* with God."[33] *The Aquarian Gospel of Jesus the Christ* quotes Jesus as saying, "What I can do all men can do. Go preach the gospel of the omnipotence of Man."[34]

Sin Is Ignorance; Salvation Is Enlightenment

The New Age worldview does not allow for sin. Since humans are viewed as divine, they are essentially a law unto themselves and cannot be held guilty of "sin."[35] Further, since monism blurs the distinction between good and evil, man has no real sin problem to deal with. And because there is no sin, any talk of salvation becomes meaningless. We should "surrender all the fallacious ideas of forgiveness, . . . divine mercy, and the rest of the opiates which superstition offers to the sinner."[36]

Further, we are told, Jesus did not die on the cross to provide salvation from sin. Benjamin Creme writes, "To my way of thinking, the Christian churches have released into the world a view of the Christ which is impossible for modern people to accept: as the one and only Son of God, sacrificed by a loving Father to save us from the results of our sins—a blood sacrifice, straight out of the old Jewish dispensation."[37]

So why did Jesus have to die? One popular New Age theory is that there was so much bad karma on the earth at the time Jesus lived, the planet was in danger of self-destruction. Jesus therefore needed to be crucified to help balance the planetary karma.

Though man does not have a sin problem, he does nevertheless have a *perception* problem. Man's problem is that he is ignorant of his divinity: "We are all manifestations of Buddha consciousness, of Christ consciousness, only we don't know it."[38]

The only thing human beings need is *enlightenment* regarding their divinity. This enlightenment or change of consciousness is called various things, such as *attunement, personal transformation, new consciousness, self-realization, God-realization,* and *at-one-*

ment. To cause this change of consciousness, various consciousness-altering techniques can be used, including meditation, guided imagery, tantric yoga, hypnosis, chanting, and ecstatic dancing. These means of altering consciousness are sometimes called "psycho-technologies."

One final aspect of New Age "salvation" involves reincarnation. New Agers believe that reincarnation eventually can lead to one's reuniting with "God." The process of reincarnation allegedly continues until the soul has reached a state of perfection and merges back with its source (God or the Universal Soul). As one New Ager put it, "Reincarnation is like show business. You just keep doing it until you get it right."[39] New Agers assure us that Jesus himself taught reincarnation or "cyclical rebirth." In Matthew 11:14, for example, Jesus said, "And if you are willing to accept it, he [John the Baptist] is the Elijah who was to come." Further, in John 3:3 Jesus affirmed, "I tell you the truth, no one can see the kingdom of God unless he is born again."

The Second Coming of Christ

New Agers typically hold to one of two views in regard to the second coming of Christ:

1. Maitreya Is the Christ

Some New Agers, such as Benjamin Creme, believe in a singular Second Coming involving an individual known as Maitreya, who will take the primary leadership role in the New Age. From 1977 to the present Creme has traveled worldwide proclaiming that the manifestation of Maitreya (the Christ) is imminent (it will take place on the "Day of Declaration"). Maitreya is said to be the leader of the "Planetary Hierarchy"—a group of exalted Ascended Masters who guide humankind's spiritual evolution.[40] So far, human apathy—as evidenced by the media's apathy in reporting on Maitreya—has allegedly prevented Maitreya's appearance. Nevertheless, Creme has continued to assure fellow New Agers that the Christ will soon reveal himself. The Day of Declaration will yet come.

2. The Second Coming Is a Mass "Incarnation" of the Cosmic Christ in All of Humanity

This is the view of New Agers such as David Spangler and George Trevelyan. Spangler says, "The Second Coming is occurring now in the hearts and minds of millions of individuals of all faiths as they come to realize this spiritual presence within themselves and each other."[41] Spangler refers to this Second Coming as a "mass" coming. He writes, "The second coming of the Christ in our age will be fundamentally, most importantly, a mass coming. It will be the manifestation of a consciousness within the multitudes."[42] Jesus "was the prototype or the expression of the reality of the Christ consciousness which is inherent in us all."[43] As such, human beings can actually become "the Word made flesh"—that is, *all flesh.*

NEW AGE DOCTRINES DISTINGUISHED FROM CHRISTIANITY

	New Age View	Christian View
God	Pantheism	Personal Creator-God
Jesus Christ	Jesus = human, Christ = divinity	One person, the human-divine Messiah
The Atonement	Balanced world karma	Atoned for human sin
Sin	Involves ignorance of divinity	Moral rebellion against God
Salvation	Enlightenment about divinity	Based on faith in Christ alone
Second Coming	Cosmic Christ comes on all humankind	Jesus will personally return

CHALLENGING NEW AGE BELIEFS

New Age Esotericism Is Unreliable

As noted in the chapter on the mind sciences, the Bible is not a book of esoteric symbols full of hidden meanings (see page 121). It is true that there are figures of speech in the Bible, but what is understood to be a figure of speech and what is taken literally should be based on the biblical text itself—such as when Jesus used obviously figurative parables to express spiritual truth.

That Jesus taught openly and with clarity is attested by the doctrinal influence He had on His followers. Scholars have noted that if Jesus had intended to teach "esoteric Christianity," He was a failure as a teacher, for His words led those who followed Him in the precise opposite direction than He would have intended.[44] For example, instead of becoming *pantheists,* Jesus' followers were *theists* who believed in a personal Creator-God distinct from creation.

Though New Agers appeal to Matthew 13 in support of esotericism, their interpretation of this passage is untenable. In
Matthew 13 Jesus said, "The knowledge of *the secrets* of the kingdom of heaven has been given to you [believers], but not to them
[unbelievers]" (v. 11, inserts mine, emphasis added). The Greek
word for "secret" in this passage simply means "mystery." A mystery in the biblical sense is a truth that was unknown to people living in Old Testament times but is now revealed to humankind by
God (Matt. 13:17; Col. 1:26). In Matthew 13 Jesus provides information to believers about the kingdom that has never been revealed
before.

The parables of the Sower (Matt. 13:3–9) and the Tares (13:24–30)
show that Jesus wanted His parables to be clear to those who were
receptive. In fact, Jesus Himself provided the interpretation of these
parables for His disciples. He did this not only so there would be no
uncertainty as to their meaning, but to guide believers as to the proper
method to use in interpreting the other parables. The fact that Christ
did not interpret His subsequent parables shows that He fully
expected believers to understand what He taught by following the
methodology He illustrated for them. Clearly, then, Matthew 13 does
not support but rather argues against esotericism.

Critic Douglas Groothuis suggests that the Golden Rule
applies regarding how New Agers interpret the Bible: "Interpret
others' texts as you would have them interpret your own."[45] Certainly an esoteric interpreter would object if an orthodox Christian
interpreted New Age books so that they came out sounding like
they support orthodox Christianity. The Christian would be guilty
of reading something into the Eastern text that simply is not there
and would be rightly reprimanded by the esotericist. Consider the
following mock conversation:

Christian: So, when Shirley MacLaine—in her book *Dancing in the
Light*—said, "You are unlimited. You just don't realize it," what she
was really talking about was the orthodox Christian doctrine of total
depravity. You see, she was really saying that people are unlimited in
terms of their evil nature. In fact, they are so evil that they are completely blind to it. That is why she said, "You just don't realize it."

New Ager: Now, wait just one minute! That is not at all what
MacLaine was saying. What she was saying—if you care to look at

her words in context and according to her intended meaning—is that human beings have an unlimited potential because of their divine nature. And because human beings do not "realize" their divine nature, she was saying they need enlightenment. You are really not being fair, because you're reading something into MacLaine's words that is not there at all!

Certainly New Agers seem to assume the truth of objective interpretive methodology when reading their own books. When David Spangler reads the books of Rudolf Steiner (his mentor), for example, he does not esoterically twist Steiner's words to mean something other than what Steiner intended. To be consistent, New Agers should not esoterically twist the words of the biblical writers to mean something other than what they intended.

The World Religions Do Not Teach the Same "Core" Truth

Contrary to New Age claims, the leaders of the various world religions did not teach the same "core" truth. Consider the doctrine of God, which is the most fundamental doctrine of any religious system. Jesus Christ taught that there is one personal God who is triune in nature (Mark 12:29; John 4:24; 5:18–19). Muhammad taught that there is only one God but that God cannot have a son. Confucius was polytheistic. Krishna believed in a combination of polytheism and pantheism. Zoroaster held to religious dualism— that is, there is both a good god and a bad god. Buddha taught that the concept of God was essentially irrelevant. Clearly, the leaders of the world's major religions held completely contradictory views regarding the nature of God. And since the doctrine of God is the most fundamental doctrine of any religious system, it cannot legitimately be said that the leaders of all the world religions taught the same core truth.

Further, Jesus was exclusivistic in His truth claims—indicating that what He said took precedence over all others. Jesus said He is exclusively man's only means of coming into a relationship with God: "I am the way, the truth, and the life; no one comes to the Father, except through me" (John 14:6). Jesus' exclusivity caused Him to warn, "Watch out that no one deceives you. For many will come in my name, claiming, 'I am the Christ,' and will deceive many" (Matt. 24:4–5, 23).

God Condemns Spiritistic Revelations

In the Bible, God categorically condemns all spiritistic activities as a heinous sin against Him. Deuteronomy 18:10–11 is clear: "Let no one be found among you . . . who is a medium or spiritist or who consults the dead. Anyone who does these things is detestable to the LORD."

Scripture indicates that Satan masquerades as an angel of light, seeking to deceive people (2 Cor. 11:14). Demons are more than willing to masquerade as "spirit guides" and "Ascended Masters" if the result will be that tens of thousands of people will be deceived and drawn away from Jesus Christ in the process. The reality is that departed humans are not available for contact by New Age channelers. Departed Christians are in the presence of Christ in heaven (Phil. 1:23). Departed unbelievers reside in a place of great suffering (Luke 16:19–31), confined until the future day of judgment (Rev. 20:11–12).

The Pantheistic View of God Is Untenable

A pantheistic view of God poses many problems, some of which I pointed out in the chapter on the mind sciences (see page 123). I will not repeat that earlier material, but I do want to draw attention to a few key factors. First, pantheism contradicts common sense. If all is truly God, then there is no difference between myself and anything else in the world. And if there is no difference between myself and anything else, then I should not call myself "myself." As one apologist noted, "To call myself 'myself' is to assume that there is a difference between myself and anything else. . . . Common sense tells me that I am different from others."[46]

Further, Jesus certainly did not teach an impersonal pantheistic idea of God as New Agers claim. Though "Jesus" is quoted as teaching a pantheistic concept of God in *The Aquarian Gospel of Jesus the Christ*, this "gospel" is clearly man-made, derived from occultism, loaded with historical errors, permeated with contradictions, and completely untrustworthy as a source of truth. The Jesus of the Bible repeatedly affirmed the personal nature of God. This is most vividly expressed in His many references to God as "my Father." Jesus' ministry at the Jordan commenced with a verbal testimony of love from the Father: "You are my Son, whom I love; with you I am well pleased" (Mark 1:11). Throughout His earthly sojourn, Jesus' fellowship with the Father was uninterrupted. He said to some of His disciples, "You will leave me all alone. Yet I am not alone, for my Father is with me" (John 16:32). Near the end of Jesus' three-year ministry, we again hear the Father speaking of His love for the Son, this time to the disciples during the Transfiguration: "This is my Son, whom I love. . . . Listen to him" (Matt. 17:5). Clearly, Jesus perceived God not as an "it" or a "cosmic force," but as a person with whom personal relations can be entered. A cosmic, impersonal force does not speak and surely cannot love.

Finally, we should note that some former New Agers have conceded that the one factor that got their attention (and led them to the true God of the Bible) was the failure of the pantheistic worldview to adequately explain the problem of evil. In their book *The Infiltration of the New Age,* Yutaka Amano and Norman Geisler provide an excellent example of how evil is problematic for the New Age worldview:

> When Francis Schaeffer spoke to a group of students at Cambridge University, there was a Hindu who began criticizing Christianity. Schaeffer said, "Am I not correct in saying that on the basis of your system, cruelty and noncruelty are ultimately equal, that there is no intrinsic difference between them?"
>
> The Hindu agreed. One of the students immediately caught on to what Schaeffer was driving at. He picked up a kettle of boiling water that he was going to use to make tea and held the steaming pot over the Indian's head.
>
> This young Hindu looked up and asked the student what he was doing.
>
> The student said with a cold yet gentle finality, "There is no difference between cruelty and noncruelty." Thereupon the Hindu walked out into the night.[47]

Jesus Did Not Train Under Hindu Gurus

I discussed the alleged disjunction between Jesus and the Christ in the chapter on the mind sciences (see page 127). Here I will briefly assess the New Age claim that Jesus was trained by Hindu gurus as a child. F. Max Müller, an orientalist at Oxford University, thoroughly debunked Nicholas Notovitch's claims regarding the alleged *Issa* manuscript. Among other things, Müller cites a woman who visited the very Buddhist monastery that contained the alleged manuscript, and according to her testimony, "there is not a single word of truth in the whole story! There has been no Russian here.... There is no life of Christ here at all!"[48]

J. Archibald Douglas, a professor at Government College in Agra, India, retraced Notovitch's steps at the Buddhist monastery in 1895. When the chief monk was asked if he was aware of a scroll on the life of Issa, he asserted, "There is no such book in the monastery."[49]

Yet another scholar, Edgar J. Goodspeed at the University of Chicago, examined Notovitch's *Life of Saint Issa* in 1926 and, among other things, pointed out factual and historical errors as well as literary dependence on the New Testament Gospels.[50] Every scholar that examines Notovitch's claims dismisses his work as a sheer fabrication.

One must wonder—if Jesus did learn how to do sensational miracles like healing, controlling the weather, casting out demons, and raising people from the dead from various gurus in the East, why didn't these gurus become well known like Jesus for having such powers? Why didn't throngs of people follow and worship them like they did Jesus of Nazareth?

Certainly the New Testament Gospels contradict the Jesus-goes-East theory. Luke 4:16 specifically says Jesus was "brought up" in Nazareth. Further, the gospel accounts indicate that Jesus was well known in His community as a carpenter (Mark 6:3) and as a carpenter's son (Matt. 13:55). How could Jesus have been known in this way if He had been away in India during the years before His public ministry?

It is also highly telling that Jesus' Jewish opponents never accused him of Eastern teaching. Had Jesus actually gone to India to study under "the great Buddhas," this would have been excellent grounds for disqualifying Him regarding His claim to be the promised Jewish Messiah. If the Jewish leaders could have accused Jesus of this, they certainly would have.

Jesus Did Not Teach that Man Is God

I discussed the alleged divinity of man in the previous chapters on the mind sciences (see page 125) and Mormonism (see page 72). But what about the New Age claim that Jesus taught that human beings are gods in John 8:58: "Before Abraham was born, I am"? When Jesus said this, He was not saying that all human beings have an "I AM" presence within them. Rather, Jesus implicitly and uniquely ascribed the divine name Yahweh to Himself alone. The backdrop of this is that "I AM" and "Yahweh" are equated in Exodus 3:14–15. The phrase I AM is not the word *Yahweh;* however, I AM (in v. 14) and *Yahweh* (in v. 15) are both derivatives of the same verb, "to be." The name I AM WHO I AM—which God revealed to Moses in verse 14—is intended as a full expression of His eternal nature and is then shortened to *Yahweh* in verse 15.

The Jews immediately picked up stones with the intention of killing Jesus, for they recognized He was uniquely identifying Himself as Yahweh. The Jews were acting on the prescribed penalty for blasphemy in Old Testament Law: death by stoning. (Note that the Jews did not understand Jesus to be teaching that they too were identified as "I AM." Nor did Jesus inform them, "*You too* have the I AM presence.")

Many scholars believe the name *Yahweh* conveys the idea of eternal self-existence. Jesus in John 8:58 deliberately contrasted the created origin of Abraham with His own eternal, uncreated nature. This adds significance to Jesus' encounter with the Jews, granting how much they venerated Abraham. Notice that in contrasting Himself with Abraham, Jesus was clearly revealing that Abraham was not "I AM" as He was. Clearly, then, Jesus' claim to be "I am" distinguished Him from all humanity.

Man Has a Sin Problem, Not an Ignorance Problem

Christian morality begins with God *as a personal being.* This is directly contrary to the monistic/pantheistic worldview, which does away with God's personality. As one New Age critic put it, "Moral terms such as right and wrong simply do not apply to an impersonal force, any more than we hold a hurricane morally responsible for its actions."[51] Moral issues are irrelevant when relating to an impersonal force. Lying and stealing, for example, are nonissues when it comes to relating to electrical energy, and the same is true of the New Age god. However, because the God of Scripture is a personal being, moral terms do apply in regard to how we relate to Him. And because the person of God is holy (Matt. 5:48) and we are not holy (Rom. 3:23), alienation is real and we are morally culpable (Rom. 6:23).

The biblical Jesus did not teach that human beings have an ignorance problem; rather, he taught that humans have a grave sin problem that is altogether beyond their means to solve (Matt. 12:34; Luke 11:13). The biblical Jesus further taught that salvation is found not by enlightenment but by placing faith in Him (John 3:16) who is the Light of the World (John 8:12). And the present life is the only opportunity we have to place faith in Him, for the doctrine of reincarnation is nothing but a false man-made doctrine. (I address this issue in chapter 8, "Hindu-Based Cults" [see page 184]).

Jesus Himself Will Come Again

New Agers present contradictory, irreconcilable scenarios and interpretations of the Second Coming based on their alleged "revelations" from the other side (the spirit world). Rudolf Steiner claimed in the 1920s (based on "revelations" from the other side) that the Christ would not come again as an individual but would instead *spiritually* come again in all humanity. Responding to Steiner's scenario, Benjamin Creme, in his book *The Reappearance of the Christ and the Masters of Wisdom*, said that the Christ later decided (by 1945, some 20 years after Steiner's death) that he would come again not in all humanity but in his own "body of manifestation."[52] Creme learned of this change in plans by receiving "revelations" from the Christ. Ironically, David Spangler, a modern-day disciple of Steiner, is also allegedly receiving current "revelations" from "the Christ" indicating that the Christ is not coming again in one body, but—like Steiner said—in all of humanity. Who's "revelation" would New Agers say is correct?

From a scriptural perspective, the very same Jesus who ascended into heaven will come again at the Second Coming (Acts 1:11). Moreover, the Second Coming of Christ will not be a coming of an invisible cosmic Christ in all of humanity but will rather be a *visible, physical* coming of the glorified Jesus (see Matt. 16:27–28; 24:30; Dan. 7:13; Zech. 9:14; 12:10; Mark 1:2; John 1:51; 2 Tim. 4:1). Revelation 1:7 speaks prophetically: "Look, he is coming with the clouds, and every eye will see him, even those who pierced him; and all the peoples of the earth will mourn because of him." It will be a glorious event that is accompanied by magnificent signs in the heavens (Matt. 24:29–30). Then the real "New Age" will begin (Christ's millennial reign).

7

THE CHURCH OF SCIENTOLOGY

This chapter should not be construed as an attack against the right of Scientologists to believe as they choose. This chapter simply summarizes some of the central teachings of Scientology, as set forth in Scientology books, and then contrasts them with historic Christianity, using the standard of the Bible. As the seventh article of the Creed of Scientology states, "All men have the inalienable rights to think freely, to talk freely, to write freely on their own opinions and to counter or utter or write upon the opinion of others."[1] It is in that invitational spirit that the following chapter is offered.

One of the more controversial new religions to emerge on American soil is the Church of Scientology, founded by the late Lafayette Ronald Hubbard (1911–86). Hubbard authored numerous novels (over 200)[2] as well as nonfiction books, the most popular being *Dianetics: The Modern Science of Mental Health,* which has reportedly sold over 3 million copies.[3] (*Publisher's Weekly* reports that the book sold 55,000 copies in the first two months after it was published in 1950).[4] Scientology literature states that this book marked a turning point in human history, as it provided the "first workable approach to solving the problems of the mind," enabling man to overcome irrational behavior.[5]

In the eyes of Scientology members, Hubbard is the world's most influential author, educator, research pioneer, explorer, humanitarian, and philosopher.[6] Few people, they believe, have achieved so much in such a wide variety of different fields.[7] Yet some critics have alleged that Hubbard was a "con man."[8] Both admirers and critics acknowledge that, at the very least, he was an interesting man.

Hubbard was born in Tilden, Nebraska, in 1911. As a 12-year-old child, he purportedly read a number of the world's great classics, and therein his interest in philosophy and religion was born.[9] Later, during his high school years, he allegedly traveled throughout Asia with his father, who was in the navy, and studied Eastern religions.[10] It was there that he became interested in the spiritual destiny of man. Biographical material in Hubbard's books claims he studied science and mathematics in the Department of Engineering at George Washington University and later attended Princeton University. In World War II he was allegedly crippled and blinded and was twice pronounced dead.[11]

Critics, however, have called into question details related to Hubbard's vita.[12] Walter Martin's *The Kingdom of the Cults* reports that "Hubbard attended high school in America while he was claiming to have been traveling in Asia."[13] George Malko, in his book *Scientology: The Now Religion*, claims, "The facts are that Hubbard never received a Bachelor of Science degree in civil engineering. He flunked freshman physics, was placed on probation in September of 1931, and failed to return to the university after the 1931–32 academic year."[14] Russell Miller's book, *Bare-Faced Messiah: The True Story of L. Ron Hubbard*, claims Hubbard's medical records do not show that Hubbard was crippled, blinded, or twice pronounced dead.[15]

In any event, as an adult Hubbard became quite a prolific author, producing a veritable deluge of literature (some of which I will cite below as related to Scientology doctrines). In his later years Hubbard apparently went into seclusion, and very little is known of his activities during that time. He died of a cerebral vascular accident (stroke) on January 24, 1986.[16] A high-ranking Scientology church leader announced Hubbard's death to a large gathering of Scientologists at the Hollywood Palladium.

> [Hubbard] has now moved on to the next level of OT [Operating Thetan] research. It's a level beyond anything any of us ever imagined.
>
> This level is in fact done in an exterior state. Meaning that it is done completely exterior from the body. At this level of OT, the body is nothing more than an impediment and encumbrance to any further gain as an OT.
>
> Thus at 2000 hours, the 24th of January, AD 36 (After Dianetics), L. Ron Hubbard discarded the body he had used in this lifetime for 74 years 10 months and 11 days.[17]

WHAT IS SCIENTOLOGY?

L. Ronald Hubbard once described Scientology as "the Western Anglicized continuance of many earlier forms of wisdom."[18] These "earlier forms of wisdom" Hubbard refers to include a variety of religious and philosophical belief systems, such as Confucianism, Hinduism, Buddhism, Taoism, Judaism, Gnosticism, the teachings of Jesus, and the writings of more recent intellectuals, such as William James, Sigmund Freud, and Friedrich Nietzsche.[19] Scientology is therefore a very eclectic religion.[20]

Scientology focuses heavily on self-empowerment and self-improvement.[21] Hubbard wrote in *Scientology: The Fundamentals of Thought* that Scientology "is a religious philosophy containing pastoral counseling procedures intended to assist an individual to gain greater knowledge of self."[22] He claimed that Scientology "can and does change behavior and intelligence, and it can and does assist people to study life."[23] Scientology allegedly equips people to handle conditions which were once considered hopeless.[24]

One might wonder what the difference is between Scientology and Dianetics (recall that Hubbard wrote a book on Dianetics years

> "Though drawing upon the wisdom of some 50,000 years, Scientology is a new religion, one which has isolated fundamental laws of life and, for the first time, developed a workable technology that can be applied to help one achieve a happier and more spiritual existence" ("Scientology: Its Backgrounds and Origins," Scientology web site).

before Scientology was founded). Dianetics, Hubbard's first major discovery, is man's "most advanced school of the mind."[25] It is a method for alleviating unwanted sensations and emotions, irrational fears, and psychosomatic illnesses (that is, illnesses caused or aggravated by mental stress).

Within a year and a half of the release of Hubbard's *Dianetics*, Hubbard began studying the human spirit rather than just the mind. This study would span the next two decades. "As breakthrough after breakthrough was codified, the philosophy of Scientology was born, giving man, for the first time, a route to higher levels of awareness, understanding, and ability that anyone could travel."[26] Scientology is said to be an applied *religious* philosophy that offers "methods and principles by which the able can become more able."[27] "Dianetics was the ultimate development of the mind of human beings. Scientology is the road from there to Total Freedom."[28]

It is important to note the religious claims of Scientology. We are told that with the discovery that man was neither his body nor his mind, but a spiritual being, L. Ron Hubbard founded the religion of Scientology, "for he had moved firmly into the field traditionally belonging to religion—the realm of the human soul."[29] Because Hubbard's findings were inherently religious, "it was only natural that those surrounding him would come to see themselves, not only as students of a new philosophy but also as students of a new religion."[30] Hence, in 1954 Scientologists in Los Angeles established the first Church of Scientology. Scientology claims to be a religion "by its basic tenets, practice, historical background and by the definition of the word *religion* itself."[31] Further, Scientology is said to have the qualities important to any religion—including a view of salvation, a preservation of "orthodoxy," the establishing of ethical and moral codes, a spiritual healing element, and the aiding of members in overcoming personal problems.[32]

The Church of Scientology opens its doors seven days a week. Many churches have both a day staff and evening/weekend staff so that help is always available. The church even has its own "chaplains" or "ministers" who conduct weddings, christenings, and funeral services.[33] Sunday sermons generally focus on primary teachings of Scientology.

The "Mother Church" for Scientology is located in Los Angeles, California, and supervises Scientology churches around the world.

The structure is said to be like that of the Catholic church.[34] At present the head of the church is David Miscavige.[35] Scientologists claim their religion now involves some 3,000 churches, missions, related organizations, and groups, and allegedly more than 8 million people in 100 countries who speak 30 languages.[36]

In recent years the Church of Scientology has received tremendous publicity due to the growing number of Hollywood celebrities joining the church. These have included such luminaries as Tom Cruise, Kirstie Alley, Mimi Rogers, Anne Archer, Sonny Bono, John Travolta, and Chick Corea. Many of these (and others) are regular visitors to Scientology's seven-story Celebrity Centre in Hollywood. Travolta once said that Scientology "contains the secrets of the Universe."[37]

SCIENTOLOGY BELIEFS

Scientology claims it is not authoritarian and "there is no enforced belief." Rather, a maxim in Scientology is that "only those things which one finds true for himself are true. In Scientology you learn to think for yourself—it is a voyage of self-discovery."[38] According to a Scientology publication, no attempts are made to change anyone's beliefs or to persuade them away from their present religion.[39] Nevertheless, as one reads Scientology literature (Hubbard's books are considered scripture),[40] one does find a particular view of man, man's problem, and how that problem is to be resolved. Hence, Scientology does have "doctrine" that one learns and to which one subscribes.

Man in His True Identity Is a "Thetan"

In the theology of Scientology, every human being in his true identity is a "thetan" (pronounced "thay´-tn"), an immortal spirit. This term is derived from the Greek letter *theta*, which Scientologists say has long served as a symbol for thought or spirit.[41]

According to Scientology literature, "Man is not the limited and pitiful body and ego he mistakenly imagines himself to be. He is a thetan whose fundamental nature is basically good and divine. He is not morally fallen; rather he is simply ignorant of his own perfection. His only 'fall' was into matter, not sin."[42]

How did this dire situation come about? It all goes back to the thetans' original creation (or mental emanation) of the physical universe. As summarized by researcher Richard Abanes:

Trillions of years ago, long before anything as we know it existed, there were countless immortal beings known as "thetans," who found themselves bored with eternal life. In an effort to rid themselves of the doldrums, they decided to collectively create the universe and everything in it. Their hope was to have a realm in which to play the "Game of Life" and pass the time. But the thetans soon faced a problem on which they had not planned. As *spiritual* beings, they could not function within their *physical* creation. The thetans solved this dilemma by building bodies for themselves, the human form being only one of many different appearances.[43]

Man Became Enslaved to "Engrams"

The problem that developed for these thetans is that they eventually became entranced with their creation so that they lost awareness of their true identity as thetans (immortal spirits). They forgot their true identity as spiritual beings.[44] In other words, they came to believe they were *merely* physical beings. "They got caught in their own trap and got stuck in their creation—and especially in Man—i.e., in matter, energy, space and time (MEST, the physical universe), even forgetting that they were the creators."[45] Tragically, according to Scientology literature, since that time they have returned *life after life* through reincarnation, inhabiting different bodies. In each new body, the "engrams" (sensory impressions stored in the mind that can cause various emotional and physical symptoms) from past lives stick with them, only to cause more problems with each new reincarnation.

Because of the process of reincarnation, wherein the thetan enters a new human body at the point of death, the thetans have now accumulated countless engrams throughout the trillions of years of their existence. And in each new body, not only does enslavement to materiality continue, but damage occurs from the accumulation of engrams in the mind. Engrams are viewed as counterproductive to man's survival,[46] which is man's basic goal according to Scientology. Engrams threaten survival by causing pain, psychosomatic illness, and irrational behavior.

This is related to the Scientology view that the human mind has two components—the *analytic* mind and the *reactive* mind. The analytic mind refers to man's conscious and rational mind.[47]

the part that thinks, observes data, remembers that data, resolves problems with data, and promotes survival with data.

The reactive mind, by contrast, is believed to be the place where painful memories are stored.[48] Scientologists believe that when a person experiences something painful in life, this causes a sensory impression or "engram" to be recorded in the reactive mind.[49] These recorded sensory impressions cause emotional and other kinds of pain, as well as inappropriate behavior.[50] Scientologists believe the reactive mind is active below the level of consciousness. "It is the literal stimulus-response mind. Given a certain stimulus it gives a certain response."[51]

Scientology literature indicates that these engrams lay dormant in the reactive mind until they become restimulated by a similar incident. When this happens, a stimulus-response behavior is produced that causes pain and is counterproductive. Even if no real threat exists, the sensory impression that has been stored in the mind causes the reactive mind to react as if there is a threat. These "engrams" can thus cause inappropriate behavior.

To illustrate, let us suppose a boy is riding his bike, and right at the moment he crashes and bruises up his entire body—scraping his elbows and knees and bumping his head—he sees a dog playing in a neighbor's front lawn. As an adult, he seems to always feel uncomfortable around dogs and is not sure why. Every dog he sees restimulates the sensory impression that was stored in his reactive mind as a child and causes an irrational, inappropriate response.

Some of the most damaging engrams can allegedly come to us while we are in our mother's womb. "Mama runs lightly and blithely into a table and baby gets its head shoved in. Mama has constipation and baby . . . gets squashed. Papa becomes passionate and baby has the sensation of being put into a running washing machine. . . . People have scores of prenatal engrams."[52]

Because of the many supposed engrams that have been stored in our reactive minds, not just in this life but in multiple past lives as well, we are conditioned to respond in a variety of inappropriate ways and to experience painful emotions when there is no need for them. Human beings are thus viewed as being *in bondage* to an "aberrated" (reactive) mind.[53] (An "aberration" is any departure from rationality.)[54] We need to be set free.

Man Can Become "Clear" of Engrams through "Auditing"

According to Scientology, man's bondage to the reactive mind and his slavery to MEST (the matter-energy-space-time physical universe) continued until L. Ronald Hubbard uncovered man's true nature and devised a solution to the problem. Through a process called "auditing,"[55] engrams can supposedly be discovered and then neutralized. This is accomplished with the help of an *auditor*, a person who applies Scientology technology to another individual.[56] *Auditor* is defined as "*one who listens* from the Latin *audire*, meaning to *hear* or *listen*. An auditor is a minister or minister-in-training of the Church of Scientology."[57]

Through the process of auditing, engrams can purportedly be exposed and then "erased" so that a person becomes "clear."[58] In other words, auditing facilitates the deleting of those sensory impressions that have been stored in the person's reactive mind through life's painful experiences. Just as one can "clear" wrong numbers from an adding machine, so one can become clear of engrams. (One who is not yet "clear" is a "*preclear*.") A person who is clear is in control of his behavior instead of being controlled by engrams.[59] He is no longer at the mercy of the stimulus-response mechanisms of the reactive mind[60] but can think independently and experience life unencumbered by the past. A clear can *act* rather than *react*.

The actual process of auditing involves the auditor asking an exact set of questions to help the preclear find out things about himself and improve his condition. Hubbard is said to have isolated the exact questions and directions to invariably bring about improvement.[61]

The process of auditing is assisted by use of a meter that allegedly helps the auditor locate areas of spiritual distress (engrams) in the preclear. This instrument is called an *Electropsychometer*, or *E-Meter*. As the preclear holds in his hands the electrodes of this "religious instrument"[62] (metal cylinders attached to wires),[63] a current of about 1.5 volts flows through the wires to the person's body and back into the E-Meter. The current is so small that there is no physical sensation. The meter is said to indicate bodily changes in electrical resistance when different questions are asked.[64] The pictures in the mind can be painful, and the changes in the mind can allegedly "influence the tiny flow of electrical energy generated by the E-Meter, causing the needle on its dial to move."[65] Scientologists claim that different needle movements have precise meanings and that it takes the skill of a trained auditor to understand all of the meter's needle movements.[66]

Hubbard said of the process, "The meter tells you what the preclear's mind is doing when the preclear is made to think of something. If they're emotionally disturbed about cats, and they're talking about cats, the needle flies about. If they're not disturbed about cats, the needle doesn't fly about. So you let them talk about cats until they're no longer disturbed about cats, and then the needle no longer flies about."[67]

Once an area of charge or upset has been located in the reactive mind via the E-Meter, the auditor can then give the directions needed to assist the preclear in examining it. The questions and directions provided by the auditor help the preclear discharge the harmful energy associated with the painful incidents or situations in his or her past. Ideally, all the forgotten details of the incident should come to light, the emotion experienced in the past should be re-experienced in the auditing session, and its force fully discharged.[68] Once this happens, the incident is said to be erased from the reactive mind and can no longer negatively affect the preclear's life.

The more data pulled out of the reactive mind and returned to one's analytical awareness, the better. As awareness increases in regard to a particular engram, that portion of the reactive mind ceases to register on the E-Meter. "This increase of awareness builds from auditing session to auditing session and the preclear gradually becomes more and more aware of who he is, what has happened to him and what his true potentials and abilities are."[69]

This, then, is "salvation" in the religion of Scientology. "Salvation is attained through increasing one's spiritual awareness."[70] And as a person's spiritual awareness increases through auditing, so does his ability to determine his own answers and solutions about life.[71] Moreover, the initiate can, through auditing, come to recognize his true identity as a thetan, an immortal spirit, that is separate from the MEST body. He can also discover how to control the MEST universe around him by the power of the mind. Since the material universe is really nothing more than a mental projection of the thetans, it stands to reason that this universe can be controlled by the mental power of an enlightened thetan.

In addition to the auditing process whereby one can supposedly become clear, one can participate in many training courses offered by Scientology.[72] Though one becomes "free" through auditing, this state of freedom must be supplemented by information regarding how to remain free.[73] The variety of available Scientology courses range from introductory (teaching basic principles) to more advanced ones that train professional auditors, including courses that can take one through the "eight dynamics of life"—*self, creativity, group survival, species, life forms, physical universe, spiritual dynamic,* and *a Supreme Being.*[74] These Scientology courses can be very expensive. A 1990 *Los Angeles Times* article on Scientology estimated that to go from the initial free test to the Operating Thetan 8 level costs between $200,000 and $400,000.[75]

"God" Can Be Interpreted However One Wants

Scientology claims that it does not set forth a specific dogma regarding God; individuals are free to interpret God as they wish.[76] "The author of the universe exists. How God is symbolized or manifested is up to each individual to find for himself."[77] Yet the church does refer to God variously in nebulous terms like "Nature," "Infinity," the "Eighth Dynamic," and "All Theta."[78] Certainly there is no *worship* of a divine being in Scientology services: "Scientology practices do not include worship, supplication or veneration, which are primarily religious practices of the Judeo-Christian tradition."[79]

Jesus is rarely mentioned in Scientology literature. Hubbard once said that neither Buddha nor Jesus were Operating Thetans, but rather were just a shade above "clear."[80] (An Operating Thetan is a thetan who possesses complete spiritual ability, freedom, independence, and serenity, and has attained *full* awareness.[81] Operating Thetans also have the ability to project themselves out of their bodies.)[82] Yet Scientology does claim to share Christ's goals for humanity's attainment of "wisdom, good health and immortality."[83] One Scientology book asserts, "Though crucified, the hope that Christ brought to man did not die. Instead, his death became symbolic of the triumph of the spirit over the material body and so brought a new awareness of man's true nature."[84]

CONTRASTING SCIENTOLOGY WITH CHRISTIANITY

Using the Holy Bible as the standard of measurement, we find that there are a number of areas where Christianity and Scientology diverge doctrinally. As a preface to touching on some specific divergences below, it is interesting to note that when we read Scientology books, we are always advised right up front not to go past any word that is not understood. That is a good principle to use also when considering the Christian Bible.[85] Indeed, by following that principle with the Bible *and* with Scientology books side by side, it comes clear that Scientology and Christianity have many incompatibilities.

SCIENTOLOGY AND CHRISTIANITY CONTRASTED

	Scientology View	Christian View
Scientology	Writings of L. Ron Hubbard	Bible
God	"All Theta," "Eighth Dynamic"	Personal Creator-God
Jesus	Just a shade above "clear"	The divine Messiah
Man	Thetan (immortal spirit)	Finite creature
Universe	Mentally emanated by thetans	Created by God
Sin	None (man is basically good)	Man is fallen in sin
Salvation	Involves increasing awareness	By trusting in Christ alone
Reincarnation	Yes	No

A Different Basis of Authority

Foundationally, Scientology and Christianity disagree over what constitutes the proper basis of authority for one's religious beliefs. Christians maintain that the Bible alone constitutes God's Word to humankind (Ps. 119; 2 Tim. 3:16). Scientologists, by contrast, view the writings of L. Ron Hubbard to be Scripture. Christians view the books of Hubbard as nothing more than the writings of a prolific man. His writings do not constitute Scripture any more than any other book one might pick from the *New York Times* bestseller list. From a biblical viewpoint, only those writings inspired by the living God ("God-breathed") constitute Scripture (2 Tim. 3:16)—and that Scripture was completed when the last book of the New Testament was written.

Because these two religions have a different basis of authority (that is, different Scriptures), it is understandable why they have differing beliefs. For example, whereas Scientology holds to reincarnation, Christianity rejects such a belief (Heb. 9:27) and holds to resurrection of the body. Whereas Scientology says man is basically good, Christianity teaches that man is plagued by original sin (Rom. 5:12). Whereas Scientology dismisses belief in a hell as a place of future suffering, the Christian Bible is clear that all who reject Jesus Christ in this life will spend eternity in this place of suffering (Rev. 20:10–14). Whereas Jesus in Scientology is not even an "Operating Thetan" but is just a "shade above clear," in Christianity He is absolute deity (John 1:1), the divine Messiah who is the Savior of humankind (Titus 2:13–14). Whereas Scientology is apparently open to what many[86] would classify as occultism (out-of-body experiences of thetans), God in the Christian Bible condemns all forms of occultism (Deut. 18:10–12).

The key question, then, is: Which set of Scriptures is the more reliable? Is it the Christian Bible, written by God's prophets and apostles and shown to be historically accurate by over 25,000 archaeological discoveries, with virtually tens of thousands of manuscript copies to prove its accurate transmission?[87] Or is it the books of author L. Ron Hubbard, who has written not just Scientology books but numerous fictional works as well? Which is the more *credible* Scripture? Christians believe it is the Bible.

Thetans Versus the Creator-God of Christianity

The Bible says there is only one true God. There are *no* other gods besides the one true God of Scripture—*and there are no thetans with godlike power.* During Moses' time, God affirmed, "See now that I myself am He! There is no god besides me" (Deut. 32:39). We find the same thing emphasized in Isaiah 44:6: "This is what the LORD says—Israel's King and Redeemer, the LORD Almighty: I am the first and I am the last; apart from me there is no God." Isaiah 46:9 likewise quotes God as saying, "I am God, and there is no other; I am God, and there is none like me." Scripture portrays this God as being absolutely sovereign over the affairs of humanity (Ps. 135:6; Eph. 1:11).

Further, the God of the Bible is a knowable, personal being, not "Nature," "Infinity," the "Eighth Dynamic," or "All Theta." A person is a conscious being—one who thinks, feels, and purposes, and carries these purposes into action. A person engages in active relationships with others. You can talk to a person and get a response. You can share feelings and ideas with him. You can argue with him, love him, and even hate him. Surely by this definition the biblical God must be understood as a person. After all, God is a conscious being who thinks, feels, and purposes—and He carries these purposes into action. He engages in relationships with others. You can talk to God and get a response from Him. The biblical picture of God is that of a loving, personal Father unto whom believers may cry, "Abba" (Rom. 8:15). (Abba is an Aramaic term of great intimacy, loosely meaning "Daddy.") God is the "father of compassion" of all believers (2 Cor. 1:3). He is often portrayed in Scripture as compassionately responding to the personal requests of His people (see Ex. 3:7–8; Job 34:28; Ps. 81:10; 91:14–15; 2 Cor. 1:3–4; Phil. 4:6–7). Such ideas are foreign to the pages of Scientology literature.

The biblical account says that this personal God, not thetans, created the universe—a universe *that included matter*—and He declared that "it was very good" (Gen. 1:31). The world of matter is not an illusion, but is real and is a part of God's good creation. Further, Scripture points to the reality of a future new heaven and a new earth (Rev. 21:15), so our ultimate destiny involves an eternal realm that accommodates our eternally material bodies.

Biblically speaking, man is not an immortal spirit who, because of a fall into MEST, now thinks he is a body. Rather, when God created man, He created him from the dust of the ground and then breathed the breath of life into him (Gen. 2:7). Man was hence created with both a material and immaterial nature (Eccl. 12:7). Man had a spirit and body from the beginning. The book of James indicates that the body without the spirit is dead (2:26). The Bible affirms that disembodied human spirits go either to heaven or Hades to await the resurrection of the just and unjust (John 5:29), whereupon they will be judged (Matt. 25:31–32). Human beings are not complete again until the resurrection, when the body is reunited with the spirit (see 1 Cor. 15).[88]

Contrary to Scientology's portrayal of man as a powerful thetan, the Bible indicates that human beings are intrinsically weak, helpless, and dependent on God. The apostle Paul affirmed, "Not that we are competent in ourselves to claim anything for ourselves, but our competence comes from God" (2 Cor. 3:5). Jesus said, "I am the vine; you are the branches. If a man remains in me and I in him, he will bear much fruit; *apart from me you can do nothing*" (John 15:5, emphasis added).

A point we must not miss is that man is a finite creature (Ps. 100:3)—and because he is a creature, he is puny when measured against the matchless and incomparable one true God. No one on earth comes even remotely close to God's greatness and majesty. God Himself affirmed to Moses that He would do mighty miracles in Egypt "so that you may know that there is no one like Me in all the earth" (Ex. 9:14). Contrary to the prideful interpretation of man as an immortal thetan, the recognition of creaturehood should lead to a sense of humility and a worshipful attitude toward the one true God. "Come, let us bow down in worship, let us kneel before the LORD our Maker; for he is our God and we are the people of his pasture, the flock under his care" (Ps. 95:6–7). Scripture affirms that "God opposes the proud but gives grace to the humble" (James 4:6). It is thus good advice to "humble yourselves, therefore, under God's mighty hand" (1 Peter 5:6).

Man Fell into Sin, Not Materiality

Since God created the world of matter (which was a "good thing" [Gen. 1:31]) and created man as a being with material and immaterial aspects (a body and spirit [see Gen. 2:7]) man's fall was not a "fall into materiality." Biblically, man's fall was a fall into sin, and this sin caused an alienation from God (Gen. 3:6–24).

Scripture says that when Adam and Eve sinned, they broke their relationship and fellowship with God, and a nature of sin and rebellion against God was introduced into them and through them into all their descendants (Rom. 5:12). This nature is the source of all our individual "acts" of sin and is the major reason why we are rendered unacceptable for a relationship with a holy God. *Sin*, not engrams, is our real problem.

Adam's own initial sin caused him to fall, and in the fall he became an entirely different being from a moral standpoint. Every child of Adam is born with the Adamic nature and is prone to sin. Unlike Scientology's claim regarding the "clearing" of engrams, sin is never said to be removed or eradicated in this life (Rom. 8:4; Gal. 5:16–17). It is only in the next life, when we (as Christians) reach heaven, that sin will be utterly eradicated (see 2 Peter 3:13; Rev. 22:15).

Biblically, of course, it is impossible for God to receive into His presence those who do not measure up to His perfect character. In 1 John 1:5 we read, "This is the message we have heard from him and declare to you: God is light; in him there is no darkness at all." God, who is light, cannot fellowship with the darkness of human sin. Sin has put up a barrier—a wide chasm—between humanity and God. But through Jesus Christ that fellowship can be restored. A. W. Tozer explains it this way:

> The whole work of God in redemption is to undo the tragic effects of that foul revolt, and to bring us back again into right and eternal relationship with Himself. This required that our sins be disposed of satisfactorily, that a full reconciliation be effected, and the way opened for us to return again into conscious communion with God and to live again in His Presence as before.[89]

Whereas sin caused estrangement, the cross of Christ brought reconciliation (Col. 1:20). Whereas sin bred enmity between us and God, the cross brought peace (Rom. 5:1). Whereas sin created a gulf between humans and God, the cross bridged that gulf (John 14:6). Whereas sin broke the fellowship between us and God, the cross restored it (Eph. 2:13). The great thing about all this, according to the Bible, is that *it is totally free*. Unlike the large amounts of money one must shell out to take Scientology courses, one can come to Jesus and drink freely of the water of life. Jesus said, "To him who is thirsty I will give to drink without cost from the spring of the water of life" (Rev. 21:6).

Science and Scientology

The claims of Scientology also have been challenged and undermined by certain authorities outside the realm of theology and religion. The legitimacy of the E-Meter, for example, has been called into question by some researchers. One report claims that "none of the Scientology theories associated with, or claims made for, the E-meter is justified. They are contrary to expert evidence."[90] Abanes says it is widely recognized that "the battery-operated contraption is simply an electrogalvanometer that measures changes in the electrical resistance of one's skin based on how moist it is. When the skin moisture of the person holding the cans fluctuates, so does the E-meter."[91]

Scientology has also been called into question by experts in the mental health field. According to a report in *Publisher's Weekly*, the 8,000 members of the American Psychological Association, at a September 1950 meeting, resolved that Hubbard's claims for Dianetics "are not supported by empirical evidence of the sort required for the establishment of scientific generalizations."[92]

8

HINDU-BASED CULTS

Approximately 700 million Hindus live in India, constituting 82 percent of India's population.[1] And approximately 13 percent of the world's population is Hindu. More than one million Hindus live in North America alone, and that number is steadily growing.[2]

The religious landscape in the West has been powerfully impacted by Eastern ideas. As Os Guinness said, "The East is still the East, but the West is no longer the West. Western answers no longer seem to fit the questions. With Christian culture disintegrating and humanism failing to provide an alternative, many are searching the ancient East."[3] But how did Americans acquire such an interest in Eastern thinking? We look to the 1960s for the answer.

THE COUNTERCULTURE OF THE 1960s

The counterculture of the 1960s played a key role in the explosive growth of Eastern religions in the West. James Sire, author of *The Universe Next Door*, believes that the openness to Eastern ideas among the Western youth of the 1960s was largely a reaction against traditional Western values. These values include high technology, reason and rationalism, materialism, economics, and the like.[4] Sire says that "with its antirationalism, its syncretism, its quietism, its lack of technology, its uncomplicated lifestyle, and its radically different religious framework, the East is extremely attractive."[5] Vishal Mangalwadi agrees, noting that Eastern enthusiasts reacted against the materialistic values, dehumanizing technology, valueless politics, and hypocritical morality of much of the West.[6] Many Americans have concluded that the East, that quiet land of meditating gurus and simple life, has the answer to our craving for meaning and significance.[7]

Thirty years ago in the United States, one might have thought a *guru* was an exotic animal. Today, because of Zen and other Eastern disciplines, it is practically a household word.[8] A guru is an enlightened master—even a godman.[9] Many view him as a man who is in his last of many thousands of reincarnations. "He is believed to have accumulated an enormous wealth of spiritual power and knowledge as a result of having logged countless years over many lifetimes as he struggled along the spiritual path."[10]

Maharishi Mahesh Yogi was one of the more prominent gurus in the 1960s with his greatly popular Transcendental Meditation. Other Eastern gurus that left their mark include Yogi Bahaman (who founded the Healthy, Happy, Holy Organization), Swami Muktananda (a guru who taught Siddha Yoga), Sai Baba (who headed the Spiritual Advancement of the Individual Foundation), Sri Chinmoy (who taught various techniques of yoga), Bhagwan Rajneesh (who taught a veritable hodgepodge of Eastern ideas), and Guru Maharaj Ji (the "Lord of the universe" who headed up the Divine Light Mission).[11]

All these gurus contributed to bringing the East to the West, especially in terms of the Eastern doctrines of *monism* (all is one) and *pantheism* (all is God). These doctrines not only helped set aside the idea of a personal Creator-God (as taught in Christianity), but also contributed greatly to the growth of moral relativism in America. Since "all is one" and "all is God," the distinction between good and evil is blurred if not obliterated.

HINDUISM'S ROOTS

A detailed history of Hinduism is far beyond the scope of this chapter. I do, however, want to note the basic factors in Hindu history that will help us understand some of the popular forms of Hinduism today. Hinduism has no specific founder, and no specific date can be cited for its founding. Scholar Bruce J. Nicholls observes that "of all the world's great religions, Hinduism is the most difficult to define. It did not have any one founder.... It has many Scriptures which are authoritative but none that is exclusively so. Hinduism is more like a tree that has grown gradually than like a building that has been erected by some great architect at some definite point in time."[12]

Starting about 1500 B.C., Vedic literature was composed over a 1,000-year period. *Veda* is a Sanskrit word that means "knowledge" or "wisdom."[13] The Hindu Vedas (the Rigveda, Samaveda, Yajurveda, and Artharvaveda)[14] are the earliest Hindu scriptures. They communicate spiritual knowledge—mainly giving priests instructions for performing rituals and providing information regarding the mystical and symbolic meaning of these rituals. Originally this knowledge was transmitted orally, but it was subsequently preserved in written form. Ancient Hindu Brahmin priests believed that Sanskrit was a language of the gods. The gods, through the Sanskrit language, supposedly conferred the Vedas to the ancient sages of India.

Ancient Hindu religion was polytheistic in nature, meaning adherents believed in many gods. Strong emphasis was placed on giving ritual offerings to various deities. Some of these gods were viewed as personifications of natural forces, such as the storm, the sun, the moon, and the fertility of the soil.[15] Eventually, certain gods became preeminent—especially Brahma, Vishnu, and Siva. By 1000 B.C. a class of priests known as Brahmins emerged who were devoted to the ultimate reality, Brahman.

During this time, Indian society began to be segregated into classes according to a system of classification known as *Varian*, which means color. These classes included the *Brahmins* (priests),

Ksatriyas (warriors or rulers), *Vaisyas* (merchants), and *Sudras* (laborers/servants). There were also "untouchables" who were forbidden contact with the other groups because they were regarded as impure. Eventually this evolved into the caste system that is predominant in India today. This caste system is based on Hinduism's belief in reincarnation. One's social status is dictated by the law of karma.[16] *Karma* comes from a root meaning "to do or act"; karma thus involves the idea that every action yields a consequence.[17] According to this law, then, one will be born in a higher status in the next life if one builds up good karma in the present life. One will be born in a lower status in the next life if one builds up bad karma in the present life.

This continual cycle of death and rebirth is known as *samsara* (transmigration),[18] a word that literally means "to wander across." Scholar Lewis M. Hopfe tells us that "Indian religions believe that the life force of an individual does not die with the death of the body. Instead it 'wanders across.' The life force moves on to another time and body where it continues to live."[19] Every person is viewed as being on the wheel of life, and salvation essentially involves breaking away from this wheel of life via reincarnation. The goal is to break the cycle of karma and samsara and be free from the burden of life. Salvation comes when one realizes that one's individual soul *(atman)* is identical with the Universal Soul *(Brahman)*.

The Brahmin priests were held in especially high regard during this time because they were the ones who engaged in the crucial rituals and by those rituals could control the gods. Inevitably, because the Brahmin priests were the highest caste in Indian society, abuses soon developed. The Brahmins "lorded it over" those of lesser castes. World religion specialist Dean Halverson tells us that as a result of the emphasis on the rituals, "the priests became the sole means by which people could approach and appease the gods. . . . The priests gained an increasing amount of power and control over the lives of the people."[20]

By the sixth century B.C., people could tolerate the abuse no longer, and they revolted against the spiritual tyranny of the Brahmins. Out of this conflict, new religions were born, such as Buddhism and Jainism. In addition, revival took place within Brahmanism. Relationships between gurus and students soon emerged, with spiritual knowledge being passed on to individual seekers. Much more emphasis was placed on internal meditation than on performing external rituals.

Though six major schools of Hindu thought were dominant in the first century in India (Nyaya, Vaisesika, Samkhya, Yoga, Mimamsa, and Vedanta), Vedanta became the predominant school. It was primarily based on the Upanishads (Hindu scriptures—literally "end or conclusion of the Vedas"—composed between 800 and 600 B.C.). The Upanishads fundamentally teach that behind the many gods of Hinduism stands the one monistic reality of Brahman. "Every aspect of the universe, both animate and inanimate, shares the same essentially divine nature. There is actually only one Self in the universe."[21]

According to this school of thought, every person possesses an individual soul known as *atman* that is related to the Universal Soul *(Brahman)*. Most Hindus believe they are in their true selves *(atman)* extended from and one with *Brahman*.[22] Through seemingly endless deaths and rebirths, one finally comes to realize that *atman is Brahman*. Indeed, "human beings are souls *(atman)* that are a part of the great ocean of souls that make up the Brahman."[23]

Because Vedanta Hinduism is monistic, distinctions are considered unreal. When one perceives distinctions, it is nothing more than a mental illusion *(maya)*. A person's individuality apart from the Brahman—the everyday world in which one lives, that which one sees, hears, and touches—is an illusion, a dream. As scholar Mark Albrecht puts it, "Hinduism holds that the world is really 'Brahman in disguise'—all matter, especially biological and human life, is merely a temporary, illusory manifestation of this universal spirit."[24]

The big problem for human beings, according to Hinduism, is that they are ignorant of their divine nature. People have forgotten that they are an extension of Brahman. "Humans have a false knowledge *(maya)* when they believe that this life and our separation from Brahman are real."[25] They have mistakenly attached themselves to the desires of their separate selves (or *egos*). For this reason, people have become subject to the law of karma. You reap (in the next life) what you sow (in the present life). Hindus sometimes argue that the early Christian church—and even the Christian Bible (Jer. 1:5; Matt. 11:14; John 3:3)—taught reincarnation and the law of karma.[26]

Liberation from this continual cycle of rebirths (samsara) is called *moksha*, which comes through the enlightened realization that the very idea of an individual self is *maya* (an illusion), and that only undifferentiated oneness with Brahman is real. When true knowledge of the illusion of life is realized, one can be freed from the bondage of life and achieve unity with the Brahman.

There are at least three paths to enlightenment one can pursue. They are (1) *karma marga* (the way of action and ritual—involving prescribed ceremonies, duties, and religious rites); (2) *jnana marga* (the way of knowledge and meditation—one must dispel ignorance and come to experientially know that the only reality is Brahman); and (3) *bhakti marga* (the way of devotion—involving private and public acts of worship). Whichever way one attains enlightenment, the goal of such enlightenment is for one's separate self or ego to lose its separate identity in Brahman, the Universal Soul.

While the Vedas are said to contain the purest form of truth, Hinduism also advocates the idea that the various religions are all custodians of spiritual truth. While all religions are said to contain truth, no one religion can claim that its teachings are *exclusively* true or are *absolute* for all people. After all, truth is in flux. It is not a concrete reality. Truth is relative.

The leaders of these religions—including Jesus—are said to have attained God-realization. In fact, Jesus' teachings are said to reflect Vedic philosophy. It is suggested that Christians have misunderstood the teachings of Jesus and that Hindu sages have a better grasp of them.

Hindus view Jesus as one of many holy men who communicated spiritual truth. He certainly was not humankind's only savior, nor was he uniquely the Son of God. Rather, he was a great master, in a league with other great masters.[27] Hindus believe there were holy men greater than Jesus, one being Prabhupada, who founded the Hare Krishna movement. Some Hindus have suggested Jesus may have been an avatar (an incarnation of a god), but he is nevertheless lower than the great Brahman.

Hindus often assert that Jesus was not perfect. They respect him and honor him, but his imperfection is evident in (among other things) the anger he showed in driving moneychangers out of the temple (Mark 11:15–19) and in causing the fig tree to wither (Matt. 21:19). Still, despite such imperfections, he was a great sage.

Hindus also teach that Jesus did not suffer when he was crucified on the cross, for he was a man who attained enlightenment and was beyond the possibility of physical pain. Maharishi Mahesh Yogi said, "It's a pity that Christ is talked of in terms of suffering."[28]

The two most prominent Hindu sects on American soil are the Hare Krishna sect and Transcendental Meditation, to which we will now turn.

HARE KRISHNA

In the 1960s the Hare Krishnas were easily recognizable. With their bright saffron robes and shaved heads and two perpendicular marks on their foreheads (signifying slavery to Krishna), chanting devotees pounded drums on street corners and hounded travelers in airports with *Back to Godhead* literature proclaiming that the transcendental bliss of Lord Krishna's paradise was the everlasting answer to mankind's religious cravings. Today Hare Krishnas dress more conventionally.

Krishna: Supreme Personality of the Godhead

Hare Krishna relates to one of the more preeminent gods in Hinduism—Vishnu, the preserver and protector of the universe.[29] Vishnu accomplishes this role through various avatars (people in whom Vishnu incarnates). Among the most famous avatars of Vishnu is Krishna (which is often spelled *Krsna*). He is the eighth avatar of Vishnu[30] and is presently adored and worshiped even more than Vishnu. In fact, contrary to traditional Hinduism, within Hare Krishna circles Vishnu is considered a "plenary expansion" of Krishna.

Krishna is viewed as the "Supreme Personality of the Godhead," the essence of all existence, and is "present everywhere, even within the atom and within the heart of every living creature."[31] Jesus Christ is seen as subordinate to Krishna and has even been called Krishna's son.

Hare Krishnas believe that the best way to burn off karma, dispel ignorance, and achieve bliss is "to express loving devotion *(bhakti)* through dancing and chanting to Krishna."[32] The "ignorance" that needs dispelling is that in which people identify themselves with their material bodies and thus become entangled in illusion *(maya)*. Until this ignorance is dispelled, one will continue to be reincarnated over and over again (either as a human being, or perhaps as a dog, hog, bird, cat, or lower species, depending on what kind of karma one has built up).[33]

Before one can engage in devotional service to Krishna through chanting, however, one must first be established in a relationship with Krishna. This can only happen by placing oneself under a spiritual master directly connected to Krishna via discipic succession (the Hindu version of Roman Catholic apostolic succession). "We connect ourselves with the guru through initiation, without which the cultivation of Krishna consciousness is impossible. From the devotee's side, initiation means that he accepts the guru as his spiritual master and agrees to worship him as God."[34]

Following this, the devotee goes about his day chanting the mantra described below, thereby attaining Krishna consciousness. Chanting removes one's consciousness from material desires and anxieties and fixes it on Krishna alone. This slowly enlightens one and helps one to realize one's true nature and identity—as an eternal servant of the supreme personality of the Godhead. Once one attains this realization and Krishna consciousness, one is thereby delivered from the cycle of births and deaths and is transported to a spiritual world called Goloka-Vrindavan, where Krishna is said to live eternally. Unlike typical Hindus who look forward to merging with the Absolute (Brahman) in the future, Hare Krishna devotees look forward to a transcendental love and fellowship with their Lord Krishna. "This is salvation—to live forever in the joy of Krishna's service."[35]

The Krishna devotional method involving chanting while dancing with the accompaniment of small brass hand-cymbals is called *sankirtana*. In developing Krishna consciousness, Hare Krishnas are expected to chant at least 16 rounds each day—a "round" consisting of singing the mantra once on each of 108 prayer beads. (The 16 words in the chant are "Hare Krishna, Hare Krishna/Krishna, Krishna, Hare, Hare/Hare Rama, Hare Rama/ Rama, Rama, Hare, Hare.") *Hare* refers to the "pleasure potency of Krishna," while *Rama* is another name for Krishna. The chant is supposed to be so powerful that it can produce divine influence wherever it is said, even cleansing one's heart of all "contaminated dust and garbage."[36]

Withdrawal from Worldly Living

Understandably, some Hare Krishna devotees feel it is in their best interest to withdraw from worldly living in order to focus devotion exclusively on Krishna. Therefore, they live in a rather strict commune setting. Monks and priests, for example, live inside the Krishna temple. In temple life, no gambling, games, sports, or discussions unconnected with Krishna consciousness are permitted. Furthermore, as apologist Kenneth Boa notes, "Anything having to do with science, education, violence, or carnality is spurned. There are no drugs, alcohol, tobacco, coffee, tea, or illicit sex. Dietary regulations prohibit meat, fish, and eggs. Everyone must sleep on the floor, usually in sleeping bags."[37] Many congregation members, however, live outside the temple though they are nevertheless committed to Krishna.

The Hare Krishna sect has strict rules regarding sexual abstinence, though it is possible to have children within the sect. The rules of celibacy are broken for couples desiring to have children. "They may have sexual relations once a month on the most auspicious day for conception. Because sex like everything is performed for Krsna's pleasure, the couple must chant fifty rounds on their japa beads for purification before engaging in sexual activity."[38] Such chanting prior to sexual relations can take four or five hours. At birth, children are given Sanskrit names and, once they reach the age of five, they are typically taken from parents and sent to Hare Krishna boarding schools.[39]

Some have noted the irony of such strictness regarding sexual relations in view of what Hindu literature tells us about Krishna himself. Indeed, as Mangalwadi notes, it is taught that when Krishna walked in human shape on the earth five thousand years ago, "he danced with about a hundred gopis [women] at one time, all of them lost in orgiastic bliss, each convinced that he was making love to her alone."[40]

Women are considered inferior in the sect. Cult specialist Ronald Enroth notes that women in the sect are expected to submit and be a servant to their husbands. They are discouraged from doing things on their own and must seek their husband's permission to do things beyond prescribed temple duties.[41] They are regarded as "prone to degradation, of little intelligence, and untrustworthy."[42]

Understandably, the Hare Krishna sect has come under heavy fire from the feminist movement.

Historical Roots

In terms of historical roots, the Hare Krishna sect first began with the great guru Chaitanya, born in 1486, who taught that Krishna was the supreme Lord over all other deities. Chaitanya danced and chanted the name of Krishna in the streets and amassed a large following, and Krishna consciousness was born. Others danced and chanted with him. "Before long, these devotees became so overwhelmed and intoxicated by the chanting of the holy names of God that they burst out of their homes into the streets."[43] Chaitanya was reportedly a man of great charisma, and many followers worshiped him as the incarnation of Krishna. His sect flourished in Bengal and northeastern India.

Four hundred years later, a guru who could be traced directly back to Chaitanya through a succession of gurus, initiated Abhay Charan De Bhaktivedanta Swami Prabhupada (1896–1977) and commissioned him to spread the teachings of Chaitanya. (*Prabhupada* means "at whose feet masters sit.") Prabhupada had graduated from the University of Calcutta where he studied English, philosophy, and economics. He then married and took a job at a pharmaceutical company.

Prabhupada continued his job at this company until his retirement in 1954. He did not completely renounce the world (according to Hindu custom) until 1959. But eventually he would fulfill the commission he had received. Indeed, he would later found the International Society for Krishna Consciousness (ISKCON) in the United States and establish a magazine entitled *Back to Godhead*, which has since become a major voice for the promotion of Hare Krishna beliefs.

Coming to New York City as a 70-year-old man in 1965 (with allegedly only eight dollars in his possession), Prabhupada gathered disciples among Greenwich Village's counterculture, teaching them about Krishna consciousness. The colorful robes and intoxicating dancing and chanting caught the attention of the media.

Prabhupada's following grew. He eventually established a Hare Krishna temple in New York, and others soon emerged in other major U.S. cities. Just six years after ISKCON was founded, there were 68 centers and about 3,000 followers in the United States, Canada, Mexico, the West Indies, Japan, Hong Kong, India, Sweden, France, Germany, Holland, Switzerland, England, Scotland, New Zealand, and Australia. In 1968 Prabhupada began a prolific writing effort, concentrating on translations of and commentaries on some of the Hindu scriptures.

Before Prabhupada died in 1977, he selected senior devotees who would continue to direct the organization. Since that time, these senior devotees and the rest of ISKCON have continued to disseminate the teachings of their master throughout the world. They received attention as a result of ex-Beatle George Harrison becoming a Krishna devotee. (His song "My Sweet Lord" was about Krishna. He has also donated some royalties and concert income to the sect.) Funds are generated from the sale of incense and the sect's lavishly illustrated literature, including the *Bhagavad-Gita: As It Is*, and its periodical, *Back to Godhead*. (Leaders claim a monthly circulation of 300,000 for *Back to Godhead*.) The actual number of ISKCON devotees in the United States is probably less than 10,000.[44]

TRANSCENDENTAL MEDITATION

One of the most influential gurus of the mid 1960s was Maharishi Mahesh Yogi, who taught his followers Transcendental Meditation (TM), into which a million Americans have now been initiated. One observer said that "what McDonald's has done for the hamburger, TM has done for Eastern mysticism."[45] TM has succeeded in making Eastern mysticism acceptable, fashionable, and desirable to the American public. About 6,000 doctors in the United States practice TM or recommend it to their patients, and TM chapters meet on about 95 percent of all public university campuses.

Maharishi Mahesh Yogi was born in 1911 in Jabalpur, Madhya Pradesh, India. He graduated with a degree in physics from Allahabad University in the 1940s. While working in a factory, he met and became a disciple of Swami Brahmananda Saraswati ("Guru Dev"). Maharishi learned a revolutionary yogic meditation technique from Guru Dev that would be foundational to his entire future. Prior to his death, Guru Dev commissioned Maharishi to develop and spread the meditation technique to the West.[46] For two years after Guru Dev's death, Maharishi remained in seclusion in a cave in the Himalayas, contemplating and assimilating what he had learned. When he emerged from solitude, he intended to change the world. He began teaching the meditation technique in India but soon realized that at this present rate of teaching, it would take him 200 years to bring TM to the world. So he headed for the West, where transportation and communication were much more efficient and his message could spread more quickly.

Maharishi arrived in the United States in 1959 and attempted to teach his ideas on meditation. The initial excursion was less successful than he hoped, largely because he did little to mask the religious nature of his teachings. At the time, he called his enterprise the "Spiritual Regeneration Movement." Many people seemed wary of anything "religious." So in 1960 he founded the more neutral-sounding International Meditation Society and in 1965 the Student's International Meditation Society. Eventually Maharishi's technique would be known as Transcendental Meditation.

Maharishi's meditation typically employs techniques such as concentrating on objects, exercising "controlled" breathing, and uttering mantras (holy words) with a view to emptying the mind of all distractions. The mantra is repeated until all awareness of the external world vanishes, enabling a person to reach an altered state of consciousness—a state of supreme harmony with oneself and the universe.

This is in keeping with Maharishi's basic doctrinal beliefs. He views God as "the one eternal unmanifested absolute Being [that] manifests itself in many forms of loves and existences in creation."[47] He sees everything in creation as a manifestation of the unmanifested absolute impersonal being of God, which he often referred to as "Creative Intelligence."

"A small man with long, dark hair and beard just beginning to turn gray, wearing traditional white silk robes, the Maharishi moved and spoke with an extraordinary combination of gentleness and strength. His words were carefully chosen and his speech, though simple, was highly articulate. He had a quick and lively wit, and a hearty laugh.... One thing was obvious: He was a happy man. Serene. At peace with himself and the world" (Jack Forem, *Transcendental Meditation: Maharishi Mahesh Yogi and the Science of Creative Intelligence*, 2).

Maharishi does not believe man has sinned against this pantheistic god, but rather has become separated from his true being. This sense of separation is caused by ignorance of one's true nature—*being divine*. Each individual is, in his or her true nature, the impersonal God.

Salvation is achieved by practicing Transcendental Meditation, which leads practitioners to realize their union with the Creative Intelligence. By reaching a state of bliss-consciousness, or happiness through meditation, TM claims people can free themselves from endless cycles of reincarnations. "Salvation" occurs when persons raise themselves from the gross levels of consciousness to the highest level, which is "Unity consciousness." (There are seven levels—dreamless sleep, dreaming, wakefulness, consciousness of one's soul or transcendental consciousness, cosmic consciousness, God consciousness, and Unity consciousness.) At this highest level, one's consciousness is completely absorbed into Brahman. "One sees that there is no difference between myself, other selves, and the material world. It is all one."[48] If persons manage to achieve Unity consciousness, they are thereby freed from the endless cycle of successive reincarnations. Maharishi has described Transcendental Meditation as a "path to God."

Maharishi was soon catapulted into the mainstream of American religion by virtue of his affiliation with various celebrities in the 1960s. When the Beatles, the Beach Boys, the Rolling Stones, and Mia Farrow began to utilize his meditation technique, he attained worldwide press coverage. For a while, TM was all the rage. Popularity declined a bit in the late 1960s but rebounded in the mid 1970s when Maharishi's technique began to be marketed as a "scientifically proven" method of attaining relaxation and inner peace. During the height of TM's popularity, Maharishi was taking in a reported $20 million per year.[49]

The claim by TM instructors that one could practice this meditation technique without violating or going against one's personal religious beliefs appealed to the American public. And, since science was said to back up the claims of TM, this appeared to be the perfect self-help technique.

Typically a prospective meditator is invited to two free TM lectures advertised in local media. TM is presented as a nonreligious mental technique for deep relaxation. Those interested in continuing then pay initiation and training fees. They are told to bring flowers, fruit, and a white handkerchief to the initiation ceremony, at which time these items are offered to Guru Dev on an altar with his image. The teacher then sings a Sanskrit hymn known as the Puja. At the end of the initiation, the initiate is given a secret mantra, a Sanskrit word that is to be repeated over and over again during times of meditation. The meditator then attends meditation classes three days in a row and is taught to meditate 20 minutes in the morning and again in the evening. Advanced courses are also available.

In the late 1970s TM again declined in popularity, partially because U.S. courts ruled that TM was in fact religious in nature. The technique is built upon Hindu Scriptures (the Vedas); the mantra each person is assigned is actually the name of a Hindu deity (and Maharishi later admitted that the use of mantras invokes gods and spirits from the spirit world); in the initiation ceremony homage is paid to Guru Dev; and a hymn is recited in Sanskrit, which—though unbeknown to the initiate—involves worship of Hindu gods. The following excerpt (translated into English) illustrates the religious nature of TM:

> To Lord Narayana, to lotus-born Brahma the Creator, to Vashishta, to Shakti, and to his son, Parashar, to Vyasa, to Shukadava, to the great Gaudapada, to Govinda, ruler among yogies, to his disciple, Shri Trotika and Varttika-Kara, to others, to the tradition of our masters I bow down. To the abode of the wisdom of the Shrutis, Smritis and Puranas, to the abode of kindness, to the personified glory of the Lord, to Shankara, emancipator of the Lord, I bow down. To Sharkaracharya, the redeemer, hailed as Krishna and Badarayana, to the commentator of the Brahma Sutras, I bow down again and again.[50]

This religious aspect of TM not only turned off many individual practitioners (they were angry because they had been deceived about the nature of TM), but also served to cut off penetration into public schools and the receiving of federal and state aid. Further, the growth of religious pluralism in America—including a plethora of other experience-inducing Eastern religions—depleted the ranks of TM devotees. Nevertheless, about a million TM enthusiasts can be found in America today.

The Maharishi International University also continues to flourish. The university, founded by the guru in 1971, seeks to empower students to attain success and fulfillment in life. It offers degrees in a broad range of disciplines and boasts of a positive, unusually serene campus atmosphere free of crime, drugs, and other problems common among colleges. Maharishi now lives in the Netherlands.

CHALLENGING HINDU BELIEFS

Truth Is Not Relative

In contrast to the Hindu emphasis on *relative* truth, Christianity rests on a foundation of *absolute* truth (1 Kings 17:24; Ps. 25:5; 43:3; 119:30; John 1:17; 8:44; 14:17; 17:17; 2 Cor. 6:7; Eph. 4:15; 6:14; 2 Tim. 2:15; 1 John 3:19; 3 John 4, 8). Moreover, the view that all truth is relative is not logically satisfying. One might understand the statement "all truth is relative" to mean that it is an *absolute* truth that all truth is relative. Of course, such a statement is self-defeating (since there are supposedly no absolute truths) and is therefore false. Or one could understand this as saying that it is a *relative* truth that all truth is relative. Such a statement is ultimately meaningless. No matter which way you understand this statement, it is logically unsatisfying.

The suggestion that all the religions are "custodians" of the truth is unreasonable in view of the significant doctrinal differences between them. I noted in a previous chapter that the leaders of the different world religions set forth different and contradictory ideas about God (some are theists, some are pantheists, some are polytheists, and so on). Beyond this, in Christianity a person is saved by placing personal faith in Jesus Christ with no works involved, while in other religions (including Hinduism) people must try to attain salvation by works. In terms of the soul, Christians believe that we *live once* and *die once* (Heb. 9:27) and look forward to a future day of bodily resurrection after which we will live forever with a personal God. Hindus, by contrast, say the soul is born over and over again in human bodies with the ultimate goal of escaping from the wheel of karma and being absorbed into the impersonal Universal

Soul. Such differences make it impossible to say all religions are "custodians" of the truth. If one of these religions is right, then the others must necessarily be wrong, for contradictory truth claims cannot be true at the same time.

Even within the Hindu Vedas there are contradictory truth claims. After all, part of the Vedas speak of belief in and worshiping many gods, while other parts espouse pantheistic monism (the idea that all is God and all is one). Both of these positions cannot be true at the same time. If all is God, then there cannot be many distinct gods.

CONTRASTING HINDUISM WITH CHRISTIANITY

	Hindu View	Christian View
Truth	Relative	Absolute
God	Many gods	One God—Yahweh
Jesus	Holy man, not a Savior	Divine Messiah, Savior
Man's Problem	Ignorance of divine nature	Sin against holy God
Solution	Enlightenment	Trust in Christ for salvation
Reincarnation	Yes	No
Goal	Merge with Universal Soul	Eternal life with God in heaven

Reincarnation Is a View Plagued by Problems

The Hindu hope in salvation via reincarnation is problematic on a number of levels. First, one must ask, Why does one get punished (via karma) for something he or she cannot remember having done in a previous life? Further, if the purpose of karma is to rid humanity of its selfish desires, then why has there not been a noticeable improvement in human nature after all the millennia of reincarnations? Still further, if reincarnation and the law of karma are so beneficial on a practical level, as Hindus claim, how do they explain the immense and ever-worsening social and economic problems—including widespread poverty, starvation, disease, and horrible suffering—in India, where reincarnation has been systematically taught throughout its history?

Scripture indicates that each human being lives once as a mortal on earth, dies once, and then faces judgment (see Heb. 9:27). He or she does not have a second chance by reincarnating into another body. Scripture indicates that at death believers in the Lord Jesus go to heaven (2 Cor. 5:8) while unbelievers go to a place of punishment (Luke 16:19–31). Moreover, Jesus taught that people decide their eternal destiny in a single lifetime (Matt. 25:46). This is precisely why the apostle Paul emphasized that "now is the day of salvation" (2 Cor. 6:2).

Contrary to the claim of some Hindu gurus, Christianity has never espoused a belief in reincarnation. Nor do the verses they typically cite from the Bible support reincarnation.

John 3:3 Does Not Teach Reincarnation

In John 3:3 Jesus said to Nicodemus, "I tell you the truth, no one can see the kingdom of God unless he is born again." Some Hindus argue that Jesus was referring to "cyclical rebirth" in this verse. The context, however, clearly shows that Jesus was referring to a *spiritual* rebirth or regeneration. In fact, the phrase "born again" carries the idea of "born from above" and can even be translated that way. Nicodemus could not have understood Jesus' statement in any other way, for Jesus clarified His meaning by affirming that "flesh gives birth to flesh, but the Spirit gives birth to spirit" (v. 6).

Matthew 11:14 Does Not Teach Reincarnation

Matthew 11:14 says, "If you are willing to accept it, he [John the Baptist] is the Elijah who was to come." Some Hindus claim that John the Baptist was a reincarnation of Elijah. Luke 1:17, however, clarifies any possible confusion on the proper interpretation of this verse by pointing out that the ministry of John the Baptist was carried out "in the spirit and power of Elijah." Nowhere does it say that John the Baptist was a reincarnation of Elijah. Hindus ignore the fact that John the Baptist, when asked if he was Elijah, flatly answered, "No" (John 1:21). And besides, Elijah does not fit the reincarnation model because he did not die. He was taken to heaven like Enoch, who did not see death (2 Kings 2:11; cf. Heb. 11:5). According to traditional reincarnation, one must first die before he or she can be reincarnated into another body.

Jeremiah 1:5 Does Not Teach Reincarnation

In Jeremiah 1:5 God said to Jeremiah, "Before I formed you in the womb I knew you, before you were born I set you apart; I appointed you as a prophet to the nations." Contrary to Hindu claims, this verse does not speak of reincarnation or of the soul pre-existing before birth. Rather, it speaks of God calling and setting apart Jeremiah for the ministry long before he was born. "I knew you" does not refer to a preexistent soul, but to the prenatal person. Jeremiah was known by God *in the womb* (Jer. 1:5; cf. Ps. 51:6; 139:13–16). The Hebrew word for know *(yada)* implies a special relationship of commitment (cf. Amos 3:2). It is supported by words like *sanctified* (set apart) and *ordained,* which reveal that God had a special assignment for Jeremiah even before birth. "Know" in this context indicates God's act of making Jeremiah the special object of His sovereign choice.

Concerning eternal destiny, one cannot help but observe that an ultimate goal of absorption into Brahman, thereby losing one's personal identity, has little appeal when compared to the possibility of living eternally, side-by-side, with the living, personal God of the universe (Rev. 22:1–5). Instead of being absorbed into a "Universal Soul," Scripture points to the reality that we will be given a resurrection body that will never again get sick, age, suffer pain, or die (1 Cor. 15:35–58). Is this not an infinitely better and more appealing prospect?

Enlightenment to Divinity Does Not Make Sense

I have already critiqued pantheism in the chapters on the mind sciences (see page 123) and the New Age movement (see page 148), and will not repeat that material. Here I merely want to call attention to the problem that exists when Hindus argue that all is God (Brahman) on the one hand and that human beings are ignorant and in need of enlightenment (regarding their divinity) on the other hand. Scholar David Johnson explains it well:

> If the world is but one vast spirit, why do we share the ignorant conclusion that it is made up of many things? Where did this conclusion come from? What is its cause? Who is ignorant? Who makes the mistake? Is Brahman (ultimate reality) making the mistake? Is it being said that the one vast spirit has made a mental error by suggesting to me that I am an individual? Has Brahman erred? How could what is described as ultimate "intelligence" make a mistake?[51]

Further, as I noted in a previous chapter, man's ignorance of his alleged divinity proves that he is not God. The fact that a person "comes to realize" his identity as God proves he is not God, for if he were God, he never would have passed from a state of ignorance to a state of enlightenment as to who he is.[52] To put it another way, "God cannot bud. He cannot blossom. God has always been in full bloom. That is, God is and always has been God."[53] And God has always been distinct from finite creatures like human beings (see Num. 23:19; Hos. 11:9; Rom. 1:22–23).

Jesus Christ Was the *Suffering* Messiah

Numerous points could be made in response to the Hindu view of Jesus Christ. One should be ready and willing to share these facts with a Hindu, for Gandhi once said, "I shall say to the Hindus that your lives will be incomplete unless you reverently study the teachings of Jesus."[54]

First, contrary to the Hindu teaching that Jesus (as an enlightened man) could not suffer, it is abundantly clear not only that Jesus suffered cruelly on the cross, but also that the whole reason He was born as a human being was to go to the cross to suffer for the sins of humankind. To deny the suffering of Christ is to deny both the Old and New Testament witnesses regarding Christ's mission. Isaiah 53:3 prophetically speaks of Christ, "He was despised and rejected by men, a man of sorrows, and familiar with suffering." We read in Matthew 16:21, "Jesus began to explain to his disciples that he must go to Jerusalem and suffer many things at the hands of the elders, chief priests and teachers of the law, and that he must be killed and on the third day be raised to life." Acts 1:3 speaks of the resurrection of the suffering Messiah: "After his suffering, he showed himself to these men and gave many convincing proofs that he was alive." Jesus *did* suffer—and He voluntarily did so for the salvation of humankind. This salvation is appropriated not by enlightenment, but by placing personal faith in Him who is the Light of the World—Jesus Christ (John 8:12).

Hindus are also wrong to attribute imperfection to Jesus simply because He expressed righteous indignation against that which was evil (for example, throwing moneychangers out of the temple). The fact that Jesus expressed righteous anger is no more a proof that He is imperfect than the fact that God Himself will express anger on the Day of Judgment shows that He is imperfect (2 Thess. 1:8–9). (One could forcefully argue that to stand idly by and turn one's face from blatant sin would be a sign of imperfection.) Further, if a Hindu criticizes Jesus for expressing anger, why do they not criticize their own gods for expressing anger (such as Brahma and Siva)?[55]

Contrary to the Hindu claim, the Scriptures indicate that Jesus was "without sin" (Heb. 4:15) and "had no sin" (2 Cor. 5:21). He is "holy, blameless, pure" (Heb. 7:26) and has been "made perfect forever" (Heb. 7:28). One cannot get more perfect than that.

Moreover, Scripture portrays Jesus as unique. The Greek word used to describe Jesus in John 3:16 (God's "*only begotten* Son" [KJV]) is *monogenes*, meaning "unique" or "one of a kind." Jesus is uniquely God's Son because, like the Father, *Jesus is God by nature.* Further, Jesus proved the veracity of all He said by rising from the dead (Acts 17:31; Rom. 1:4). None of the other leaders of the different world religions—including the grandest of the Hindu gurus—ever did that.

WARNING: Altered States of Consciousness May Be Dangerous to Your Health

Altered states of consciousness—such as those that result from practicing Transcendental Meditation and attaining "Krishna consciousness"—can be dangerous and can lead to harmful consequences. Kenneth Boa mentions an increasing number of reports regarding people who found the practice of TM to be harmful.[56] Among other things, altered states of consciousness can lead to contact with spirits.[57] And Leon Otis of Stanford Research Institute notes that some meditators developed increased anxiety, confusion, and depression.[58] Following his study, Otis concluded, "The number and severity of complaints were positively related to the duration of meditation. That is, people who had been meditating for the longest period of time reported the most adverse effects."[59] Researcher Gary Schwartz found that too much meditation can hinder logical thought processes.[60] Researcher Arnold Ludwig found that "as a person enters or is in an ASC [altered state of consciousness], he often experiences fear of losing his grip on reality, and losing his self-control."[61]

Of course, as Christians we must be careful not to write off all meditation simply because it is practiced in an unbiblical way by Hindus. Unlike Eastern meditation, biblical meditation does not involve mysticism or emptying the mind. Rather, biblical meditation involves objective contemplation and deep reflection on God's

Word (Josh. 1:8) as well as on His person and His faithfulness (Ps. 119; cf. Pss. 19:14; 48:9; 77:12; 104:34; 143:5). Christian meditation calls us to look upward to God so that our minds may be filled with godly wisdom and insight, and so that our hearts may be filled with comfort, happiness, and joy. To echo the opening words of the psalmist, "Blessed is the man . . . [whose] delight is in the law of the LORD, . . . on his law he meditates day and night" (Ps. 1:1–2).

9

THE UNIFICATION CHURCH

In a survey conducted in 1970, 1,000 Americans born between 1940 and 1952 were given a list of 155 names—and, amazingly, only 3 percent had not heard of Reverend Sun Myung Moon.[1] Moon's notoriety is due in no small part to the tremendous controversy that has surrounded him and his Unification Church.

Sun Myung Moon was born in northwestern Korea on January 6, 1920. The fifth of eight children of a rural farmer, Moon was just 10 years old when his family converted to Christianity.[2]

Moon claims that when he was 16 he had a dramatic spiritual experience in which Jesus appeared to him and requested that he complete the mission he had started almost 2,000 years earlier.[3] Jesus allegedly told Moon that Korea was the new Israel, the land God chose for the Second Coming.[4] Upon realizing that he was the sole person on earth who could deliver humankind from Satan's domain, Moon accepted the call.[5] According to Unification literature, Moon spent the next nine years on a "spiritual path of devotion, study and service,"[6] and engaged in spiritual warfare with Satan.

Satan reportedly tried to thwart Moon's mission by getting Moon to sin and disqualify himself as the Messiah. But Moon claims he was victorious and defeated the Devil, fulfilling the initial demands required for being the Messiah. During this same period, Moon is said to have received spiritual communications from such religious figures as Moses, the Buddha, and even God himself.

Mose Durst, a close companion of Reverend Moon, observes that when Moon went to Japan in these early years, he did not keep himself from political action and he ended up paying for it.[7] While there, Moon joined an underground liberation movement that sought to bring freedom to his Korean homeland and was arrested by the Japanese police several times. Eventually American forces defeated Japan, and Korea was liberated.

Returning to Korea, Moon then made preparations for ministry and got married. This first wife, however, divorced Moon and sought to destroy his ministry. Moon says that "with the Christian people opposing our movement, my first wife was influenced and, being weak, that caused the rupture in my family and I got divorced."[8] Former Unificationist Nansook Hong says that Moon's wife believed that at the Second Coming the Messiah will come in the clouds as Christianity has traditionally taught.[9]

In 1946 Moon went to North Korea to teach about God and confront "the godless ideology of communism."[10] Not popular with North Korean (communistic) authorities, Moon was arrested in 1947. He was allegedly beaten, tortured, and left for dead, but was nursed back to health by followers who found him.

Even at this early juncture, Moon apparently had illusions of grandeur and compared his sufferings to those of Christ during New Testament times. Moon claims he was being persecuted because of his faith just as Jesus was persecuted for his faith. As soon as Moon was well, he began preaching again.

Moon was arrested a second time in 1948 on charges of advocating social chaos. He was sentenced to five years of hard labor at a concentration camp in North Korea but escaped during the

Korean War, after just two and one-half years of imprisonment, when United Nations forces arrived at the camp and liberated the prisoners. He then fled to South Korea.

Settling in Pusan, South Korea, Moon began developing a following in the 1950s. He started a church in a small mud hut and while there began to be called "Reverend" because he was viewed as the pastor.[11]

In 1953 Moon moved to Seoul, the capital of South Korea, and continued his work of ministry. He formally established a church in 1954, which he dubbed The Holy Spirit Association for the Unification of World Christianity, more popularly known as the Unification Church. Moon did not seek to establish a new denomination. Rather, he wanted his church to be the foundation for unity for all Christian denominations and, in fact, for virtually all religions—East and West. Church membership quickly grew in Seoul, but so did persecution.

In 1955 Moon and other Unification Church members were arrested, this time on false charges of draft evasion. The charges were soon dropped, however, for Moon had been imprisoned in a North Korean concentration camp during the war and was therefore ineligible for conscription by the South Korean army.

Critics provide a different account of this arrest. In her book *The Making of a Moonie: Choice or Brainwashing?* Eileen Barker claims "his indictment was initially draft dodging but was later changed to adultery and promiscuity." She notes that "similar rumors (which persist to this day in Korea) alleged that he was engaging in ritual sexual practices."[12] This type of purification rite is known as *p'i kareun* and involves a church member having sexual intercourse with the messianic leader.[13] The Unification Church responded that these charges were unfounded, and that because of curfews at night, some people could not return home after long services and had to spend the night at the church center.[14] In 1993, however, Chung Hwa Pak—who is said to have traveled to South Korea in 1951 with Moon—wrote a book entitled *The Tragedy of the Six Marias*, in which he said that Moon not only practiced *p'i kareun*, but that his first wife left him because of sexual activities with other women.[15] There was enough evidence for this practice that the Korean National Council of Churches condemned the movement and refused it membership.

In any event, just a few years later (1957) Moon published the *Divine Principle*, a document shaped over many years by revelations he claimed to have received and which sets forth the basic teachings of Unification. Although it is not known how many copies of this book have been distributed, it has been translated into different languages, and critics estimate that the number of copies distributed is vast. Since its initial publication, multiple editions of this book have been published in which doctrinal changes have been introduced.

Moon married a second time in 1960 to Hak Ja Han. Continuing the illusions of grandeur, the wedding is said to have been "the marriage of the Lamb" referenced in Revelation 21:9.[16] They have since had 13 children.

Before long the Unification Church began to spread beyond South Korea. The movement expanded not only to Japan, where Moon now has a large following, but to the United States, as a result of Moon's missionary representative, Young Oon Kim, who was sent to the U.S. in 1959.

During the turbulent 1960s, Moon visited the United States, though he attracted little attention. It was not until the early to mid 1970s that the Unification Church started to draw significant numbers of people in the United States. The reason for this, observers say, is that Moon began to make headlines across the country. One thing that fascinated the Western media was Moon's conducting mass marriages, in which he personally chose and united marriage partners. In a single ceremony in 1975, Moon married some 1,800 couples from 25 countries. (In Unification theology, marriage is a sacrament like communion and baptism. Thus there is religious significance to these mass marriages.)

Another reason Moon made the headlines during the 1970s was that he publicly supported Richard Nixon during the Watergate scandal.[17] As a result of this public support, Moon was invited to the White House by Nixon. The visit was picked up by the evening news, and Moon became a star.

As the movement continued to mushroom, troubling reports began to surface. There were allegations of brainwashing, concerns over the finances of the organization, and, of particular concern to Christians, hints in Moon's comments that he was the Messiah[18] and that Jesus had not completed his mission.[19]

This spurred a backlash against the Unification Church from various Christian groups during the 1970s. An increasing number of evangelical Christian organizations and individuals publicly denounced Moon, declaring that his church was not Christian but cultic. Moon often responded that just as religious people took a stand against Jesus during His day, so religious people were taking a stand against him. He believed that many would come to embrace him just as Paul (who once persecuted Jesus) came to embrace Jesus (Acts 9:5).

In the early 1980s, however, Moon found himself in trouble with the law again. He was found guilty of tax evasion charges and was sentenced to 18 months in jail.[20] He got out 5 months early for good behavior. His time in prison set him up as a martyr in the eyes of his followers.[21]

Presently the Unification Church is a worldwide movement with its heaviest concentrations of members in Korea, Japan, and the United States. Moon is convinced that the United States is pivotal to his global influence, because the United States is the most powerful economic, political, and military nation in the world. Moon believes that the United States is the perfect platform from which to influence the rest of the world.

The best estimate of membership in the Unification Church is between 1 and 2 million members worldwide. There are an estimated 30,000 or less living in North America.[22]

JOINING THE MOONIES

Prospective converts are typically invited to an evening at a local Unification Center, after which they are invited to a three-day weekend workshop where they hear lectures on Unification theology.[23] In a typical workshop in California, perhaps 100 people might come to a camp—about half potential converts and half Unification members. Guests awaken around 7:00 A.M., have breakfast, and participate in some exercise. Then each guest is allocated to a group of about 12 people (perhaps five guests and the rest Moonies). They get to know each other well. Potential converts are never left alone. Sessions begin with singing, which is followed by a Unification lecture. People then disperse to join their small groups and have a sharing time ("How did you hear about our group?" and so on). Sometimes when a guest says something, Moonie members applaud, making guests feel welcomed and accepted. At the end of the weekend stay, each person is asked if he or she would like to join. Those who decline cease to receive personal attention.[24]

Once a person is drawn into the Unification Church, his or her life dramatically changes. Researcher Isamu Yamamoto notes that Unification members in the past have been pressured to work long hours raising funds for the church and enlisting new members. Over the past 20 years many millions of dollars have been collected for Moon's cause in the United States alone. A single Moonie can bring in between $90 and $160 a day selling candy and flowers on street corners.[25]

Moonies often experience little sleep and a poor diet. Moreover, one is no longer in control of one's life, for one must now live to please "Father" Moon. Unificationists must recite a pledge: "I will fulfill our father's [Moon's] will, and the responsibility given me. I will become a dutiful son and a child of goodness to attend to our father [Moon] forever."[26] This commitment to Reverend Moon is understandable in view of the Unification belief that Moon is the Messiah. There have been reports of insulation and isolation, whereby converts no longer watch television or listen to the radio, and contact with family members and friends is broken off. Those who express interest in leaving may be told they are yielding to Satan.[27]

In serving Reverend Moon, members have often participated in "heavenly deception."[28] This entails the use of lying and dishonesty for the sake of drawing somebody into "the kingdom of God" (Moon's Church) or raising funds. Isamu Yamamoto writes, "I personally have observed Unificationists practice heavenly deception on numerous occasions. For example, I have encountered Unificationists in wheelchairs soliciting funds for social programs that did not exist, and when I asked them why they pretended to be disabled as they walked to their van, they used their concept of heavenly deception to defend their actions."[29]

UNIFICATION "FRONT GROUPS" AND CONFERENCES

The Unification Church sponsors numerous "front groups" that may be considered "backdoors" into church involvement. Numerous people become affiliated with what they think is a professional or academic organization—an activist group at a college, for example—and are unaware that the group is affiliated with the Unification Church. It is estimated that the Unification Church operates over 200 front groups in the United States alone.[30] The ultimate aim of these organizations is the conversion and indoctrination of people into the cult. These groups include The International Federation for Victory over Communism, Freedom Leadership Foundation, World Freedom Institute, American Youth for a Just Peace, International Cultural Foundation, One World Crusade, Project Unity, Creative Community Project, Professors Academy for World Peace, Committee for Responsible Dialogue, and The Collegiate Association for the Research of Principles. Many of these groups sound inviting and beneficial. Tragically, however, many unsuspecting people have been drawn into the Unification Church by joining one of these organizations.

Another common tactic used by the Unification Church to lend respectability to itself and gain members is sponsoring conferences. Cult watcher Ruth Tucker, professor at Trinity Evangelical Divinity School in Deerfield, Illinois, is correct in saying that "through scientific, philosophical, and religious conferences offered free of charge to ministers and educators at posh resorts, the organization has been able to win influential friends that would not otherwise have offered support."[31] Sociologist Eileen Barker was invited to one such conference, and she commented that it "turned out to be disappointingly respectable. In fact, by academic standards, it was even rather a good conference."[32] The church is vying for respectability.

The Unification Church has also sought legitimacy by associating with evangelicals and respectable leaders. The likes of former President George Bush, vice presidential candidate Jack Kemp, Marilyn Quayle, Bill Cosby, and Barbara Walters have participated at Unification Church–sponsored events (having been paid hefty honorariums).[33] Sometimes Reverend Moon will have himself photographed with a famous leader, and that picture will then be run in Unification publications, thereby boosting Moon's credibility.

UNIFICATION BELIEFS
Reverend Moon's Revelations Supersede the Bible

According to Unification theology, human history can be divided into three ages, and in each one God gave revelation suitable for that age. God gave the law of Moses for those living during the Old Testament age. He gave the teachings of Christ for those living during the New Testament age. And he allegedly gave the Reverend Moon's book, *Divine Principle,* for us who are living in the Completed Testament age.

The revelations communicated through Reverend Moon take precedence over both the Old and New Testaments. Furthermore, the Old and New Testaments are not viewed as the absolute, inerrant, inspired Word of God, but instead are viewed as mere "textbooks" that teach God's truth. Moon's writings are elevated to supreme authority, and any who reject the *Divine Principle* may be destined for hell.

Unificationists set forth a twisted interpretation of Jesus' words in John 16:12–13: "I have much more to say to you, more than you can now bear. But when he, the Spirit of truth, comes, he will guide you into all truth. He will not speak on his own; he will speak only what he hears, and he will tell you what is yet to come." Unificationists believe the words Jesus left unuttered are presently being revealed through the Holy Spirit as "new truth," that is, through Moon's revelations.

Man Fell Both Physically and Spiritually

Moon teaches that after God created the universe He desired to establish the kingdom of God on earth among human beings. God intended for Adam and Even to continually mature and attain spiritual perfection before engaging in a sexual union. Had they done this, they would have given birth to sinless offspring, and the kingdom of heaven would have been established on earth. They would have established what in Unification theology is called the Four Position Foundation. "In this idea a husband and wife lives [*sic*] in a loving relationship with God and produce children. God, the parents, and the child make up a Four Position Foundation. This ideal for family life would be multiplied throughout the earth, fulfilling God's intentions and bringing him joy."[34] Had Adam and Eve obeyed God, they would have become "True Parents," and their children and children's children would have populated the world, bringing about the kingdom of God on earth.

Things did not go as God desired, however. Lucifer—who had been assigned by God to look after Adam and Eve—disrupted God's plan. Lucifer saw how special Adam and Eve were in the eyes of God. Lucifer also saw how beautiful Eve was. He lusted after her and desired to seduce her. He sought a sexual union with her not only because it would bring pleasure to him, but because it would also grieve God spiritually. Therefore, Lucifer seduced Eve and had an illicit (spiritual) sexual relationship with her.

When Eve submitted to Lucifer's advances, the two committed fornication by means of their spirit bodies in the spirit world. This resulted in the spiritual fall of the human race. From this point forward, man's spiritual nature was corrupted and had a propensity for evil. It was also at this time that Lucifer became the Devil.

Eve then realized through a spiritual insight that she had gone astray and had deviated from God's ideal plan.[35] In a misguided attempt, she sought to rectify things. She physically seduced Adam. She reasoned that she might be able to get back on track with God's ideal plan by engaging in a husband-and-wife relationship with Adam. Her strategy backfired, however, because Adam and Eve had not yet reached spiritual maturity.

Because of Eve's spiritual fornication with Satan, she inherited satanic "love"—so that when she and Adam engaged in physical sexual relations, their relationship was motivated by satanic "love." Hence, their children were born of a satanic "love," meaning that all people are the "children" of Satan.

This sexual union constituted yet another deviation from God's perfect plan and represented the physical fall of man. At this point humankind's physical nature became corrupted and the process of aging, disease, and eventual physical death began. Unificationists argue that Adam and Eve's sin was clearly sexual because they immediately sought to cover their bodies after committing their treason against God.

Original sin thus involves a tainted blood lineage that goes back to Eve's illegitimate sexual liaison with Satan and her premature physical seduction of Adam. The fall was the result of the misuse of the most powerful of forces—love. The ultimate result is that all love experienced on earth is rooted in Satan. No one since the fall has been free of original sin except Jesus Christ.

Restoration to God would be possible only through the Messiah, who would faithfully fulfill the role in which Adam had failed. The Messiah was to marry, and he and his wife were to become the

"True Parents" of a perfect humanity and give rise to the kingdom of God on earth.

Because man fell both spiritually and physically, man must be redeemed both spiritually and physically. It would be impossible for the kingdom of God to be established on earth without both a spiritual and a physical redemption. According to Moon, Jesus, at the cross, accomplished the spiritual redemption of humankind but failed to accomplish man's physical redemption because he failed to get married and have children. Thus, it would be the task of the Lord of the Second Advent to accomplish man's physical redemption. This would be Moon's task.

Man Must Be Redeemed Physically and Spiritually

One cannot understand the Unification view of salvation without understanding the significant role Jesus himself was to play in attaining this salvation. So important was the role of Jesus that God supposedly prepared for his coming by sending such religious leaders as Gautama the Buddha, Socrates, and Confucius to prepare the hearts of the people. Ultimately, followers of these religions and philosophies were to unite under a single messiah.

When Jesus finally arrived on the scene, he was supposed to establish the kingdom of heaven on earth by redeeming humanity both spiritually and physically. According to the *Divine Principle*, Jesus' basic purpose was to get married and bear children, and in doing this, he would redeem humanity both spiritually and physically.

The plan of redemption was disrupted, however, because the Jews did not believe Jesus was the Messiah. The *Divine Principle* tells us that it was John the Baptist who was responsible for the Jews rejecting Jesus as the Messiah. John was sent in the spirit and power of Elijah to prepare the hearts of the Jewish people to receive the Messiah, but he allegedly failed to fulfill his mission because of his disbelief. When he was in prison, John publicly expressed his doubts about Jesus being the Messiah (Luke 7:20). Had John been faithful, Jesus would have been recognized as the Messiah and the Jewish people would have believed in him.

As a result of John botching his mission, the Jews did not believe in Jesus, and therefore Jesus was forced to go to the cross. By going to the cross, Jesus redeemed humanity spiritually but not physically. In view of this, the *Divine Principle* tells us, Jesus himself said that the

Lord must come again to complete humanity's restoration to its original state of sinlessness. Even though the death of Jesus on the cross brought spiritual redemption to people, that death did not remove original sin, for followers of Christ obviously still sin and are therefore subject to sin in their flesh. To overcome this bondage to sin and regain a state of sinlessness, the Lord of the Second Advent must come.

Unification literature asserts that this Lord of the Second Advent will succeed in establishing the kingdom of heaven on earth by redeeming human beings *physically*. The time of arrival for the Lord of the Second Advent appears to be our own day. Unificationists claim there were 2,000 years between Adam and Abraham, during which time God dealt with his people Israel. There were 2,000 years between Abraham and Jesus, the second Adam, during which time Israel was supposed to prepare for the coming of the Messiah. Further, there was to be 2,000 years between Jesus and the Lord of the Second Advent, the third Adam. During this time, Christians are supposed to lay the foundation for the coming of the second Messiah.[36] In view of these facts, it is clear that the timing of the coming of the second Messiah *is now*.

Unificationists point to Revelation 7:2–4, which prophesies that an angel will come from the East with a seal of God, and say that this verse indicates that the second Messiah will be born somewhere in the East.[37] They argue that Korea is the only logical country that could possibly be referred to, because Japan worships pagan gods and China is a communist country. Korea is viewed as a suitable birthplace for the Messiah because people there have a strong faith in God.

According to Unificationists, once the Messiah is born in Korea, he will perfect himself, his family, his nation, and the entire

"Adam and Eve were supposed to be the True Parents of mankind in God's plan. When they failed, God intended Jesus to be the True Parent of mankind. When he was crucified on the cross, God promised another messiah. He is coming to consummate the ideal of God-centered True Parents. He will generate a new family of God through restoring the family unit under God's ideal. When we have True Parents of God, we can all become true brothers and sisters" (Reverend Moon, cited in Frederic Sontag, *Sun Myung Moon and the Unification Church*, 142–43).

world. He will perfect himself by defeating the Devil and removing himself from Satan's lineage. He will perfect his family by getting married and having children. (Moon presently has 12 living children who not only represent but are said to actually stand in the place of the 12 tribes of Israel and the 12 apostles of Jesus. His dead son, Heung Jin Nim, is said to be carrying on his father's work in heaven as the "King of Heaven," in authority over Jesus.)[38] He will perfect the nation of Korea by defeating communism, which is based on the demonic principle of Satan. He will perfect the world by uniting all religions under the Lord of the Second Advent, defeating communism, and uniting all nations into one kingdom on earth, centered on God.

Like other cults, works come into the picture in the Unification system of salvation, despite the work accomplished by the first Messiah (Jesus) and that which will be accomplished by the second Messiah (Moon). The Unification doctrine of indemnity involves atoning for our own sins through specific acts of penance. While God does the majority of the work in regard to human salvation, people still have to do their part. "The providence of restoration cannot be fulfilled by God's power alone, but it is to be fulfilled by man's joint action with God."[39] We are told, "As one atones for his own sins through constant effort, he can build up enough indemnity merit to be freed from guilt."[40]

Another Jesus, Another Trinity

In the theology of Reverend Moon, Jesus is not eternal deity. Rather, we are told, "after his crucifixion, Christianity made Jesus into God."[41] In other words, the absolute deity of Christ was something the early church fabricated. Though Jesus is not absolute deity, Moon believes Jesus attained a lesser level of deity. This is based on Moon's teaching that God originally created humanity to be perfect and sinless. According to Moon, the first human being to become perfect also becomes the tree of life, which is viewed as a symbol of eternal life in God. Had Adam become perfect, he would have become the tree of life and assumed deity. Yet it was Jesus who first attained spiritual perfection and therefore attained deity and became the tree of life. So Jesus is "God," but his deity is an attained deity and is a lesser deity than that of the Father.

The fact that Jesus was tempted by the Devil shows that Jesus is not God in the ultimate sense, because God cannot be tempted (see Matt. 4:1–11). The fact that Jesus is portrayed as praying to God on several occasions indicates that he is not God in the ultimate sense, because God cannot pray to Himself (see John 17). Further, if Jesus were God in the ultimate sense, he would never have been defeated and nailed to the cross.

As for Christ's resurrection, in Unification theology Jesus was not physically raised from the dead. No human body can be resurrected following death, because the body decays. Moon believes that at the resurrection Jesus became a being transcendent of the material world. This is inferred from a number of New Testament verses. For example, we are told in John 20:19 that Jesus suddenly appeared in the midst of a room where the disciples were gathered. Moreover, Luke 24:15–16 says that the two disciples on the road to Emmaus did not initially recognize Jesus as they walked together with him, thereby indicating that Jesus had not physically risen in the same body in which he died.

Concerning the Trinity, Moon's rendition bears virtually no resemblance to the biblical account.[42] According to Moon, it was God's original intention in creating Adam and Eve to form a Trinity by uniting them into one body with himself (that is, God, the "True Father" [Adam], and the "True Mother" [Eve]). This plan was foiled because Adam and Eve did not perfect themselves and fell into sin. Because of the fall, a Satanic trinity was formed with Satan, Adam, and Eve (false parents). Later, once Jesus perfected himself spiritually, God formed a spiritual Trinity with Jesus and the Holy Spirit (who is a female spirit; hence Jesus and the Holy Spirit supposedly took the roles of "Second Adam" and "Second Eve"). But because Jesus died on the cross before getting married, God could not form a physical trinity with Jesus and the woman he might have married. Moon claims that the members of the physical Trinity will be God, the Lord of the Second Advent, and the Lord of the Second Advent's wife. Moon teaches that when this physical Trinity is formed, the kingdom of heaven will be established on earth.[43]

All Humans Will Eventually Become Divine Beings

Unification literature speaks of both an earthly hell and a spiritual hell. "Spiritual hell" refers to where wicked people go when they die, while "earthly hell" refers to any place where people succumb to their evil nature and serve Satan. In Moon's theology, anybody who rejects the Lord of the Second Advent and anybody who rejects the *Divine Principle*, goes to spiritual hell. Yet spiritual hell is only a temporary abode. Even people in hell will come to realize the truth about the Lord of the Second Advent and will be delivered. Ultimately, every person will be redeemed. At some point in the future, after hell has been emptied, God will abolish hell.

In accordance with this, in Unification theology all human beings will eventually become divine beings. Those obedient to the law of Moses during the Old Testament age went into the spirit world as "form spirits" at the moment of death. (Such spirits have *formed* a relationship with God even though they have not yet perfected themselves.) Those obedient to Christ during the New Testament age went into the spirit world as "life spirits" at the moment of death. (These spirits are closer to God than form spirits, but they too have not yet reached perfection.) Those who serve the Lord of the Second Advent and die during this Completed Testament age enter the spirit world as "divine spirits." Through continuing perfection, all humans will at last become divine beings.

CHALLENGING UNIFICATION BELIEFS

The *Divine Principle* Is Not God's Word

Former Unificationist Nansook Hong notes that for a heavenly inspired document, the *Divine Principle* is very derivative: "The 556-page sacred text of the Unification Church is a synthesis of Shamanism, Buddhism, neo-Confucianism, and Christianity. It borrows from the Bible, from Eastern philosophy, from Korean legend, and from the popular religious movements of the Reverend Moon's youth to stitch together a patchwork theology, with the Reverend Moon at its center."[44]

Further, a number of revisions of the *Divine Principle* have been made to correct theological problems in the book. Since God does not make mistakes, we can assume that the source of the material in the *Divine Principle* is not God, for if it were, there would be no need for revision. While Unificationists often claim that the revisions only corrected errors of transcribers and translators of Moon's teachings, theological changes have been made as well.[45]

Contrary to Unification claims, the Bible is not just a textbook but is in fact the inspired Word of God. Certainly Jesus held that

Scripture alone (the Bible) is the supreme and infallible authority for the believer. Jesus said, "Scripture cannot be broken" (John 10:35). He also said, "I tell you the truth, until heaven and earth disappear, not the smallest letter, not the least stroke of a pen, will by any means disappear from the Law until everything is accomplished" (Matt. 5:18; cf. Luke 16:17). Jesus used Scripture as the final court of appeal in every matter under dispute. He said to some Pharisees, "You nullify the word of God by your tradition that you have handed down" (Mark 7:13). To the Sadducees He said, "You are in error because you do not know the Scriptures or the power of God" (Matt. 22:29). To the Devil, Jesus consistently responded, "It is written..." (Matt. 4:4–10). Following Jesus' lead, the Scriptures alone are our supreme and final authority, not any man-made book that has to go through numerous revisions to correct its errors.

Spiritism Is Condemned by God

Not only has Moon claimed to be in contact with people who have died, but the same is said to be true of his followers. People in the spirit world are allegedly helping Moon and his followers establish the kingdom of heaven on earth. In Scripture, however, God explicitly condemns all forms of Spiritism (Lev. 19:26, 31; 2 Kings 23:24). Deuteronomy 18:10–11 is clear: "Let no one be found among

CONTRASTING THE UNIFICATION CHURCH WITH CHRISTIANITY		
	Unification View	**Christian View**
Scripture	Highest=*Divine Principle*	Bible alone
Bible	Uninspired textbook of God's truth	Inspired Word of God
Trinity	God, Moon, and his wife	Father, Son, and Holy Spirit
Jesus	Attained lesser level of deity	Absolute deity
Messiah	Moon is Second Messiah	Jesus is only Messiah
Fall	Spiritual fall and physical fall	A single fall
Adam/Eve's Sin	Sexual in nature	Ate forbidden fruit
Redemption	Physical and spiritual	A single redemption
Second Coming	Reverend Moon	Jesus
Resurrection	Nonphysical	Physical

you . . . who is a medium or spiritist or who consults the dead." Further, we must keep in mind that departed human beings are not hovering around in the "great beyond" available for contact from human beings on earth. Departed Christians are in the presence of Christ in heaven (Phil. 1:23), whereas departed unbelievers are in a place of suffering (Luke 16:19–31), *confined* until the future day of judgment (Rev. 20:11–12).

Moon's Family Is Not "Perfect"

Despite Unification claims that Reverend Moon would establish a perfect family on earth, the facts reveal otherwise. In her book *In the Shadow of the Moons: My Life in the Reverend Sun Myung Moon's Family*, Nansook Hong chronicles what life was like for her in her marriage to one of Moon's sons, and the picture she paints is disconcerting. She portrays Moon's son—Hyo Jin Moon—as a substance abuser with a high interest in pornography, and she claims that he sometimes beat her, even when she was seven months pregnant. She tells how her problems with the Moon family escalated to the point that she decided to "leave behind the man who beat me and the false Messiah who let him, men so flawed that I now knew that God would never have chosen Sun Myung Moon or his son to be his agents on earth."[46]

The Fall Was Not Sexual In Nature

The idea that the Devil seduced Eve sexually is completely foreign to the pages of Scripture. History reveals that this idea did not emerge with Moon, but was borrowed from the man Moon studied under in 1945—Baek Moon Kim at the Israel Monastery in Seoul. Kim was not the only one who held to this theory back then. Another "pastor," Kim Seongdo, founder of the Holy Lord Church in Chulson in North Korea, made the same false claim.[47]

Moreover, the Bible never describes the sexual relationship between Adam and Eve as sinful. Their sin is always described in terms of eating the forbidden fruit. Moreover, there is no indication in Scripture that Adam and Eve were supposed to mature to spiritual perfection before engaging in sexual union. After creating Adam and Eve, God instructed them to be fruitful and multiply (Gen. 1:28). No waiting period was stipulated.

Scripture also stands against the view that the spiritual part of the fall related to Eve's sin (spiritual fornication with Satan) while the physical part related to Adam's sin (premature sexual relations with Eve). The apostle Paul said that "sin entered the world through one man, and death through sin, and in this way death came to all men, because all sinned" (Rom. 5:12). Indeed, "through the disobedience of the one man the many were made sinners..." (Rom. 5:19; see also 1 Cor. 15:21–22). There was a single fall based on a single act of disobedience.

The Kingdom Arrived with Jesus Christ

The teaching that the kingdom of heaven could not be established on earth until Jesus married a perfect mate and then produced children is nonsense. Scripture indicates that the kingdom of heaven was already present in Christ's own ministry. In Luke 17:21, Jesus affirmed that "the kingdom of God is *in your midst*" (NASB, emphasis added). Jesus said this because Christ (the King) is "in your midst." The kingdom is present because the King is present. Jesus further indicated that his very act of casting out demons from people was concrete proof that God's kingdom had come with power (Matt. 12:28; Luke 11:20). Not a single reference can be found in Scripture to support the claim that Jesus had to marry before establishing the kingdom of heaven on earth.

John the Baptist Did Not Fail

The Unification claim that the Jews failed to believe Jesus was the Messiah as a result of the faithlessness of John the Baptist is also unfounded. That John did not fail is clear from Jesus' own statement about him: "I tell you the truth: among those born of women there has not risen anyone greater than John the Baptist.... He is the Elijah who was to come" (Matt. 11:11, 14). Jesus would not have said such a thing if John had failed. Further, Scripture indicates that John indeed did point the people to Jesus as the Savior (see, for example, John 1:15–34). In reality, many Jews believed in Jesus (John 1:12). The Bible often describes Jesus as being overwhelmed by large crowds of Jews who wanted to get close to Him (Matt. 5:1; 8:1; 12:15; 13:2; 14:13–14, 21; 15:10, 35–38; 17:14; 19:1–2; 20:29; 21:8).

Jesus Is the One True Messiah

Contrary to Unification theology, Jesus did not "become perfect" and "attain deity"; rather, He is eternal deity, just as the Father is. A look at John's gospel alone proves Christ's eternal deity.

He is called eternal God in John 1:1. He is portrayed as the divine Creator in John 1:3 (only God can be the Creator—see Isa. 44:24). He is identified as the great I AM (Yahweh) in John 8:58 (cf. Ex. 3:14). He is seen to have the same divine nature as the Father in John 10:30. He is recognized as God by doubting Thomas in John 20:28. He is portrayed as having the divine attributes of omnipresence (John 1:47–49), omniscience (John 2:25; 16:30; 21:17), and omnipotence (John 1:3; 11:1–44). These verses represent the tip of the iceberg when it comes to proofs for the eternal deity of Christ.

Praying to the Father

The fact that Jesus prayed to the Father does not mean He is not fully God, as Moon claims. One must keep in mind that prior to the incarnation, Christ, the second person of the eternal Trinity, had only a divine nature. But in the incarnation Christ took on human nature (and was therefore fully God *and* fully man). It is in His humanity alone that Christ prayed to the Father. Since Christ came as man—and since one of the proper duties of man is to worship, pray to, and adore God—it was perfectly proper for Jesus to address the Father in prayer. As a man, as a Jew, and as our high priest ("made like his brothers in every way," Heb. 2:17), Jesus could pray to the Father, but this in no way takes away from His intrinsic deity.

The Temptation of Christ

The fact that Jesus was tempted does not argue against His full deity, as Moon asserts. It was *in His humanity* that Jesus was subject to temptation, distress, weakness, pain, sorrow, and limitation. But even though tempted, there was no chance (in my view) Jesus could have succumbed to temptation and sinned. As the God-man, Christ could not have sinned because:

1. In His divine nature, He is immutable and does not change.
2. In His divine nature, He is omniscient, knowing all the consequences of sin.
3. In His divine nature, He is omnipotent in His ability to resist sin.
4. While He experienced real temptations, He never succumbed and always remained without sin (Heb. 4)

5. Christ had no sin nature like all other human beings and was perfectly holy from birth (Luke 1:35).
6. There is an analogy between the written Word of God (the Bible) and the living Word of God (Christ). Just as the Bible has a human element and a divine element and is completely without error, so Christ in the incarnation is fully divine and fully human and is completely without (and unable to) sin.

This does not mean Christ's temptations were not real. Christ was genuinely tempted, but the temptations stood no chance of luring Christ to sin. It is much like a canoe trying to attack a U.S. battleship. The attack is genuine, but it stands no chance of success.

Jesus' Death

Contrary to the Unification view that Jesus died because of circumstances beyond His control, Scripture indicates that it was God's plan from the very beginning for Jesus to die on the cross. In fact, Jesus was born into the world with a specific purpose of dying (see Matt. 26:42; Luke 24:25–26; Heb. 10:5–10). We are told in 1 John 4:10, "This is love: not that we loved God, but that he loved us and sent his son as an atoning sacrifice for our sins." In Acts 2:23, Peter declares to the crowd, "This man [Jesus] was handed over to you *by God's set purpose and foreknowledge*; and you, with the help of wicked men, put him to death by nailing him to the cross" (emphasis added).

At Jesus' birth we find evidence that it was not Jesus' ultimate intention to marry but to suffer. When the devout Simeon blessed Mary and the infant Jesus in the temple, he also informed her that a sword would pierce her soul—an obvious allusion to the cross (Luke 2:35). It makes no sense to think that Mary's soul would be pierced because Jesus would get married and have a family.

In addition, Scripture indicates that Jesus died of His own accord (see John 10:18) because He had a specific goal to accomplish—that is, humankind's redemption. And Scripture indicates that He did in fact complete that mission. Recall what Jesus said on the cross in regard to His sacrificial death: "It is finished" (John 19:30). This proclamation from the Savior's lips is full of meaning. The Lord was doing more than announcing the termination of His physical life—that fact was self-evident. What was not known by those carrying out the brutal business at Calvary was that somehow, despite the sin they were committing, God through Christ had completed the final sacrifice for sin. The work long contemplated, long promised, long expected by prophets and saints was done (Isa. 53:3–5; Zech. 12:10).

Thus, Jesus' words on the cross do not constitute a moan of defeat or a sigh of patient resignation. Rather, His words were a triumphant recognition that He had now fully accomplished what He came into the world to do. The work of redemption was completed at the cross. Nothing further needed to be done. He had paid in full the price of our redemption (2 Cor. 5:21). And "after he had provided purification for sins, he sat down at the right hand of the Majesty in heaven" (Heb. 1:3), where He remains to this day.

Scripture is emphatic that Jesus completed the work of redemption at the cross with a single, once-for-all sacrifice. No more sacrifices—and no more work from a "second Messiah"—would occur. It was a "done deal," a finished transaction, at that point. Consider the book of Hebrews. God assures believers that "their sins and their lawless deeds I will remember no more" (Heb. 10:17). And "where these have been forgiven, there is no longer any sacrifice for sin" (10:18). Christ made a sacrificial offering "once for all when he offered himself" (7:27). He did so "not. . .by means of the blood of goats and calves; but he entered the Most Holy Place once for all by his own blood, having obtained eternal redemption" (9:12). So, by the death of Christ "we have been made holy through the sacrifice of the body of Jesus Christ once for all" (10:10).

Jesus Was Physically Resurrected from the Dead

Contrary to the Unification view, the Bible is clear that Jesus was *physically* resurrected from the dead. Jesus asserted to some Jews that He would be physically resurrected (John 2:19–21), and following His resurrection, He affirmed that His resurrection body was flesh and bones (Luke 24:39). The resurrected Christ ate physical food on four different occasions as a means of proving that He had a real physical body (Luke 24:30; 24:42–43; John 21:12–13; Acts 1:4). He also allowed people to touch his resurrected body (Matt. 28:9; Luke 24:39; John 20:17).

In view of the above, how are we to interpret the verse Moon cites to prove Jesus was not physically resurrected—John 20:19:

"On the evening of that first day of the week, when the disciples were together, with the doors locked for fear of the Jews, Jesus came and stood among them"? This is not difficult to answer. Jesus' resurrection body was essentially and continuously *material* (see Luke 24:34). The fact that Jesus could get into a room with closed doors in no way proves His body was immaterial. One must keep in mind that if He chose to do so, Jesus could have performed this same miracle *before* His death in His preresurrection material body, for as the Son of God, His miraculous powers were just as great before the resurrection. Moreover, even before His resurrection Jesus performed miracles with His physical body that transcended natural laws, such as walking on water (John 6:16–20). But walking on water did not prove His preresurrection body was immaterial. Otherwise, Peter's preresurrection walk on water would mean his body was immaterial (Matt. 14:29)! Further, although physical, the resurrection body is by its very nature a supernatural body (1 Cor. 15:44). Hence, it should be expected that it can do supernatural things, such as appearing in a room with closed doors.

Jesus Himself Is Coming Again

Moon's doctrine of the Second Coming is plagued with problems. To begin, there is no biblical basis for his chronology involving three sets of 2,000-year periods (that is, 2,000 years between Adam and Abraham during which God dealt with Israel, 2,000 years between Abraham and Jesus during which Israel was to prepare for the coming of the Messiah, and 2,000 years between Jesus and the alleged Lord of the Second Advent, during which Christians were to lay the foundation for the coming of the second Messiah). Biblical experts challenge Moon's assertion that Abraham was called by God *exactly* 2,000 years after Adam's creation.

Further, Moon's interpretation of Revelation 7:2–4 is absurd. As noted previously, he teaches that this passage prophesies the coming of the Lord of the Second Advent from a country in the East. Reverend Moon was born in Korea and is purportedly the fulfillment of this verse.

Such an interpretation is faulty at numerous points. First, the text is speaking of an angel, not a Messiah or Christ. Second, this angel is said to come from the *direction* of the east, not from a country in the East. Unificationists are reading something into this verse that simply is not there. Other references to "east" in the book of

Revelation always mean the *direction* of the east (see Rev. 16:12; 21:13). Third, even if it was granted that this verse was referring to a country, how can it legitimately be narrowed down to Korea? It seems odd that Korea would be singled out as the sole option when this country has far more Buddhists than Christians. Fourth, the Scriptures indicate that at the Second Coming, the *same* Jesus who ascended into heaven will physically come back again (Acts 1:9–11). There will not be a second Christ who comes from Korea. Finally, the one and only true Messiah is Jewish, not Korean (see Matt. 1).

WHEN THE LORD OF THE SECOND ADVENT DIES...

Reverend Sun Myung Moon, the alleged Lord of the Second Advent, is around 80 years old at this writing. Statistically speaking, the man will likely not live much longer. And when he dies, many expect that he will take the Unification movement down with him. How bitter it will be for those who have lived their lives in perpetual service to Moon.

10

THE BAHA'I FAITH

The Baha'i Faith has been popular with many people. Leo Tolstoy spoke glowingly of their "spirit of brotherhood."[1] Woodrow Wilson's daughter became a convert.[2] Rock music superstars Seals and Crofts in the 1970s often wove the Baha'i message into their songs and spoke of their faith at concerts.[3] Members of Crosby, Stills, Nash, and Young also promoted the faith.[4] Today there are some 17,148 Local Spiritual Assemblies of the Baha'i Faith in the world and 4,515 in the United States alone.[5]

Baha'is claim to have members in 235 countries, and their literature is presently translated into over 700 different languages.[6] Total world membership is estimated at 5 million. The Baha'i Faith is active on many college campuses, seeking to reach the under-25 age group.[7]

When asked what a "Baha'i" is, Abdul Baha (a Baha'i leader) succinctly replied, "To be a Baha'i simply means to love all the world; to love humanity and try to serve it; to work for universal peace and universal brotherhood."[8] Baha'ism upholds the unity of God, espouses a unity of His prophets, and inculcates the principle of the oneness and wholeness of the entire human race.[9] "If you imagine all people as the leaves on one tree, though we are of different size, shape, and hue, the same sun warms us and the same rain nourishes us. Imagine us all as drops in one ocean or waves of one sea. 'Your souls are as waves on the sea of the spirit; although each individual is a distinct wave, the ocean is one, all are united in God.'"[10]

These statements from Baha'i publications emphasize the unity that is at the very heart of the Baha'i Faith. All the people of the world are viewed as belonging to one large, loving family, having been created from a single origin. There is thus no room for anything that divides human beings, including religion. Baha'i Scripture teaches, "Love ye all religions and races with a love that is true and sincere and show that love through deeds."[11] The world's religions are viewed not as contradictory and competitive, but are considered to be successively updated versions of the same basic religious beliefs.[12] They are believed to be different only in inconsequential details.

> There can be no doubt whatever that the peoples of the world, of whatever race or religion, derive their inspiration from one heavenly source, and are the subjects of one God. The difference between the ordinances under which they abide should be attributed to the varying requirements and exigencies of the age in which they were revealed. All of them ... were ordained of God, and are a reflection of His Will and Purpose.[13]

In view of its emphasis on Unity, the Baha'i Faith stands for the promotion of gender, racial, and economic equality; the advancement of universal education; the establishment of harmony between science and religion; the maintenance of balance between nature and technology; and the development of a world federal system.[14] The foundational belief that undergirds these goals is the brotherhood of man.

Baha'i grew out of Islam.[15] Indeed, we might consider Baha'i to be somewhat of a despised stepchild of Islam. Muslims hate Baha'is because they believe Baha'is have committed apostasy by their doctrine that not Muhammad but Baha'u'llah is the greatest prophet.[16] *Time* magazine reports that Baha'is in Iran have suffered a reign of terror in the land where their faith was born, with many being executed, hundreds being imprisoned, and thousands losing their homes and possessions.[17]

The Baha'i Faith was born in 1844, when Mizra Ali Muhammad, known among Baha'is simply as "the Bab" (meaning "the Gate"), proclaimed that he was the greatest manifestation of God yet to appear in human history.[18] The Bab purported to be a direct descendent of the prophet Muhammad. Even as a child, he is said to have exhibited innate wisdom "that astonished both his teacher and other adults";[19] and as a young boy, he spent long periods in meditation and prayer. The Bab eventually placed himself in a greater role than Muhammad and claimed to have fulfilled the prophecies of the Scriptures of the various world religions.[20] The Bab—claimed by Baha'is to be a man of exceptional piety—had a relatively short ministry of less than six years, much of which he spent in a long series of imprisonments, scourgings, and various indignities.

The Bab spoke of yet another manifestation of God that would follow him, and he would be the greatest manifestation yet. The Bab thus played a role similar to that of John the Baptist regarding this coming manifestation. He was to be a herald and prepare for the coming of this great one.[21]

In 1850 persecution came to a head, and the Bab was led to be executed in Tabriz. According to Baha'i literature, "A regiment of 750 Armenian soldiers, arranged in three files of 250 each, opened fire in three successive volleys. So dense was the smoke raised by the gunpowder and dust that the sky was darkened and the entire yard obscured."[22] When the smoke cleared, the Bab was not to be seen, and his ropes had been rent into pieces. Baha'i accounts say the Bab was found back in his cell, giving final instructions to a follower. Shortly after this, the Bab calmly announced to his captors, "Now you may proceed to fulfill your intention."[23] Following his execution, a fierce black whirlwind reportedly swept into the city, reminiscent of the darkness that came across the land when Jesus was crucified.

In 1863 a follower of the Baha'i Faith in its early unfoldings, Mirza Husayn Ali, proclaimed that he was the great Prophet of whom the Bab had spoken and took the title "Baha'u'llah," meaning "The Glory of God."[24] His followers became known as the "Baha'is," or "Followers of the Glory." Even as a young person, Baha'u'llah was viewed as being special. Baha'i literature states,

> From childhood He was extremely kind and generous. He was a great lover of outdoor life, most of His time being spent in the garden or the fields. He had an extraordinary power of attraction, which was felt by all. People always crowded around Him. Ministers and people of the Court would surround Him, and the children also were devoted to Him. When He was only thirteen or fourteen years old He became renowned for His learning. He would converse on any subject and solve any problem presented to Him.[25]

Baha'u'llah claimed to be the second coming of Christ, the promised Spirit of truth of John 14:16, and a new revelation from God, following in the footsteps of such spiritual luminaries as Moses, Buddha, Jesus, and Muhammad. Not only is Baha'u'llah viewed as the second coming of Christ, he is viewed as the coming of Maitreya the Buddha (prophesied in Buddhist scripture), the new incarnation of Krishna for the Hindus, and a fulfillment of the "Day of God" spoken of in the Muslim Koran.[26] Allegedly, all the world's major religions have been pointing to the coming of Baha'u'llah. He alone is "the Promised One of all these Prophets—the Divine Manifestation in Whose era the reign of peace will actually be established."[27]

The writings of Baha'u'llah are revered as scripture in the Baha'i Faith.[28] They are looked upon as the Word of God and have been translated into hundreds of languages. Baha'u'llah's laws relate to prayer, marriage, divorce, fasting, inheritance, and a variety of other subjects. (I will draw from Baha'u'llah's writings later in the chapter when I discuss Baha'i theology.)

In late 1891—almost 30 years after he proclaimed himself the great "manifestation" of God of which the Bab spoke—Baha'u'llah told his followers his work was done and he wished to "depart from this world."[29] In 1892 he contracted a fever and died. Following his death, the leadership of the Baha'i Faith passed to his son, Abbas Effendi (1844–1921).[30] Abbas sought to rightly interpret his father's writings (about 200, including the most important *Kitab-i-Aqdas* [literally, "Book of Certitude"]) for the masses. Though he did not claim to be a manifestation of God like his father, he did assume exclusive authority to interpret his father's teachings and claimed infallibility for his interpretations. He eventually took the name of Abdul Baha (Servant of the Baha'i) and brought the Baha'i Faith to the United States by 1912.[31] He was often referred to as "the Master" among Baha'is.

Following Baha's death in 1921, the mantle of leadership for the Baha'i Faith passed to Baha's Oxford-educated grandson, Shoghi Effendi (the "Guardian of the Faith").[32] (A "Guardian" interprets Baha'i teachings for the masses and guides the Baha'i community.) Shoghi Effendi's writings have enjoyed substantial circulation. Under Effendi's leadership, the Baha'i Faith became a global religion and spread to some 35 countries. One of his unique contributions was his elaboration on the relationship of the Baha'i Faith to the other religions.[33]

Contrary to Baha'i law, Effendi did not leave a will stipulating a successor. He died in 1957, and six years later, the first Baha'i Universal House of Justice was elected. This nine-person board has since been the supreme legislative and executive governing body of Baha'i.[34] It promotes and applies the laws of Baha'u'llah. The establishment of this body was a landmark event for Baha'is inasmuch as its nine members were from four continents and represented three major religious backgrounds—Judaism, Christianity, and Islam—as well as several ethnic backgrounds. Thus this house symbolizes "the element which Baha'is regard as the essence of their faith: unity."[35]

Local groups of Baha'is are called "spiritual assemblies," and these meet in major cities all over the world. There are no ministers and no ecclesiastical organization. The local assemblies in each country are governed by a National Spiritual Assembly. Baha'i services are nondenominational and consist of readings and prayers from the scriptures of the world's various religions. There are no sermons or other attempts to cast these teachings in a mold of specifically Baha'i interpretation. Scripture selections are often set to music and sung by trained a cappella choirs.[36]

The famous Baha'i nonagon (nine-sided) temple is located in Wilmette, Illinois. The building's nine sides represent the world's nine living religions. The architecture of the building is a combination of synagogue, mosque, and cathedral, symbolizing the unity of all religions.

In keeping with their emphasis on unity, Baha'is ultimately seek for the world to become a single super-state with Baha'i as its religion. Shoghi Effendi portrayed this as a commonwealth in which all the peoples of the world would be subject to a single global authority. Nations would wave national sovereignty and relinquish rights to the Baha'i world super-state.[37] Then there would be cooperation, peace, and sharing among the peoples of the world. Baha'i literature proclaims,

> National rivalries, hatreds, and intrigues will cease, and racial animosity and prejudice will be replaced by racial amity, understanding and cooperation. The causes of religious strife will be permanently removed, economic barriers and restrictions will be completely abolished, and the inordinate distinction between classes will be obliterated. Destitution on the one hand, and gross accumulation of ownership on the other, will disappear.[38]

BAHA'I BELIEFS

Progressive Revelation Comes from Various "Manifestations" of God

The Baha'i Faith advocates continuing revelation. One might say that Baha'is have applied the evolutionary principle to revelation, for revelation is an evolving reality in the unfolding of the world's religions.[39] Baha'i leader Shoghi Effendi said, "The Fundamental principle which constitutes the bedrock of Baha'i belief [is] the principle that religious truth is not absolute but relative, that Divine Revelation is orderly, continuous, and progressive and not spasmodic or final."[40] Baha'i literature thus affirms,

> God has always watched over humankind. Throughout history, He has sent us blessed souls, perfect mirrors which manifest and reflect the glory and perfection of the heavenly kingdom. Each of these Messengers or Prophets renews the Word of God and lifts humanity to new heights of spiritual development. The spiritual foundation of all religions is the same—God. The laws and social teachings of each religion change depending on the time and place the Messenger appears.[41]

Throughout history there have purportedly been a number of key manifestations of God, though Baha'is do not agree as to how many.[42] Both the Bab and Baha'u'llah believed there were six previous manifestations of God: Adam, Noah, Abraham, Moses, Jesus, and Muhammad. Abdul Baha (Baha'u'llah's son) added to this mix both Zoroaster and the Buddha. Present-day Baha'is have taken Adam and Noah off the list and believe there are a total of between 9 and 12 manifestations: an unknown prophet, Krishna, Abraham, Hud, Salih, Moses, Zoroaster, Buddha, Christ, Muhammad, the Bab, and Baha'u'llah.[43]

These various manifestations of God are supposed to reveal progressively larger increments of truth. And because each of these manifestations communicate revelation from the same God, they do not contradict each other. According to Baha'u'llah, "Baha'is view religion as a progressive, evolutionary process which needs to be updated as humanity evolves mentally, socially, and spiritually. Every so often a new prophet is sent to humanity to update religion to the current needs of mankind."[44] There may appear to be some differences among the religions, but that is only because the needs of humankind at that time were different.[45] The core teachings of the religions are viewed as being the same. Further, though God is viewed as being unknowable (more on this below), Baha'is believe that one can learn about God and His attributes through each of these manifestations of God.[46] "Our knowledge of the Manifestation is, in fact, the closest we can come to the knowledge of God."[47]

It is important to understand that, strictly speaking, the Baha'is do not claim that theirs is a *new* religion; rather, it is a *renewal* of the true teachings of each religion, which, over time, have become corrupted. They do not wish to be seen as being merely one among many other religions. Their goal is to harmonize all religions under Baha'i teachings. Baha'u'llah once said of the various manifestations: "If thou wilt observe with discriminating eyes, thou wilt

"Light is good in whatsoever lamp it is burning! A rose is beautiful in whatsoever garden it may bloom! A star has the same radiance if it shines from the east or the west. Be free from prejudice so you will love the Sun of Truth from whatsoever point in the horizon it may arise!" (*Uniting the Human Family: The Baha'i Faith,* 11)

behold them all abiding in the same tabernacle, soaring in the same heaven, seated upon the same throne, uttering the same speech, and proclaiming the same faith."[48]

Baha'ism Claims to be Compatible with Christianity

Baha'is claim that the Baha'i Faith is compatible with Christianity.[49] And, indeed, when one reads Baha'i literature, there are places in which the Baha'i Faith sounds Christian. For example, Baha'is affirm belief in Jesus Christ. But as one continues reading Baha'i literature, it becomes clear that the teachings of the Bible are radically reinterpreted to fit Baha'i theology. For example, the references to the second coming of Christ in the Bible are said to be fulfilled in the coming of Baha'u'llah. He is the promised Messiah, and his teachings are said to supersede those of Jesus and the New Testament.

Baha'is realize that Christians continue to talk about the Second Coming in terms of the personal return of Jesus but think they are mistaken. The Christian Bible has purportedly been misunderstood for several millennia by Christian clergy, and the proper understanding comes through Baha'i, which is viewed as the *true* form of Christianity.

Baha'is often argue that just as the ancient Jews misunderstood the Old Testament Scriptures and therefore opposed Jesus, so Christians today have misunderstood Scripture and oppose Baha'u'llah. "Today, Christians make the same mistake the Jews made 2,000 years ago. They are so concerned with their own ideas of what Christ is that they cannot see the spirit of Christ in Baha'u'llah."[50]

God Is Unknowable

The Baha'i Faith is clearly monotheistic. In Baha'i thinking, whether one calls God Allah or Yahweh or Brahma does not matter, for all these names refer to the same being.[51] However, God is viewed as essentially unknowable and is therefore undefined by Baha'is.[52] "God is so far beyond his creation that, throughout all eternity, man will never be able to formulate any clear image of him or attain to anything but the most remote appreciation of his superior nature."[53] God is variously referred to as "the Most Exalted, the Inaccessible," "the Invisible and Unknowable Essence," "the All-Pervading, the Incorruptible," among other descriptive terms.[54] Such terms place

God so far beyond humans that one really has no idea what God is like.[55]

In Baha'i thought people can never really know this high and exalted God personally. Baha'u'llah once said that God "is and hath ever been veiled in ancient eternity of His Essence, and will remain in His Reality everlastingly hidden from the sight of men."[56] We are told, "His nature is limitless, infinite and all-powerful. It is therefore impossible for mortal men and women, with limited intellect and finite capacities, to directly comprehend or understand the Divine reality."[57] One cannot help but observe that such a nebulous concept of God makes it easier to subsume all religions under the umbrella of the Baha'i Faith.

The only way God can be known at all, as noted previously, is through the various manifestations of God. God's "attributes and qualities are completely immanent in the Manifestations."[58] Note, however, that these manifestations are not considered incarnations of God, for God cannot incarnate himself.

Baha'is also reject the Christian concept of the Trinity. Baha'u'llah described God as a "supreme singleness." The doctrine of the Trinity is viewed as an irrational concept. When asked about the Trinity, one Baha'i leader said, "If by the Trinity you mean the Christian concept that the three persons—Father, Son, and Holy Spirit—are all the one God, the answer is no. . . . We believe that God is one person in agreement with Judaism and Islam. We cannot accept the idea that God is both three and one and find this foreign to the Bible, which Christianity claims as its source. Not a few Jewish scholars are in complete agreement with us on this point, as is the Koran."[59]

Jesus Christ Was One of Many "Manifestations" of God

Baha'is view Jesus as merely one of many manifestations or prophets of the divine. "Jesus was the way, the truth, and the life for His time but certainly not for all time."[60] And since Baha'is deny that God can incarnate himself in anyone, they consider the incarnation of Jesus Christ a myth. Baha'is also deny the deity of Christ and his miracles, and they argue that Jesus never claimed to be God's only Son. They further deny that Jesus was God the creator.[61]

Baha'i theology views Jesus as being inferior to Baha'u'llah—and Baha'is believe there is biblical support for this view.[62] As noted previously, Baha'is believe that biblical references to the Second Coming are fulfilled in Baha'u'llah. They also argue that such standard messianic passages as Isaiah 9:2–7; 11:1–2; 40:1–5; and 53 are references to Baha'u'llah. Indeed, Baha'u'llah himself asserted, "I am the one whom the tongue of Isaiah hath extolled."[63] They further believe Baha'u'llah is "the Spirit of truth" of whom Jesus spoke in the Upper Room Discourse in John 14–16.[64]

Jesus' death is said to hold no eternal significance. His death may be an encouragement and an example of self-sacrifice, but Jesus did not bring about salvation by that death. Nor did he physically rise from the dead. Abdul Baha tells us the true significance of the resurrection: "The disciples were troubled and agitated after the martyrdom of Christ. . . . The Cause of Christ was like a lifeless body; and, when after three days the disciples became assured and steadfast . . . his religion found life, his teachings and his admonitions became evident and visible."[65] Thus, the resurrection basically refers to something that happened in the minds of the disciples.[66]

Humans Are Imperfect but Not Fallen

Baha'is deny the doctrine of original sin, though they concede that no one is "perfect." Though people err to some extent, they do not have intrinsically evil elements in their nature. Baha'is typically argue that the doctrine of original sin was not taught by the messengers of God but rather emerged in the sixteenth century.[67] "We accept the fact that no one is perfect, but by the practice of principles laid down by Baha'u'llah and by making every effort through prayer and personal sacrifice to live in accord with the character of the divine being revealed in him, we can arrive at eventual salvation as you like to term it."[68]

Baha'is believe people "learn" sin. People can accordingly unlearn sin and keep the law and return to a state of perfection. Through enlightenment one can develop goodness and eliminate evil. As long as proper education and ethical teachings are available, humanity can fix all its problems. Baha'i scripture, written by Baha'u'llah, sets forth the ethical system by which people are expected to live.[69]

Baha'i Is a Religion of the Law

Baha'is reject the apostle Paul's doctrine of justification by faith alone and instead argue that salvation depends on personal merit and keeping the law. Baha'i is very much a religion of the law. The only salvation in any age, Baha'is believe, is to "turn again towards God, to accept his Manifestation for that day, and to follow his teachings."[70] "Only in striving to fulfill the law does [one] come into the right relationship with God."[71] One must not only render external obedience to the law, but one must keep the law inwardly as well. In view of this emphasis on the law, the Baha'i Faith teaches that no person can be sure that he or she is in a saved state.

Baha'is agree that a person must be "born again," but they believe Christians have misunderstood what Jesus meant by this term. Baha'u'llah said that to be "born again" simply refers to believing in the manifestations of God. When one comes to know God because of revelation communicated through one of his messengers, one is thereby born again.

Heaven and Hell Are Not Literal Places

Baha'is do not believe heaven and hell are literal places. Rather, they say heaven and hell are states of being. "Heaven is knowing about God and doing what he wants. Hell is not knowing about God or not doing what he wants. A person who is happy and is obeying God is in heaven. A person is in hell when he dislikes others or himself, or is always unhappy."[72] We also read, "In the final analysis, heaven can be seen partly as a state of nearness to God; hell is a state of remoteness from God. Each state follows as a natural consequence of individual efforts, or the lack thereof, to develop spiritually."[73] Hence, we can experience our own heaven or hell while yet on earth. "Heaven is harmony with God's will and. . . . Hell is the want of such harmony."[74]

In regard to the afterlife, Baha'is believe that one can attain personal immortality as a result of engaging in good works. But what that afterlife involves is not clearly defined. Baha'i literature says that "the exact nature of the afterlife remains a mystery."[75] As Baha'u'llah put it, "the nature of the soul after death can never be described."[76] Yet we do find hints of Islam in that Baha'is expect to one day be in paradise: "We do believe in the paradise of God, which will be the abode of the righteous. . . ."[77] "Know thou of a truth that the soul, after its separation from the body, will continue to progress until it attainest the presence of God."[78]

CHALLENGING BAHA'I BELIEFS

Baha'i Is a Religion

The claim that the Baha'i Faith is not a religion, but is rather a uniting factor among religions, is a hollow one. The reality is that final and ultimate truth is found in the teachings of Baha'u'llah (whose writings are considered "scripture")—and this prophet's teachings set forth a definite view of God, God's messengers, man's problem, the means of attaining a right relationship with God, the afterlife, and other elements typical of religions, such as rituals and services. The Baha'i Faith is just as much a religion as Christianity, Islam, or Hinduism.

The Attempt to Unite the World Religions Is Futile

The Baha'i goal of unifying world religions under one umbrella (that is, the Baha'i Faith) is futile in view of the fact that each religion conflicts with every other religion on key doctrines. I noted earlier in the book how each of the world religions conflict on the fundamental doctrine of God (see page 147). I will not repeat that earlier material, but I do want to draw attention to Dr. Francis Beckwith's point that "though Shoghi Effendi has said that the manifestations disagree on 'nonessential aspects of their doctrine,' it would stretch credulity to the limit to suppose that the nature of

CONTRASTING THE BAHA'I FAITH AND CHRISTIANITY		
	Baha'i View	**Christian View**
Scripture	Writings of Baha'u'llah	Bible alone
God	Unknowable	Knowable and personal
Jesus	Manifestation of God	Absolute deity
Jesus' death	No salvific value	Atoned for sins of man
Second Coming	Baha'u'llah	Jesus Himself
Spirit of Truth (John 14:16)	Baha'u'llah	The Holy Spirit
World religions	Truth in all	Only Christianity true
Sin	Man imperfect, not fallen	Man fallen in sin
Salvation	Keep Baha'i law	Trust in Christ alone

God is one of these nonessential aspects. God cannot be impersonal, personal, transcendent, polytheistic, pantheistic, monotheistic, able to beget, not able to beget, relevant, and irrelevant all at the same time."[79]

One can also observe that the Baha'i Faith denies fundamental doctrines held by each major world religion. For example, while religions such as Hinduism and Buddhism teach reincarnation, the Baha'i Faith denies this doctrine. While Christianity teaches that Jesus is absolute deity, the Baha'i Faith calls him a mere manifestation of God. While Islam teaches that Muhammad is the final and greatest prophet, the Baha'i Faith teaches that Baha'u'llah is the greatest prophet. I could mention many other contradictions, but these are sufficient to show the folly of the Baha'i attempt to unify the religions under one umbrella.

Baha'i Makes Hollow Claims of Tolerance

Baha'is profess respect for all the religions of the world and therefore view themselves as tolerant. Yet the very act of setting themselves up as the unifying factor of the different religions—along with the claim that Baha'u'llah is the greatest of all the prophets—must ultimately lead them to believe they are right and others are wrong. Furthermore, the various religions are forced into conformity with Baha'i through reinterpretation of their teachings. For example, Baha'is say Christian clergy have misunderstood the Bible from the beginning and only Baha'i offers the correct interpretation. Christianity is thus *recreated* in the image of Baha'i, as are other religions. In the end, Baha'is are only "tolerant" of fictional caricatures of the world religions.

The Bible Does Not Speak of Baha'u'llah

Contrary to Baha'i claims, the Bible never speaks of Baha'u'llah, except indirectly when Jesus and the apostles warned of the coming of false prophets and false Christs (Matt. 7:15–16; 2 Cor. 11:13–15). It is impossible that the messianic references cited by Baha'is refer to Baha'u'llah, because, among other things, Baha'u'llah was of Iranian descent, whereas the Messiah was to be Jewish (see Matt. 1; cf. Gen. 12:1–3; 2 Sam. 7:12–13). Moreover, the New Testament repeatedly (as in Matt. 1:1; 3:16; 8:17; Luke 1:31; Rev. 5:5) cites the fulfillment, in the person of Jesus, of Isaiah's prophecies (see, for example, Isa. 7:14; 9:6–7; 11:1–2; 40:1–5; 53:4–5). It is clear, then, that Baha'is are practicing *eisogesis*—that is, they are reading a meaning into the text of Scripture that is not there.

As to the Second Coming, Scripture indicates that the *very same* Jesus who ascended into heaven will one day personally return (Acts 1:9–11). Scripture also prophesies a number of dramatic and highly visible signs that will accompany the Second Coming (sun darkened, stars falling from the sky, heavenly bodies shaken; Matt. 24:29), and none of these were present when Baha'u'llah arrived on the scene. Scripture further indicates that at the Second Coming the Messiah will come to Jerusalem (his feet will physically touch the Mount of Olives; Zech. 14:4), but Baha'u'llah never did this.

In addition, Jesus was not referring to Baha'u'llah in John 16:12–13 when He said to the disciples, "I have much more to say to you, more than you can now bear. But when he, the Spirit of truth, comes, he will guide you into all truth. He will not speak on his own; he will speak only what he hears, and he will tell you what is yet to come." An examination of the context of John 14–16 shows how unfounded the Baha'i interpretation is. First, Jesus clearly identifies the Spirit of truth as being the Holy Spirit (John 14:16–17, 26). And Jesus said almost 2,000 years ago that His promise of the Holy Spirit would be fulfilled "in a few days" (Acts 1:5), not in the 1800s when Baha'u'llah was born. The fulfillment came in Acts 2 on the Day of Pentecost. Moreover, Jesus said one function of the Holy Spirit would be to make known *Jesus'* teaching, not replace His teachings with those of another prophet (John 16:14). And finally, Jesus said the Holy Spirit will "be with you forever" (John 14:16). Baha'u'llah lived a mere 75 years and died in 1892. This hardly constitutes "forever."

The Baha'i Jesus Is a Counterfeit Jesus

In 2 Corinthians 11:4 the apostle Paul spoke of those who would believe in "another Jesus," a Jesus *other than* the Jesus of the Bible. The Baha'i rendition of Jesus clearly falls into this category.

Jesus Did Claim to Be God's Unique Son.

Contrary to Baha'i claims, Jesus referred to Himself as God's "one and only Son" (also translated "only-begotten son") in John 3:16. The words "only begotten" in the Greek carry the idea of "unique" or "one of a kind." According to Reformed scholar Benjamin Warfield, "The adjective 'only begotten' conveys the idea, not of derivation and subordination, but of uniqueness and consubstantiality: Jesus is all that God is, and He alone is this."[80] Jesus is the "Son of God," which means He has the same nature as the Father—a *divine* nature. For this reason, whenever Christ claimed to be the Son of God in the New Testament, His Jewish critics tried to stone Him because they correctly understood Him as claiming to be God and thought He was guilty of committing blasphemy (see John 5:18).

Jesus Was God the Creator.

Contrary to Baha'i claims, Jesus is God the creator. Of course, the Old Testament revealed that only God Almighty is the creator. God Himself asserted in Isaiah 44:24, "I, the LORD [Yahweh], am the *maker of all things,* stretching out the heavens *by Myself,* and spreading out the earth *all alone*" (NASB, emphasis added). Against this backdrop, it is highly significant that the New Testament says that Christ is the agent of creation: "For by him all things were created: things in heaven and on earth, visible and invisible, whether thrones or powers or rulers or authorities; all things were created by him and for him" (Col. 1:16). The little phrase, "all things," means that Christ created *the whole universe of things.* Notice that in the space of five verses in Colossians 1 (vv. 16–20), the apostle Paul mentions "all creation," "all things," and "everything"—thereby indicating that Christ is supreme over all. "Every form of matter and life owes its origin to the Son of God, no matter in what sphere it may be found, or with what qualities it may be invested. . . . Christ's creative work was no local or limited operation; it was not bounded by this little orb [earth]."[81] Everything—whether simple or complex, visible or invisible, heavenly or earthly, immanent or transcendent—is the product of Christ.

Other passages that speak of Christ as the Creator, including John 1:3; Hebrews 1:2; 1:10; and Revelation 3:14, reveal that the Son's role as Creator is at the very heart of New Testament revelation. And Christ's role in creation reveals His divine nature. As apologist Norman Geisler wrote, "There is no doubt that the Old Testament presents God alone as Creator of the universe (Gen. 1, Isa. 40, Ps. 8). And when the disciples of Christ declare Jesus to be the one through whom all things were created, the conclusion that they were thereby attributing deity to him is unavoidable."[82]

Jesus Was an Incarnation of God.

Contrary to Baha'i claims, Jesus *was* an incarnation of God (see Isa. 7:14; John 1:1, 14, 18; Heb. 10:1–10; Phil. 2:5–11). Scripture says that to deny either the undiminished deity or the perfect humanity of Christ in the incarnation is to put oneself outside the pale of orthodoxy (see 1 John 4:2–3). The apostle Paul affirmed that "in Christ all the fullness of the Deity lives in bodily form" (Col. 2:9). In the incarnation, Jesus was 100 percent God and 100 percent man. The incarnate Christ was thus truly Immanuel—"God with us" (Matt. 1:23).

Jesus Was the Greatest Revelation of God.

Jesus was the single greatest revelation of God precisely because He was 100 percent God and 100 percent man. We read, "No one has ever seen God, but God the One and Only [Jesus], who is at the Father's side, has made him known" (John 1:18). That is why Jesus could say, "When [a person] looks at me, he sees the one who sent me" (John 12:45, insert added), and "Whoever accepts me accepts the one who sent me" (13:20).

Jesus was a perfect revelation of God in many ways. God's awesome power was revealed in Jesus (John 3:2) as was God's incredible wisdom (1 Cor. 1:24). God's boundless love was revealed and demonstrated by Jesus (1 John 3:16), and so was God's unfathomable grace (2 Thess. 1:12). Certainly Jesus set forth revelation in the words He spoke to the masses. Jesus even affirmed that while heaven and earth will pass away, His words will never pass away (see Matt. 24:35).

It is highly revealing that, as one reads the New Testament, Jesus' teachings are always presented as being ultimate and final. He unflinchingly placed His teachings above those of Moses and the prophets—and in a Jewish culture at that!

Jesus always spoke in His own authority. He never said, "Here is what the LORD says . . ." as did the prophets; He always said, "*I tell you the truth. . . .*" He never retracted anything He said, never guessed or spoke with uncertainty, never made revisions, never contradicted Himself, and never apologized for what He said.

Understandably, the teachings of Jesus always had a profound effect on people. His listeners always seemed to surmise that these were not the words of an ordinary man. When He taught in Capernaum on the Sabbath, the people "were amazed at his teaching" (Luke 4:32). After the Sermon on the Mount, "the crowds were amazed at his teaching, because he taught as one who had authority, and not as their teachers of the law" (Matt. 7:28–29). When some Jewish leaders asked the temple guards why they had not arrested Jesus when He spoke, they responded, "No one ever spoke the way this man does" (John 7:46).

One cannot read the Gospels long before recognizing that Jesus regarded Himself and His message as inseparable. The reason Jesus' teachings had ultimate authority was that He was and is God. *Jesus' words are the very words of God!* The words of Baha'u'llah, by contrast, are the words of a mere man.

The Bible Exalts Jesus from Beginning to End.

Jesus, not Baha'u'llah, is exalted throughout the Christian Bible. Not only is there no indication in Scripture that a greater prophet than Jesus would come, but Scripture is emphatically clear that Christ has been exalted to the highest level. Philippians 2:9–11, for example, tells us that Christ was given a name above every name, "that at the name of Jesus every knee should bow, in heaven and on earth and under the earth, and every tongue confess that Jesus Christ is Lord." It is significant that the apostle Paul in this verse was alluding to Isaiah 45:22–24: "I am God, and there is no other. By myself I have sworn, my mouth has uttered in all integrity a word that will not be revoked: Before me every knee will bow; by me every tongue will swear." Paul was drawing on his vast knowledge of the Old Testament to make the point that what is true of Yahweh (in His exaltation) is also true of Christ (in His exaltation). *Jesus is the exalted one.*

In keeping with this, the Bible indicates that the Father raised Jesus from the dead "and seated him at his right hand in the heavenly realms, far above all rule and authority, power and dominion, and every title that can be given, not only in the present age but also in the one to come" (Eph. 1:19–21). Notice that Jesus is supreme now and in the age to come. Jesus is on the center stage of glory—both now and forever more!

Dr. William Miller Has Thoroughly Debunked the Baha'i Faith

Dr. William Miller has written perhaps the greatest single polemic against the Baha'i Faith—*The Baha'i Faith: Its History and Teachings* (1974). It is far beyond the scope of this chapter to do justice to the many significant points made in this book. In a nutshell, however, Miller convincingly demonstrates that the founder of Baha'i, the Bab, believed (as of 1844) that he would be the only manifestation of God for at least the next 1,500 years. Yet Baha'u'llah soon emerged (by 1863) as the next manifestation. At least one of these manifestations was therefore wrong. If indeed another manifestation of God was not to appear for another 1,500 or so years, one can only conclude that Baha'u'llah must have been an impostor.[83] One must also wonder how the needs of humanity changed so much between the death of the Bab and Baha'u'llah's time that a new revelation from God was required.[84] It does not make sense.

Further, Miller points out, one must raise the question as to whether Baha'u'llah can legitimately be considered a contemporary manifestation of God for our time. After all, Baha'u'llah died in 1892, before automobiles, atom bombs and other weapons of mass destruction, and all the other technological advances of our day were invented. Yet Baha'u'llah said there will not be another "manifestation" until A.D. 2866.[85] So that the point is not lost, I will reiterate that between the time of the Bab and Baha'u'llah very little had changed in the world, yet a new revelation from God was given in the person of Baha'u'llah. Since Baha'u'llah's time, there have been unprecedented changes on the world scene, taking place at an exponential pace, yet there will be no new revelation until A.D. 2866. Miller is right to say that this stretches all credulity.

Finally, Miller capably demonstrates moral failure on the part of Baha'i's founders, documents excessive errors made by "infallible" Baha'i leaders, proves there have been deliberate changes and omissions in the official Baha'i translation of its own Scriptures, and documents how Shoghi Effendi clearly contradicts the teachings of Baha'u'llah.[86] How can Baha'i hope to unify the world religions when there is a lack of harmony even among Baha'i's leaders?

11

UNITARIAN UNIVERSALISM

Today there are over 1,000 Unitarian Universalist congregations around the world,[1] with over 210,000 registered members—mostly in the United States.[2] The actual number of people affiliated with Unitarian Universalism (unregistered) may be far larger, with as many as half a million Americans considering themselves part of the group.[3] Unitarian Universalism is presently growing at a rate of 4 percent annually, partially due to the group's growing interest in evangelism as a way to blunt the progress of the "religious right."[4]

While these numbers may not seem overly impressive, Dr. Alan Gomes, who has done considerable research on Unitarian Universalism, points out that this group has exerted an influence in this country that extends beyond its numbers. Indeed, Gomes notes that "anyone who has been told that truth is relative; that 'tolerance' of 'alternative lifestyles' and beliefs—including homosexuality, radical feminism, and abortion on demand—is the highest virtue; that reason, conscience, and experience are the ultimate guides to truth; and that the Bible is a myth and Jesus Christ is but one of many inspirational (but fallible) teachers, has encountered cherished Unitarian Universalist dogmas."[5]

Certainly Unitarian Universalism has influenced many prestigious individuals. Past Unitarian Universalists include five U.S. presidents (John Adams, Thomas Jefferson, John Quincy Adams, Millard Fillmore, and William Taft); famous literary figures such as Henry Wadsworth Longfellow, Ralph Waldo Emerson, Henry David Thoreau, and Charles Dickens; eight U.S. Supreme Court justices; famous women like Florence Nightingale and Susan B. Anthony; and various other famous people like Charles Darwin, Alexander Graham Bell, and Paul Revere. Unitarian Universalist members comprise approximately 25 percent of those listed in the American Hall of Fame.[6]

Today Unitarian Universalists gather under the umbrella of the Unitarian Universalist Association (UUA). The UUA has been defined as "an association of fellowships, churches, or societies that subscribe to certain broad principles and purposes and affiliate themselves organizationally with the UUA denomination, headquartered in Boston, Massachusetts."[7] This Association is the result of a 1961 merger that took place between the American Unitarian Association (incorporated 1825) and the Universalist Church of America (incorporated 1793).[8]

The Unitarians are so named because they deny the doctrine of the Trinity.[9] This movement rose to prominence during the sixteenth-century Reformation and spread from Europe to England and then on to America.

The Universalists are so named because they believe in the salvation of all human beings.[10] They strongly oppose the doctrine of hell and eternal punishment, finding such concepts incompatible with a loving God. "Universalism's principal theological contribution lies in striking hell from the theological menu."[11] Universalist teaching spread from England to America in the eighteenth century.

Both Universalism and Unitarianism gained popularity among intellectuals in America in the eighteenth century as the Age of

Reason (the Enlightenment) gained ground.[12] People in both religions rejected the Calvinistic ideas of predestination, total depravity, and eternal damnation.[13] They were convinced that people were not born in a state of corruption but rather had the potential for good or evil, and also that in the end all people will be saved instead of just those God has "elected" to salvation. A loving God would never send anyone to hell to suffer for all eternity.

It is beyond the scope of this chapter to give a detailed history of each individual who contributed to the emergence of Unitarian Universalism. However, it is critical to briefly note at least several of the more influential thinkers instrumental in the development of the movement in continental Europe, England, and America. (Those who wish a more detailed treatment are urged to consult other available resources.)[14]

Continental Europe

Spanish-born Arian Michael Servetus (1511–53) is considered the founder of Unitarianism in continental Europe. Servetus denied Jesus was the Son of God, and he wrote a strong polemic against the doctrine of the Trinity entitled *On the Errors of the Trinity in Seven Books* (1531). In this book he asserted, "Your Trinity is the product of subtlety and madness. The Gospel knows nothing of it."[15] This book brought swift condemnation from religious authorities—so much so that he had to flee to France, change his name, and live there in exile. He thus escaped an inquisition for several decades, only to be later executed for his beliefs by Reformer John Calvin in 1553—something that gave him martyr-like status among his followers.[16]

Another individual who contributed to the growth of Unitarianism in continental Europe was Faustus Socinus (1539–1604). Socinus immigrated to Poland "in quest of religious liberty"[17] and was a major force in Poland in standing against the Trinity and the deity of Christ, both in writing and oral debate.[18] Socinus believed the Scriptures should be interpreted rationally. He believed God was one essence and this essence contained one person—the Father. He also believed, however, that Jesus, because of his perfect obedience during life, was rewarded with what might be called a delegated divinity following his resurrection.

England

John Biddle (1615–62), an Oxford graduate, is considered the Father of English Unitarianism.[19] To refute the doctrine of the Trinity logically and biblically, he wrote *A Confession of Faith Touching the Holy Trinity According to the Scripture.* He also argued that the doctrine of the deity of Christ was repugnant to both sound reason and Holy Scripture. In arguing for this viewpoint, he often cited verses concerning the Incarnate Christ (Jesus as a man) and His dependence on the Father (for example, John 14:9–14).[20] Biddle was eventually sent into exile for his heretical beliefs and died in prison in 1662.[21]

Theophilus Lindsey (1723–1808) is another who promoted the cause of Unitarianism in England. Because of his Unitarian views, he objected to being required to worship Christ and the Holy Spirit. At one point he circulated a petition that received 250 signatures asking that clergymen be relieved from having to subscribe to the Thirty-Nine Articles (which required belief in the Trinity). The English Parliament refused to receive the document, and it was following this (in 1773) that Lindsey founded a church in London— the Essex Street Chapel—which was used as a platform to spread Unitarianism.

America

Unitarianism did not make inroads into Christian churches in America until the late eighteenth century, having been outlawed in the colonies during the seventeenth century. The Congregational churches were especially affected by the movement, with approximately 125 churches eventually swinging over to the Unitarian side.[22]

A number of individuals were responsible for the growth of Unitarianism in America. Jonathan Mayhew (1720–66), for example, openly preached against the Trinity and wrote about the strict unity of God. Joseph Priestley (1733–1804)—eminent chemist and discoverer of oxygen—was a distinguished and influential Unitarian who denied both the Virgin Birth and Christ's sinlessness. He established a Unitarian church in Northumberland, Pennsylvania, in 1794 and one in Philadelphia in 1796.

William Ellery Channing (1780–1842) was perhaps one of the most influential American Unitarians. He became a leader in the movement "away from a harsh and dogmatic Calvinism and toward a more liberal and liberating theology. . . . He preached not retribution, but the love of God. . . . He spoke of Jesus less as the second person of a metaphysical trinity than as a human example of human life lived to the fullness of its spiritual capacity."[23]

Channing eventually became known as an "apostle of Unitarianism," holding that Christ was more than a man but less than God.[24] He denied that Christ in the incarnation had both a human and a divine nature, arguing instead for a "unity" in Christ's person. In his famous sermon "Unitarian Christianity," he argued biblically against the Trinity and sought to demonstrate the irrationality of the idea.[25] Published and reprinted seven times as a popular pamphlet, the sermon affirmed the Unitarian belief that the ultimate authority is not the voice of the past as revealed in Scripture, but the "living voice" of experience and reason.[26] His commitment to reason also led to a commitment to universalism, for reason dictates that a loving God could never damn one eternally to hell.

Also paving the way for Unitarianism was the Transcendentalism of the nineteenth century. Ralph Waldo Emerson (1803–82) denied the ultimate authority of the Bible and elevated intuition over the senses as the means of finding "truth."[27] Man's inner intuition—not the external Word of God, and not the historic traditions of the church—became the final authority. Emerson placed heavy emphasis on self-reliance in all things. The way was thus opened for Unitarian Universalists to develop their own unique belief system.[28]

Eventually the America Unitarian Association was founded in 1825 by a dozen graduates of Harvard Divinity School.[29] At this early juncture, however, the association seems to have received a less than enthusiastic response. Some time later, in 1867, the more radical Unitarians formed the Free Religious Association, emphasizing complete freedom of beliefs.

In the early 1900s humanism emerged among a number of Unitarians.[30] This school of thought, which emphasized the sufficiency of human beings to solve their own problems rather than having to seek outside divine assistance, caused no small measure of friction with the theist Unitarians (like Channing). But humanism would not go away. It is significant that about half the signers of the 1933 Humanist Manifesto I were Unitarians.[31] These Unitarian Universalists placed a heavy premium on science and believed religion must be reasonable to scientific minds. Eventually, the humanists and the theists within Unitarianism learned to get along, emphasizing freedom of thought.

Universalism also flourished in America during the eighteenth and nineteenth centuries. Among the early movers and shakers responsible for the growth of Universalism were John Murray (1741–1815), who founded the first Universalist Church in America (the Independent Christian Church), and Hosea Ballou (1771–1852), who became pastor of the Second Universalist Church in Boston.[32] Ballou denied such doctrines as original sin, miracles, the Trinity (he was Unitarian),[33] and eternal punishment by the fires of hell. Murray and Ballou emphasized God's infinite love, man's potential good, and salvation for all. Contrary to Calvinism, which spoke of the "elect," these men emphasized that all human beings were elect in God's eyes. Ballou was even "deterministic" about his universalistic beliefs, arguing that the Father was determined that all human beings be saved.[34]

Unitarianism and Universalism thus developed along parallel tracks in America. Then in 1961, because both groups took similar approaches and had many similar beliefs, they merged under a single denominational umbrella, the Unitarian Universalist Association.

Today Unitarian Universalist ministers are trained at one of three principle universities: Harvard University, Meadville-Lombard (affiliated with the University of Chicago), and Starr King School of the Ministry in California. The UUA is well positioned for future growth.

UNITARIAN UNIVERSALIST BELIEFS

The UUA Embraces a Diversity of Beliefs

Instead of basing their beliefs on some holy book with absolute authority, Unitarian Universalists base their beliefs on their own experiences. "Ours is a faith whose authority is grounded in contemporary experience, not ancient revelation."[35] Some within the UUA are led by their experience to liberal Christianity, some to humanism, some to earth-centered spiritualities, and some to New Age spiritualities.[36]

Unitarian Universalists are not committed to any one religious system of thought. They believe one should feel free to follow whatever religious path one desires. And whatever path one chooses, it is important not to infringe on the path someone else has taken. Every person has the right to decide for himself or herself what to believe. "We believe in the authority of reason and conscience. The ultimate arbiter in religion is not a church, a document, or an official, but the personal choice and decision of the individual."[37]

Unitarian Universalism has moved progressively further away from Christianity and toward acceptance of a variety of other religious persuasions. As one Unitarian Universalist put it, "The UUA is unique in the annals of church history—it being perhaps the only branch of the Body of Christ ever to vote itself out of Christendom and declare itself no longer a Christian denomination, but an interfaith Association."[38] In view of this, Unitarian Universalists are noncreedal and nondoctrinal in the sense that no one is required to subscribe to a doctrinal creed of any type.[39] They reject creeds because creeds imply "that religious beliefs are fixed and uniform, rather than subject to growth through a person's lifetime, and through history itself."[40]

Accordingly, Unitarian Universalists abhor religious exclusivism and believe religious tolerance is a virtue.[41] Within their church they feel free to express their individual religious opinions without fear of censure or reprisal. They claim to have a universal viewpoint that "excludes all exclusiveness."[42] In their thinking, there is no such thing as absolute truth. Rather, they embrace and tolerate many different religious perspectives. One Unitarian Universalist publication stated, "Unitarian Universalists believe that no religion—including their own—has exclusive possession of the truth. All ought to be honored and respected for the truth in them. The following of almost any religion can help a dedicated individual find a better and more meaningful life."[43]

Within Unitarian Universalism it would not be uncommon to encounter liberal Christians, neopagans (who worship the Goddess), atheists, agnostics, humanists, New Age pantheists, or liberal Jews, among many others.[44] In fact, a 1997 poll of 10,000 Unitarian Universalists reveals the following breakdown: 46.1 percent humanist, 19 percent earth/nature-centered, 13 percent theist, 9.5 percent Christian (liberal), 6.2 percent mystic, 3.6 percent Buddhist, and less than 1 percent Muslim and Hindu.[45]

"The opposite of freedom is authoritarianism. I reject it. I affirm freedom's synonym, openness. The opposite of reason is narrow literalism. I reject it. I affirm reason's equivalent, sensible applicability to life's here and now. The opposite of tolerance is exclusivity. That, too, I reject. I affirm tolerance's synonym, inclusiveness" (George Beach, *Catechism with an Open Mind*, 69).

The important thing for Unitarian Universalists is that we are to act on the ethics of whatever religious persuasion we hold to. Ethical living is viewed as the supreme witness of all religion.[46] So long as one does that, it does not matter what religion one subscribes to.

Although Unitarian Universalists are open to a wide variety of religious viewpoints, it is important to note that they do take a stand against certain beliefs that violate ethical living. People are not free to believe absolutely anything or to believe in nothing at all. "Clearly, one could never advocate racism or genocide, for example, and still in any meaningful sense call oneself a Unitarian Universalist."[47] One cannot believe whatever one wants if it means "disregarding the ethical consequences of those beliefs."[48]

Because Unitarian Universalists are free to view things differently, the rest of the doctrines I will discuss below are generalizations that are true of many Unitarian Universalists but not necessarily all.

The Bible Is One Among Many Religious Books

Unitarian Universalists have little respect for the Christian Bible. While some would say there are some inspiring truths in it, most say it is a fallible human book. It is viewed as one among many other religious books—right alongside the Hindu Vedas and the Muslim Koran.[49] "We regard the Bible as one of many important religious texts but do not consider it unique or exclusive in any way."[50] The Bible "is not a central document in our religion."[51]

Drawing on liberal higher criticism, Unitarian Universalists believe there are textual errors in the "very imperfect" Bible so that we cannot trust that it accurately records the actual words of Jesus. The Jesus of the four Gospels is said to be more a reflection of the theological biases of the gospel writers (who were fallible and ignorant men) than of historical reality. In addition, the Bible is said to contain primitive ideas about God that are not relevant to modern scientific man.[52] Some Unitarian Universalists say there are ethical barbarisms in the Bible, while others simply say that the ethical teachings in the Bible are too strict (for example, dealing with divorce or homosexuality).[53]

In any case, Unitarian Universalists are unanimous that the Bible should not be interpreted in a literal fashion.[54] After all, they say, this is a human book that contains inspiring myths, and no book of myths should be taken literally.

Instead of the Bible being in the place of authority, human reason, conscience, and personal experience are elevated to the position of authority in regard to all religious truth claims. This means the Bible and all other religious books must be judged according to human reason. Thus, teachings such as miracles and a belief in hell where people suffer for all eternity are rejected because they do not make sense to human reason.

"God" Can Be Interpreted Many Ways

In keeping with their religious diversity, Unitarian Universalists have a variety of viewpoints regarding the doctrine of God.[55] "We do not have a defined doctrine of God. Members are free to develop individual concepts of God that are meaningful to them. They are also free to reject the term and concept altogether."[56] Thus, while some accept a "God" (whether a personal God, the Mother Goddess, or the idea that all is God), many others simply reject the idea. One can believe anything or nothing about God. One can be an atheist, pantheist, polytheist, agnostic, deist, theist, or anything else. Some Unitarian Universalists interpret God as a higher power or "divine spark" within themselves. Others view "God" as the ordering principle in nature (the "sustaining order of the universe"). Still others hold to a view of God akin to that of process theology (involving a changeable and evolving God). And still others hold to a neopagan understanding of God as the Mother Earth or Goddess.

In most UUA church services, there is little if any mention of a deity. Indeed, most Unitarian Universalists do not believe in any kind of supernatural being that miraculously intervenes in the lives of creatures. "We do not believe in miracles in any supernatural way since our ideas of God generally do not include a deity who has the ability to alter the workings of the natural world."[57]

All Unitarian Universalists reject the biblical concept of a triune God.[58] William Ellery Channing, an early Unitarian, said, "We are astonished that any man can read the New Testament, and avoid the conviction that the Father alone is God."[59]

Jesus Was a Great Moral Teacher

In Unitarian Universalist theology, Jesus is typically respected as a moral teacher and influence but is not revered as God. He is viewed as "one of a number of great moral and ethical teachers who have lived on earth."[60] Unitarian Universalists "admire and respect the way he lived, the power of his love, the force of his example, and his values."[61] He is respected as "one sent from God to show us how to live better lives."[62] In the Unitarian Universalist book *A Chosen Faith*, we read, "Most of us would agree that the important thing about Jesus is not his supposed miraculous birth or the claim that he was resurrected from death, but rather how he lived. The power of his love, the penetrating simplicity of his teachings, and the force of his example of service on behalf of the disenfranchised and downtrodden are what is crucial."[63]

Jesus is thus viewed not as divine in any special sense but rather as a human being who attained significant spiritual heights. He was really no different from us. Indeed, just as Jesus had a divine spark within him, so we today have a divine spark within us. What Jesus did, *all* of us can do. If Jesus was different at all, it was a difference involving degree only. But others can nevertheless attain the same spiritual heights that he did.

Some Unitarian Universalists describe Jesus in New Age terms. They make reference to "the Christ" as a divine principle that Jesus embodied, just as we today can embody the Christ. Like Jesus, all people can attain a Christ consciousness.[64]

Appealing to human reason, Unitarian Universalists reject Christ's miracles, his virgin birth, and his resurrection from the dead as mythological.[65] Such things, we are told, have long been disproved by science. The miracle stories recorded in the four Gospels essentially involved embellishments on the part of the biased gospel writers.[66]

Unitarian Universalists are "universal" in their emphasis that Jesus did not die for the sins of humankind. "Because UUs have long rejected the idea of Original Sin, the belief that Jesus atoned for the sins of the world by his death has little relevance for us."[67] "No Savior can carry away the sin and punishment. No Savior can bear the penalty in our place."[68] Such an idea is said to be "pernicious."[69] Rather, we must save ourselves (see below). We become "saved" when we raise ourselves to a higher moral plane.

Man Is Essentially Good

In Unitarian Universalist theology, man is not viewed as a fallen sinner. As noted above, the doctrine of original sin is outright denied, and, in fact, one seldom hears the word *sin* in UUA church services.[70] Instead, they "assert the goodness of the individual person."[71] Human beings have "great potential for further growth" and even now possess "evidence of the divine."[72]

Unitarian Universalists thus emphasize human goodness, dignity, and worth. Instead of focusing on human shortcomings and weaknesses, they focus on human strengths. This is one reason Unitarian Universalism is so popular among humanists. Humans by use of reason can solve any problem that confronts them; by their own power, they can make good things happen in the world. They have no need of supernatural intervention.

Some Unitarian Universalists would interpret "sin" more in terms of making mistakes and then suffering the consequences of those mistakes. But there is no sin for which human beings are held morally accountable to God. Even when sin is viewed as a mistake, it is a relative concept; what is "sin" to one Unitarian Universalist would not be considered a "sin" by another.

We "Save" Ourselves by Improving Ourselves

In Unitarian Universalism, all people in the world are viewed as the children of God. The exclusivist claim by Christians that they alone are children of God and that Jesus is the only way to salvation is considered the height of arrogance. All human beings are viewed as good, and the same spark of the divine that dwelt in Jesus dwells in all people.

Unitarian Universalists sometimes speak of salvation in the sense of cultural reconstruction—"saving" the world and making it a better place to live. People can be "saved" in the sense of being delivered from some of the injustices in this world (for example, racism or sexism).

Others speak of salvation as mere "character improvement." We can "save" ourselves by improving our character from an ethical point of view.[73] "Religious liberals usually reject the idea of salvation as rescue of the soul from the world, or its passage from earth to heaven at death. We usually speak of salvation in and for this world—as a quality of human wholeness, or being at one with ourselves and others in heart, mind, and will."[74]

Salvation is also sometimes interpreted as simply waking up to the wonder of life all around us. We are told that "part of being born again, in a Unitarian Universalist way, lies in waking up to the fact that all of life is a gift.... Redemption has little to do with escaping death. Instead, it involves discovering and acting upon life's hidden yet abundant richness."[75]

There Is No Afterlife

In keeping with a commitment to humanism, it is not surprising that most Unitarian Universalists deny that there is an afterlife (heaven or hell). "Very few UUs believe in a continuing, individualized existence after physical death. Even fewer believe in the physical existence of places called heaven and hell where one goes after dying."[76] Most Unitarian Universalists view death "as the final and total end of our existence."[77]

Some Unitarian Universalists would go so far as to say that the very ideas of heaven and hell are immoral. Inducing people to be good because of promises of a future reward or punishment is "pernicious."[78] Moreover, "it is totally unthinkable for God, as a loving Father, to damn any of his children everlastingly to hell."[79] A small minority of Unitarian Universalists, however, do say they believe in some kind of life after death—but they are not sure what it entails.

Most Unitarian Universalists prefer to spend most of their time focusing their attention on living in the present rather than worrying about some alleged afterlife. They focus on the *here and now* instead of the *hereafter*. Unitarian Universalists do not see death in a morbid and despairing sense, but "view the finality of death as a compelling reason to live life as fully as possible."[80] "We look not to the heavens or an afterlife for our meaning, but to the exuberance of life's unfolding. Whatever abundance there may be is lodged right here on earth."[81]

Unitarian Universalists universally deny bodily resurrection. Resurrection does not make sense in view of the fact that when a person dies his or her body immediately begins to decay. After a time, a person's remains are little more than dust. For Unitarian Universalists, "immortality" lies in the positive effect one has had in the lives of others. Leaving a good legacy serves to immortalize a person.[82]

CHALLENGING UNITARIAN UNIVERSALIST BELIEFS

A 1997 poll of 10,000 Unitarian Universalists found that 60 percent had considered leaving the Unitarian Universalist Association.

They gave four primary reasons: (1) lack of spirituality, warmth, and joy; (2) congregational conflict; (3) "too arrogant and cerebral"; and (4) too much political correctness.[83] These are important facts to keep in mind as one engages Unitarian Universalists in dialogue. One should emphasize the Unitarian Universalist claim of "openness"—for if they are really open, they will at least consider challenges to their belief system.

Because the UUA embraces a variety of individuals—including humanists, neopagans, New Agers, and the like—there is no single "apologetic response" one can offer. Rather, depending on the variety of Unitarian Universalism one encounters, one can deal with the specific issues that will overcome his or her objection to evangelical Christianity. Below I briefly elaborate on some of the more important points on which evangelical Christians should focus.

Unitarian Universalists Are Ultimately Intolerant

Although Unitarian Universalists claim to be tolerant of all religions, in reality they are *intolerant* of Christians who worship Jesus as the one way of salvation. While they speak in accepting terms of other religions—including New Age religions and neopaganism—the words reserved for evangelical Christianity include "myth," "rubbish," "sham," "primitive," and "nonsense."[84] Christian doctrines are often viewed as mere superstitions. Those who

CONTRASTING UNITARIAN UNIVERSALISM WITH CHRISTIANITY		
	Unitarian Universalist View	**Christian View**
Authority	Reason and experience	The Bible
Bible	One of many holy books	Inspired Word of God
Truth	Relative	Absolute
Miracles	Myth	Historical reality
God	Open to many interpretations	One true God—Yahweh
Jesus	Great moral teacher	Divine Messiah, Savior
Sin	No sin (man is good)	Man is a sinner
Salvation	We "save" ourselves	By faith in Christ alone
Belief in afterlife	No, death ends all	Yes

believe the Bible is the infallible Word of God are considered imbeciles. In their intolerance of Christians, it seems clear that Unitarian Universalists are most guilty of what they condemn in others. Their tolerance is limited to that which does not offend them.

Unitarian Universalists would do well to reconsider their intolerance of the idea that man is fallen in sin and therefore is in need of a Savior. After all, a reasonable look at the empirical evidence seems to support the Christian teaching on man's depravity and fallenness instead of man's alleged innate goodness. John Ankerberg and John Weldon observe that "since 3,600 B.C. the world has known only 292 years of peace. In that period, stretching more than 55 centuries, there have been an incredible 14,531 wars in which over 3.6 billion people have been killed."[85] Being intolerant of a view supported by empirical facts—that is, the harsh reality of human sin—is not reasonable!

A Relativistic View of Truth Is Not Satisfying

The view that all truth is relative, as Unitarian Universalists hold, is not logically satisfying (and since Unitarian Universalists claim to hold to reason, this criticism should be of concern). As noted earlier, one might understand the statement "all truth is relative" to mean that it is an *absolute* truth that all truth is relative. Of course, such a statement is self-defeating (since there are supposedly no absolute truths) and is therefore false. One could also understand this as saying that it is *relative* truth that all truth is relative. But such a statement is ultimately meaningless. Also meaningless is the Unitarian Universalist claim that truth "changes over time." Indeed, what if the position that truth changes over time is itself one of the "truths" that change over time?[86] Such a position is unreasonable.

Biblical Christians believe there are absolute morals grounded in an absolutely moral God. Moral law flows from the moral Lawgiver of the universe (see Matt. 5:48). God stands against the moral relativist whose behavior is based on "whatever is right in his own eyes" (Deut. 12:8; Judg. 17:6; 21:25; Prov. 21:2). Since there is an absolutely moral Creator-God (Isa. 44:24) who has communicated precisely what He expects of us in terms of moral behavior (see, for example, Ex. 20:1–17), then we as His creatures are responsible to render obedience.

The New Testament Writers Were Not Untrustworthy

Unitarian Universalists say the four gospel writers were biased by theological "motives." The gospel writers' intent was to convince readers of Jesus' deity, we are told, and hence their historical testimony is untrustworthy.

The fallacy here is to imagine that to give an account of something one believes in passionately necessarily forces one to distort history. This is simply not true. In modern times some of the most reliable reports of the Nazi Holocaust were written by Jews who were passionately committed to never seeing such genocide repeated.

The New Testament is not made up of fairy tales but is based on eyewitness testimony. In 2 Peter 1:16 we read, "We did not follow cleverly invented stories when we told you about the power and coming of our Lord Jesus Christ, but we were eyewitnesses of his majesty." First John 1:1 affirms, "That which was from the beginning, which we have heard, which we have seen with our eyes, which we have looked at and our hands have touched—this we proclaim concerning the Word of life."

One cannot help but be impressed that the Bible's historical accuracy and reliability have been proved and verified over and over again by archaeological finds presented by both believing and nonbelieving scholars and scientists. This includes verification for numerous customs, places, names, and events mentioned in the Bible. Scholar Donald J. Wiseman notes, "The geography of Bible lands and visible remains of antiquity were gradually recorded until today more than 25,000 sites within this region and dating to Old Testament times, in their broadest sense, have been located."[87] Nelson Glueck, a specialist in ancient literature, did an exhaustive study and concluded, "It can be stated categorically that no archaeological discovery has ever controverted a biblical reference."[88] Scholar William Albright, following a comprehensive study, wrote, "Discovery after discovery has established the accuracy of innumerable details, and has brought increased recognition of the value of the Bible as a source of history."[89] This hardly sounds like the error-packed book Unitarian Universalists make it out to be.

It is important to understand that the Bible is not a mere man-made document, but is inspired by God. Biblical inspiration may be defined as God's superintending of the human authors so that, using their own individual personalities and even their writing styles, they composed and recorded without error His revelation to humankind. The writers of Scripture were not mere writing machines. God did not use them like keys on a typewriter to mechanically reproduce His message. Nor did He dictate the words page by page. The biblical evidence makes it clear that each writer had a style of his own. Isaiah had a powerful literary style; Jeremiah had a mournful tone; Luke's style had medical overtones; John had a simple, straightforward approach. The Holy Spirit infallibly worked through each of these writers, through their individual styles, to inerrantly communicate His message to humankind.

Second Peter 1:21 provides a key insight regarding the human-divine interchange in the process of inspiration. This verse informs us that "prophecy [or Scripture] never had its origin in the will of man, but men spoke from God as they were carried along by the Holy Spirit." The phrase "carried along" in this verse literally means "forcefully borne along." Even though human beings were used in the process of writing down God's Word, they were all literally "borne along" by the Holy Spirit. The human wills of the authors were not the originators of God's message. God did not permit the will of sinful human beings to misdirect or erroneously record His message. Rather, "God *moved* and the prophet *mouthed* these truths; God *revealed* and man *recorded* His word."[90]

Interestingly, the Greek word for "carried along" in 2 Peter 1:21 is the same as that found in Acts 27:15–17. In this passage the experienced sailors could not navigate the ship because the wind was so strong. The ship was being *driven*, *directed*, and *carried along* by the wind. This is similar to the Spirit's driving, directing, and carrying the human authors of the Bible as He wished. The word is strong, indicating the Spirit's complete superintending of the human authors. Yet, just as the sailors were active on the ship (though the wind, not the sailors, ultimately controlled the ship's movement), so the human authors were active in writing as the Spirit directed.

Science Does Not Disprove Miracles

Science does not disprove the miracles of the Bible as Unitarian Universalists claim. Science depends on observation and replication. Miracles, such as the Incarnation and the Resurrection, are by their very nature unprecedented events. No one can replicate these events in a laboratory. Therefore, contrary to what Unitarian Universalists say, science simply cannot be the judge and jury of whether or not these events occurred.

The scientific method is useful for studying nature but not *super*nature. Just as football stars are speaking outside their field of expertise when they appear on television to tell you what kind of car you should buy, so scientists are speaking outside their field when they address theological issues like miracles or the Resurrection.

The world of nature and Scripture, properly interpreted, do not conflict. God has communicated to humankind both by *general* revelation (nature, or the observable universe) and *special* revelation (the Bible). Since both of these revelations come from God—and since God does not contradict Himself—we must conclude that these two revelations are in agreement. While there may be conflicts between one's interpretation of the observable universe and one's interpretation of the Bible, there is no ultimate contradiction.

We might say that science is a fallible human interpretation of the observable universe while theology is a fallible human interpretation of the Scriptures. If the Unitarian Universalist challenges the idea that science can be fallible, remind him or her of what (secular) science historian Thomas Kuhn proved in his book *The Structure of Scientific Revolutions*—that is, science is in a constant state of change. New discoveries have consistently caused old scientific paradigms to be discarded in favor of newer paradigms.

Here is the point: The *world of nature* and *Scripture* don't contradict; rather, *science* (man's fallible interpretation of nature) and *theology* (man's fallible interpretation of Scripture) sometimes conflict. Therefore, the Unitarian Universalist cannot simply dismiss biblical miracles because "science and the Bible contradict."

Occasionally, Unitarian Universalists might say that the miracles recorded in the Bible involved the misguided conclusions of ancient people who were ignorant of the laws of science (or laws of nature), but this is not a fair allegation. People in biblical times did know enough of the laws of nature to recognize bona fide miracles. As C. S. Lewis wrote, "When St. Joseph discovered that his bride was pregnant, he was 'minded to put her away.' He knew enough biology for that. Otherwise, of course, he would not have regarded pregnancy as a proof of infidelity. When he accepted the Christian explanation, he regarded it as a miracle precisely because he knew enough of the laws of nature to know that this was a suspension of them."[91]

Moreover, Lewis observed, "When the disciples saw Christ walking on the water they were frightened: they would not have been frightened unless they had known the laws of nature and known that this was an exception. If a man had no conception of a regular order in nature, then of course he could not notice departures from that order."[92] Nothing can be viewed as "abnormal" until one has first grasped the "norm."

It Is Reasonable to Believe in God

Unitarian Universalists often speak as if Christians have no reasonable basis for their faith that God exists. This allegation is untrue, however, for—even aside from the historical and archaeological evidences for the veracity of the Bible, which speaks of God's existence—Christian thinkers since the first century have addressed a number of logical and reasonable arguments for God's existence.

1. The Cosmological Argument

This argument says that every effect must have an adequate cause. The universe is an "effect." Reason demands that whatever caused the universe must be greater than the universe. That cause is God (who Himself is the uncaused First Cause). As Hebrews 3:4 puts it, "Every house is built by someone, but God is the builder of everything."

2. The Teleological Argument

This argument says that there is an obvious purposeful and intricate design of the world. If we found a watch in the sand, the assumption would have to be that someone created the watch, because, with its intricate design, it is obvious that all the parts of the watch could not have just jumped together to cause itself. Similarly, the perfect design of the universe argues for a Designer, and that Designer is God.

3. The Ontological Argument

This argument says that most human beings have an innate idea of a perfect being. Where did this idea come from? Not from man, for man is an imperfect being. Some perfect being (God) must have planted the idea there. God cannot be conceived of as not existing, for then one could conceive of an even greater being that did exist. Thus God must in fact exist.

4. The Moral Argument

This argument says that every human being has an innate sense of oughtness or moral obligation. Where did this sense of oughtness come from? It must come from God. The existence of a moral law in our hearts demands the existence of a moral Lawgiver (see Rom. 1:19–32).

5. The Anthropological Argument

This argument says that man has a personality (mind, emotions, and will). Since the personal cannot come from the impersonal, there must be a personal cause, and that personal cause is God (see Gen. 1:26–27).

Are these arguments convincing to a nonbeliever? Perhaps Reformer John Calvin's view of these arguments was the best. He said that the unregenerate person sees these evidences for God in the universe with blurred vision. It is only when one puts on the "eyeglasses" of faith and belief in the Bible that these evidences for God's existence come into clearest focus. Nevertheless, these arguments do illustrate that belief in the God of the Bible is reasonable.

God Is a Trinity

I have set forth evidence earlier in the book that God by nature is a Trinity (see page 94). Here I simply wish to remind the reader that the doctrine of the Trinity makes sense when one considers all the data about God in the Bible. The doctrine of the Trinity is based on three very clear lines of evidence in the Bible: (1) evidence that there is only one true God (Isa. 44:6, 9; John 5:44; 17:3; Rom. 3:29–30; 16:27; Gal. 3:20; Eph. 4:6; 1 Tim. 2:5; James 2:19); (2) evidence that there are three persons who are God—the Father (1 Peter 1:2), the Son (John 20:28; Heb. 1:8), and the Holy Spirit (Acts 5:3–4); and (3) evidence that indicates three-in-oneness within the Godhead (Matt. 28:19; 2 Cor. 13:14).

Matthew 28:19 is particularly revealing, for it says, "Go therefore and make disciples of all the nations, baptizing them in the *name* of *the* Father and *the* Son and *the* Holy Spirit" (emphasis added). The word *name* is singular in the Greek, indicating that there is one God but three distinct persons within the Godhead—*the* Father, *the* Son, and *the* Holy Spirit, each preceded by a definite article ("the"), thereby pointing to the distinctness of each. In view of the biblical evidence, the Unitarian Universalist claim that the Trinity cannot be found in the Bible is unreasonable.

Jesus Was Not Just a Good Moral Teacher

Jesus was not just a good moral teacher, as Unitarian Universalists claim. No mere "example" or "moral teacher" would ever claim that the destiny of the world lay in His hands, or that people would spend eternity in heaven or hell depending on whether they believed in Him (John 6:26–40). The only "example" this would provide would be one of lunacy. And for Jesus to try to convince people that He was God (John 8:58) and the Savior of the world (Luke 19:10) when He really was not would be the ultimate *immorality.* Hence, to say that Jesus was just a good moral teacher *and nothing more* is unreasonable. As C. S. Lewis put it, "A man who was merely a man and said the sort of things Jesus said would not be a great moral teacher. He would either be a lunatic—on the level with the man who says he is a poached egg—or else he would be the Devil of Hell. You must make your choice. Either this man was, and is, the son of God: or else a madman or something worse."[93]

Jesus Is "the Only Way"

Jesus claimed that what He said took precedence over all others. He said He is humanity's *only* means of coming into a relationship with God (John 14:6), which His followers confirmed (Acts 4:12; 1 Tim. 2:5). Further, Jesus proved the veracity of all He said by rising from the dead (for which I provide evidence below). None of the other leaders of the different world religions did that. Jesus' resurrection proved that He was who He claimed to be—the divine Messiah (Rom. 1:4).

Though Unitarian Universalists claim to give high status to rationality and reason, their position on "excluding all exclusiveness" is unreasonable. Dr. Alan Gomes rightly notes that "it is impossible for Unitarian Universalists to exclude all exclusivistic positions since the very act of excluding these positions is itself an act of exclusivism."[94] We return here to the intolerance of Unitarian

Universalists: though they condemn intolerance in evangelical Christians, they themselves are clearly manifesting the very intolerance they condemn in others.

Sometimes Unitarian Universalists claim Christians are being arrogant in claiming exclusivity. But when Christians assert that Jesus Christ is the only way to God, they are not suggesting they are better than anyone else. They are putting themselves in the same camp as the rest of humanity in affirming that all humanity—Christians included—need a Savior. Accepting and proclaiming God's way is therefore not arrogance; it is genuine humility. *All* of us are lost; *all* of us need the one true Savior, Jesus Christ.

Christians recognize that they have nothing in themselves that saves. It is the way of Jesus that saves, not their way. Christians merely repeat the claim made by Jesus Himself: "I am the way and the truth and the life. No one comes to the Father except through me" (John 14:6). Christians are not the authors of Jesus' words, nor even the editors. They are only the mail-carriers. There is no arrogance in merely "delivering the mail." What is truly arrogant is to put oneself in the place of correcting Almighty God and saying that what He has revealed in the Bible is mere myth.

Sometimes Unitarian Universalists claim that Christians are "narrow-minded" in saying Jesus is "the only way." But is being "narrow" in some things necessarily evil? Many things in life are narrow that are not bad. We want the airline pilot to land on the right runway. We want our spouses to remain faithful to their one and only spouse. There is often only one road out of the forest. There is only one correct formula for Pepsi. There is only one operation that can save your life. There is only one antidote to a particular poison.

While it is true that God's way of salvation is narrow (that is, faith in Christ alone), God's heart is infinitely wide; He is full of love for all people—men and women, rich and poor, fat and thin, kings and peasants, socialites and social outcasts (see Isa. 45:22; Ezek. 18:23; 1 Tim. 2:3–4). He offers the same gift to everyone—salvation in Jesus Christ. Jesus Himself wants all people to receive this wonderful gift (see Matt. 28:19; John 3:17), as did the apostles (Acts 26:28–29; Rom. 1:16). This is the predominant emphasis in Scripture.

Christ's Resurrection Is a Historical Reality

Abundant evidence exists that Christ truly did rise from the dead. The biblical testimony tells us that Jesus first attested to His resurrection by appearing to Mary Magdalene (John 20:1–18)—a fact that is a highly significant indicator of the authenticity and reliability of the resurrection account. The resurrection story could not have been fabricated by the disciples, for no one in a first-century Jewish culture would have invented it this way. In Jewish law a woman's testimony was unacceptable in any court of law except in a very few circumstances. A fabricator would have been much more likely to portray Peter or the other male disciples at the tomb. But our biblical text tells us that the Lord appeared first to Mary because that is the way it actually happened.

Following her encounter with Jesus, Mary promptly told the disciples the glorious news. That evening the disciples had gathered in a room with the doors shut for fear of the Jews (John 20:19). This fear was well founded, for after Jesus had been arrested, Annas the high priest specifically asked Jesus about the disciples (18:19). Jesus had also previously warned the disciples in the Upper Room, "If they persecuted me, they will persecute you also" (15:20). These facts no doubt lingered in their minds after Jesus was brutally crucified.

But then the disciples' gloom turned to joy. The risen Christ appeared in their midst and said to them, "Peace be with you" (John 20:19). This phrase was a common Hebrew greeting (1 Sam. 25:6). But on this occasion Jesus' words had special significance. After the disciples' shameful conduct on Good Friday (they all scattered like a bunch of cowards after Jesus' arrest), they may well have expected a rebuke from Jesus. Instead, He displayed compassion by pronouncing peace upon them.

Jesus immediately showed the disciples His hands and His side (John 20:20). The risen Lord wanted them to see that it was truly He. The wounds showed that He did not have another body but the same body. He was dead, but now He is alive forevermore.

Now, consider this: By all accounts, the disciples came away from the crucifixion frightened and full of doubt. Yet, following Jesus' resurrection appearance to the disciples, their lives were transformed. The cowards became bulwarks of courage, fearless defenders of the faith. The only thing that could account for this incredible transformation was the resurrection.

As the days passed, Jesus continued to make many appearances and proved that He had truly risen from the dead. Acts 1:3 says, "He showed himself to these men and gave many convincing proofs that he was alive. He appeared to them over a period of forty days and spoke about the kingdom of God." Jesus appeared to *too many people* (over 500 people on a single occasion—see 1 Cor. 15:6), on *too many occasions* (12), over *too long a time* (40 days), for the resurrection to be dismissed as mere myth, as Unitarian Universalists do. The appearance to 500 people at a time is especially relevant, for if Paul had misrepresented the facts, wouldn't one of these 500 have come forward to dispute his claims? No one came forward to dispute anything because the resurrection really occurred.

Further, one cannot help but be impressed by the honest character of the New Testament witnesses. It is hard to believe that these followers—predominantly Jewish and therefore aware of God's stern commandments against lying and bearing false witness—would make up such a lie and then suffer and give up their lives in defense of it. Moreover, if Jesus' followers concocted events like the resurrection, wouldn't Jesus' critics have immediately come forward to debunk these lies and put an end to Christianity once and for all?

These and many other evidences point to the historical veracity of the resurrection accounts in the New Testament. Though Unitarian Universalists claim to appeal to human reason in dismissing the resurrection as a myth, in reality they must deny extensive historical evidence and in the process go against reason to maintain their position.

12

ONENESS PENTECOSTALISM

The Oneness Pentecostal movement has its roots in the Assemblies of God in the early part of the twentieth century. From 1913 to 1916 several Pentecostal leaders affiliated with the Assemblies of God, including John Sheppe, Frank J. Ewart, and Garfield Haywood, began to teach—based on Acts 2:38—that baptism must be "in the name of the Lord Jesus Christ" and not "in the name of the Father, and of the Son, and of the Holy Spirit."[1] These individuals assumed a modalistic understanding of the nature of God—meaning that "Father," "Son," and "Holy Spirit" are modes of manifestation of the one God, who is Jesus.[2] "Father, Son, and Holy Spirit are manifestations, modes, offices, or relationships that the one God has displayed to man."[3]

This Oneness teaching met with great resistance from other Assemblies of God leaders, and a polarization occurred within Pentecostal ranks. In 1915 the Assemblies of God Third General Council opposed the teaching, and the Fourth General Council in 1916, held in St. Louis, strongly affirmed belief in the Trinity in its "Statement of Fundamental Truths." This action resulted in the immediate withdrawal of 156 out of 585 ministers (and their congregations) affiliated with the Assemblies of God.[4]

In 1916 some of the Oneness ministers who had left the Assemblies of God formed the General Assembly of Apostolic Assemblies (the GAAA). This formally marked the beginning of the Oneness Pentecostal movement. From that point forward, other Oneness denominations began to emerge as a result of doctrinal schisms, offshoots, and mergings. Eventually the GAAA merged with the Pentecostal Assemblies of the World (PAW), retaining the latter name (PAW). One challenge the PAW faced was the racial tension that developed within its ranks. Other Oneness denominations at that time remained segregated.

In November of 1931 a merger involving various segregated Oneness sects resulted in the founding of the Pentecostal Assemblies of Jesus Christ (PAJC). Yet a number of the black leaders did not trust that the arrangement was in their best interests (they were suspicious of the motives behind the merger) and decided to remain with the PAW. Over a decade later, in 1945, the largest white Oneness organizations—the Pentecostal Church, Inc. (PCI) and the PAJC—merged to form the largest of the Pentecostal Oneness groups, the United Pentecostal Church (UPC).[5]

Today about 90 denominations in 57 countries are affiliated with Oneness Pentecostalism. There are more than 5 million advocates of Oneness theology in the world (some estimates are higher),[6] with about 1 million of these living in the United States.[7] The single greatest and most influential Oneness organization is the United Pentecostal Church, International, with which approximately 75 percent of Oneness Pentecostals are affiliated. This group is growing at a rate of 10 to 15 percent per year, making it one of the fastest-growing religious movements on American soil. The UPC embraces some 3,800 churches in the United States.[8]

Aside from the fact that most Oneness Pentecostals are affiliated with the UPC, it is also true that the denomination is aggressive in terms of publishing (Word of Flame Press has published more than 100 titles), Bible colleges (including the Apostolic Bible Institute and the United Pentecostal Bible Institute), evangelism, missions, and media outreaches.

Because of the size and influence of the denomination, this chapter focuses specifically on the UPC and on the three primary doctrinal distinctives of Oneness theology: (1) the view that Jesus is the one true God (He is the Father, the Son, and the Holy Spirit), (2) a denial of the Trinity, and (3) a view of salvation that entails faith, repentance, water baptism in the name of Jesus only, and baptism in the Holy Spirit as evidenced by speaking in tongues.

ONENESS PENTECOSTAL BELIEFS

Jesus Is the Father, Son, and Holy Spirit

Oneness Pentecostals believe Jesus is the one true God—He is the Father, the Son, and the Holy Spirit. Jesus is God *in His totality*, and "Father," "Son," and "Holy Spirit" are simply different roles that this one divine person temporarily assumed.

In arguing that Jesus is God, Oneness Pentecostals often use some of the same verses evangelicals do. Jesus is called God (John 1:1; 20:28; Titus 2:13; 2 Peter 1:1; 1 John 5:20) and Lord (John 20:28; Rom. 10:9–13; Phil. 2:9–11); is worshiped as God (Matt. 28:17; Heb. 1:6); and is prayed to as God (Acts 7:59; 1 Cor. 1:2; 2 Cor. 12:7–10).[9]

The Scriptures also indicate, according to Oneness Pentecostals, that God is absolutely *one*.[10] After all, Deuteronomy 6:4 says, "Hear, O Israel: The LORD our God, the LORD is one." This same truth about God's oneness is asserted hundreds of times in Scripture (see Isa. 42:8; 43:10–11; 44:6; 1 Cor. 8:4–6; Eph. 4:4–6; 1 Tim. 2:5).

In view of the fact that there is only one God and that Jesus Christ is God, it is concluded that Jesus is the one God of which Scripture speaks. This means that Jesus is the Father, Son, and Holy Spirit. Oneness theologian David Bernard writes, "If there is only one God and that God is the Father (Mal. 2:10), and if Jesus is God, then it logically follows that Jesus is the father."[11] It is likewise argued that if there is only one God, and the Holy Spirit is God, then Jesus must be the Holy Spirit.

In support of the claim that Jesus is the Father, Oneness Pentecostals note that Jesus is called "Mighty God, Everlasting Father" in Isaiah 9:6.[12] It follows, then, that Jesus is the Father. Moreover, in John 10:30, Jesus said, "I and the Father are one," pointing to their common identity.[13] In a number of passages, Jesus indicated that if anyone saw Him, they were actually seeing the Father (see John 8:19; 12:45; 14:7–11).

Further, there are a number of verses that Oneness Pentecostals believe, if translated correctly, indicate that Jesus is the Father. For example, in Romans 1:7 we read Paul's salutation, "Grace to you and peace from God our Father and the Lord Jesus Christ" (NASB). Oneness Pentecostals argue that the word "and" (Greek *kai*) in the phrase "God our Father and the Lord Jesus Christ" should be translated "even." It should thus read, "God our Father, *even* the Lord Jesus Christ."[14] Translated this way, Jesus and the Father are seen to be one and the same person.[15] The same is said to be the case with Paul's salutation in 1 Corinthians 1:3.

Because the Father and the Son are portrayed as engaging in identical activities throughout the Bible, Oneness Pentecostals reason that they are one and the same person. For example, both the Father and Jesus are said to raise Jesus from the dead (John 2:19–22; Gal. 1:1). Both the Father and Jesus answer prayer (John 14:14; 15:16). Both the Father and Jesus sent the Holy Spirit (John 14:16; 15:26). Both the Father and Jesus draw people to Jesus (John 6:44; 12:32). Both the Father and Jesus raise other people from the dead (John 6:40; Rom. 4:17).[16]

To prove Jesus is the Holy Spirit, Oneness Pentecostals often cite 2 Corinthians 3:17: "Now the Lord is the Spirit; and where the Spirit of the Lord is, there is liberty" (NASB). They argue that Jesus is the *Lord* in this verse, and He is explicitly identified as the *Holy Spirit* who opens up the heart of believers.[17] Therefore, Jesus is the Holy Spirit.

Also, because Scripture portrays Jesus and the Holy Spirit doing the same kinds of activities throughout Scripture, their common identity seems clear. For example, both Jesus and the Holy Spirit raised Jesus from the dead (John 2:19–21; Rom. 8:9–11). Both Jesus and the Holy Spirit dwell in the hearts of believers (John 14:16; Col. 1:27). Both Jesus and the Holy Spirit pray for believers (Rom. 8:26; Heb. 7:25).

Therefore, in Oneness Pentecostal theology, the Holy Spirit is another term for the one God (who is Jesus). He is not a separate person with a separate identity, but is the one God who assumes

· Church of Scientology ·

◀ A Scientology center in Los Angeles.
Courtesy Personal Freedom Outreach

Scientology Testing Center in
Los Angeles (circa 1980s).
Courtesy Personal Freedom Outreach
▶

◀ Some representative Scientology books.
Copyright © 2001 Jack Roper

· Hindu-based Cults ·

Bhagwan Shree Rajneesh, a popular Hindu guru who renamed himself Osho shortly before his death in 1990. *Courtesy George Mather*

Maharishi Mahesh Yogi, founder of the Transcendental Meditation movement. *Courtesy George Mather*

Some Krishna idols. *Copyright © 2001 Jack Roper*

Maharishi International University in Fairfield, Iowa. *Courtesy George Mather*

· Hindu-based Cults ·

◄ Statue of Swami Prabhupada (1896–1977), founder of the Hare Krishnas (ISKCON). *Courtesy Personal Freedom Outreach*

The Hare Krishna "Palace of Gold" at New Vrindaban, West Virginia. *Courtesy Personal Freedom Outreach* ►

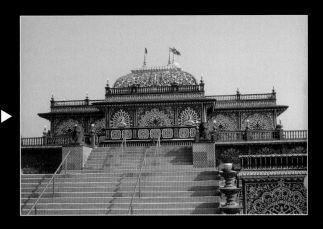

◄ Some representative Hare Krishna literature. *Copyright © 2001 Jack Roper*

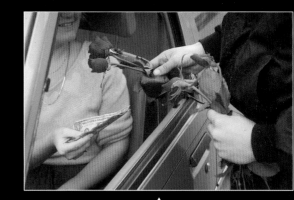

Unification members often raise funds on street corners. *Courtesy Personal Freedom Outreach*

Reverend Sun Myung Moon, founder of the Unification Church. *Courtesy George Mather*

A Unification Church flyer for the God Bless America Festival held at Yankee Stadium, New York City, June 1, 1976.

· Baha'i ·

▲

The Baha'i House of Worship in Wilmette, Illinois
Courtesy Personal Freedom Outreach

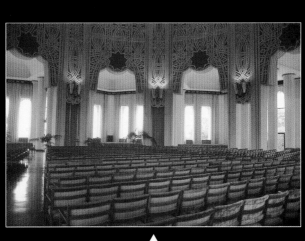

▲

The interior of the Baha'i House of Worship in
Wilmette, Illinois. *Courtesy Personal Freedom Outreach*

▲

United Pentecostal Church International headquarters
in Hazelwood, Missouri. *Courtesy Personal Freedom Outreach*

▲

Gateway College of Evangelism in Florissant, Missouri,
an affiliate of the United Pentecostal Church.
Courtesy Personal Freedom Outreach

· Masonic Lodge ·

The entrance to the Shriner Tripoli Temple in Milwaukee. *Copyright © 2001 Jack Roper*

The Scottish Rite Center in Milwaukee. The Scottish Rite is one branch of advanced Masonry. *Copyright © 2001 Jack Roper*

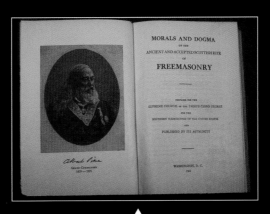

Morals and Dogma, a book written by Albert Pike, a respected authority in Masonic circles. *Copyright © 2001 Jack Roper*

The Shriner Tripoli Temple in Milwaukee. Shriners are high-level Masons.

• Satanism •

The Church of Satan in San Francisco,
founded by Anton Szandor LaVey in 1966.
Copyright © 2001 Jack Roper

Anton Szandor LaVey (1930–97),
founder of the Church of Satan.

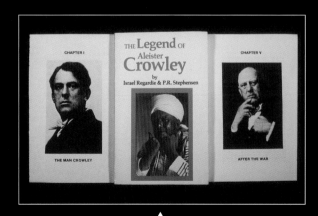

Occultist Aleister Crowley (1875–1947),
who laid the groundwork for modern Satanism.
Copyright © 2001 Jack Roper

A Satanic ritual altar.
Copyright © 2001 Jack Roper

the particular role of "God in activity."[18] So, for example, God (Jesus) as the Holy Spirit is active in the hearts of people, working His sanctifying influence.

Further support for the idea that Jesus is the Father, Son, and Holy Spirit is found in comparing Matthew 28:19 with Acts 2:38. In Matthew 28:19, Jesus instructs His followers, "Therefore go and make disciples of all the nations, baptizing them in the *name* of the Father and the Son and the Holy Spirit" (emphasis added). But in Acts 2:38 we find reference to baptizing "in the *name* of Jesus" (emphasis added). Putting these verses together, Oneness Pentecostals believe that "Jesus" must be the name of the Father, Son, and Holy Spirit. Because the word *name* is singular in Matthew 28:19, this must mean that the Father, Son, and Holy Spirit are one person—the person of Jesus Christ.[19] The *Father* is God in a universal sense. The *Son* is God in manifestation, particularly as revealed in human flesh. The *Holy Spirit* is God imparting Himself to humankind in various ways.

According to Oneness Pentecostals, the distinction between the Father and the Son is identical to the distinction between the deity and the humanity of Jesus. Jesus, as the Father and the Son, is divine and human. "Both identities, father and son, were in the same one [person]."[20] The Father refers to deity.[21] "The omnipresence of the Son is the Father."[22] Indeed, "the Father is the Omnipresence, Omniscience, and Omnipotence of the Son."[23] We are told that the Son is "the flesh or humanity. The Father is the great eternal Spirit who indwelt the Son."[24] "They were not two persons but two natures—human and divine, Son and Father—all in Jesus Christ."[25]

Most Oneness Pentecostal theologians teach that the term "Son of God" is said to refer only to the incarnate Christ. The "son" is the "flesh or humanity" of Jesus. The "son" is the human body of the Father.[26] "The Son" always refers to the incarnation, and "we cannot use it in the absence of the human element."[27] "Son of God" refers to "a specific role that God temporarily assumed for the purpose of redemption."[28]

Note, however, that in Oneness literature the "Son" can refer either to the human nature alone, or it can refer to God manifested in the flesh—that is, deity dwelling in the human nature. Note also that even though Jesus is the Father and Jesus is the Son, this does not mean that the Father is the Son. As Bernard notes, "Since Father refers to deity alone, while 'Son of God' refers to deity as incarnated in humanity, we do not believe that the Father is the Son. The distinction is pivotal.... The deity in the Son is the Father."[29]

Oneness Pentecostals argue that Scripture never indicates that Jesus' sonship is an eternal sonship. The term "eternal Son" is never found in the Bible. Nor is the term "God the Son" in the Bible.[30] Instead, we are told that the "Son" was "begotten" (John 3:16 KJV), which indicates that Jesus became the Son at a point in time. The words *eternal* and *begotten* are in direct contradiction to each other. "If someone is eternal he has never been begotten. If he has been begotten then he is not eternal.... He cannot at the same time be the 'eternal Son' and the 'begotten Son.'"[31]

Hence, in Oneness theology Jesus is both the Father who sent his Son, and the Son who obeyed the Father. "He was both the *Son* who prayed to the Father, and the *Father* who answered the Son. He was both the *man* who experienced God-forsakenness, and the *God* who at least appeared to forsake his Son on the cross."[32] Yet Jesus was and is just one person.

The sonship of Christ is viewed as a temporary role that will one day end (1 Cor. 15:28). According to Oneness Pentecostalism, when the millennium is completed, Jesus' Sonship ministry will be finished. "When the reasons for the Sonship cease to exist, God (Jesus) will cease acting in His role as Son, and the Sonship will be submerged back into the greatness of God, who will return to His original role as Father, Creator, and Ruler of all."[33]

What about those verses in the New Testament that seem to indicate that the Son of God was involved in the creation of the universe? Bernard answers that "the verses of Scripture that speak of creation by the Son cannot mean the Son existed substantially at creation as a person apart from the Father. The Old Testament proclaims that one individual being created us, and he is Jehovah, the Father."[34] According to Oneness Pentecostalism, when Scripture speaks of God creating the world through the Son of God, it should be interpreted to mean that God created the world "with a view towards" or "for the sake of" Jesus Christ, the *future* Son in whom he planned to dwell. "Although the Son did not exist at the time of creation except as the Word in the mind of God, God used

His foreknowledge of the Son when He created the world."[35] When-ever we encounter verses that seem to point to the preexistence of the Son, it is mere preexistence *in the mind of the Father.*[36]

The Trinity Is a False Doctrine

Typical antitrinitarian groups like the Jehovah's Witnesses deny the doctrine of the Trinity because they deny the full deity of Christ. Oneness Pentecostals are different, for they strongly affirm the full deity of Christ. They deny the Trinity by denying that Jesus is in any sense distinct from the Father or Holy Spirit.

Oneness Pentecostals argue against the doctrine of the Trinity from Scripture, from reason, and from history. They begin by not-ing that Scripture speaks of only one God (Deut. 6:4; 1 Tim. 2:5). While they acknowledge that Scripture indicates that the Father is God (Mal. 2:10), the Son is God (John 1:1), and the Holy Spirit is God (Acts 5:3–4), their conclusion is that Jesus *is* the Father, Son, and Holy Spirit. They typically characterize Trinitarianism as a form of Tritheism (belief in three distinct gods) and point out that the word *Trinity* is not even in the Bible.

Realizing that Trinitarians often appeal to Matthew 3:16–17 in support of the Trinity (Jesus is baptized, the Father speaks, and the Holy Spirit descends on Jesus), Oneness Pentecostals say this is no real support at all. They argue that Jesus was both the Son (human) and the Father (God). "The man who was baptized by John was also the omnipresent God, and *He* was responsible for the voice."[37] Jesus was thus on earth and in heaven at the same time, engaging in differ-ent activities. "It was not at all difficult for the Spirit of Jesus to speak from heaven and to send a manifestation of His Spirit in the form of a dove even while His human body was in the Jordan River."[38]

Appealing to reason, Oneness Pentecostals argue that if one denies that Jesus is the Father and the Holy Spirit, this would mean the fullness of God did not dwell in Christ, as Colossians 2:9 affirms.[39] Further, the Trinitarian belief that an alleged second person

"If there existed three distinct and separate Omnisciences, Omni-presences and Omnipotences for each of the three alleged persons in the Deity, there would, of course, be three Gods without argu-ment" (Kenneth Reeves, *The Godhead*, 38).

of the Godhead prays to an alleged first person of the Godhead is said to be nonsensical (Heb. 7:25). How could an alleged divine person pray without undeifying himself? "A divine person does not need help: only men need help."[40] Thus Scripture indicates that "the human nature of Jesus prayed to the eternal Spirit of God. The divine nature did not need help; only the human nature did."[41]

Moreover, Mark 13:32 indicates that the Son does not know the day or the hour of the Second Coming; only the Father does. If the Son were, in himself, a separate divine person from the Father, would he not know the day and hour of the Second Coming?[42]

Yet another argument against the Trinity is that there are many Bible passages where the Father and the Son are mentioned, but not the Holy Spirit. First John 1:3, for example, says, "Our fellowship is with the Father and with his Son, Jesus Christ." Many of Paul's opening salutations mention the Father and Jesus, but not the Holy Spirit (for example, 1 Cor. 1:3; 2 Cor. 1:2). This is not what one would expect if God were a Trinity, with each of the three persons being equal.[43]

For Oneness Pentecostals the Trinitarian argument that the Hebrew word for God, *Elohim*, is plural and therefore teaches the Trinity is weak. Instead, they argue this is simply a plural of majesty and indicates the greatness and majesty of God, not his alleged plurality.[44] Such arguments are meant to show how unreasonable it is to believe in the Trinity.

Appealing to history, Oneness Pentecostals argue that the doctrine of the Trinity is rooted in paganism.[45] The Assyrians, Babylonians, and other pagan nations allegedly believed in some form of the Trinity, and therefore the idea of the Trinity did not originate in Christianity. Some of the early theologians in church history were purportedly influenced by pagan ideas and introduced heresy into Christian creeds. Oneness Pentecostals point to church fathers Clement of Rome (A.D. 100), Ignatius (A.D. 110–15), and Justin (A.D. 150) as early examples of those who taught Oneness doctrine as opposed to the doctrine of the Trinity.[46]

Salvation Does Not Come Easy

In Oneness Pentecostalism salvation is difficult to achieve. In their theology, faith, repentance, water baptism (by immersion) in the name of Jesus only, and baptism in the Holy Spirit (as evidenced by speaking in tongues) are all necessary for the new birth. These last two elements—water baptism and spirit baptism—are of particular concern to evangelical Christians. Of further concern is the teaching that after one has been saved, one must continue to live a strictly regimented life of holiness according to "holiness standards" if one is to remain saved.

The holiness standard involves living a life of victory, free from sin. While individual Oneness Pentecostal congregations vary on their holiness requirements, they are in general agreement on forbidding smoking and dancing, drinking alcoholic beverages, and attending movie theaters. Watching television is often looked down on. Women are supposed to avoid wearing makeup, jewelry, and pants and are not to cut their hair. Men, by contrast, are to wear their hair very short. These and other requirements are viewed as necessary for maintaining a life of holiness.

As for the necessity of baptism, Oneness Pentecostals believe that John 3:5, among other verses, teaches that water baptism is the means by which God regenerates a person. Water baptism makes a person part of the kingdom of God and is also the only means by which sins can be remitted.[47] Water baptism, then, is indispensable in the Oneness Pentecostal view of salvation.

Citing Acts 2:38, Oneness Pentecostals argue that baptism must be administered "in the name of Jesus" and not "in the name of the Father, and the Son, and the Holy Spirit."[48] "Since water baptism is 'for the remission of sins' and since the name of Jesus is the only name that saves from sin (Acts 4:12), it is needful for the name of Jesus to be spoken in water baptism."[49] Oneness Pentecostals argue that baptism in the name of Jesus was practiced by the early church, and that baptism in the name of the Father, and the Son, and the Holy Spirit emerged only after the church abandoned true monotheism.

Also necessary for salvation is baptism in the Holy Spirit, which always carries the initial evidence of speaking in tongues. "Anyone who has never spoken in tongues has never been baptized with the holy ghost."[50] In Acts 2:1–4; 10:44–48; and 19:1–7, the initial evidence of being baptized in the Holy Spirit was speaking in tongues. What was true in the first century is true today. If one has not spoken in tongues, one is urged to continue seeking this gift until it comes, even if it takes years.

Clearly, salvation in Oneness Pentecostal theology involves following a rather strict formula. Deviating from this formula can rob one of salvation.

CHALLENGING ONENESS PENTECOSTAL BELIEFS

Jesus Is Not the Father or the Holy Spirit

Scripture is clear that the Father, Son, and Holy Spirit are distinct persons. Regardless of the convoluted interpretations Oneness Pentecostals offer of specific Bible verses, a natural and unforced reading of Scripture indicates that the Father *sent* the Son (John 3:16–17), the Father and Son *love* each other (John 3:35), and the Father and Son *speak* to each other (John 11:41–42). Moreover, the Father *knows* the Son and the Son *knows* the Father (Matt. 11:27), and Jesus is our advocate with the Father (1 John 2:1).

Furthermore, it is clear that Jesus is not the Holy Spirit, for the Holy Spirit descended upon Jesus at His baptism (Luke 3:22). The Holy Spirit is said to be *another* comforter (John 14:16 KJV), whom Jesus sent (John 15:26) and who seeks to glorify Jesus (John 16:13–14). In view of such evidence, it is impossible to argue that Jesus is the Father and the Holy Spirit as Oneness Pentecostals do. These are clearly distinct persons within the Godhead.

Jesus Was the Preexistent, Eternal Son of God

In John 1:1 we read, "In the beginning was the Word, and the Word was with God, and the Word was God." When heaven and earth came into being at the Creation, Christ the *Logos* already existed in the closest association with the Father, for "the Word was *with* God" (John 1:1). The Greek preposition for the English word *with* is *pros* and carries the idea of intimate, unbroken fellowship and communion. Christ the *Logos* spent eternity past in company with and in intimate, unbroken fellowship with the Father in an eternal loving relationship. Both the Word (Jesus) and His relationship to the Father are eternal.

Moreover, contrary to the Oneness position, Scripture indicates that Christ is *eternally* the Son of God.[51] Though "Son of . . ." can refer to "offspring of," it carries the more important meaning "of the order of."[52] The phrase is often used this way in the Old Testament. For example, "sons of the prophets" meant "of the order of prophets" (1 Kings 20:35). "Sons of the singers" meant "of the order of singers" (Neh. 12:28). Likewise, the phrase "Son of God" means "of the order of God" and represents a claim to undiminished deity.

Ancient Semitics and Orientals used the phrase "Son of. . ." to indicate likeness or sameness of nature and equality of being.[53] Therefore, when Jesus claimed to be the Son of God, His Jewish contemporaries fully understood that He was making a claim to be God in an unqualified sense. In fact, the Jews insisted, "We have a law, and according to that law he [Christ] must die, because he claimed to be the Son of God" (John 19:7; see also 5:18). Recognizing that Jesus was identifying Himself as God, the Jews wanted to kill Him for committing blasphemy.

Evidence for Christ's eternal Sonship is found in Hebrews 1:2, which says God created the universe through His "Son," implying that Christ was the Son of God prior to the Creation. (The feeble suggestion that the Son merely preexisted in the mind of the Father at the Creation is completely unconvincing.) Moreover, Christ as the Son is explicitly said to have existed "before all things" (Col. 1:17; see also vv. 13–14). Jesus, speaking as the Son of God (John 8:54–56), also asserted His eternal preexistence before Abraham (v. 58). The fact that the Son of God was "sent into" the world implies He was the Son before He was sent (see John 3:16).

CONTRASTING ONENESS PENTECOSTALISM WITH CHRISTIANITY

	Oneness Pentecostal View	Christian View
Nature of God	One God (Jesus), three modes	One God, three persons
Jesus	Is the Father, Son, and Holy Spirit	Second person of the Trinity
Father	Refers to the deity of the Son	First person of the Trinity
Son	Refers only to the incarnation	Eternal Son, second person
Holy Spirit	Refers to God in activity (mode)	Third person of the Trinity
Salvation	Strict requirements	Faith in Christ alone
Water Baptism	In the name of Jesus only	Trinitarian
Spirit Baptism	Speaking in tongues required	Tongues not required
Holiness	Required to maintain salvation	Follows salvation

Scripture Must Be Interpreted with Integrity

Isaiah 9:6 Does Not Prove Jesus Is the Father

Though Jesus is called "Everlasting Father" in Isaiah 9:6, the Oneness Pentecostal contention that this proves Jesus is "the Father" is incorrect. Foundationally, Jesus speaks of the Father as someone other than Himself over 200 times in the New Testament. And over 50 times in the New Testament the Father and Son are distinct within the same verse (for example, Rom. 15:6; 2 Cor. 1:4; Gal. 1:2–3; Phil. 2:10–11; 1 John 2:1; 2 John 3).[54] The word *Father* as a title of God did not emerge into prominence until New Testament times when Jesus taught that God was a "Father." It certainly was not a common title for God in Old Testament times. This would argue against the idea that the use of "Father" in Isaiah 9:6 was intended to be a New Testament–like reference to God.

If the Father and the Son are distinct, then in what sense can Jesus be called "Everlasting Father" (Isa. 9:6)? This phrase is better translated "Father of eternity," and carries the meaning "possessor of eternity." *Father of eternity* is used here in accordance with a Hebrew and Arabic custom in which he who possesses a thing is called the father of it. Thus, *the father of strength* means "strong"; *the father of knowledge,* "intelligent"; *the father of glory,* "glorious."[55] According to this common usage, the meaning of *Father of eternity* in Isaiah 9:6 is "eternal." Christ as the "Father of eternity" is an eternal being.

The Targum, a simplified paraphrase of the Old Testament Scriptures used by the ancient Jews, rendered Isaiah 9:6 (as translated into English): "His name has been called from of old, Wonderful Counselor, Mighty God, He who lives forever...."[56] The ancient Jews considered the phrase "Father of eternity" as indicating the eternality of the Messiah. Therefore, Jesus, although distinct from the Father, can be called "Everlasting Father."

Former Oneness Pentecostal Gregory Boyd raises this important question: "Why are the New Testament writers so remarkably clear in communicating the sonship of Jesus—to the point that no one has ever missed this—yet so remarkably opaque in communicating the (supposed) fatherhood of Jesus—to the point that the vast majority of Bible readers have never even suspected this?"[57] If we are to believe Oneness Pentecostals, 99.99 percent of all believers throughout church history have gotten it wrong in terms of Jesus being the Father, and hence, they are all lost, having believed in a false Trinitarian God.

John 10:30 Does Not Prove Jesus Is the Father

In John 10:30, Jesus affirmed, "I and the Father are one." This verse does not mean Jesus and the Father are one and the same person. We know this to be true, because in the phrase "I and the Father are one," a first person plural "we are" (Greek *esmen*) is used. The verse literally reads from the Greek, "I and the Father *we are* one." If Jesus intended to say that He and the Father were one person, He would not have used the first person plural, which clearly implies two persons.

Moreover, the Greek word for "one" *(hen)* in this verse refers not to personal unity (the idea that the Father and Son are one person), but to unity of essence or nature (that the Father and Son have the same divine nature). This is evident in the fact that the form of the word in the Greek is neuter, not masculine. Further, the verses that immediately precede and follow John 10:30 distinguish Jesus from the Father (see John 10:25, 29, 36, 38).

John 14:6–11 Does Not Prove Jesus Is the Father

In John 14:6–11, Jesus affirms that one who has seen Jesus has seen the Father. These verses prove only that the Father and the Son are one in *being,* not that they are one *person.* Contextually, notice that in John 14:6 Jesus clearly distinguishes Himself from the Father when He says, "No one comes *to* the Father, except *through* me" (emphasis added). The words *to* and *through* would not make any sense if Jesus and the Father were one and the same person. They only make sense if the Father and Jesus are distinct persons, with Jesus being the Mediator between the Father and humankind. Furthermore, when Jesus said "Anyone who has seen me has seen the Father" (John 14:9), He was not saying He was the Father. Rather, Jesus is the perfect revelation of the Father (1:18).

First Corinthians 1:3 Does Not Prove Jesus Is the Father

In 1 Corinthians 1:3 we read the salutation, "Grace to you and peace from God our Father and the Lord Jesus Christ." Oneness Pentecostals argue that the latter part of the verse should read, "God our Father, *even* the Lord Jesus Christ." Translated this way, Jesus and the Father are seen to be one and the same person.

While it is true that the Greek word *kai* can be translated "even" in certain verses, context is always determinative in how the word is translated. Greek scholars universally agree that, in context, *kai* in 1 Corinthians 1:3 should be translated "and," not "even." Further, most of the occurrences of the word *kai* in the New Testament are translated as "and," not "even." This means that the burden of proof is on Oneness Pentecostals to demonstrate that the word must be translated with its secondary meaning ("even") and not its primary meaning ("and") in 1 Corinthians 1:3. Moreover, the verses immediately prior to and immediately after 1 Corinthians 1:3 point to the distinction between the Father and Jesus Christ (see vv. 2, 4). Contextually, then, the Oneness Pentecostal interpretation does not fit.

Colossians 2:9 Does Not Prove Jesus is the Father

In Colossians 2:9 the apostle Paul said of Christ, "For in him dwelleth all the fullness of the Godhead bodily" (KJV). As noted previously, Oneness Pentecostals believe that because the fullness of the Godhead is said to dwell in Jesus, this must mean that Jesus is the Father and the Holy Spirit. That this interpretation is incorrect is clear in the fact that the term "Godhead" simply means *Deity*, as translated in the New International Version. The word indicates that the fullness of deity—the very divine essence itself, including all the divine attributes—dwells fully in Jesus. The verse indicates, then, that Jesus is fully God, but it does not say that Jesus is the only person who is God. A fundamental hermeneutical principle is that Scripture interprets Scripture. And Scripture indicates that in the unity of the one God (Deut. 6:4) there are three distinct persons, each of whom is in full possession of the divine essence (Matt. 28:19; 2 Cor. 13:14).

Second Corinthians 3:17 Does Not Prove Jesus Is the Holy Spirit

As noted previously, Oneness Pentecostals often cite 2 Corinthians 3:17 to "prove" Jesus is the Holy Spirit: "Now the Lord is the Spirit: and where the Spirit of the Lord is, there is liberty." Of course, the verse does not say that Jesus is the Holy Spirit. That is something Oneness Pentecostals are reading into the verse. The text says "the Lord is the Spirit." Most expositors interpret this verse as saying the Holy Spirit is "Lord," not in the sense of being Jesus, but in the sense of being Yahweh (the Lord God). The verse is not saying Jesus is the Holy Spirit, for earlier in 2 Corinthians 3 Paul clearly distinguishes between Jesus and the Holy Spirit (see vv. 3–6). The immediate context, then, stands against the Oneness Pentecostal view.

Oneness Arguments against the Trinity Fail

The Trinity Is Not Illogical

The Trinity may be beyond our means to fully understand, but this does not mean it is illogical or false. For human beings to be able to understand everything about God, they would need to have the very mind of God. Scripture itself indicates that finite human beings cannot possibly understand everything about an infinite God or His ways (Isa. 55:8–9; Rom. 11:33; 1 Cor. 13:12).

The doctrine of the Trinity may be *beyond* reason, but it is not *against* reason. The doctrine of the Trinity does not entail three Gods in one God or three persons in one person. Such claims would be nonsensical. There is, however, nothing contradictory in affirming three persons in one God, as Scripture does (Matt. 28:19; 2 Cor. 13:14). More than one Christian apologist has noted the irony of Oneness Pentecostals claiming the Trinity doctrine is illogical in view of their own convoluted arguments that Jesus is the Father, the Son, and the Holy Spirit.

The Trinity Is Not Rooted in Paganism

The Babylonians and Assyrians believed in triads of gods who headed up a pantheon of many other gods. But these triads included three separate gods (polytheism), which is utterly different from the doctrine of the Trinity—which maintains that there is only one God (monotheism) with three persons within the one Godhead. Therefore the suggestion that Christianity borrowed the Trinitarian concept from pagans is quite infeasible.

It is interesting to note that pagans taught the concept of a creator. They also taught the concept of a great flood that killed much of humankind and the idea of a messiah-like figure (named Tammuz) who was "resurrected." Therefore, if Oneness Pentecostals were consistent in their reasoning, they would have to reject the creator, the flood, the Messiah, and the resurrection because there are loose parallels among pagan religions. Simply because pagans spoke of a concept remotely resembling something found in Scripture does not mean the concept was stolen from pagans.

The Church Fathers Held Trinitarian Viewpoints

Though Oneness Pentecostals cite church fathers like Clement of Rome, Ignatius, Justin, and others in arguing against the Trinity, it is a historical fact that the writings of the church fathers do not support Oneness Pentecostalism, but imply Trinitarianism. For example, they taught that there is but one God; they taught that the Father is God; they taught that Jesus is God; they taught that the Holy Spirit is God; they taught that the Father and the Son are distinct persons; they taught that the Son and the Spirit are distinct persons; they taught that the Father and the Spirit are distinct persons; and they referred to all three together as distinct persons. History thus argues against Oneness Pentecostalism.[58]

The Biblical Case for the Trinity

In arguing against the Trinity, Oneness Pentecostals often cite Trinitarian arguments that, frankly, are weak. A case in point is the use of the plural word *Elohim* to support the doctrine of the Trinity. Knowledgeable evangelicals do not argue that the word *Elohim* proves the doctrine of the Trinity, but Oneness Pentecostals speak as if this were a sine qua non of Trinitarianism. Oneness Pentecostals often avoid dealing with the stronger biblical evidences that support the Trinity. In what follows, I offer a summary of some of these evidences.

To begin, we must note that simply because the word Trinity is not found in the Bible does not mean the Trinity is unbiblical. While the word is not in the Bible, the concept definitely is. As Calvin Beisner notes, "That the Bible does not use *Trinity* (or any other term) is no more evidence against Trinitarianism than the absence of the word *Oneness* in the Bible is evidence against Oneness theology. When Oneness writers argue this way, they indulge in special pleading."[59] Oneness Pentecostals also make reference to "modes" and "manifestations" of God, neither word being in the Bible.

The question is, does the word *Trinity* reflect a biblical teaching or concept? If it does, then it is legitimate to use the shorthand term to describe a biblical doctrine. Biblically, the doctrine of the Trinity is based on three lines of evidence: (1) evidence that there is only one true God; (2) evidence that there are three persons who are God; and (3) evidence that indicates three-in-oneness within the Godhead.

1. Evidence for one God. The fact that there is only one true God is the consistent testimony of Scripture from Genesis to Revelation. It is a thread that runs through every page of the Bible. God positively affirms through Isaiah the prophet: "This is what the LORD says—Israel's King and Redeemer, the LORD Almighty: I am the first and I am the last; apart from me there is no God" (44:6). God also says, "I am God, and there is no other; I am God, and there is none like me" (Isa. 46:9). These and a multitude of other verses (including John 5:44; 17:3; Rom. 3:29–30; 16:27; 1 Cor. 8:4; Gal. 3:20; Eph. 4:6; 1 Tim. 2:5; James 2:19) make it clear that there is one and only one God.

2. Evidence for three persons who are called God. Although Scripture indicates there is only one God, in the unfolding of God's revelation to humankind, it also becomes clear that there are three distinct persons who are called God in Scripture.

- *The Father is God.* Peter refers to the saints "who have been chosen according to the foreknowledge of God the Father" (1 Peter 1:2).
- *Jesus is God.* When Jesus made a post-resurrection appearance to doubting Thomas, Thomas said, "My Lord and my God" (John 20:28). In addition, the Father said of the Son, "Your throne, O God, will last for ever and ever, and righteousness will be the scepter of your kingdom" (Heb. 1:8).
- *The Holy Spirit is God.* In Acts 5:3–4 we are told that lying to the Holy Spirit is equivalent to lying to God.

Moreover, each of the three persons on different occasions is seen to possess the attributes of deity. For example, all three are said to be *omnipresent:* the Father (Jer. 23:23–24), the Son (Matt. 28:18), and the Holy Spirit (Ps. 139:7). All three are *omniscient:* the Father (Rom. 11:33), the Son (Matt. 9:4), and the Holy Spirit (1 Cor. 2:10). All three are *omnipotent:* the Father (Gen. 18:14; Ps. 24:8; Jer. 32:17), the Son (Matt. 28:18), and the Holy Spirit (Rom. 15:19). Furthermore, *holiness* is ascribed to each person: the Father (Rev. 15:4), the Son (Acts 3:14), and the Holy Spirit (John 16:7–14). *Eternity* is ascribed to each person: the Father (Ps. 90:2), the Son (Mic. 5:2; John 1:2; Rev. 1:8, 17), and the Holy Spirit (Heb. 9:14). And each of the three is individually described as the *truth:* the Father (John 7:28), the Son (Rev. 3:7), and the Holy Spirit (1 John 5:6).

3. Three-in-oneness in the Godhead. In the New American Standard Bible, Matthew 28:19 reads, "Go therefore and make disciples of all the nations, baptizing them in the name of *the* Father and *the* Son and *the* Holy Spirit" (emphasis added). It is highly revealing that the word *name* is singular in the Greek, indicating that there is one God, but three distinct persons within the Godhead—the Father, the Son, and the Holy Spirit. Theologian Robert Reymond draws our attention to the importance of this verse for the doctrine of the Trinity:

> Jesus does not say, (1) "into the names [plural] of the Father and of the Son and of the Holy Spirit," or what is its virtual equivalent, (2) "into the name of the Father, and into the name of the Son, and into the name of the Holy Spirit," as if we had to deal with three separate Beings. Nor does He say, (3) "into the name of the Father, Son, and Holy Spirit" (omitting the three recurring articles), as if "the Father, Son, and Holy Ghost" might be taken as merely three designations of a single person. What He does say is this: (4) "into the name [singular] of *the* Father, and of *the* Son, and of *the* Holy Spirit," first asserting the unity of the three by combining them all within the bounds of the single Name, and then throwing into emphasis the distinctness of each by introducing them in turn with the repeated article.[60]

The "Absent" Holy Spirit Does Not Disprove the Trinity

The Oneness Pentecostal argument against the Trinity based on the "absent" Holy Spirit in many passages is weak at best. This is nothing more than an argument from silence and is therefore an invalid argument. An omission is not the same as a denial. Boyd beautifully illustrates this for us:

> If I am with my two daughters at a public speaking engagement and I introduce them as "my children, Denay and Alisha," this does not mean that I do not have a son. To conclude that I don't have a son because I didn't mention him would be an argument from silence. In truth my omission only means that I, for whatever reasons, didn't deem it expedient to mention him. Nor does the fact that I didn't mention my wife, my father, or my grandfather imply that I don't have a wife, a father, or a grandfather. Since an omission does not constitute a denial, arguments from silence are never valid.[61]

In like manner, simply because the Holy Spirit is not always mentioned alongside the Father and Jesus is not an argument against the fact that the Holy Spirit is a person who is fully God on an equal par with the Father and Jesus. A number of key passages of Scripture do mention all three together (for example, Matt. 28:19; 2 Cor. 13:14; et al.).

It is also noteworthy that Scripture reveals the role of the Holy Spirit to be one in which He points away from Himself and toward Christ (John 16:13–14). In view of the fact that the Holy Spirit Himself inspired Scripture (2 Tim. 3:16), it is not surprising to find these Scriptures primarily exalting Jesus the divine Messiah in His salvific mission on behalf of the Father.

Problems with the Oneness Pentecostal View of Salvation

Baptism Does Not Have to Be "In the Name of Jesus" Only (Acts 2:38)

The idea of baptism "in the name of Jesus only" is primarily based on a misinterpretation of Acts 2:38: "Peter replied, 'Repent and be baptized, every one of you, *in the name of Jesus Christ* for the forgiveness of your sins. And you will receive the gift of the Holy Spirit'" (emphasis added). In answering the Oneness Pentecostal interpretation, we must first note that the phrase "in the name of" in biblical times often carried the meaning "by the authority of." Seen in this light, the phrase in Acts 2:38 cannot be interpreted to be some kind of a magic baptismal formula. The verse simply indicates that people are to be baptized according to the authority of Jesus Christ. The verse does not mean that the words "in the name of Jesus" must be liturgically pronounced over each person being baptized. If Acts 2:38 was intended to be a baptismal formula, then why is this formula never repeated in exactly the same way in the rest of Acts or the New Testament (cf. Matt. 28:19)?

If we were consistent in using Oneness Pentecostal logic, we would have to pronounce the words "in the name of Jesus" over everything we did, for Colossians 3:17 instructs us, "Whatever you do in word or deed, do all *in the name of the Lord Jesus*, giving thanks through Him to God the Father" (NASB, emphasis added). Clearly the words "in the name of Jesus" are not intended as a formula.

Moreover, a baptism in the name of Jesus makes good sense in the context of Acts 2, because the Jews ("men of Judea" [v. 14], "men of Israel" [v. 22]), to whom Peter was preaching, had rejected

Christ as the Messiah. It is logical that Peter would call on them to repent of their rejection of Jesus the Messiah and become publicly identified with Him through baptism. Baptism in the "name of Jesus" would serve to distinguish this baptism from all the other baptisms that were part of Judaism at the time.

From a historical perspective, the Trinitarian baptism (Matt. 28:19) was certainly dominant from the time of the second century. Are we to conclude that all those who were baptized from the second century to the present century in this manner are unsaved? The suggestion is preposterous. Furthermore, it is highly revealing that no church leaders quibbled over the Trinitarian baptism in the early centuries of Christianity. If salvation depended on one being baptized in the name of Jesus, there certainly would have been major debate when the Trinitarian baptism was widely practiced in the early centuries of Christianity. But church history reveals there wasn't even a ripple in the ocean of theological debate on this issue. Clearly the early believers did not consider "in the name of Jesus" or "in the name of the Father, Son, and Holy Spirit" to be rigid formulas.

Finally, one could argue that the use of such a strict "formula" to bring about a desired result (salvation) reeks of ancient paganism. Among the ancient pagans, deities could be manipulated to bring about a desired result by reciting a precise incantation. In Oneness Pentecostalism, one recites a specific formula ("in the name of Jesus") so that God brings about the desired result, salvation.[62] Such a view cannot be sustained from Scripture.

Water Baptism Is Not a Requirement for Salvation

Aside from citing Acts 2:38 in support of the idea that baptism must be "in the name of Jesus only," Oneness Pentecostals also cite this verse to prove that *one cannot be saved without water baptism* ("repent and be baptized... for the forgiveness of your sins"). Properly understood, however, this verse does not teach that baptism is a requirement for salvation.

Admittedly, this is not an easy verse to interpret. But a basic principle of Bible interpretation is that difficult passages are to be interpreted in light of the easy, clear verses. One should never build a theology on difficult passages alone. The great majority of passages dealing with salvation in the New Testament affirm that salvation is by faith alone (for example, John 3:16–17; 5:24; 7:38; 20:29).

In view of such self-explanatory passages, how is Acts 2:38 to be interpreted?

A single word in the verse gives us the answer. The verse reads, "Peter replied, 'Repent and be baptized, every one of you, in the name of Jesus Christ *for* the forgiveness of your sins. And you will receive the gift of the Holy Spirit'" (emphasis added). Students of Greek often point out that the Greek word translated "for" *(eis)* is a preposition that can indicate causality ("in order to attain") or a result ("because of"). An example of using "for" in a resultant sense is the sentence, "I'm taking an aspirin for my headache." Obviously this means I am taking an aspirin *as a result of* my headache. I am not taking an aspirin *in order to obtain* a headache. An example of using "for" in a causal sense is the sentence, "I'm going to the office for my paycheck." Obviously this means I am going to the office *in order to obtain* my paycheck.

In Acts 2:38 the word *for* is apparently used in a resultant sense. The verse might be paraphrased, "Repent, and be baptized every one of you in the name of Jesus Christ *because of* (or *as a result of*) the remission of sins." The verse is not saying, "Repent, and be baptized every one of you in the name of Jesus Christ *in order to attain* the remission of sins." If the "resultant" interpretation is correct, the verse is seen to be compatible with the hundreds of New Testament verses that say salvation comes by *faith alone* (for example, John 3:16; Acts 16:31) and indicates that baptism *follows* the salvation experience.

Another verse Oneness Pentecostals sometimes cite in favor of their view that water baptism is necessary for salvation is John 3:1–5, which refers to being "born of water." Critical to a proper understanding of John 3:1–5 is verse 6: "That which is born of the flesh is flesh, and that which is born of the Spirit is spirit" (NASB). Flesh can only reproduce itself as flesh and flesh cannot pass muster with God (cf. Rom. 8:8). The law of reproduction is "after its kind" (see Gen. 1). So, likewise, the Spirit produces spirit.

In Nicodemus's case, we find a Pharisee who would have been trusting in his physical descent from Abraham for entrance into the Messiah's kingdom. The Jews believed that because they were physically related to Abraham, they were in a specially privileged position before God. Christ, however, denied such a possibility. Parents can transmit to their children only the nature they themselves possess. Since each parent's nature, because of Adam's sin, is sinful, each parent transmits a sinful nature to the child. And what is sinful cannot enter the kingdom of God (v. 5). The only way one can enter God's kingdom is to experience a spiritual rebirth, and this is precisely what Jesus was emphasizing to Nicodemus. Nicodemus, however, did not initially comprehend Jesus' meaning. He wrongly concluded that Jesus was speaking of something related to physical birth but could not understand how a person could go through physical birth a second time (John 3:4). Jesus picked up on Nicodemus's line of thought and sought to move the argument from physical birth to spiritual birth.

Notice how Jesus went about His explanation to Nicodemus. He first spoke about being "born of water and the Spirit" in John 3:5 and then explained what He meant by this in verse 6. It would seem that "born of water" in verse 5 is parallel to "born of the flesh" in verse 6, just as "born of . . . the Spirit" in verse 5 is parallel to "born of the Spirit" in verse 6. Jesus' message, then, is that just as one has had a physical birth to live on earth, so one must also have a spiritual birth in order to enter the kingdom of God. One must be "born from above." The verse thus has nothing whatsoever to do with water baptism as a requirement for salvation.

Speaking in Tongues Is Not Required for Salvation

Contrary to the Oneness Pentecostal claim, the unbending requirement of speaking in tongues cannot be sustained from Scripture. Speaking in tongues is not the definitive evidence of the baptism of the Holy Spirit, for not all the Corinthians spoke in tongues (1 Cor. 14:5) even though all had been baptized by the Spirit (12:13). Further, the fruit of the Holy Spirit (Gal. 5:22–23) does not include speaking in tongues. Therefore, Christlikeness does not require speaking in tongues. A number of passages in the book of Acts record conversions of people being baptized or filled with the Holy Spirit in which no mention is made of speaking in tongues (see Acts 2:37–41; 4:31; 6:3–6; 7:55; 11:24; 13:52). It seems clear from such texts that speaking in tongues is not an indispensable evidence of being baptized in the Spirit.

Maintaining Holiness Is Not a Condition of Salvation

The view that one must maintain holiness to sustain one's salvation goes against God's gospel of grace as clearly delineated in

Scripture (for example, Eph. 2:8–9). A key verse refuting this idea is Romans 8:1, where the apostle Paul writes, "There is *now* no condemnation for those who are in Christ Jesus" (emphasis added). Salvation is said to be by faith alone close to 200 times in the New Testament (for example, John 3:15; 5:24; 11:25; 12:46; 20:31). If salvation were not by faith alone, these almost 200 verses would be deceptive, saying there is one condition for salvation when there are many conditions. While we are saved *by* faith, we are saved *for* works. Works are not the *condition* of our salvation, but a *consequence* of it. A life of holiness is important, but it follows salvation; it does not cause it.

In view of the fact that Oneness Pentecostals set forth a different God, a different Jesus, and a different gospel, the group is properly categorized as a cult. Their differences with mainstream historic Christianity are not mere peripheral issues but relate to the foundational doctrines on which Christianity rests.

13

FREEMASONRY

Freemasonry is a centuries-old fraternal order and secret society deeply entrenched in symbolism, secret oaths, and secret rituals. Key themes include the universal fatherhood of God and the brotherhood of man.

Some very famous Americans have been Masons—including 14 United States presidents (George Washington, for one), 18 vice presidents, 5 chief justices of the Supreme Court, Paul Revere, Benjamin Franklin, James Monroe, Alexander Hamilton, General Douglas MacArthur, J. Edgar Hoover, and Barry M. Goldwater. Also to be counted as Masons were John Philip Sousa, Mark Twain, W. C. Fields, Henry Ford, Harry Houdini, Cecil B. DeMille, John Wayne, Clark Gable, Ernest Borgnine, Roy Rogers, Red Skelton, J. C. Penney, and Norman Vincent Peale. Some noted non-American Masons were

Wolfgang Amadeus Mozart, François Voltaire, Franz Joseph Haydn, Sir Arthur Conan Doyle, Oscar Wilde, and Sir Winston Churchill.[1]

Today millions of people are involved in the various orders of Freemasonry. There are probably about 3 million Masons in the Blue Lodge, over a quarter million in the York Rite, close to a million in the Scottish Rite, and perhaps another million in the various other orders affiliated with Freemasonry.[2] There are presently about 33,700 Masonic Lodges (meeting places for Masons) in 164 countries in the world, with about 15,300 in the Unites States alone. Clearly this is a movement to take seriously.

People join the Freemasons for a variety of reasons. Some like the idea of belonging to a secret society where they are privileged to learn secret mysteries. Some are fascinated by the symbolism. Some join because they appreciate the emphasis on the brotherhood of man and the accompanying humanitarianism. Still others join because they think it is a good place to make business contacts.[3]

The origin of Freemasonry is shrouded in deep mystery and wild legends. Some Masons claim that Freemasonry goes back to the time of Adam and Eve, arguing that the fig leaves referenced in Genesis 3:7 were actually the first Masonic "aprons" (which are used in Masonic initiatory ceremonies).[4] Other Masons claim that Freemasonry dates back to the time of Solomon, who utilized the skills of stone masons in building the temple in Jerusalem.[5]

Contrary to such claims, history reveals that Freemasonry formally began in London, England, in 1717, due to the efforts of James Anderson, George Payne, and Theopholis Desaguliers.[6] The earliest recorded minutes of a Masonic meeting date back to 1723. It was just a matter of time before additional lodges sprang up across England, Ireland, Scotland, Holland, Germany, France, and other European countries.[7]

Spreading rapidly, Freemasonry arrived on American soil by 1733, just 16 years after it first emerged in England. Throughout the 1800s virtually thousands of Masonic Lodges mushroomed throughout the United States.[8] Understandably, Freemasonry grew to become a powerful influence in American religion, politics, and social life. Today about half the Grand Lodges and two-thirds of the Freemasons in the world are in the United States.

No single definition of Freemasonry will be acceptable to all Masons. There are so many degrees in Freemasonry, with different levels of mysteries revealed to initiates, that what constitutes Freemasonry to one person may be quite different from how another Mason sees it. Some low-level Masons may view Freemasonry as little more than a social club or fraternal fellowship that is beneficial for business contacts. For others, particularly those in more advanced degrees, Freemasonry takes on much more significance and can even become a way of life.[9]

Some Masons believe that one cannot understand *true* Masonry outside of the higher degrees. The lower degrees are merely the "cover of the book," so to speak, and to understand what Masonry really is requires opening that book and exploring the mysteries.[10] Nonetheless, no one Mason speaks for another. "Freemasonry has no 'official voice' and that freedom of thought and expression is one of the fundamental principles of the Order."[11]

Yet Freemasonry is a historical movement that has produced a large body of literature and acknowledges certain leaders within the movement whose writings are recognized as representative. Therefore, this chapter will focus on the "core" beliefs expressed in respected and representative Masonic literature—especially that produced by Masonic leaders like Henry Wilson Coil, Joseph Fort Newton, Albert G. Mackey, and Albert Pike. Masonic Grand Masters across the United States consider such leaders authoritative spokesmen.

MASONIC FAMILIES

There is not just one kind of Mason. There are *families* of Masons, each with distinctive characteristics. When a person first becomes a Mason, he is initiated into the Blue Lodge. This is the starting point for anyone wishing to become a Mason. (In what follows, I will provide only basic summary facts about the various Masonic families. I will discuss specific Masonic beliefs later in the chapter.)

The Blue Lodge

Membership in the Blue Lodge is restricted to males 21 years of age or older. One must be recommended by a lodge member in order to be accepted. Following such a recommendation, a vote is taken. Should the member receive what is called a "blackball" (a negative vote), a "foul" is announced and a second vote is taken.

Barring any further blackballs, the candidate is accepted. If he receives a second blackball, he is rejected.[12]

Once accepted, the candidate begins to earn the degree of Entered Apprentice. Upon acceptance, one is required to bow before "The Worshipful Master" and say something to the effect, "I am lost in darkness, and I am seeking the light of Freemasonry. . . ."[13]

After Entered Apprentice, there are two additional degrees within Blue Lodge Freemasonry—Fellow Craft and Master Mason. One must participate in required rituals to attain each of these degrees. Before being accepted in either, the candidate must swear a blood oath: "I promise and swear, that I will not write, print, stamp, stain, hew, cut, carve, indent, paint, or engrave it [Masonic secrets] on anything moveable or immovable . . . binding myself under no less penalty than to have my throat cut across, my tongue torn out by the roots, and my body buried in the rough sands of the sea at lower water mark."[14]

When seeking entrance into the Fellow Craft degree, the oath includes additional words: "Binding myself under no less a penalty than that of having my left breast torn open, my heart plucked out and given as prey to the wild beasts of the fields and the fowls of the air." When seeking entrance into the third degree—the Master Mason's degree—the oath adds, "Binding myself under no less a penalty than that of having my body severed in twain, my bowels taken from thence and burned in ashes."[15]

Though it is highly doubtful that such threats have ever been carried out, the very fact that such words are spoken within the confines of Masonic Lodges is nothing less than barbaric. Most Masons probably do not take such oaths literally. One pro-Mason historian noted, "No Mason believes that the penalties of his oath will be visited upon him, and every candidate would hurry out of the room if ever told that he must help to inflict those penalties on someone else."[16] Nevertheless, the very spirit of such oaths is exceedingly offensive to the consciences of many outsiders.

The York Rite

Having completed the three degrees in the Blue Lodge, the Mason is then free to pursue higher degrees in either the York Rite or the Scottish Rite. The York Rite is named after York, England, the seat of the Ancient York Grand Lodge.[17] According to Masonic literature, one can attain four "Chapter" degrees that are awarded by the General Grand Chapter of the York Rite: Mark Master (fourth degree), Past Master (fifth degree), Most Excellent Master (sixth degree), and Royal Arch Mason (seventh degree). One can then opt to pursue "Council" degrees: Royal Master (eighth degree), Select Master (ninth degree), and Super Excellent Master (unnumbered degree).

The Scottish Rite

The Scottish Rite branch of Freemasonry—perhaps the most popular form of Freemasonry—may be pursued after one has completed the Master Mason degree in the Blue Lodge. The Scottish Rite confers an additional 29 degrees, the highest of these being the 33rd-degree Mason, which is called the "Knight Commander."[18] An example of a well-known 33rd-degree Mason is positive-thinking author Norman Vincent Peale.

Special Interest Masonic Orders

Aside from the Blue Lodge, the York Rite, and the Scottish Rite, there are a number of minor orders within Freemasonry that cater to what one might call "special interest groups" within Freemasonry. Following is a brief summary of some of the more notable of these.[19]

Ancient Arabic Order of the Nobles of the Mystic Shrine

This Order was founded in 1872 for the primary purpose of "extracurricular fraternization." Shriners, as they are called, are high-level York Rite and Scottish Rite Masons who gather for fun and socializing apart from the normal meetings in Masonic Lodges. Today Shriners are well known for their charitable work for children's hospitals and burn centers.

The Order of the Eastern Star

This Order was founded in 1850 by Dr. Robert Morris. It is open to women who are related to Masons—including wives, daughters, mothers, sisters, granddaughters, and other female relatives. The order supports both the causes and the doctrines of Masonry. The five degrees attainable within this order are named after women of the Bible: Adah (the first degree, which stresses obedience), Ruth (the second degree, which stresses devotion), Esther (the third degree, which stresses fidelity), Martha (the fourth degree, which stresses faith), and Electa (the fifth degree, which stresses charity). (Masons believe Electa is the "chosen lady" mentioned in 2 John 1.)

It is not surprising, in view of the male exclusivity of Freemasonry, that some Masons reacted less than charitably when this order was formed. One well-known Mason, Albert Mackey, thought the idea was reprehensible and was aghast that women could be permitted to learn the sacred secrets of Freemasonry. Others view it as more beneficial, since Masonic education of wives and other family members can help them better support the man of the house.

Daughters of the Eastern Star

This Order is for girls ages 14 to 20 whose fathers are Masons or whose mothers are members of the Eastern Star. The order was founded in 1925 and confers three degrees—Initiatory, Honorary Majority, and Public.

The Order of DeMolay

This Order is named after Jacques DeMolay, leader of the Knights Templar, who was burned at the stake in the fourteenth century. It is an order for males ages 14 to 21 and focuses on such noble things as citizenship, patriotism, morality, cleanliness, and faith in God.

The International Order of Job's Daughters

This Order was founded in 1920 by Ethel T. W. Mick and is obviously named from the book of Job: "Nowhere in all the land were there found women as beautiful as Job's daughters, and their father granted them an inheritance along with their brothers" (Job 42:15). This order is for girls between the ages of 11 and 20 and focuses heavily on moral and spiritual development. They are also involved in charity in the community.

The International Order of Rainbow for Girls

This Order was founded in 1922 by Reverend Mark Sexson. The goal of this order is to prepare girls for eventual membership in the Eastern Star. Membership is limited to females, ages 12 to 20, and requires a recommendation by a Mason or a member of the Eastern Star. The "Rainbow" ritual is built on the foundation of faith, hope, and charity.

Masonic College Fraternities

There are a number of fraternal organizations on college campuses that are directly affiliated with Freemasonry—including Acacia, The Square and Compass, Sigma Mu Sigma, The Order of the Golden Key, and Tau Kappa Epsilon. Most of these emerged in the late 1800s or early 1900s. Many college campuses across the country sponsor these and other fraternal organizations.

Prince Hall Freemasonry

In view of the fact that blacks had been consistently denied membership in the various orders of Freemasonry, it is not surprising that an all-black lodge eventually emerged. Prince Hall Freemasonry emerged due to the efforts of Prince Hall, a black man, in the late 1700s. His petition for a charter was granted by the Grand Lodge of England in 1784.[20]

MASONIC BELIEFS

Freemasonry as a Religion

One of the more controversial aspects of Freemasonry relates to the question of whether it is a religion or not. Even Masons disagree among themselves on this issue. Well-known Masonic authors such as Albert Mackey and H. W. Coil say Freemasonry is a religion. Such authors appeal to the fact that Freemasonry requires a belief in a Supreme Being and contains a creed, temples, doctrines, altars, worship, and even chaplains. Such factors point to the reality that Freemasonry is a religious organization.[21] Coil said, "Freemasonry is undoubtedly a religion,"[22] and he compared the Masonic Lodge to a church.[23] Albert Pike said that "every Masonic Lodge is a temple of religion, and its teachings are instruction in religion."[24]

Other Masonic authors—in fact, the majority of Freemasons—deny that Freemasonry is a religion. Freemasonry does require belief in a Supreme Deity and the immortality of the soul, but the differences between Freemasonry and religion are said to be far greater than any similarities that may exist. These Masons argue that the term *religion* implies new revelation, a plan of salvation, a theology, dogmas, sacraments, clergy, and ways of communicating with God, none of which are part of Freemasonry, according to its members.[25] "There is nothing better understood among Masons than that [Masonry] is not a religion."[26] Indeed, "Freemasonry is not a religion, it is a philosophy."[27]

Moreover, the fact that each Mason is free to interpret religious ideas as he chooses goes against the claim that Freemasonry is a religion. How the individual Mason perceives and worships the Supreme Being in which he believes is said to be his own business, as is the means by which he hopes to attain immortality, and no brother Mason is permitted to attempt to dissuade him from those beliefs.

In Freemasonry, then, one is free to follow his own personal religious beliefs—whether he is a Christian, a Jew, a Muslim, or a Hindu. "He may believe the teachings of any organized religion, or he may even have religious convictions that are his alone—as did Thomas Jefferson and John Locke—so long as he believes in a Supreme Being. On that basis, Masonry has welcomed Jews, Moslems, Sikhs, and others, all of whom take the oaths on their own Holy Books."[28] Masonry brings together people of different persuasions to enjoy a "common fellowship," despite different personal religious beliefs.[29]

Some Masons argue that if Freemasonry were a religion it would specifically define the Supreme Being, but it does not do this. Dr. Norman Vincent Peale, a Mason, wrote, "Freemasonry is not a religion, though, in my experience, Masons have predominantly been religious men and for the most part, of the Christian faith. . . . All Masons believe in the deity without reservation. However, Masonry makes no demands as to how a member thinks of the great architect of the universe."[30]

Freemasonry is said to be more about ethics and doing good in the world than about religion.[31] One Mason asserts, "An honest interpretation of the teachings of Freemasonry will show that instead of teaching men what to believe, men are simply asked to put the religion they already have, when they become a Mason, into everyday practice."[32] Another Mason says Freemasonry "teaches Masons that their daily life should reflect the principles of their own religion, whatever their religion might be."[33]

Despite the controversy over this issue, most Masons today believe Freemasonry is not a religion. One likely reason for this is that it would be hard to draw people into its ranks from a variety of religious persuasions if it positioned itself as a new religion.

The Bible Is One of Many Symbols of God's Will

Masons believe that even though the Bible is a significant book, it is not the exclusive Word of God. It is not viewed as God's *only* revelation to humankind, but as one of many holy books that contains religious and moral truth. Masons often refer to the Bible as a symbol of God's will.[34] "The prevailing Masonic opinion is that the Bible is only a symbol of Divine Will, Law, or Revelation, and not that its contents are Divine Law, inspired, or revealed. So far, no responsible authority has held that a Freemason must believe the Bible or any part of it."[35] Other symbols of God's will include the Koran (used by Muslims), the Vedas (used by Hindus), and the Torah (used by Jews).

All holy books are acceptable within the confines of the Masonic Lodge. All these books are said to provide not just religious truth, but moral truth, and hence they constitute ethical guides by which to govern one's life. Quite clearly the Masonic view of the Bible is in keeping with the Masonic openness to all religions.

God Is the Great Architect of the Universe

A key requirement of joining a Masonic Lodge is that one must subscribe to belief in a Supreme Being. It does not matter what one calls that deity, but one must believe in a deity. No atheist can be a Mason.[36] God is often described by Masons as the "Great Architect of the Universe," "Supreme Being," "Grand Geometrician of the Universe," "Grand Artificer of the Universe," and "God, the Creator, Author, and Architect of the Universe, Omnipotent, Omniscient, and Omnipresent."[37] The Supreme Being of the Masonic Lodge is essentially unknowable and, consequently, inoffensive. If God is infinitely beyond our ability to comprehend, then it is inappropriate for us mere humans to fight over how to define Him.

Masons believe that Jews, Christians, Hindus, Muslims, and those of other faiths are all worshiping the same God using different names. Therefore, God is known as "the nameless one of a hundred names."[38] People worship God under different names only because they do not know any better; they are in spiritual darkness. Freema-

"Masonry knows, what so many forget, that religions are many, but Religion is one.... Therefore it invites to its altar men of all faiths knowing that, if they use different names for 'the Nameless One of a hundred names,' they are yet praying to the one God and Father of all" (cited in *Holy Bible [Temple Illustrated Edition]*, 3–4).

sonry claims it can remove this darkness by revealing that all people are actually worshiping the same God. As Albert Mackey put it, "God is equally present with the pious Hindoo [sic] in the temple, the Jew in the synagogue, the Mohammedan in the mosque, and the Christian in the church."[39]

Though different Masons refer to God using different names, Freemasonry does not affirm the Christian belief in the doctrine of the Trinity. Masons believe that if Freemasonry affirmed belief in the Trinity, that would amount to sponsoring the Christian religion, since Christianity is the only religion that holds to this doctrine. The Masonic policy is that "no phrase or terms should be used in a Masonic service that would arouse sectarian feelings or wound the religious sensibilities of any Freemason."[40]

One cannot help but observe that even though Freemasonry teaches that one is free to hold to one's own view of God, Masonry does in fact teach a concept of God—that is, that *all religions believe in the same God*. So despite the fact that Masonry denies teaching a doctrine of God, it is in fact doing just that. This is nowhere more evident than in the Royal Arch Degree of the York Rite, in which the Mason is told that the real name of God is *Jabulon*. This is a compound word derived from *Ja* (for Jehovah), joined with *Bel* or *Bul* (for Baal, the ancient Canaanite God), and *On* (for Osiris, the ancient Egyptian mystery god). As Martin Wagner put it, "In this compound name an attempt is made to show by a coordination of divine names ... the unity, identity, and harmony of the Hebrew, Assyrian, and Egyptian god-ideas."[41]

Jesus Was a Great Moral Teacher

Not surprisingly, the deity of Christ is either denied or greatly downplayed within Masonic circles. Those who are Christians within the Masonic Lodge may consider Jesus the divine Son of God, but they typically choose not to invoke his name when praying. After all, not all Masons believe in Jesus, so invoking the name of Jesus might be offensive to some. Further, if the name of Jesus were invoked, others from different religious persuasions would seek to invoke the name of their deity during prayer. To avoid religious disputes, Masons avoid invoking any name—including that of Jesus. Rather, they are instructed, "Prayers in the lodges should be closed with expressions such as 'in the Most Holy and Precious name we pray,' using no additional words which would be in conflict with the religious beliefs of those present at meetings."[42]

For the most part, Masons regard Jesus as a great moral teacher and ethical philosopher, putting him in the same league as other great men like Socrates, Plato, and Muhammad. Similar to other great religious leaders, Jesus stood for morality and virtue—but he is not unique. Certainly any suggestion that Jesus is the only way to God is rejected outright by Masons. Such a viewpoint is considered intolerant, and intolerance is not a characteristic allowed within the halls of Masonic Lodges. (Intolerance is not tolerated!)

It is highly revealing that when Scripture verses are quoted in the Masonic Lodge, the name of Jesus is always deleted. For example, whereas 1 Peter 2:5 actually reads, "...offering spiritual sacrifices acceptable to God *through Jesus Christ*" (emphasis added), the Masonic ritual reads, "...To offer up spiritual sacrifices acceptable to God." Likewise, whereas 2 Thessalonians 3:12 actually reads, "Now such persons we command and exhort *in the Lord Jesus Christ* to work in quiet fashion and eat their own bread" (NASB, emphasis added), the Masonic ritual reads, "Now them that are such, we command and exhort, that with quietness they work and eat their own bread."[43] One wonders how "Christian" Masons can in good conscience go along with this, in view of the teaching of Deuteronomy 4:2: "Do not add to what I command you and do not subtract from it, but keep the commands of the LORD your God that I give you."

Man Is Not a Sinner; Salvation Comes through Ethical Living

Masons deny the Christian doctrine of original sin and reject any suggestion that human beings are depraved.[44] They believe that human beings can, in and of themselves, improve their somewhat flawed or unpolished character and behavior and attain the moral perfection necessary to go to heaven.[45] Masonry's purpose is "to make good men better."[46] Albert G. Mackey, in the *Revised Encyclopedia of Freemasonry*, writes, "All [Masons] unite in declaring it to be a system of morality, by the practice of which its members may advance their spiritual interest, and mount by the theological ladder from the Lodge on earth to the Lodge in heaven."[47]

Masons believe that moral and spiritual perfection lie within every human being and may be discovered and surfaced through the education that takes place in the Masonic Lodge. Thus, Freemasonry can provide what every man needs to attain moral perfection. This heightened morality is evidenced in the fact that Masons are typically involved in charity and engage in civic duties.[48] In short, Freemasonry helps men to become better people who help the world become a better place.

The Masonic view of salvation is clearly works-oriented, even though they would deny this. In their view, one earns salvation by ethical living based on whatever holy book one subscribes to. Jack Harris, a former Worshipful Master Mason, affirms that "in all the rituals that I taught for eleven years, Masonry did teach how to get to heaven. They taught it with the apron that I wore, by my purity [of] life and conduct. . . . Never at any Masonic ritual did they point out that Jesus is the way of salvation."[49]

The lambskin is often used as a symbol of the purity expected from Masons: "In all ages the lamb has been deemed an emblem of innocence; he, therefore, who wears the Lambskin as a badge of Masonry is continually reminded of that purity of life and conduct which is necessary to obtain admittance into the Celestial Lodge above, where the Supreme Architect of the universe presides."[50]

CHALLENGING MASONIC BELIEFS

Masons do not like it when "fundamentalist" Christians criticize their movement. They feel they are misrepresented and misunderstood. For this reason Masons set forth some rather unflattering caricatures of evangelical apologists who have taken a stand against Freemasonry.[51] Mason Richard Thorn, in his book *The Boy Who Cried Wolf: The Book that Breaks Masonic Silence*, seeks to unmask "some of those who pretend to be Christians, but who evidently lack the love and tolerance stressed by the Man from Galilee."[52]

Of course, Jesus is a man of love, compassion, and meekness. But He is also the divine Judge of humankind (for example, 2 Tim. 4:1). This man of "tolerance," as Thorn describes Him, took an unbending stand against false prophets and false Christs (Matt. 7:22–23; 24:4–5, 23–25). And this same Jesus will one day come again and separate the sheep from the goats, inviting the sheep (true Christians) into His kingdom but dooming the goats (all others) to suffer eternally in hell (Matt. 25:31–46). Thorn has clearly portrayed Jesus in a way favorable to Freemasonry but foreign to the pages of Scripture.

FREEMASONRY CONTRASTED WITH CHRISTIANITY

	Masonic View	Christian View
Bible	One symbol of God's will	Unique Inspired Word of God
Jesus	Good moral teacher	Absolute deity, divine Messiah
God	Supreme Architect, no Trinity	One God, three persons
Sin	Man not fallen in sin	Man fallen in sin
Salvation	Earned by ethical living	By faith in Christ alone

Freemasonry Is a Religion

There can be no denying that Freemasonry has a religious nature by virtue of the fact that belief in a deity is required and that atheists are barred from membership. Furthermore, the fact that one finds such things as altars and pulpits and "Worshipful Masters" in Masonic Lodges—and the fact that rituals, prayers, pledges, sacred vows, sacred literature reading, hymn singing, and funeral services take place within Masonic Lodges—constitutes a strong argument that Freemasonry is a religion. In fact, if one argues that despite these things Freemasonry is not a religion, one could by that same virtue argue that Christianity is not a religion. It is highly revealing to note that just as Christianity refers to the need for a "new birth," so one of the rituals in Freemasonry involves being delivered from the pollution of the profane world and receiving "new birth."

Many Masons argue that because Freemasonry is open to all religions, it in itself is not a religion. However, such thinking is fallacious. As George Mather and Larry Nichols point out, Hinduism also believes that all paths lead to God, yet this tolerance on the part of Hinduism does not in any way negate the fact that it is a religion.[53] One Masonic publication concedes that Freemasonry "is a religion without a creed, being of no sect but finding truth in all."[54] In other words, it is a *religion* finding truth in *numerous religions*.

Because of the strongly religious nature of Freemasonry, it is hard to see how a Christian can in good conscience join a Masonic Lodge. After all, when persons first become Masons, the first ritual they must agree to go through describes them as being "in darkness, helplessness, and ignorance," and being "covered with the pollution of the profane world," and "seeking the new birth." Born-again Christians could not say this in good conscience, because from the moment they were saved by trusting in Christ, they were already born again (1 Peter 1:22–23) and had already escaped the defilement of the world system (2 Peter 1:3–4).

It seems inconceivable that a Christian could, in good conscience bow before "The Worshipful Master" and say, "I am in darkness and I am in need of the light of Freemasonry." After all, the Christian has received the Light of the World (Jesus Christ) and has been redeemed by His blood. Through Christ, we have been delivered from the kingdom of darkness and brought into the kingdom of God's Son, which is the kingdom of light (see Col. 1:12–14). As God's children, we walk in the light, not in darkness (see 1 John 1:4–7). In John 12:46, Jesus said, "I have come into the world as a light, so that no one who believes in me should stay in darkness." He also said, "I am the light of the world. Whoever follows me will never walk in darkness, but will have the light of life." The apostle Paul affirmed, "You were once darkness, but now you are light in the Lord. Live as children of light" (Eph. 5:8).

It is understandable that many Christian denominations in both Europe and America have forbidden their members to join the Masons. These include the Roman Catholic Church, the Greek Orthodox Church, and many Protestant denominations in various doctrinal traditions—Lutheran, Presbyterian, Baptist, Church of God, Wesleyan, Pentecostal, Nazarene, Quaker, Adventist, and Mennonite.[55] Such churches take exception to the ideas that all religions are true, that Christ is not truly God, that Christ is not the only way of salvation, and that the Bible is merely one among many "symbols" of religious truth. They further take exception to the Masonic teaching that all people of all religions are part of a single brotherhood. Scripturally, one does not become a part of the family of God without believing in the one true Savior, Jesus Christ (John 3:16; Acts 16:31; Titus 2:13–14).

The Bible Alone Is God's Word

The Bible is not merely one among many symbols of religious truth in a league with the Muslim Koran and the Hindu Vedas. In fact, it is fair to say that if one of these books is correct, then the others are necessarily wrong, since they set forth diametrically opposing ideas on basic religious concepts such as the doctrine of God. The Christian Bible teaches a triune concept of God; the Muslim Koran denies the Trinity, says God cannot have a Son, and says Allah is the one true God; the Hindu Vedas recognize the existence of many gods. Further, the Koran and the Vedas set forth a works-oriented salvation, whereas the Bible says salvation is a free gift for those who trust in Christ (Eph. 2:8–9). There are many radical and irreconcilable points of difference between these books such that if one is right, the others must be wrong.

Unlike other "holy books," the Bible's accuracy and reliability have been proved and verified repeatedly by archaeological finds presented by both believing and nonbelieving scholars and scientists. This includes archaeological verification for numerous customs, places, names, and events mentioned in the Bible. Over 25,000 discoveries have established the amazing accuracy of innumerable details in the Bible. Moreover, we possess more than 24,000 partial and complete manuscripts of the New Testament alone, as well as tremendous manuscript support for the Old Testament. In short, the historical support for the Bible is unmatched by any other alleged holy book.[56]

Christians view the Bible as having the same authority as God Himself, for these writings were inspired by God ("God-breathed") (2 Tim. 3:16). In the Bible, God speaks, God teaches, and God communicates. To disobey the Bible is to disobey God Himself.

Jesus and the apostles often gave testimony to the absolute authority of the Bible as the Word of God. They constantly turned to the Old Testament as the final court of appeal. They often indicated this by the introductory phrase, "It is written," which is repeated some 90 times in the New Testament. Jesus used this phrase three times when appealing to Scripture as the final authority in His dispute with Satan (Matt. 4:4, 7, 10). And in *all* His disputes with Jewish religious leaders, Jesus referred to the authority of the Bible.

Solomon warned that "every word of God is flawless. . . . Do not add to his words, or he will rebuke you and prove you a liar" (Prov. 30:5–6). The Bible ends with John issuing the same exhortation, declaring, "I warn everyone who hears the words of the prophecy of this book: If anyone adds anything to them, God will add to him the plagues described in this book. And if anyone takes words away from this book of prophecy, God will take away from him his share in the tree of life ..." (Rev. 22:18–19). It is clear that God does not wish anything that claims divine authority to be added to His inspired words. Those who set forth other holy books that are in reality man-made fall under God's condemnation.

Even if one hypothetically granted that God did wish to reveal additional truths through other holy books (which I do not), that revelation would have to be consistent with previous divine revelation. The apostle Paul said that "even if we or an angel from heaven should preach a gospel other than the one we preached to you, let him be eternally condemned" (Gal. 1:8). Paul spoke of the importance of making sure that new claims to truth be measured against what we know to be true from Scripture (cf. Acts 17:11; 2 Tim. 3:16). Since the "revelations" in the Hindu Vedas and the Muslim Koran and other such books directly contradict the revelation found in the Christian Bible, we can assume they did not come from the same source. If the Bible came from God (as indicated above), then these other books did not. For these books to be put on an equal level of authority in the Masonic Lodge is an outrage against the one true God.

Yahweh Is the One True God

In view of my earlier point that the Bible teaches the Trinity, the Koran denies the Trinity and exalts Allah, and the Vedas espouse many gods, the teaching of Freemasonry that the different religions are worshiping the same God using different names shows incredible ignorance. If one of these concepts of God is correct, the others must necessarily be incorrect. If Yahweh is the one true God, as the Bible teaches (Ex. 3:14–15), then the god of Islam and the god(s) of Hinduism cannot be the true God.

Even though the names these different religions use for God actually point to false gods, the Christian Bible does in fact use a variety of names of the one true God. For example, two common names used of God in the Old Testament are Elohim and Yahweh. In the New Testament God is often called "Father." These various names indicate something about the character of the one true God. Yet the one true God referenced by these names is distinct from the false gods of Hinduism, Islam, and other false religious systems.

The Masonic claim that God's true name is Jabulon is atrocious. The attempt to relate the God of the Bible with Baal is nothing less than blasphemy. Baal worship is perhaps the epitome of evil idol worship in the ancient world, involving such things as ritual prostitution (Judg. 2:17), self-mutilation (1 Kings 18:28), and the sacrificing of children (Jer. 19:4–5). In Judges 3:7 we read, "The Israelites did evil in the eyes of the LORD; they forgot the LORD their God and served the Baals and the Asherahs." From this we can easily surmise that the Masonic view that God is Jabulon is detestable to the Lord.

It is interesting to note that the one sin for which God judged the people of Israel more severely than any other was that of participating in false heathen religions (for example, Ex. 20:4–6; Lev. 19:4; 26:1; Deut. 4:15–19; 2 Sam. 7:22). The Bible repeatedly implies and states that God hates, despises, and utterly rejects anything associated with heathen false religions and practices. Those who follow such idolatry are not regarded as groping their way to God but as having turned their backs on Him, following the ways of darkness. This means that those today who participate in false religions like Hinduism and Islam are not viewed by God as groping their way toward Him, but are viewed as worshiping a false God.

Jesus Christ Is the "Only Way" to Salvation

Contrary to the Masonic claim that Jesus was just a great moral teacher and was not unique, the Bible reveals Jesus to be the unique Son of God with whom there is no equal. The Jesus of the Bible is unique in every way, especially in view of the fact that He is absolute deity (see John 1:1; 8:58; 10:30; 20:28). Jesus did not just claim to have a way to God, like the founders of the other world religions; Jesus claimed to *be* God. Moreover, Jesus and His message were inseparable. The reason Jesus' teachings had absolute authority was that He *was* and *is* God. This is not the case with the leaders of the other world religions. The Buddha taught that his ethical teachings were the important thing, not he himself. He emphasized that these ethical teachings were important whether or not he himself existed. But Jesus said, "Verily, verily *I* say unto you...," with the authority of God.

Jesus claimed that what he said took precedence over the words of all others. He said he is humanity's only means of coming into a relationship with God (John 14:6). This was confirmed by those who followed him (Acts 4:12; 1 Tim. 2:5). Jesus also warned His followers about those who would try to set forth a different "Christ" (Matt. 24:4–5).

Jesus proved the veracity of all He said by rising from the dead (Acts 17:31), something none of the leaders of the other world religions did. Jesus' resurrection proved that He was who He claimed to be—the divine Messiah (Rom. 1:4).

Jesus affirmed that those who do not honor him cannot honor the Father who sent Him (John 5:23). We are told in 1 John 2:23 that "no one who denies the Son has the Father." Of particular significance to those Christians who choose to attend Masonic Lodges and participate in the devaluing of Jesus Christ, is Jesus' assertion in Luke 9:26, "If anyone is ashamed of me and my words, the Son of man will be ashamed of him when he comes in his glory and in the glory of the Father and of the holy angels." (See pages 99–101 for more on the scriptural identity of Jesus Christ.)

Man Is a Sinner in Need of Salvation

The Masonic contention that human beings can in themselves move toward spiritual perfection is seriously misled. On the one hand, it is true that human knowledge is increasing tremendously decade by decade. But if there is one thing we have learned by observing culture and history, it is that man's new technological discoveries become new vehicles for the expression of the perverse sin that is in the human heart. The Internet is a perfect example. While it is truly a technological wonder, at the same time, there are few places one can go to find more empirical evidence for the fallen nature of man. I am referring, of course, to the plethora of pornography and cybersex freely available on the Internet.

C. H. Spurgeon once said, "He who doubts human depravity had better study himself."[57] Jesus said, "for out of the heart come evil thoughts, murder, adultery, sexual immorality, theft, false testimony, slander..." (Matt. 15:19). While Freemasonry focuses attention on external ethics, it can do virtually nothing to cure the ills of the human heart. Only Christ can do that. People's lives do not need an external Masonic tune-up, they need a brand new engine. They need to become brand new creatures (2 Cor. 5:17), and that can happen only with a personal relationship with Christ that begins with the new birth (John 3:3–5).

Let us not forget that Jesus taught that people without exception are sinful, that human beings have a grave sin problem that is altogether beyond their means to solve. He taught that human beings are evil (Matt. 12:34) and that man is capable of great wickedness (Mark 7:20–23). Moreover, He said that man is utterly lost (Luke 19:10), that he is a sinner (Luke 15:10), that he is in need of repentance before a holy God (Mark 1:15), and that he needs to be born again (John 3:3, 5, 7). Jesus often spoke of sin in metaphors that illustrate the havoc sin can wreak in one's life. He described sin as blindness (Matt. 23:16–26), sickness (Matt. 9:12), being enslaved (John 8:34), and living in darkness (John 8:12; 12:35–46). Jesus taught that this is a universal condition and that all people are guilty before God (Luke 7:37–48).

God is fully aware of every person's sins, both external acts and inner thoughts (Matt. 5:28); nothing escapes His notice (Matt. 22:18; Luke 6:8; John 4:17–19). In view of such facts, moral perfection among human beings hardly seems attainable.

Even in those who become Christians, there remains a fountain of evil continually producing unnatural and evil desires (read the book of Romans). This warfare inside each human being will be terminated only by death or the second coming of the Lord. While sanctification and growth in Christlikeness will take place (see, for example, Titus 2:12), moral perfection will not be attainable on this side of eternity. We read in 1 John 1:8, "If we claim to be without sin, we deceive ourselves and the truth is not in us."

Because of man's dire sin problem, man can do nothing to merit salvation, as Masons seek to do. Salvation in the Bible is something that is rooted in God's wonderful grace. Paul writes, "For it is by grace you have been saved, through faith—and this not from yourselves, it is the gift of God—not by works, so that no one can boast" (Eph. 2:8–9). Titus 3:5 tells us, "He saved us, not because of righteous things we had done, but because of his mercy." Galatians 2:16 tells us, "Man is not justified by observing the law, but by faith in Jesus Christ. So we, too, have put our faith in Christ Jesus that we may be justified by faith in Christ and not by observing the law, because by observing the law no one will be justified."

As for the Masonic view of the fatherhood of God and the brotherhood of man, Scripture indicates that while there is a general sense in which God is the Father of all people as their creator (Acts 17:24–28), there is a unique sense in which only those who believe in Jesus Christ become a part of God's family. John 1:12–13 tells us, "To all who received him [Jesus], to those who believed in his name, he gave the right to become children of God—children born not of natural descent, nor of human decision or a husband's will, but born of God." Galatians 3:26 says, "You are all sons of God through faith in Christ Jesus." So there is no universal Fatherhood of God in the sense of being in His eternal family, for entrance into this family is only by faith in Christ.

A glaring omission from all Masonic literature is the doctrine of hell. Although the Masons make no mention of hell, the Bible is full of references on this subject. The Scriptures use a variety of words to describe the horrors of hell—including fire, fiery furnace, unquenchable fire, the lake of burning sulfur, the lake of fire, everlasting contempt, perdition, the place of weeping and gnashing of teeth, eternal punishment, darkness, the wrath to come, exclusion, torments, damnation, condemnation, retribution, woe, and the second death. Hell is a horrible destiny (see, for example, Matt. 25:31–46; Jude 7; Rev. 20:14).

God, of course, does not want to send anyone to hell (2 Peter 3:9). That is why He sent Jesus to pay the penalty for man's sins by dying on the cross (John 3:16–17). Unfortunately, not all people turn to Christ, and God lets them suffer the consequences of their choice (see Luke 16:19–31). C. S. Lewis once said that in the end there are two groups of people. One group of people says to God, "Thy will be done." These are those who have placed their faith in Jesus Christ and will live forever with God in heaven. The second group of people are those to whom God says, sadly, "*Thy* will be done!" These are those who have rejected Jesus Christ and will spend eternity apart from Him. Many Masons likely fall into this latter category.

No One Should Swear Blood Oaths

Some legitimate oaths are mentioned in both the Old Testament (Ex. 20:7; Lev. 5:1; 19:12; Num. 30:2–15; Deut. 23:21–23) and the New Testament (Acts 2:30; Heb. 6:16–18; 7:20–22). Even the apostle Paul said, "I call God as my witness. . ." (2 Cor. 1:23), and "I assure you before God that what I am writing to you is no lie" (Gal. 1:20). On another occasion Paul said, "God can testify how I long for all of you with the affection of Christ Jesus" (Phil. 1:8). Hence, there are some cases in which oaths can be made.

The problem with Masonic oaths is not the fact that oaths are taken but the content of those oaths. No Christian has any business taking oaths that speak of cutting the throat or tearing out one's tongue. Many Masons argue that such words are only to be understood symbolically, but even with the most generous interpretation of the alleged symbol, it cannot be understood in any way acceptable to a Christian.

If a Christian joins a Masonic Lodge and takes this bloody oath and then later realizes the terrible mistake he has made, he is best off breaking his oath and leaving the Masonic Lodge (see Lev. 5:4–6). It is better to break an oath than to remain committed to one that is clearly against God's will.

Beware of Masonic Occultism

Christian apologists have noted that there is an occult connection to some of the rituals in Freemasonry, though perhaps some Masons may be unaware of this. The nineteenth through the twenty-eighth degrees of the Scottish Rite are deeply occultic, involving such things as the development of psychic powers, telepathy, altered states of consciousness, mysticism, Kabbalism (an occult art that began among the Jewish people in the first century A.D.), Rosicrucianism (a mystical brotherhood that involves pursuit of occultic powers and spirit contact), hermetic philosophy (alchemy), and the pursuit of esoteric truths.[58] Further, there is a connection between the ceremonies that take place in Freemasonry and the ancient mystery religions that worshiped pagan gods and promoted occultic ideas. These facts alone should be enough to dissuade any Christian from participating in Freemasonry.

14

SATANISM

Satanism is not a monolithic organization made up of individuals who all share identical beliefs.[1] Rather, Satanism involves a diversity of beliefs, and Satanists come in many different shapes and sizes. This is rooted in the fact that Satanists are self-serving and therefore define Satanism according to their own criteria.[2]

One research team has defined Satanism as "a form of religious belief and expression holding to the worship of Satan, whether Satan is defined as a supernatural person, a deity, the Devil, a supernatural force, a natural force, an innate human force, or, most commonly, the self."[3] Another researcher has defined it as "the cognizant belief in and deliberate invocation and worship of Satan as a supernatural personal being, or an impersonal force or energy, or a religious symbol representing the material world and carnal nature of mankind."[4] These definitions reflect the reality that there is no single type of Satanist, that, in fact, Satanists often have different opinions as to who (or what) Satan actually is.

Some Satanists believe what the Bible says about Satan (and God), but they have given allegiance to Satan even though they understand they may have to suffer eternal punishment in hell after death for doing so. Other Satanists hold to a more dualistic concept, believing that both God and Satan constitute equal and opposite spiritual forces—either of which human beings can use to achieve their goals in life. Still other Satanists interpret Satan to be a force that governs the world of nature.[5] This force can be harnessed to achieve one's personal desires in life. And still other Satanists—unquestionably the majority—use the term *Satan* as a metaphorical way to symbolize their rejection of the Christian faith, which they interpret to be a powerless religion involving nothing more than self-sacrifice, self-denial, and oppression.

Those in this latter category of Satanists do not believe in the actual existence of either Satan or God, but rather focus on the power of self and how to gratify self.[6] These Satanists interpret Satan as a symbol or personification of fleshly human desires and appetites. They react against the Christian notion that the desires of the flesh should be suppressed in the interest of pursuing spiritual values.[7] They pursue self-gratification and in this sense represent a deliberate reversal of the Christian faith. In place of Christian virtues like humility, self-sacrifice, and purity are "satanic virtues" like pride, greed, and lust. For these individuals, Satanism is essentially "you-ism."[8]

Because Satanism is not a monolithic system, researchers have divided Satanists into a number of general categories. There is some overlap in these categories, but they are nevertheless helpful in distinguishing among different kinds of Satanists.

The first group might be categorized as *traditional Satanists*. These Satanists are very secretive and usually operate in association with a satanic or occultic group. They engage in various rituals based on traditional Christianity (more precisely, Roman Catholicism), only everything is reversed or perverted. For example, they say the Lord's Prayer backwards. They put animal blood (or perhaps urine) in the communion cup.[9] These individuals hold Christianity in disdain and mock the Christian church.

The second category are *self-styled Satanists* who are not affiliated with any satanic or occultic group but rather make up their own brand of Satanism based on books they have read on the subject. They are typically alienated teenagers who find it difficult to socialize, and the rituals they perform are geared to secure such things as money, popularity, romance, or sex.[10] One FBI report states that these teenagers "turn to Satanism and the occult to overcome a sense of alienation, to obtain power, or to justify their antisocial behavior. For these teenagers, it is the symbolism, not the spirituality, that is important."[11] Often drug use and heavy metal music are part of this form of Satanism.

A third category of Satanists are the *religious Satanists* who are members of satanic churches like Anton LaVey's First Church of Satan or Michael Aquino's Temple of Set (which I will discuss later in the chapter). These Satanists prohibit the ritualistic harming of living beings and prohibit illegal activities. "They advocate egotism, indulgence, and the acquisition and use of personal and political power, have well-defined theologies and authority structures, and recruit members openly."[12] Most Satanists in this category are hedonists. What the Christian church terms the seven deadly sins (greed, pride, envy, anger, gluttony, lust, and sloth) are fully indulged in by these Satanists because such things gratify self.

A fourth category of Satanists are *dabblers*. Usually this category involves young people who are not totally committed to Satan, but rather experiment with satanic literature (such as *The Satanic Bible*), satanic rock music (heavy metal music with satanic lyrics), and occult-related games (such as Ouija Boards, and Dungeons and Dragons).[13] They love to attend horror/satanic movies. Sometimes they engage in homemade rituals involving blood pacts and occasional animal sacrifices.

A fifth category might be called *outlaw Satanists*. These Satanists worship the Devil and focus on drugs, vandalism, and heavy metal music. One researcher notes that "the members are usually young (fifteen to twenty-five), socially alienated, and held together by a charismatic leader. Meetings are generally sporadic and lack any coherent theology; the rituals . . . tend to be slapped together from movies and books on black magic."[14] These are generally socially deviant individuals who use drugs and sometimes commit violent acts. The group is more or less a means to vent youthful hostilities.

A final category might be called *psychotic Satanists*. These are individuals who are mentally deranged. Sometimes they claim to hear voices and think Satan is directing them to do something destructive, cause injury, or perhaps even brutally murder someone. Some of these Satanists engage in extreme violence as what they consider service to Satan. Richard Ramirez, the "Night Stalker" of 1985, would, for example, sneak into homes in Southern California and murder the residents, leaving a bloody pentagram as a "calling card." Journalist Jon Trott notes that "at his arraignment he held up his manacled left hand, revealing a crudely drawn pentagram inside a circle. 'Hail Satan,' he mumbled, then louder, 'Hail Satan!'"[15]

Even though there is a variety of Satanists, one should not conclude that Satanism is a movement involving millions of people. This is an important point because some people, whose stories have been reported in the newspaper and on national television, believe there is a massive satanic conspiracy involving Satanic Ritual Abuse (more on this later in the chapter). The reality is that the total number of people in the world who describe themselves as Satanists probably comes to fewer than 6,000, though it is hard to be precise because of the highly clandestine character of many Satanists.[16]

ROOTS OF SATANISM

The early roots of Satanism are extremely difficult to trace.[17] Cult researcher Richard Abanes has noted that "the developmental history of Satanism is a long and twisting path that winds back through centuries of witchcraft, superstition, religious folklore, and ancient paganism. It was a blending of these elements by persons seeking to fight Christianity's growing theological and moral influence (c. A.D. 400s–1600s) that led to the birth of Satanism, which has since come to represent the ultimate expression of rebellion against God."[18]

It is well beyond the scope of this chapter to provide a thorough history of Satanism. For our purposes, attention will focus on two of the most prominent individuals who have contributed to the emergence and growth of Satanism in more recent history, Aleister Crowley and Anton LaVey.

Aleister Crowley (1875–1947)

Aleister Crowley grew up in a strict, fundamentalist Plymouth Brethren Church in England. Early on, however, he seems to have preferred the evil characters in the Bible instead of the good ones. At one point he cheerfully accepted his mother's comment that he was the Great Beast 666 of Revelation.[19] As a young man he rejected his parents' faith and became heavily interested in magic and occultism as a means of attaining personal power.[20]

Crowley's modus operandi can be summed up as, "Do whatever you want."[21] He lived an exceedingly depraved lifestyle. He mixed into his magic and occultism ritual sex, and participated in group sex, bestiality, and homosexuality.[22] He claimed that through some of these sex rituals he came into contact with demonic spirits and even had sex with some of them. Crowley further enhanced his contact with demonic spirits by the use of drug-induced trances.[23]

A world traveler, Crowley claimed to have received revelation from a guardian angel while in Cairo, Egypt. He wrote down these revelations, and these became the basis for his book, *The Book of the Law.* He later wrote another book entitled *Equinox* (1909), and many of the ideas in this book are foundational to modern Satanism.[24] Most (if not all) of the satanic books I examined in preparing for this chapter cite the writings of Crowley. His influence is considerable.

Self-fulfillment and self-indulgence were the driving forces in Crowley's life. As researchers Gretchen and Bob Passantino note, Crowley's magical system "combined the three elements of (1) rejection of Christianity, (2) assumption of the supremacy of the self, and (3) the use of magic to enhance one's experiences and reach one's goals."[25] These elements became fundamental to contemporary Satanism.

Anton LaVey (b. 1930)

Perhaps the most famous individual in Satanist circles today is Anton LaVey. At a young age, LaVey became quite cynical toward Christians and Christianity. He witnessed the hypocrisy of certain Christians and concluded that Christianity was an irrelevant and powerless religion. LaVey once said,

> On Saturday night I would see men lusting after half-naked girls dancing at the carnival, and on Sunday morning when I was playing organ for the tent-show evangelists at the other end of the carnival lot, I would see the same men sitting in the pews with their wives and children, asking God to forgive them and purge them of carnal

desires. And the next Saturday night they'd be back at the carnival or some other place of indulgence. I knew then that the Christian church thrives on hypocrisy, and that man's carnal nature will out no matter how much it is purged or scorched up by any white-light religion.[26]

During the 1950s, the Church of Satan slowly evolved. LaVey and his wife would entertain other like-minded nonconformists in their home, and LaVey would engage in lectures and magic acts that, over the next decade, became formalized. He came up with a number of lectures on a variety of occultic subjects.[27] LaVey said his Church of Satan was to be "a temple of glorious indulgence that would be fun for people. . . . But the main purpose was to gather a group of like-minded individuals together for the use of their combined energies in calling up the dark force in nature that is called Satan."[28] LaVey says Satanism is a "blatantly selfish, brutal religion. It is based on the belief that man is inherently a selfish, violent creature, that life is a Darwinian struggle for survival of the fittest, that the earth will be ruled by those who fight to win."[29]

LaVey eventually came up with a satanic creed for the Church of Satan entitled "The Nine Satanic Statements."[30] They sum up the belief system to which many modern Satanists subscribe:

1. Satan represents indulgence instead of abstinence.
2. Satan represents vital existence instead of spiritual pipe dreams.
3. Satan represents undefiled wisdom instead of hypocritical self-deceit.
4. Satan represents kindness to those who deserve it instead of love wasted on ingrates.
5. Satan represents vengeance instead of turning the other cheek.
6. Satan represents responsibility to the responsible instead of concern for psychic vampires.
7. Satan represents man as just another animal—sometimes better, more often worse than those that walk on all fours— who, because of his "divine spiritual and intellectual development," has become the most vicious animal of all.
8. Satan represents all the so-called sins, as they all lead to physical, mental, or emotional gratification.

9. Satan has been the best friend the church has ever had, as
   he has kept it in business all these years.[31]

In view of the above, it is not surprising that LaVey, like Crowley, is open to a variety of sexual indulgences, including heterosexuality, homosexuality, and adultery.[32] Whatever gratifies self is considered acceptable.

The Temple of Set

While speaking of satanic churches, I should also mention the Temple of Set. This church was founded in 1975 by Michael Aquino, who claims to have received a revelation from Satan telling him to found a new organization that would worship the true powers of darkness. The name "Set" is derived from Set-Ham, an Egyptian deity that Aquino believes to be the true source of the name Satan (they even sound alike if you pronounce them quickly). Aquino claims the Temple of Set is rooted in prehistory and therefore relates his organization to some of the ancient mystery religions of Egyptian and Greek cultures.[33]

THE USE OF RITUAL SACRIFICES

Satanic rituals often involve sacrifices of one kind or another. Abanes reports that some Satanists engage in a "sacrifice of self"—a counterpart to the apostle Paul's Christian teaching in Romans 12:1 ("offer your bodies as living sacrifices...")—which often entails sexual intercourse, homosexual acts, oral copulation, or masturbation. Other Satanists engage in "pain sacrifices," which often involve the slashing of one's arms, upper thighs, or buttocks—actions that can allegedly bring about similar physiological responses as those associated with sexual ecstasy. Still other Satanists engage in sacrifices that utilize animal or human body parts (neighbors' pets, carcasses on the roadside, or perhaps body parts obtained by grave robbing). And some allegedly engage in the sacrifice of live animals or humans. Such rituals are designed to enhance the personal power of the Satanist performing the ritual. Some Satanists—particularly religious Satanists like those affiliated with Anton LaVey's Church of Satan— strongly denounce such animal and human sacrifices.[34]

Some Satanists believe that the sacrifice of an animal releases its life-force into the surrounding atmosphere of the ritual and that this force can be harnessed by the Satanist, thus enhancing the

Satanist's chances of obtaining the full benefit of the ritual. Other Satanists believe they are sacrificing to demons, who, in return for such an act, will grant whatever the Satanist desires. The greater the desire, the greater the sacrifice must be.[35]

Perhaps the most controversial satanic ritual, though, is the Black Mass.[36] In this highly offensive ritual, it becomes clear how Satanism is, in some ways, the antithesis of Christianity (especially Roman Catholicism) in the worst sort of way. Participants typically suspend a crucifix upside down, recite the Lord's Prayer (or other prayers) backward, engage in a mock blessing using filthy water, use a naked woman as an altar, sacrifice animals, and engage in bizarre sexual acts.[37] Below is an excerpt from the Black Mass. (Sensitive readers may wish to skip over this section in view of its morally and spiritually depraved words about Christ.)

> Thou, thou who, in my capacity of Priest, I force, whether thou wilt or no, to descend into this host, to incarnate thyself into this bread Jesus, artisan of hoaxes, bandit of homages, robber of affection— hear! Since the day when thou did issue from the complaisant bowels of a false virgin, thou hast failed all thy engagements, belied all thy promises. Centuries have wept awaiting thee, fugitive god, mute god! Thou was to redeem man and thou hast not; thou wait to appear in thy glory, and thou sleepest....
>
> ...O lasting foulness of Bethlehem, we would have thee confess thy impudent cheats, thy inexpiable crimes! We would drive deeper the nails into thy hands, press down the crown of thorns upon thy brow, and bring blood from the dry wounds from thy side.
>
> And this we can and will do by violating the quietude of thy body, profaner of the ample vices, abstractor of stupid purities, cursed Nazarene, impotent king, fugitive god! Behold great Satan, this symbol of the flesh of him who would purge the earth of pleasure and who, in the name of Christian "justice" has caused the death of millions of our honored brothers. We curse him and defile his name.
>
> O Infernal Majesty, condemn him to the pit, evermore to suffer in perpetual anguish. Bring Thy wrath upon him, O Prince of Darkness, and rend him that he may know the extent of Thy anger. Call forth Thy legions that they may witness what we do in Thy name. Send forth Thy messengers to proclaim this deed, and send the Christian minions staggering to their doom. Smite him anew, O Lord

of Light, that his angels, cherubim, and seraphim may cower and tremble with fear, prostrating themselves before Thee in respect of Thy power. Send crashing down the gates of Heaven, that the murders of our ancestors may be avenged.[38]

BELIEFS OF SATANISM

As noted earlier, there is no single kind of Satanist. Since most Satanists are self-styled, they typically have different views on various doctrines. The summary of doctrines presented below is representative of those held by many Satanists.

The Bible Is a Stupid Book of Fables

Most Satanists believe no holy book is authoritative. Satanists call the Bible a "stupid book of fables,"[39] brimming with contradictions and falsehoods. It is viewed as an oppressive and enslaving book. Speaking of the doctrines derived from the Bible, Anton LaVey writes, "Christian doctrine has become outmoded and unbelievable, even to the most feebleminded. One wonders, 'How is it possible for people to be so stupid as to believe the lies they are taught by ministers and priests?'"[40]

Not only do Satanists reject the Christian Bible as an inspired book from God, they do not place themselves in submission to any holy book, including *The Satanic Bible.* If self is to remain supreme, then any book becomes secondary and must bow to the will of the individual.[41]

Satanists do, however, subscribe to the teachings in *The Satanic Bible,* even though it is not intended to be obeyed as authoritative. Rather, it is more or less a guide. It represents LaVey's "declaration of emancipation from the strictures of any organized, autocratic, centrally ordered system,"[42] declaring the supremacy of the individual in open mockery of the Christian Bible and the sovereign God of which the Bible speaks. To LaVey, the Bible is an oppressive book that thwarts individuality and independence. *The Satanic Bible* is just the opposite.

God Is Interpreted Variously

Satanists hold a variety of different views on the doctrine of God. Most deny the existence of a sovereign deity who involves himself in the lives of people. Indeed, many of them are atheists and do not believe in the existence of God at all. "There is no God . . . no supreme, all-powerful deity in the heavens that cares about the lives of human beings. There is nobody up there who gives a [expletive]. Man is the only God."[43]

Yet other Satanists hold to a dualistic concept that acknowledges the existence of both God and the Devil, who exist independently of each other and are equal in power. Researcher Craig Hawkins notes, "Within this framework, some Satanists believe the balance of power will remain the same with neither side dominating or conquering the other; others hold that Satan will eventually conquer God."[44]

Still others interpret God as the force that lies behind the world of nature that can be harnessed by people to accomplish their goals. LaVey says, "This powerful force which permeates and balances the universe is far too impersonal to care about the happiness or misery of flesh-and-blood creatures on this ball of dirt upon which we live."[45]

Jesus Is an Embarrassing Failure

Satanists do not agree regarding the doctrine of Jesus Christ. Some believe he actually existed but say he was an utter failure. LaVey asserts that "Christ has failed in all his engagements as both savior and deity."[46] He was essentially a wimp with a weak spine. He was always talking about absurd things like love, self-denial, and forgiveness. By contrast, Satanists are interested in personal power and the gratification of self. Instead of putting others first like Jesus taught, the Satanist is interested in putting self first.

As noted previously, some Satanists engage in rituals that are an open mockery of the Jesus of the Bible. LaVey once said, "I dip my finger in the watery blood of your impotent mad redeemer, and write over his thorn-torn brow: The true prince of evil—the king of the slaves!... Say unto thine own heart, 'I am mine own redeemer.'"[47]

Other Satanists deny that Jesus even existed. They say he is a mythological figure with no historical basis. Such a denial, of course, makes it easy to ignore Jesus' words about sin and the need for a Savior.

"Cursed are the weak, for they shall inherit the yoke.... Cursed are the righteously humble, for they shall be trodden under cloven hoofs. [sic] ... Cursed are the god-adorers, for they shall be shorn sheep" (*The Satanic Bible*, 33–35).

Man Is Supreme

In Satanist thinking, the individual self is supreme above all else. Self-fulfillment, self-indulgence, self-exaltation, and hedonism are top priorities.[48] Even if self-fulfillment and self-indulgence come at the expense of another human being, they are still good. Researchers George Mather and Larry Nichols note how LaVey's Satanism is essentially a modern manifestation of sadism: "The Marquis de Sade (1740–1814) had formulated this philosophy [of hedonism] several centuries earlier, namely, that natural urges should not be suppressed. Rejecting God, Sade taught that the only crimes or the only sins of humanity are those that prevent one from obeying the voice of nature."[49] Sade faulted Christianity for suppressing natural urges. Anton LaVey represents a modern and popularized form of sadism.

There Is No Sin

It is not surprising that Satanists do not believe in the biblical teaching of human sin and the need to be saved. In keeping with the Satanist's low view of the Bible and low view of Jesus Christ, sin is more or less interpreted as something invented by Christianity to keep Christianity "in business."[50] The teaching that Jesus died on the cross to save human beings from sin is considered an outrageous myth. If anything, the thought of Christ on the cross is a sorry and embarrassing picture of weakness that no one should want to emulate.

Instead of worrying about "absurd" things like sin, the wisest course of action, according to Satanists, is to do what one can to pursue self-fulfillment and self-indulgence in one's present life. If any problems develop, Satanists can solve their own problems through sheer human effort. No deity is needed. Satanism is a "can do" belief system. Man is the measure of all things.

The Afterlife Is Interpreted Variously

Satanists hold differing viewpoints regarding the afterlife. Some believe there is no afterlife at all. Since our present lives are all we have, we should live it up. Other Satanists hold to a concept of reincarnation and believe we will have an eternity of physical rebirths to continually indulge our carnal appetites. Still other

Satanists believe Satan will eventually defeat God, after which time Satanists will spend eternity in Satan's great kingdom of hell, where sensual gratification will be unbridled and enjoyed forever. Finally, there are some Satanists who concede that God will eventually judge Satan and all Satanists and cast them into eternal torment, but they still choose to the follow the Devil in this present life. Hawkins explains this perverted mentality:

> Satanists may hold this seemingly incomprehensible position because of their seething hatred and utter contempt for God and Christians. God is viewed as a contemptible, weak-willed, spineless, maudlin chump, a cosmic bore and "nerd" of infinite proportions. Christianity is viewed as a nuisance and hindrance to living; as a dreary, tedious, and lifeless religion.... They feel it would be better to fully indulge themselves in this life, and if nothing else be alive and burning with hatred for all eternity than to merely exist in heaven.[51]

THE SATANIC RITUAL ABUSE CONTROVERSY

Some people claim that there are presently 100,000 adult survivors of Satanic Ritual Abuse (SRA).[52] The survivors allegedly have had certain memories therapeutically recovered that point to satanic crimes on the part of their parents or custodians—including emotional abuse, sexual torture (including mutilation of the sexual organs), incest, physical beating, bestiality, and forcing women to have babies that are then sacrificed to Satan, among other heinous things.[53] Such satanic rituals are said to involve the drinking of blood, the use of satanic symbols, and even human sacrifice. This purportedly nationwide and perhaps worldwide satanic conspiracy is said to be almost invincible and to involve millions of people, many of whom are in powerful positions in government, religion, education, and society at large.

The typical victim in SRA is a white woman who has a history of psychological problems, generally in the 25 to 45 age group.[54] This person is highly suggestible though intelligent and well-learned. Often the person has sought counseling for some unrelated problem, such as an eating disorder, when memories of SRA surface. Generally these memories surface as a result of either the therapist or the client raising the possibility of repressed memories of SRA. These memories are believed to have been repressed as a form of self-protection. Researchers Bob and Gretchen Passantino note, "At first the client may deny a past history of Satanic Ritual Abuse or may not remember anything or may have fragments of almost meaningless images of Satanic Ritual Abuse. After long-term, intensive therapy with a therapist committed to believing the client no matter what, the alleged adult survivor and therapist will gradually piece together a complex personal Satanic Ritual Abuse history."[55]

When challenged with the lack of evidence for a widespread SRA conspiracy, true believers often respond that conspiracies are by their very nature secretive. It is also often stated or implied that anybody who argues against the conspiracy is a part of the conspiracy. Further, only a massive conspiracy involving millions of people has the capability of destroying all the evidence.

Of course, such arguments hold little weight when evaluated logically. For one thing, it is fallacious to argue that a conspiracy of this magnitude could suppress all the evidence. If a gun has been fired, there will be a smoking gun—that is, there will be a trail of evidence. One would think that if there had been over 100,000 people victimized by SRA, there would be at least *some* substantive evidence to verify the claim. But the evidence is lacking. While true believers in SRA argue that only a large conspiracy can suppress all the evidence, a more logical interpretation of the data is that because the evidence is not there, neither is the conspiracy.

One survey that included 6,910 psychiatrists, psychologists, and clinical social workers, and 4,655 district attorneys, police departments, and social service agencies examined some 12,264 accusations of SRA these people had investigated. "The survey found not a single case among them in which there was clear corroborating evidence for the most common accusation—that there was 'a well-organized intergenerational satanic cult, who sexually molested and tortured children in their homes or schools for years and committed a series of murders.'"[56]

Some who formerly believed in SRA have now changed their view because of the lack of genuine evidence. Indeed, many who formerly thought they were victims of SRA have recanted their stories and reconciled with their families. Abanes suggests that a number of psychotherapists "inadvertently (some say deliberately) implanted 'false memories' of satanic ritual abuse (SRA) into the impressionable minds of their clients."[57] He cites evidence from psychologists to the effect that some people can be induced to "remember" events that never actually happened. They are "false memories" that seem real but in fact are not real.[58]

CHALLENGING SATANIC BELIEFS

The Bible Is Liberating, Not Oppressive

Most Satanists who say that the Bible is an enslaving and oppressive book have simply not read the book. The reality is that the Bible sets one free from slavery and oppression—that is, the slavery and oppression of sin (John 8:32). The Bible does not take away from good living, but rather is the source for good living (for example, Ps. 19:8; 119:32; 146:7; Gal. 5:1; 2 Tim. 3:15–17). The psalmist wrote that those who live life God's way prosper in all they do. God's commandments are liberating, not oppressive. They enable us to live the best and most fulfilling life.

As for the claim that the Bible is full of contradictions, the burden of proof is on the Satanist to back that claim up with hard evidence. While the Gospels may have some *apparent* contradictions, they do not have *genuine* contradictions. There are differences, yes, but actual contradictions, no. If all four Gospels were identically the same, with no differences, critics would be screaming "collusion" all over the place. The fact that the Gospels have differences shows there was no collusion but instead four different (but inspired) accounts of the same events.

One should not assume that a partial account in a gospel is a faulty account. In Matthew 27:5, for example, we are told that Judas died by hanging himself. In Acts 1:18 we are told that Judas burst open in the middle and all his entrails gushed out. These are both partial accounts. Neither account gives us the full picture. But taken together we can easily reconstruct how Judas died. He hanged himself, and sometime later the rope loosened and Judas fell to the rocks below, thereby causing his intestines to gush out. As one probes into alleged contradictions, one consistently sees that they are all explainable in a reasonable way.[59] It seems fair to suggest that Satanists continue to propagate the allegation of "Bible contradictions," despite contrary evidence, because it makes it easier for

Satanism Contrasted with Christianity

	Satanist View	Christian View
Bible	Stupid book of fables	Inspired Word of God
Man's Goal	Self-gratification	Serve and glorify God
God	Most deny His existence	Yahweh, Triune God
Jesus	Embarrassing failure	Divine Messiah
Satan	"Self," or Force behind nature	Fallen angel
Man	Self is supreme	Fallen sinner
Sin	Indulgence in sin is good	Sin separates us from God

them to ignore and dispose of what the Bible says about God, Jesus, human sin, and the need for a Savior, not to mention the Bible's unrelenting condemnation of immoral behavior.

God Exists, and We Are Accountable to Him

As noted previously, the majority of Satanists deny that God even exists. Earlier I provided proofs for the existence of God (see page 247), and I will not repeat that material. Here I simply want to stress that because there is a God who created humankind (Gen. 1:26–27; Isa. 44:24; Col. 1:16), all humans are therefore morally responsible to Him (Ex. 20). This accountability is one that will ultimately result in an eternity in a real place of suffering called hell for those who maintain allegiance to Satan and reject the one true Savior, Jesus Christ. This eternity in hell will involve not eternal sensual pleasures (as Satanists hope for), but rather weeping and gnashing of teeth (Matt. 13:41–42), condemnation (Matt. 12:36–37), destruction (Phil. 1:28), eternal punishment (Matt. 25:46), separation from God's presence (2 Thess. 1:8–9), and perpetual trouble and distress (Rom. 2:9). In view of this—and in view of the fact that Satanists are essentially hedonists—one would think Satanists would take all this to heart, especially since those who trust in Christ will not only escape this horrible destiny, but will live forever in a paradise heaven (Rev. 20:1–5).

Jesus Was No Myth

Jesus was certainly no myth, as some Satanists have argued. It is noteworthy that the existence and life of Christ have been verified by non-Christian witnesses, including Jewish historian Flavius Josephus (*Antiquities* 20.9.1), Roman historian Cornelius Tacitus (*Annals* 15.44), and Roman historian Suetonius (*Life of Claudius* 25.4). Further, the biblical accounts are based on eyewitness testimony (Luke 1:1–4). Indeed, John writes, "That which was from the beginning, which we have heard, which we have seen with our eyes, which we have looked at and our hands have touched—this we proclaim concerning the Word of life" (1 John 1:1). In 2 Peter 1:16 we read, "We did not follow cleverly invented stories when we told you about the power and coming of our Lord Jesus Christ, but we were eyewitnesses of his majesty."

Furthermore, Satanists' claim that the picture of Christ on the cross indicates that He was some kind of spineless wimp completely misses the import of biblical teaching. The truth is precisely the opposite of what Satanists claim. There can be no greater act of courage than to give up one's life on behalf of another (John 15:13)—and that is precisely what Christ did on the cross (1 John 3:16). Christ voluntarily sacrificed himself for our benefit. (What Satanist has the courage to give his life on behalf of another?) Furthermore, that Christ was no spineless wimp is more than evident in His constant stand against the most powerful religious influences of His day—the Pharisees, scribes, and Sadducees—and in the fact that He never backed down or retracted anything He said. While Christ was gentle and loving, He was also the epitome of strength.

If it is power the Satanist wants to see, he will have an eyeful at the Second Coming. The apostle John describes this future event:

> I saw heaven standing open and there before me was a white horse, whose rider is called Faithful and True. With justice he judges and makes war. His eyes are like blazing fire, and on his head are many crowns.... The armies of heaven are following him, riding on white horses and dressed in fine linen, white and clean. Out of his mouth comes a sharp sword with which to strike down the nations. "He will rule them with an iron scepter." He treads the winepress of the fury of the wrath of God Almighty. On his robe and on his thigh he has this name written: KING OF KINGS AND LORD OF LORDS. (Rev. 19:11–16)

The Biblical Portrait of Satan

The evidence for the existence and activity of Satan in the Bible is formidable. **Seven books in the Old Testament specifically** teach the reality of Satan (Genesis, 1 Chronicles, Job, Psalms, Isaiah, Ezekiel, and Zechariah). Every New Testament writer and 19 of the books make specific reference to him (for example, Matt. 4:10; 12:26; Mark 1:13; 3:23, 26; 4:15; Luke 11:18; 22:3; John 13:27). Jesus Himself refers to Satan some 25 times.

The Scriptures are just as certain of Satan's existence as of God's existence. They reveal that Satan is both a fallen angel and a genuine person. How do we know he is a person? For one thing, Satan has all the attributes of personality, including mind (2 Cor. 11:3), emotions (Rev. 12:17; Luke 22:31), and will (Isa. 14:12–14; 2 Tim. 2:26). Not only that, but personal pronouns are used to describe him in the Bible (Job 1; Matt. 4:1–12). In addition, Satan performs personal actions (Matt. 4:1–11; John 8:44; 1 John 3:8; Jude 9). Hence, the Satanist's view that Satan is just a "force" behind nature is unbiblical.

The Scriptures also portray Satan as a created being who, though powerful, has definite limitations. Satan does not possess attributes that belong to God alone, such as *omnipresence* (being everywhere-present), *omnipotence* (being all-powerful), and *omniscience* (being all-knowing). Satan can only be in one place at one time; his strength (though great) is limited; and his knowledge (though great) is limited. Thus, the Satanist's dualistic view that God and Satan are equal and opposite entities is unfounded. Satan is portrayed in Scripture as a created being, first known as Lucifer, who fell in sin and was cast out of heaven by Almighty God (see Isa. 14:12–17; Ezek. 28:11–19).

It is fascinating to observe the various ways the Bible speaks about Satan. We learn much about Satan and his work by the various names and titles given him. For example:

- Satan is called the *accuser of the brethren* (Rev. 12:10). The original Greek rendering of this verse indicates that accusing God's people is a continuous, ongoing work of Satan. He accuses God's people "day and night." He never lets up. Thomas Ice and Robert Dean note that "Satan opposes God's people in two ways. First, he brings charges against believers before God (Zech. 3:1; Rom. 8:33). Second, he accuses believers to their own conscience."[60] Perhaps another way he accuses Christians is by motivating his followers (Satanists) to openly mock Christians.

- Satan is called our *adversary* (1 Peter 5:8). This word indicates that Satan opposes us and stands against us in every way he can. Certainly the same is true of Satanists.
- Satan is called *Beelzebub* (Matt. 12:24). This word literally means "lord of the flies," carrying the idea "lord of filth." The Devil corrupts everything he touches. The rituals that are a part of Satanism illustrate this well.
- Satan is called the *Devil* (Matt. 4:1). This word carries the idea of "adversary" as well as "slanderer." The Devil was and is the adversary of Christ; he is the adversary of all who follow Christ. Satan slanders God to man (Gen. 3:1–7) and man to God (Job 1:9; 2:4). (A slanderer is a person who utters maliciously false reports that injure the reputation of another.)[61] Christ is perpetually slandered among Satanists.
- Satan is called our *enemy* (Matt. 13:39). This word comes from a Greek root meaning "hatred." It characterizes Satan's attitude in an absolute sense. He hates both God and His children. Satanists, too, perpetually express hatred toward God and those who follow Him.
- Satan is called the *father of lies* (John 8:44). The word *father* is used here metaphorically, meaning the originator of a family or company of persons, in this case of a family animated by a deceitful character. In other words, Satan was the first and greatest liar. Satanists, following the lead of the father of lies, lie about the Bible, Jesus, God, and other components of Christianity.
- Satan is called a *murderer* (John 8:44). This word literally means "man killer" (cf. 1 John 3:12, 15). Satan hates both God and His children, so he has a genuine motive for murder. Satanists are certainly involved in this work of Satan, for they sometimes offer live sacrifices to Satan (animals and humans).
- Satan is called the *god of this age* (2 Cor. 4:4). Of course, this does not mean that Satan is deity. It simply means that this is an evil age, and Satan is its "god" in the sense that he is the head of it. As well, as "god of this age," Satan is behind the false cults and systems that have cursed the true church through the ages.[62] He is certainly behind Satanist groups who worship him.

- Satan is compared to a *roaring lion* (1 Peter 5:8–9). This graphic simile depicts Satan's strength and destructiveness. Sadly, those involved in Satanism have no conception of the destruction that awaits them unless they repent and turn to the Savior, Jesus Christ.
- Satan is called the *tempter* (Matt. 4:3). This name points to his constant endeavor to incite people to sin. He presents the most plausible excuses and suggests the most striking advantages for sinning.[63] The hedonism that is so predominant in Satanist circles points to Satan's success here.
- Satan is called a *serpent* (Gen. 3:1; Rev. 12:9). The serpent is characterized by treachery, deceitfulness, venom, and murderous proclivities. Satanists, too, are characterized by treachery, deceitfulness, venom, and murderous proclivities.

Satan as the "Ape" of God

It was Augustine who called the Devil *Simius Dei*—"the ape of God." Satan is the great counterfeiter.[64] He mimics God in many ways. "The principle tactic Satan uses to attack God and His program in general is to offer a counterfeit kingdom and program."[65] This is hinted at in 2 Corinthians 11:14, which makes reference to Satan *masquerading* as an "angel of light."

In what ways does Satan act as "the ape of God"? Consider the following:

- Satan has his own *church*—the "synagogue of Satan" (Rev. 2:9).
- Satan has his own *ministers*—ministers of darkness that bring false sermons (2 Cor. 11:4–5).
- Satan has formulated his own *system of theology*—called "doctrines of demons" (1 Tim. 4:1; Rev. 2:24).
- His ministers proclaim his *gospel*—"a gospel other than the one we preached to you" (Gal. 1:7–8).
- Satan has his own *throne* (Rev. 13:2) and his own worshipers (13:4).
- Satan inspires *false Christs* and self-constituted messiahs (Matt. 24:4–5).
- Satan employs *false teachers* who bring in "destructive heresies" (2 Peter 2:1).

- Satan sends out *false prophets* (Matt. 24:11).
- Satan sponsors *false apostles* who imitate the true (2 Cor. 11:13).

In view of such mimicking, one theologian has concluded that "Satan's plan and purposes have been, are, and always will be to seek to establish a rival rule to God's kingdom. He is promoting a system of which he is the head and which stands in opposition to God and His rule in the universe."[66] It is noteworthy that within Satanist circles we find numerous counterfeits of Christianity—such as a counterfeit Bible *(The Satanic Bible)*, a counterfeit cross (upside down crucifix), counterfeit altar (often a nude woman), counterfeit prayer (the Lord's Prayer said backwards), and counterfeit rituals (the Black Mass). Satan truly is the ape of God.

Satan's Attempt to Thwart Christ's Mission

As we trace the history of the New Testament it becomes very clear that Satan had a dark agenda in trying to thwart the person and mission of Jesus Christ. Consider the following historical facts.

- According to Matthew 2, Joseph, Mary, and Jesus had to flee to Egypt because Herod ordered the slaughter of all male children, hoping to kill Christ in the process (vv. 13–16). The account in Matthew does not mention the involvement of Satan, but it was nevertheless a satanic act. (See Rev. 12:4–6, which seems to support the idea that Satan sought Jesus' death following His birth.)
- Following Jesus' baptism, He was led into the wilderness where He was tempted by the Devil for 40 days (Matt. 4:1–11). Of course, Christ *as God* could not be made to sin. But Satan nevertheless made the attempt in hopes of disqualifying Christ from being the Savior.
- During some of His disputes with Israel's religious leaders, Jesus identified the work of Satan in their actions. For example, when some of the Jews sought to have Jesus put to death, Jesus responded, "You belong to your father, the devil, and you want to carry out your father's desire. *He was a murderer from the beginning*" (John 8:43–44, emphasis added).
- Jesus also saw the work of Satan among those to whom He was closest. When Jesus predicted His own death, Peter

rebuked Him and said, "Never, Lord! This shall never happen to you" (Matt. 16:22). Jesus then said to Peter, "Get behind me, Satan!" Jesus recognized in Peter's words Satan's attempt to stop Jesus from going to the cross.

Satan continues his opposition to Christ today, not only by personally attacking Christians and the church, but by motivating Satanists to continually mock and assault the Christian church, which is the body of Christ (Eph. 5:30).

The Judging of Satan

As we examine what the pages of Scripture say about Satan, it becomes clear that there are six distinct judgments against him. He was cast from his original position of privilege in heaven following his rebellion against God (Ezek. 28:16). He was judged in the Garden of Eden following his role in leading Adam and Eve into sin (Gen. 3:14–15). He was judged at the cross (John 12:31; cf. Col. 2:15; Heb. 2:14).[67] He will be cast out of heaven in the middle of the future seven-year tribulation period (Rev. 12:13) and will be barred from all further access to heaven. He will be confined in the abyss during the future 1,000-year millennial kingdom over which Christ will rule (Rev. 20:2). He will be cast into the lake of fire at the end of the millennial kingdom, where he will dwell for the rest of eternity (Rev. 20:10; cf. Matt. 25:41).

What we learn from the above passages is that even though Satan is very active in our world, he is a judged being and is destined for eternal suffering. While the execution of the above judgments is not yet complete, the judgments have been pronounced, and it is just a matter of time before Satan's final doom is brought about. Those who choose to follow Satan will suffer the same consequences in the lake of fire (Matt. 25:41; Rev. 20:11–15).

Satanists desperately need to understand that the Satan they think they know is not the Satan that is (he cannot be trusted—John 8:44); the Christian God they think they know is not the God that is (He can be trusted, and He loves all people—John 3:16); and the Jesus they think they know is not the Jesus that is (He is the divine Messiah who can truly set them free—John 8:32,36). Further, hell will not be the pleasure palace they imagine it to be but will be a place of horrific suffering (see 2 Thess. 1:8–9). Satanists have listened to him who is the father of lies (John 8:44) and desperately need him who is "the way, the truth, and the life" (John 14:6).

POSTSCRIPT

Jesus said His words lead to eternal life (John 6:63). But for us to receive eternal life through His words, they must be taken as He intended them to be taken. A cultic reinterpretation of Scripture that yields another Jesus and another gospel (2 Cor. 11:3–4; Gal. 1:6–9) will yield only eternal death (Rev. 20:11–15). Cultists who believe in another Jesus and another gospel enter eternity lost.

That is why it is so critically important that every Christian "contend earnestly for the faith which was once for all delivered to the saints" (Jude 3 NASB). The word *contend* was often used in New Testament times to refer to competition in athletic contests. The idea behind the word, then, is that of an intense and vigorous struggle to defeat the opposition. Moreover, the English word *agony* comes from the noun form of *con-*

tend in Greek *(agonia)*. In ancient times, athletes would push themselves to the point of agony in their struggle to win. Likewise, believers are to engage in an intense and vigorous struggle to defend Christianity—"the faith"—against cultic challengers.

Scripture exhorts us to *"always* be prepared to give an answer to everyone who asks you to give the reason for the hope that you have. But do this with gentleness and respect" (1 Peter 3:15, emphasis added). The only way to "always be prepared to give an answer to everyone" is to become equipped with an apologetic defense. I hope that this book has helped you toward that end.

Jesus commands each of us to be salt and light in our society (Matt. 5:13–14). Salt is known for its effectiveness as a preservative. We are to have a preserving effect on the world by influencing it for Christ. And since Christ has called us to be "light," He does not want us to be "secret agent" Christians who cloak our lights. Because the darkness of the cults is hovering over Western culture as never before, there has never been a time when the light of each individual Christian has been more needed. *Every* Christian should stand out like a sparkling diamond.

The task begins with a single person—*you!* A great thinker once said, "Let him that would move the world, first move himself."[1] If you really want to see the religious climate in America improve, why not take the first step—*you,* without waiting for others to act—and commit to being an agent of change?

NOTES

INTRODUCTION: LIGHTING A CANDLE

1. J. E. Wood, "Separation of Church and State," in *Dictionary of Christianity in America* (Downers Grove, IL: InterVarsity Press, 1990), 268.

2. James Madison: cited by Wood, "Separation of Church and State," 267.

3. See Orville Swenson, *The Perilous Path of Cultism* (Caronport, Saskatchewan, Canada: Briercrest Books, 1987), 82.

4. John Ankerberg and John Weldon, *Encyclopedia of Cults and New Religions* (Eugene, OR: Harvest House, 1999), xv.

5. An example is Southern Evangelical Seminary in Charlotte, North Carolina.

6. "Letters to the Editor," Internet, *Newsweek*, 7 April 1997.

7. Paul R. Martin, "The Psychological Consequences of Cultic Involvement," *Christian Research Journal*, Winter/Spring 1989, CRI web site, www.equip.org.

8. Paul R. Martin, "Cults and Health," *Well Spring Messenger*, Winter 1996, 3.

9. Elliot Miller, "The 1993 Parliament of the Worlds Religions: The Fundamentalism of Tolerance," *Christian Research Journal*, Winter 1994, CRI web site, www.equip.org.

CHAPTER 1: DEFINING CULTS

1. See Ruth Tucker, *Another Gospel: Alternative Religions and the New Age Movement* (Grand Rapids: Zondervan, 1989), 16. See also Alan Gomes, *Unmasking the Cults*, Zondervan Guide to Cults and Religious Movements (Grand Rapids: Zondervan, 1995), 14–15.

2. I make this point in my book *The Culting of America* (Eugene, OR: Harvest House, 1995), chs. 1–2.

3. John A. Saliba, *Understanding New Religious Movements* (Grand Rapids: Eerdmans, 1995), 1.

4. Bob Passantino and Gretchen Passantino, "What Is a Cult?" Answers in Action web site, 1990.

5. See, for example, Saliba, *Understanding New Religious Movements*, ch. 1.

6. Ibid., 22.

7. Passantino and Passantino, "What Is a Cult?"

8. Cited in Orville Swenson, *The Perilous Path of Cultism* (Caronport, Saskatchewan, Canada: Briercrest Books, 1987), 8.

9. James Sire, *Scripture Twisting* (Downers Grove, IL: InterVarsity Press, 1980), 20.

10. Walter Martin, *The New Cults* (Ventura, CA: Regal Books, 1980), 16.

11. Swenson, *The Perilous Path of Cultism*, 10.

12. Gomes, *Unmasking the Cults*, 7. See also George Braswell, *Understanding Sectarian Groups in America* (Nashville: Broadman, 1994), 280.

13. Gomes, *Unmasking the Cults*, 7.

14. Derived from Gomes, *Unmasking the Cults*, 10–11. See also Walter Martin, *Rise of the Cults* (Santa Ana, CA: Vision House, 1977), 11.

15. See John Ankerberg and John Weldon, *Encyclopedia of Cults and New Religions* (Eugene, OR: Harvest House, 1999), xxiii.

16. For more comprehensive treatments that include secondary characteristics, I recommend Alan Gomes's series, the Zondervan Guide to Cults and Religious Movements; and Walter Martin, *The Kingdom of the Cults*, ed. Hank Hanegraaff (Minneapolis: Bethany House, 1999).

17. Journal of Discourses 16:46.

18. *Studies in the Scriptures*, vols. 1–7 (Brooklyn: Watchtower Bible and Tract Society, 1989).

19. Anthony A. Hoekema, *The Four Major Cults* (Grand Rapids: Eerdmans, 1978), 379.

20. J. Isamu Yamamoto, "Unification Church (Moonies)," in *A Guide to Cults and New Religions*, ed. Ron Enroth (Downers Grove, IL: InterVarsity Press, 1983), 160.

21. Gomes, *Unmasking the Cults*, 41.

22. Martin, *The Kingdom of the Cults*, 28.

23. Gomes, *Unmasking the Cults*, 33.

24. Swenson, *The Perilous Path of Cultism*, 51–52.

25. Ibid., 51. See also Martin, *The Kingdom of the Cults*, 40–41.

26. Ankerberg and Weldon, *Encyclopedia of Cults and New Religions*, xxiv.

27. I realize that some Christian thinkers have called into question how valuable sociology is in defining and understanding cults. Alan Gomes makes the legitimate point that some of the sociological characteristics often said to be true of cults may be falsely applied to legitimate evangelical Christian groups. (See Gomes, *Unmasking the Cults*, 48ff.)

28. See Saliba, *Understanding New Religious Movements*, 12.

29. See John Ankerberg and John Weldon, *Cult Watch* (Eugene, OR: Harvest House, 1991), vi.

30. Jim Bjornstad, "Success at What Price? The Boston (Church of Christ) Movement," *Christian Research Journal*, Winter 1993, 27.

31. Enroth, *A Guide to Cults and New Religions*, 18–19.

32. *The Watchtower*, 1 May 1957, 274.

33. *The Watchtower*, 15 January 1983, 22.

34. Ibid., 27.

35. *The Watchtower*, 15 September 1911, reprint 4885.

36. *Qualified to Be Ministers* (Brooklyn: Watchtower Bible and Tract Society, 1955), 156.

37. *The Watchtower*, 15 July 1963, 443–44.

38. "I Was an Elder with the Jehovah's Witnesses: The Personal Testimony of Chuck Love," *Christian Research Newsletter*, CRI web site, www.equip.org.

39. David A. Reed and John R. Farkas, *How to Rescue Your Loved One from Mormonism* (Grand Rapids: Baker, 1994), 23–24.

40. See Enroth, *A Guide to Cults and New Religions*, 20.

CHAPTER 2: UNDERSTANDING CULTIC GROWTH

1. See Walter Martin, *The New Cults* (Ventura, CA: Regal Books, 1980), 16. See also *World Almanac and Book of Facts 2000* (Mahwah, NJ: Primedia Reference, 1999); Eric Pement, ed., *Contend for the Faith: Collected Papers of the Rockford Conference on Discernment and Evangelism* (Chicago: Evangelical Ministries to New Religions, 1992), 262; Jehovah's Witnesses official web

site (see "Statistics"); *Deseret News 2001–2002 Church Almanac* (Salt Lake City: Deseret News, 2000), 167; Kosmin, B., and S. Lachman, *One Nation Under God: Religion in Contemporary American Society* (New York: Harmony Books, 1993), 15–17; official web site of the United Pentecostal Church; Christian Research Institute, "Cult Growth Statistics" (September 1993). Also, a good Internet resource for statistics of various religious groups in America and around the world is the Adherents web site: www.adherents.com.

2. These statistics are derived from John Ankerberg and John Weldon, *Encyclopedia of Cults and New Religions* (Eugene, OR: Harvest House, 1999), xvi.

3. See Walter Martin, *The Kingdom of the Cults*, ed. Hank Hanegraaff (Minneapolis: Bethany House, 1985), 11–37; Ronald Enroth, *The Lure of the Cults* (Downers Grove, IL: InterVarsity Press, 1987), 103–11.

4. Paul R. Martin, "Dispelling the Myths: The Psychological Consequences of Cultic Involvement," *Christian Research Journal*, Winter/Spring 1989, 11.

5. Josh McDowell and Don Stewart, *Understanding the Cults* (San Bernardino, CA: Here's Life, 1983), 20.

6. Ruth A. Tucker, *Another Gospel: Alternative Religions and the New Age Movement* (Grand Rapids: Zondervan, 1989), 25.

7. J. K. Van Baalen: cited in Martin, *The Kingdom of the Cults*, 14.

8. Russell Chandler, *Racing Toward 2001* (Grand Rapids: Zondervan, 1992), 165.

9. Chuck Colson, interview published in the *Christian Research Newsletter*, March/April 1993, 1.

10. Ken Boa, *Cults, World Religions, and You* (Wheaton, IL: Victor Books, 1979), 4.

11. J. Gordon Melton: cited in Tucker, *Another Gospel*, 25–26.

12. Orville Swenson, *The Perilous Path of Cultism* (Caronport, Saskatchewan, Canada: Briercrest Books, 1987), 14.

13. Enroth, *Lure of the Cults*, 49.

14. Robert and Gretchen Passantino: cited in Swenson, *The Perilous Path of Cultism*, 96.

15. Walter Martin, *The Rise of the Cults* (Ventura, CA: Regal Books, 1983), 24.

16. See Harold Bussell, "Why Evangelicals Are Attracted to the Cults," *Moody Monthly*, March 1985, 111.

17. Berit Kjos, *Your Child and the New Age* (Wheaton, IL: Victor Books, 1990), 39.

18. See John A. Saliba, *Understanding New Religious Movements* (Grand Rapids: Eerdmans, 1995), 74.

19. Enroth, *Lure of the Cults*, 51.

20. Ibid., 95.

21. See my book *The Counterfeit Christ of the New Age Movement* (Grand Rapids: Baker, 1990).

22. Enroth, *Lure of the Cults*, 54.

23. Martin, "Dispelling the Myths," 48.

24. *Humanist Manifesto II* (Amherst, NY: American Humanist Association, 1973).

25. James Hitchcock, *What Is Secular Humanism?* (Ann Arbor, MI: Servant, 1982), introduction.

26. *Humanist Manifesto II*.

27. Paul Kurtz, *Forbidden Fruit* (Buffalo: Prometheus Books, 1988), 243.

28. Douglas Groothuis, *Unmasking the New Age* (Downers Grove, IL: InterVarsity Press, 1986), 40.

29. Cited in Groothuis, *Unmasking the New Age*, 56.

30. Groothuis, *Unmasking the New Age*, 41.

31. Swenson, *The Perilous Path of Cultism*, 13.

32. Ankerberg and Weldon, *Encyclopedia of Cults and New Religions*, xvi–xvii.

33. Os Guinness, *The Dust of Death* (Downers Grove, IL: InterVarsity Press, 1973), 195.

34. Cited in Enroth, *Lure of the Cults*, 42.

35. James Sire, *The Universe Next Door* (Downers Grove, IL: InterVarsity Press, 1992), 138–39.

36. Ibid.

37. Douglas Groothuis, *Confronting the New Age* (Downers Grove, IL: InterVarsity Press, 1988), 19.

38. Elliot Miller, "Breaking Through the 'Relativity Barrier,'" *Christian Research Journal*, Winter/Spring 1988, 7.

39. See Ron Rhodes, *The Culting of America* (Eugene, OR: Harvest House, 1995), 78.

40. David Gershon and Gail Straub, *Empowerment: The Art of Creating Your Life As You Want It* (New York: Delta, 1989), 35.

41. Ibid., 35–36.

42. Swenson, *The Perilous Path of Cultism*, 14.

43. Ronald Enroth, *A Guide to Cults and New Religions* (Downers Grove, IL: InterVarsity Press, 1983), 20.

44. Nancy Gibbs, "Angels Among Us," *Time*, 29 December 1993, online version.

45. Timothy Jones, "Rumors of Angels," *Christianity Today*, 5 April 1993, 20.

46. For more on this, see my book *The New Age Movement* in the series Zondervan Guide to Cults and Religious Movements (ZGCRM) (Grand Rapids: Zondervan, 1997).

47. Paul Vitz, *Censorship: Evidence of Bias in Our Children's Textbooks* (Ann Arbor, MI: Servant, 1986), 18–19, 33–36, 84.

48. Kjos, *Your Child and the New Age*, 26.

49. Fritjof Capra, *The Turning Point* (New York: Simon & Schuster, 1982), 322.

50. John Ankerberg and John Weldon, *The Facts on Holistic Health and the New Medicine* (Eugene, OR: Harvest House, 1992), 5.

51. Cited in Chandler, *Racing Toward 2001*, 120.

52. George Barna, *Absolute Confusion: How Our Moral and Spiritual Foundations Are Eroding in This Age of Change* (Ventura, CA: Regal Books, 1993), 114.

53. Ibid., 105, 114.

54. Barna, *The Future of the American Family* (Chicago: Moody Press, 1993), 99.

55. "Cults and the Media," *Cult Awareness Network News*, December 1990, 6.

56. Ibid.

57. *Arizona Republic*, June 30–July 3, 1991: cited in "What's New in the Headlines," *Christian Research Newsletter*, September/October 1991, 6.

58. See the author's web site for links to many of these sites: www.ronrhodes.org.

59. Nansook Hong, *In the Shadow of the Moons: My Life in the Reverend Sun Myung Moon's Family* (Boston: Little, Brown, 1998), 25–26.

60. Matthew Fox, *The Coming of the Cosmic Christ* (San Francisco: HarperSanFrancisco, 1988), 136, 164.

CHAPTER 3: THE CHURCH OF JESUS CHRIST OF LATTER-DAY SAINTS

1. Richard N. Ostling and Joan K. Ostling, *Mormon America: The Power and the Promise* (New York: HarperSanFrancisco, 1999), xvi, 115.

2. Cited in Alan Gomes, *Unmasking the Cults*, Zondervan Guide to Cults and Religious Movements (Grand Rapids: Zondervan, 1995), 20.

3. Ostling and Ostling, *Mormon America*, xvi.

4. *Salt Lake Tribune*, 13 January 2000: cited in *The Centers for Apologetic Research January 2000 Prayer Update*, 1.

5. Joseph Smith, *History of the Church of Jesus Christ of Latter-day Saints* (Salt Lake City: Deseret, 1973), 1:17, 19.

6. Ibid., 1:28. See Gordon B. Hinckley, *Truth Restored* (Salt Lake City: Corporation of the President of The Church of Jesus Christ of Latter-day Saints, 1979), 7.

7. Jerald and Sandra Tanner, *Mormonism, Magic and Masonry* (Salt Lake City: Utah Lighthouse Ministry, 1988).

8. David O. McKay, *Gospel Ideals* (Salt Lake City: Improvement Era, 1953), 85.

9. Hinckley, *Truth Restored*, 8–9.

10. Ostling and Ostling, *Mormon America*, 267.

11. Joseph Smith, *History of the Church of Jesus Christ of Latter-day Saints* (Salt Lake City: Deseret, 1978), 1:40–42.

12. Doctrine and Covenants 57:6.

13. Smith, *History of the Church*, 3:175.

14. Ostling and Ostling, *Mormon America*, 58–59.

15. Doctrine and Covenants 132:52–54.

16. Ruth Tucker, *Another Gospel* (Grand Rapids: Zondervan, 1985), 68.

17. Ostling and Ostling, *Mormon America*, 58.

18. Walter Martin, *The Kingdom of the Cults*, ed. Hank Hanegraaff (Minneapolis: Bethany House, 1999), 189.

19. Joseph Fielding Smith, ed. *Teachings of the Prophet Joseph Smith* (Salt Lake City: Deseret, 1977), 158.

20. Robert M. Bowman Jr., "How Mormons Are Defending Mormon Doctrine," *Christian Research Journal*, Fall 1989, 26.

21. Cited by Bowman, "How Mormons Are Defending Mormon Doctrine," 26.

22. Smith, *History of the Church*, 4:461.

23. James E. Talmage, *A Study of the Articles of Faith* (Salt Lake City: The Church of Jesus Christ of Latter-day Saints, 1982), 236.

24. Orson Pratt, "Divine Authenticity of the Book of Mormon," in *A Series of Pamphlets* (Liverpool, England: n.p., 1851), 47.

25. Bruce McConkie, *Mormon Doctrine*, 2d ed. (Salt Lake City: Bookcraft, 1977), 383.

26. Joseph Smith, Genesis 40:33, Inspired Version.

27. Milton R. Hunter, *The Gospel Through the Ages* (Salt Lake City: Deseret, 1958), 104.

28. McConkie, *Mormon Doctrine*, 278.

29. Spencer W. Kimball, *The Ensign* (Mormon magazine, November 1975): 80. See James White, *Is the Mormon My Brother?* (Minneapolis: Bethany House, 1997), 105.

30. Orson Pratt, *The Seer* (Washington, DC: N.p., 1853–54), 37–38.

31. McConkie, *Mormon Doctrine*, 745.

32. Ibid., 1966 ed., 526–28.

33. *Deseret News*, Church Section, 31 July 1965, 7.

34. *Gospel Principles* (Salt Lake City: Church of Jesus Christ of Latter-day Saints, 1985), 17.

35. *The Holy Bible* (Salt Lake City: Church of Jesus Christ of Latter-day Saints, 1990), 697.

36. Spencer W. Kimball: quoted in *Book of Mormon Student Manual* (Salt Lake City: Church of Jesus Christ of Latter-day Saints, 1989), 36.

37. *Gospel Principles*, 290.

38. Ibid., 17.

39. McConkie, *Mormon Doctrine*, 601.

40. Joseph Fielding Smith, *Answers to Gospel Questions* (Salt Lake City: Deseret, 1958), 2:208.

41. Gerhard Kittel and Gerhard Friedrich, eds., *Theological Dictionary of the New Testament* (Grand Rapids: Eerdmans, 1985), 772.

42. Scott Faulring, "Changes in New Triple: Part 1—The Book of Mormon," *Seventh East Press*, Provo, Utah, 21 October 1981.

43. David Whitmer, *An Address to All Believers in Christ* ([1887] Concord, CA: Pacific Publishing, 1976).

44. Jerald Tanner and Sandra Tanner, *Major Problems of Mormonism* (Salt Lake City: Utah Lighthouse Ministry, 1990), 148–54.

45. Tucker, *Another Gospel*, 56.

46. Fawn Brodie, *No Man Knows My History* (New York: Alfred A. Knopf, 1971), 46–47.

47. Cited in Tanner and Tanner, *Major Problems of Mormonism*, 162.

48. Cited in John Ankerberg and John Weldon, *Cult Watch* (Eugene, OR: Harvest House, 1991), 38.

49. Cited in Tanner and Tanner, *Major Problems in Mormonism*, 162.

CHAPTER 4: THE JEHOVAH'S WITNESSES

1. David A. Reed, *Jehovah's Witness Literature* (Grand Rapids: Baker, 1993), 9.

2. Ibid.

3. Paul Carden, *The Centers for Apologetic Research January 2000 Prayer Update*, 1.

4. *The Watchtower*, 1 January 1993, 19b; cf. *Jehovah's Witnesses: The Organization Behind the Name*, video produced by the Watchtower Bible and Tract Society (Brooklyn, 1990).

5. Alan Gomes, *Unmasking the Cults*, Zondervan Guide to Cults and Religious Movements (Grand Rapids: Zondervan, 1997), 22.

6. *Mankind's Search for God* (Brooklyn: Watchtower Bible and Tract Society, 1990), 353.

7. David Reed, *Blood on the Altar* (Amherst, NY: Prometheus Books, 1996), 37.

8. *Jehovah's Witnesses: Proclaimers of God's Kingdom* (Brooklyn: Watchtower Bible and Tract Society, 1993); Leonard Chretien and Marjorie Chretien, *Witnesses of Jehovah* (Eugene, OR: Harvest House, 1988), 25.

9. *Zion's Watch Tower* (Brooklyn: Watchtower Bible and Tract Society, reprints), 3822.

10. Robert M. Bowman, *Jehovah's Witnesses*, Zondervan Guide to Cults and Religious Movements (Grand Rapids: Zondervan, 1995), 10.

11. *The Watchtower*, 15 September 1910, 298.

12. Chretien and Chretien, *Witnesses of Jehovah*, 32; Ruth Tucker, *Another Gospel* (Grand Rapids: Zondervan, 1989), 121; *The Harp of God* (Brooklyn: Watchtower Bible and Tract Society, 1921), 239.

13. *Jehovah's Witnesses: Proclaimers of God's Kingdom*, 59.

14. Walter Martin, *The Kingdom of the Cults*, ed. Hank Hanegraaff (Minneapolis: Bethany House, 1999), 88.

15. See David Reed, *Blood on the Altar* (Amherst, NY: Prometheus Books, 1996).

16. Ibid., 79.

17. *The New World* (Brooklyn: Watchtower Bible and Tract Society, 1942), 104.

18. Chretien and Chretien, *Witnesses of Jehovah*, 45.

19. Ibid., 58.

20. John Ankerberg and John Weldon, *The Facts on Jehovah's Witnesses* (Eugene, OR: Harvest House, 1988), 7.

21. See Reed, *Blood on the Altar*, 137.

22. Ankerberg and Weldon, *The Facts on Jehovah's Witnesses*, 7.

23. *Awake!* 8 October 1968, 13.

24. *The Watchtower*, 15 October 1980, 31.

25. *The Watchtower*, 15 May 1984, 5.

26. Rich Abanes, *Cults, New Religious Movements, and Your Family* (Wheaton, IL: Crossway Books, 1998), 243.

27. *Reasoning from the Scriptures* (Brooklyn: Watchtower Bible and Tract Society, 1989), 199.

28. *The Watchtower*, 1 March 1983, 25.

29. *The Watchtower*, 15 January 1983, 22.

30. *The Watchtower*, 15 September 1911, in *The Watchtower* reprints, 4885.

31. *Studies in the Scriptures*, vol. 5, 5, 60–61.

32. *Reconciliation* (Brooklyn: Watchtower Bible and Tract Society, 1928), 101.

33. *The Watchtower*, 15 August 1987, 29.

34. *You Can Live Forever in Paradise on Earth* (Brooklyn: Watchtower, 1982), 143.

35. *Studies in the Scriptures*, vol. 2 (1888), 129; *The Watchtower*, 1 September 1953, 518.

36. *Aid to Bible Understanding* (Brooklyn: Watchtower Bible and Tract Society, 1971), 1395.

37. *Should You Believe in the Trinity?* (Brooklyn: Watchtower Bible and Tract Society, 1989), 20.

38. *Reasoning from the Scriptures*, 380, 407.

39. *You Can Live Forever in Paradise on Earth*, 83.

40. *The Watchtower*, 1 April 1947, 204.

41. *The Watchtower*, 15 August 1972, 491.

42. *Reasoning from the Scriptures*, 308.

43. Duane Magnani, *The Watchtower Files* (Minneapolis: Bethany House, 1985), 232.

44. *Reasoning from the Scriptures*, 76.

45. Ibid., 79.

46. David Reed, *How to Rescue Your Loved One from the Watch Tower* (Grand Rapids: Baker, 1989), 20; and *Jehovah's Witnesses Answered Verse by Verse* (Grand Rapids: Baker, 1992), 12.

47. Cited in Erich and Jean Grieshaber, *Expose of Jehovah's Witnesses* (Tyler, TX: Jean Books, 1982), 30.

48. Bruce M. Metzger, *Theology Today*, April 1953.

49. William Barclay, *The Expository Times*, November 1953.

50. Raymond Franz, *Crisis of Conscience* (Atlanta: Commentary Press, 1983), 50, n. 15.

51. Martin, *The Kingdom of the Cults*, 124.

52. Walter Martin, *Jehovah of the Watchtower* (Minneapolis: Bethany House, 1974), 43.

53. Robert L. Reymond, *Jesus, Divine Messiah: New Testament Witness* (Phillipsburg, NJ: Presbyterian and Reformed, 1990), 247.

54. Bowman, *Why You Should Believe in the Trinity*, 77.

55. See Henry Clarence Thiessen, *Lectures in Systematic Theology* (Grand Rapids: Eerdmans, 1981), 96; Millard J. Erickson, *Introducing Christian Doctrine* (Grand Rapids: Baker, 1992), 263; Louis Berkhof, *Systematic Theology* (Grand Rapids: Eerdmans, 1982), 96.

Chapter 5: The Mind Sciences

1. Willa Cather and Georgine Milmine, *The Life of Mary Baker G. Eddy and the History of Christian Science* (Lincoln: University of Nebraska Press, 1993), 54.

2. Horatio W. Dresser, *A History of the New Thought Movement* (London: Harrap, n.d.), 160–61.

3. Stephen Gottschalk, *The Emergence of Christian Science in American Religious Life* (Berkeley: University of California Press, 1973), 128.

4. Ralph Waldo Trine, *In Tune with the Infinite* (New York: Crowell, 1897), 11.

5. Ibid., 13.

6. William A. Warch, *The New Thought Christian* (Anaheim, CA: Christian Living, 1977), 91.

7. *New Thought*, Spring 1979, 18.

8. Henry Wood, *New Thought Simplified* (Boston: Lee & Shepard, 1903), 182.

9. Cather and Milmine, *The Life of Mary Baker G. Eddy*, 12.

10. Ibid., 30.

11. *Quimby Manuscripts*, 389: cited in Todd Ehrenborg, *Mind Sciences*, Zondervan Guide to Cults and Religious Movements (Grand Rapids: Zondervan, 1996), 8.

12. Orville Swenson, *The Perilous Path of Cultism* (Caronport, Saskatchewan, Canada: Briercrest, 1987), 160.

13. See Walter Martin, *The Kingdom of the Cults*, ed. Hank Hanegraaff (Minneapolis: Bethany House, 1985), 128–33.

14. Todd Ehrenborg, *Speaking the Truth in Love to "The Mind Sciences"* (Visalia, CA: n.p., n.d.), 50.

15. See ibid., 10.

16. Ibid., 11.

17. *Los Angeles Times*, 16 January 1978, part 2, 4.

18. Mary Baker Eddy, *The First Church of Christ Scientist and Miscellany* (Boston: Trustees under the Will of Mary Baker G. Eddy, 1913), 238.

19. Mary Baker Eddy, *Miscellaneous Writings* (Boston: Trustees under the Will of Mary Baker G. Eddy, 1896), 311.

20. Mary Baker Eddy, *Unity of Good* (Boston: Trustees under the Will of Mary Baker G. Eddy, 1908), 50.

21. Mary Baker Eddy, *Science and Health with Key to the Scriptures* (Boston: Trustees under the Will of Mary Baker G. Eddy, 1934), 377.

22. Walter Martin, *Martin Speaks Out on the Cults* (Ventura, CA: Regal Books, 1983), 75.

23. Mary Baker Eddy, *Rudimental Divine Science* (Boston: Trustees under the Will of Mary Baker G. Eddy, 1908), 4.

24. Eddy, *Science and Health*, 331–32. See Cather and Milmine, *The Life of Mary Baker G. Eddy*, 184.

25. Eddy, *Unity of Good*, 59–60.

26. Eddy, *The First Church of Christ Scientist and Miscellany*, 297.

27. Eddy, *Science and Health*, 44.

28. Ibid., 509.

29. Ibid., 46.

30. Eddy, *The First Church of Christ Scientist and Miscellany*, 160.

31. Eddy, *Miscellaneous Writings*, 42.

32. Eddy, *Science and Health*, 291.

33. Ernest Holmes, *The Science of Mind* (New York: Putnam, 1998), 2.

34. Ernest Holmes, *Science of Mind* (magazine), February 1979, 40.

35. Holmes, *What Religious Science Teaches* (Los Angeles: Science of Mind Publications, 1975), 10.

36. Holmes, *The Science of Mind*, 98.

37. Holmes, *What Religious Science Teaches*, 61.

38. Ibid., 64.

39. Ibid., 65.

40. Holmes, *The Science of Mind*, 161–62.

41. Holmes, *What Religious Science Teaches*, 20.

42. Ernest Holmes, *Keys to Wisdom* (Los Angeles: Science of Mind Publications, 1977), 39.

43. Ernest Holmes and Fenwicke Holmes, *The Voice Celestial* (Los Angeles: Science of Mind Publications, 1979), 284.

44. Holmes, *The Science of Mind*, 104.

45. Ibid., 33–34.

46. Holmes, *What Religious Science Teaches*, 57.

47. Ernest Holmes, "What I Believe" (pamphlet), 3; emphasis mine.

48. Ernest Holmes, "What I Believe," *Science of Mind*, January 1965.

49. Ernest Holmes, *The Philosophy of Jesus* (Los Angeles: Science of Mind Publications, n.d.), 91.

50. Holmes, "What I Believe," *Science of Mind*.

51. Ernest Holmes, *Gateway to Life* (Los Angeles: Science of Mind Publications, n.d.), 19.

52. Holmes, *The Philosophy of Jesus*, 16.

53. Ernest Holmes and Alberta Smith, *Questions and Answers on the Science of Mind* (New York: Dodd, Mead, 1953), 152.

54. Swenson, *The Perilous Path of Cultism*, 225.

55. Ehrenborg, *Mind Sciences*, 60.

56. James Dillet Freeman, *The Story of Unity* (Unity Village, MO: Unity Books, 1978), 60.

57. Martin, *The Kingdom of the Cults*, 279.

58. Freeman, *The Story of Unity*, 26.

59. James Freeman, *What Is Unity?* (Lees Summit, MO: Unity School of Christianity, n.d.), 5.

60. Charles Fillmore, *The Metaphysical Bible Dictionary* (Lees Summit, MO: Unity Books, 1962), 629.

61. Cady, *Lessons in Truth*, 8.

62. Ibid., 9.

63. H. Emilie Cady, *God a Present Help* (Lees Summit, MO: Unity Books, 1938), 52–53.

64. Holmes, *What Religious Science Teaches*, 19.

65. Fillmore, *The Metaphysical Bible Dictionary*, 150.

66. Holmes, *What Religious Science Teaches*, 20.

67. Fillmore, *The Metaphysical Bible Dictionary*, 333.

68. Charles Fillmore, *Dynamics for Living* (Lees Summit, MO: Unity School of Christianity, n.d.), 145.

69. Emilie Cady, *Lessons in Truth* (Lees Summit, MO: Unity Books, 1967), 95–96.

70. Ibid., 35.

71. Fillmore, *The Metaphysical Bible Dictionary*, 554.

72. See Swenson, *The Perilous Path of Cultism*, 229.

73. *Unity Statement of Faith* (Lees Summit, MO: Unity School of Christianity, n.d.), Art. 22.

74. Marcus Bach, *The Story of Unity* (Englewood Cliffs, NJ: Prentice-Hall, 1962), 159–60.

75. Norman L. Geisler, *Explaining Hermeneutics: A Commentary* (Oakland, CA: International Council on Biblical Inerrancy, 1983), 6.

76. James Sire, *Scripture Twisting* (Downers Grove, IL: InterVarsity Press, 1980), 17.

77. Geisler, *Explaining Hermeneutics*, 7.

78. Ibid., 14–15.

79. Gordon L. Lewis, *Confronting the Cults* (Phillipsburg, NJ: Presbyterian & Reformed, 1985), 137.

80. Norman L. Geisler, *Christian Apologetics* (Grand Rapids: Baker, 1978), 187.

81. Ernest Holmes, *Sermon by the Sea* (Los Angeles: Science of Mind Publications, 1967), 8.

82. Martin, *Kingdom of the Cults*, 289.

83. Norman Geisler and Ronald Brooks, *Christianity under Attack* (Dallas: Quest, 1985), 43.

84. Swenson, *The Perilous Path of Cultism*, 51. See also Martin, *The Kingdom of the Cults*, 40–41, 248; Ruth A. Tucker, *Another Gospel: Alternative Religions and the New Age Movement* (Grand Rapids: Zondervan, 1989), 152.

CHAPTER 6: THE NEW AGE MOVEMENT

1. Marilyn Ferguson, review of *Heaven on Earth* by Michael D'Antonio, *Los Angeles Times*, 16 February 1993.

2. These statistics are documented in my book *The New Age Movement*, in the series Zondervan Guide to Cults and Religious Movements (ZGCRM) (Grand Rapids: Zondervan, 1997).

3. This definition is based on Elliot Miller, *A Crash Course on the New Age Movement* (Grand Rapids: Baker, 1989), 15.

4. George Trevelyan, *Operation Redemption* (Walpole, NH: Stillpoint, 1981), 29.

5. Benjamin Creme, *The Reappearance of the Christ and the Masters of Wisdom* (Los Angeles: Tara Center, 1980), 103.

6. Interview with Beverly Galyean conducted by Frances Adeney, "Educators Look East," *SCP Journal*, Winter 1981, 29.

7. Jessica Lipnack and Jeffrey Stamps, *Networking* (Garden City, NY: Doubleday, 1982), 227.

8. David Spangler, *Emergence: The Rebirth of the Sacred* (New York: Dell, 1984), 45.

9. Ibid., 19.

10. Ronald Nash, *Christianity and the Hellenistic World* (Grand Rapids: Zondervan, 1984), 222.

11. Russell Chandler, *Understanding the New Age* (Dallas: Word, 1991), 33.

12. H. P. Blavatsky, *The Key to Theosophy* (Pasadena: Theosophical University Press, 1972), 63.

13. Miller, *A Crash Course on the New Age Movement*, 141.

14. Wouter J. Hanegraaff, *New Age Religion and Western Culture: Esotericism in the Mirror of Secular Thought* (Albany: State University of New York Press, 1998), 23.

15. Miller, *A Crash Course on the New Age Movement*, 24–25.

16. David Spangler, in *Earth's Answer*, eds. Michael Katz, William Marsh, and Gail G. Thompson (New York: Harper & Row, 1977), 203.

17. Mark Prophet and Elizabeth Clare Prophet, *The Lost Teachings of Jesus 3* (Livingston, MT: Summit University Press, 1988), 273–74.

18. Levi, *The Aquarian Gospel of Jesus the Christ* (London: L. N. Fowler, 1947), 56.

19. Kevin Ryerson and Stephanie Harolde, *Spirit Communication* (New York: Bantam, 1989), 46–48.

20. Creme, *The Reappearance of the Christ and the Masters of Wisdom*, 115.

21. Levi, *The Aquarian Gospel of Jesus the Christ*, 56, emphasis added.

22. David Spangler, *Reflections on the Christ* (Forres, Scotland: Findhorn, 1981), 8.

23. Philip Swihart, *Reincarnation, Edgar Cayce, and the Bible* (Downers Grove, IL: Inter-Varsity Press, 1978), 18.

24. Levi, *The Aquarian Gospel of Jesus the Christ*, 87.

25. Elizabeth Clare Prophet, *The Lost Years of Jesus* (Livingston, MT: Summit University Press, 1987), 218–46.

26. Ryerson and Harolde, *Spirit Communication*, as quoted in Shirley MacLaine, *Out on a Limb* (New York: Bantam, 1984), 233–34.

27. See Joseph Gaer, *The Lore of the New Testament* (Boston: Little, Brown, 1952), 118.

28. Nicolas Notovitch: cited in Prophet, *The Lost Years of Jesus*, 219.

29. "Ramtha," with Douglas James Mahr, *Voyage to the New World* (Friday Harbor: Master-works, 1985), 24.

30. Theodore Roszak, *Unfinished Animal* (New York: Harper & Row, 1977), 225.

31. Mark Prophet and Elizabeth Clare Prophet, *The Lost Teachings of Jesus 2* (Livingston, MT: Summit University Press, 1988), 254.

32. Prophet and Prophet, *The Lost Years of Jesus*, 62.

33. Trevelyan, *Operation Redemption*, 83.

34. Levi, *The Aquarian Gospel of Jesus the Christ*, 126, 15, 263.

35. David Spangler, *Revelation: The Birth of a New Age* (Middleton, WI: Lorian, 1976), 13.

36. Annie Besant, *Karma* (London: Theosophical Publishing Society, 1904), 23.

37. Creme, *The Reappearance of the Christ and the Masters of Wisdom*, 47.

38. Joseph Campbell, *The Power of Myth* (Garden City, NY: Doubleday, 1988), 57.

39. MacLaine, *Out on a Limb*, 233.

40. Elliot Miller, "Benjamin Creme and the Reappearance of the Christ," *Forward* 6, no. 1, 3.

41. David Spangler, *Cooperation with Spirit* (Middleton, WI: The Lorian Press, 1982), 4.

42. David Spangler, *Towards a Planetary Vision* (Forres, Scotland: Findhorn, 1977), 108.

43. Spangler, *Reflections on the Christ*, 14–15.

44. E.g., Groothuis, *Confronting the New Age*, 89.

45. Ibid., 89–90.

46. Norman Geisler and Yutaka Amano, *Reincarnation Sensation* (Wheaton, IL: Tyndale, 1986), 17.

47. Ibid., 20.

48. Max Müller, "The Alleged Sojourn of Christ in India," *The Nineteenth Century* 36 (April 1894): 515–16.

49. J. Archibald Douglas, "The Chief Lama of Himis on the Alleged 'Unknown Life of Christ,'" *Nineteenth Century* 38 (April 1896), 667–77.

50. Edgar J. Goodspeed, *Modern Apocrypha* (Boston: Beacon, 1956), 5–14.

51. Dean C. Halverson, *Crystal Clear* (Colorado Springs: NavPress, 1990), 38.

52. Creme, *The Reappearance of the Christ and the Masters of Wisdom*, 54–55.

CHAPTER 7: THE CHURCH OF SCIENTOLOGY

1. Church of Scientology, "The Creed of the Church of Scientology," *Freedom*, September 1994, 35.

2. Hubbard wrote such fiction titles as *Excalibur, Slaves of Sleep, Kingslayer, Typewriter in the Sky, Fear, Death's Deputy,* and *Final Blackout.* See also *Scientology: Theology and Practice of a Contemporary Religion,* written by the Church of Scientology International Staff (Los Angeles: Bridge Publications, 1998), 90.

3. Gary Leader, "Scientology," in *Beliefs of Other Kinds: A Guide to Interfaith Witness in the United States* (Atlanta: Baptist Home Mission Board, 1984), 83.

4. Kurt Van Gorden, "Scientology," in *Evangelizing the Cults,* ed. Ronald Enroth (Ann Arbor, MI: Servant, 1990), 143.

5. *What Is Scientology?* (Los Angeles: Bridge Publications, 1992), 83.

6. Friends of L. Ron Hubbard, *L. Ron Hubbard: A Profile* (Los Angeles: CSI, 1995), 51.

7. Bent Corydon and L. Ron Hubbard Jr., *L. Ron Hubbard: Messiah or Madman?* (Secaucus, NJ: Lyle Stuart, 1987), 11–14. Prior to publication, L. Ron Hubbard Jr. sued to have his name removed as coauthor of this book.

8. Richard Kyle, *The Religious Fringe* (Downers Grove, IL: InterVarsity Press, 1993), 305. See also Joseph M. Hopkins, "Scientology: Religion or Racket? Part 1," *Christianity Today* 14, no. 3 (1969), 6; Joel Sappell and Robert W. Welkos, "The Making of L. Ron Hubbard: Defining the Theology," *Los Angeles Times,* 24 June 1990, Internet ed.

9. Ruth A. Tucker, *Another Gospel: Alternative Religions and the New Age Movement* (Grand Rapids: Zondervan, 1989), 300.

10. Ibid.

11. *What Is Scientology?* 118; *Scientology: Theology and Practice of a Contemporary Religion,* 90; George Malko, *Scientology: The Now Religion* (New York: Delacorte Press, 1970), 37.

12. See also Walter Martin, *The Kingdom of the Cults,* ed. Hank Hanegraaff (Minneapolis: Bethany House, 1999), 345; George A. Mather and Larry A. Nichols, *Dictionary of Cults, Sects, Religions and the Occult* (Grand Rapids: Zondervan, 1993), 250.

13. Martin, *The Kingdom of the Cults,* 372.

14. Malko, *Scientology: The Now Religion,* 31.

15. Russell Miller, *Bare-Faced Messiah: The True Story of L. Ron Hubbard* (London: Michael Joseph/Penguin Books, 1987), 50.

16. Martin, *The Kingdom of the Cults,* 374.

17. Quoted in Tucker, *Another Gospel,* 317.

18. John Weldon, "Scientology: From Science Fiction to Space-Age Religion," *Christian Research Journal,* from CRI web site, www.equip.org.

19. L. Ron Hubbard, *The Creation of Human Ability* (Los Angeles: The Publications Organization Worldwide, 1968), 177. See also *Scientology: Theology and Practice of a Contemporary Religion,* 132.

20. See Malko, *Scientology: The Now Religion,* 101.

21. See, for example, *What Is Scientology?* 251–311.

22. L. Ron Hubbard, *Scientology: The Fundamentals of Thought* (Los Angeles: The Church of Scientology of California, 1975), 2.

23. Ibid., 13–14.

24. *What Is Scientology?* 155–69.

25. L. Ron Hubbard, *The Problems of Work* (Los Angeles: The Church of Scientology of California, 1977), inside front jacket.

26. *What Is Scientology?* 130.

27. Hubbard, *The Problems of Work*, inside front jacket.

28. Ibid.

29. *What Is Scientology?* 147. See also *Scientology: Theology and Practice of a Contemporary Religion*, 17–18.

30. *What Is Scientology?* 130.

31. Ibid., 541.

32. *Scientology: Theology and Practice of a Contemporary Religion*, 8–9.

33. *What Is Scientology?* 235. See also *Scientology: Theology and Practice of a Contemporary Religion*, 41.

34. *What Is Scientology?* 556.

35. Mather and Nichols, *Dictionary of Cults, Sects, Religions and the Occult*, 252.

36. *Scientology: Theology and Practice of a Contemporary Religion*, v.

37. John Travolta, quoted in Richard Behar, "Scientology: The Cult of Greed," *Time*, 6 May 1991, 50.

38. *What Is Scientology?* xi.

39. Ibid., 544.

40. *Scientology: Theology and Practice of a Contemporary Religion*, 47.

41. *What Is Scientology?* 7.

42. Weldon, "Scientology: From Science Fiction to Space-Age Religion."

43. Abanes, *Cults, New Religious Movements, and Your Family* (Wheaton, IL: Crossway Books, 1998), 79. See also *Scientology: Theology and Practice of a Contemporary Religion*, 164.

44. *Scientology: Theology and Practice of a Contemporary Religion*, 164.

45. Ibid.

46. *What Is Scientology?* 142–43.

47. L. Ron Hubbard, *Dianetics: The Modern Science of Mental Health* (Los Angeles: Bridge Publications, 1992), 570.

48. Ibid., 68–91.

49. Ibid., 80.

50. Ibid., 547–48.

51. Hubbard, *Scientology: The Fundamentals of Thought*, 58.

52. Hubbard, *Dianetics: The Modern Science of Mental Health*, 167.

53. Hubbard, *Scientology: The Fundamentals of Thought*, 58.

54. Hubbard, *Dianetics: The Modern Science of Mental Health*, 531.

55. See Hubbard, *Dianetics: The Modern Science of Mental Health*, 218–24; *What Is Scientology?* 156–63.

56. L. Ron Hubbard, *Scientology: A New Slant on Life* (Los Angeles: The Church of Scientology of California, 1972), 34.

57. *What Is Scientology?* 156.

58. Hubbard, *Scientology: A New Slant on Life*, 34.

59. *What Is Scientology?* 146.

60. Ibid.

61. Ibid., 156.

62. *Scientology: Theology and Practice of a Contemporary Religion,* 37.

63. See ibid., 36–37.

64. See *What Is Scientology?* 812.

65. Ibid., 157.

66. Ibid., 159.

67. L. Ron Hubbard: cited in Malko, *Scientology: The Now Religion,* 124.

68. *What Is Scientology?* 159–60.

69. Ibid., 162.

70. *Scientology: Theology and Practice of a Contemporary Religion,* 21.

71. Ibid., 21.

72. Ibid., 38.

73. *What Is Scientology?* 164.

74. See ibid., 148–49.

75. Sappell and Welkos, "The Making of L. Ron Hubbard," Internet ed.

76. *Scientology: Theology and Practice of a Contemporary Religion,* 26.

77. *What Is Scientology?* 545. See also *Scientology: Theology and Practice of a Contemporary Religion,* xiii, 26.

78. Weldon, "Scientology: From Science Fiction to Space-Age Religion." See also *Scientology: Theology and Practice of a Contemporary Religion,* 24.

79. *Scientology: Theology and Practice of a Contemporary Religion,* 10.

80. L. Ron Hubbard, *Certainty* magazine, vol. 5, no. 10: cited in Walter Martin, *Martin Speaks Out on the Cults* (Ventura, CA: Regal Books, 1983), 119; cf. Mather and Nichols, *Dictionary of Cults, Sects, Religions and the Occult,* 252.

81. *Scientology: Theology and Practice of a Contemporary Religion,* 37.

82. Ibid.; *What Is Scientology?* 222–23.

83. *What Is Scientology?* 545.

84. Ibid., 38.

85. Hubbard, *Dianetics: The Modern Science of Mental Health,* vii; Hubbard, *Scientology: The Fundamentals of Thought,* 6.

86. See Weldon, "Scientology: From Science Fiction to Space-Age Religion."

87. For more on historical and archaeological support for the Bible, see my book *The Complete Book of Bible Answers* (Eugene, OR: Harvest House, 1997), chs. 1 and 2.

88. Van Gorden, "Scientology," 164.

89. A. W. Tozer, *The Pursuit of God* (Wheaton, IL: Tyndale House, n.d.), 35.

90. Kevin Anderson, *Report of the Board of Inquiry into Scientology* (Melbourne: AC Brooks Government Printer, 1965), no. 9, 95–97: cited in Weldon, "Scientology: From Science Fiction to Space-Age Religion."

91. Abanes, *Cults, New Religious Movements, and Your Family,* 76.

92. *Publisher's Weekly,* 16 September 1950: 1124: cited in Martin, *The Kingdom of the Cults,* 376.

CHAPTER 8: HINDU-BASED CULTS

1. J. Isamu Yamamoto, *Hinduism, TM and Hare Krishna* (Grand Rapids: Zondervan, 1996), 20; Dean C. Halverson, "Hinduism," in *The Compact Guide to World Religions* (Minneapolis: Bethany House, 1996), 87.

2. Russell Chandler, *Racing Toward 2001* (Grand Rapids: Zondervan, 1992), 189.

3. Os Guinness, *The Dust of Death* (Downers Grove, IL: InterVarsity Press, 1973), 195.

4. James Sire, *The Universe Next Door* (Downers Grove, IL: InterVarsity Press, 1992), 138–39.

5. Ibid., 138–39.

6. Vishal Mangalwadi, *The World of Guru* (Chicago: Cornerstone Press, 1992), 59.

7. Sire, *The Universe Next Door*, 138–39.

8. Ron Enroth, *The Lure of the Cults* (Downers Grover, IL: InterVarsity Press, 1987), 42.

9. Mangalwadi, *The World of Guru*, 9.

10. Mark Albrecht, "Hinduism," in *Evangelizing the Cults*, ed. Ronald Enroth (Ann Arbor, MI: Servant, 1990), 23.

11. *The New Age Rage*, ed. Karen Hoyt (Old Tappan, NJ: Revell, 1987), 28.

12. Bruce J. Nicholls, "Hinduism," in *The World's Religions* (Grand Rapids: Eerdmans, 1974), 136.

13. Josh McDowell, *A Ready Defense* (Nashville: Thomas Nelson, 1993), 272.

14. John Ankerberg and John Weldon, *The Facts on Hinduism in America* (Eugene, OR: Harvest House, 1991), 8.

15. Lewis M. Hopfe, *Religions of the World* (New York: Macmillan, 1991), 91.

16. Ken Boa, *Cults, World Religions, and You* (Wheaton, IL: Victor Books, 1979), 13.

17. Walter Martin, *The New Cults* (Ventura, CA: Regal Books, 1980), 82–83.

18. John B. Noss, *Man's Religions* (New York: Macmillan, 1974), 101.

19. Hopfe, *Religions of the World*, 100.

20. Halverson, "Hinduism," 88.

21. Martin, *The New Cults*, 82.

22. Halverson, "Hinduism," 89.

23. Hopfe, *Religions of the World*, 99.

24. Albrecht, "Hinduism," 22.

25. Hopfe, *Religions of the World*, 98.

26. Paramahansa Yogananda, *Autobiography of a Yogi* (Los Angeles: Self-Realization Fellowship, 1972), 199.

27. See George A. Mather and Larry A. Nichols, *Dictionary of Cults, Sects, Religions and the Occult* (Grand Rapids: Zondervan, 1993), 119.

28. Yogi, *Meditations of Maharishi Mahesh Yogi* (New York: Bantam, 1968), 123–24.

29. Irvine Robertson, *What the Cults Believe* (Chicago: Moody Press, 1983), 118.

30. J. Isamu Yamamoto, "Hare Krishna," in *A Guide to Cults and New Religions* (Downers Grove, IL: InterVarsity Press, 1983), 92.

31. *Back to Godhead*, no. 47, 1.

32. Yamamoto, *Hinduism, TM and Hare Krishna*, 18.

33. Ruth Tucker, *Another Gospel: Alternative Religions and the New Age Movement* (Grand Rapids: Zondervan, 1989), 275.

34. Ibid., 66.

35. Mangalwadi, *The World of Guru*, 65.

36. Robertson, *What the Cults Believe*, 119.

37. Boa, *Cults, World Religions, and You*, 181.

38. Francine Daner, *The American Children of Krsna* (New York: Holt, Rinehart & Winston, 1976), 67.

39. Orville Swenson, *The Perilous Path of Cultism* (Caronport, Saskatchewan, Canada: Briercrest Books, 1987), 181.

40. Mangalwadi, *The World of Guru*, 69.

41. Enroth, *The Lure of the Cults and New Religions*, 88.

42. Prabhupada: cited in Mangalwadi, *The World of Guru*, 69.

43. Garuda Dasa, "Sankirtana: The Perfection of Glorifying God," *Back to Godhead* 16, no. 11 (1981), 6.

44. Yamamoto, "Hare Krishna," in *A Guide to Cults and New Religions*, 95.

45. Cited in Enroth, *The Lure of the Cults*, 42.

46. Patricia Drake Hemingway, *The Transcendental Meditation Primer* (New York: David McKay, 1975), xvii; Boa, *Cults, World Religions, and You*, 156. See Peter Russell, *TM: The Technique* (Boston: Routledge & Kegan Paul, 1976), ch. 2; Harold H. Bloomfield, Michael Peter Cain, Dennis T. Jaffe, and Robert B. Kory, *TM: Discovering Inner Energy and Overcoming Distress* (Boston: G. K. Hall, 1975), 106–7.

47. Martin, *The New Cults*, 96.

48. Mangalwadi, *The World of Guru*, 77.

49. Mather and Nichols, *Dictionary of Cults, Sects, Religions and the Occult*, 277.

50. Cited in McDowell, *A Ready Defense*, 354.

51. David Johnson, *A Reasoned Look at Asian Religions* (Minneapolis: Bethany House, 1985), 97.

52. Norman L. Geisler and Ronald M. Brooks, *Christianity under Attack* (Dallas: Quest, 1985), 43.

53. Norman L. Geisler and Jeff Amano, *The Infiltration of the New Age* (Wheaton, IL: Tyndale House, 1990), 18.

54. Cited in Halverson, "Hinduism," 94.

55. Yamamoto, *Hinduism, TM and Hare Krishna*, 50.

56. Boa, *Cults, World Religions, and You*, 163.

57. See Tal Brooke, *Riders of the Cosmic Circuit* (Batavia, NY: Lion, 1986), 39–50.

58. James Hassett, "Caution: Meditation Can Hurt," *Psychology Today*, November 1978, 125–26.

59. Dr. Otis: cited in Mangalwadi, *The World of Guru*, 82.

60. Mangalwadi, *The World of Guru*, 81.

61. Arnold M. Ludwig, *Altered States of Consciousness*, 16: cited in Josh McDowell and Don Stewart, *Answers to Tough Questions: What Skeptics Are Asking About the Christian Faith* (Nashville: Thomas Nelson, 1994), 83.

CHAPTER 9: THE UNIFICATION CHURCH

1. Eileen Barker, *The Making of a Moonie: Choice or Brainwashing?* (Cambridge: Basil Blackwell, 1984), 2.

2. Mose Durst, *To Bigotry, No Sanction* (Chicago: Regnery Gateway, 1984), 62.

3. See Richard Abanes, *Cults, New Religious Movements, and Your Family* (Wheaton, IL: Crossway Books, 1998), 139.

4. Nansook Hong, *In the Shadow of the Moons: My Life in the Reverend Sun Myung Moon's Family* (Boston: Little, Brown, 1998), 18.

5. J. Isamu Yamamoto, *Unification Church* (Grand Rapids: Zondervan, 1995), 7–11.

6. Durst, *To Bigotry, No Sanction*, 63.

7. See Barker, *The Making of a Moonie*, 39. See also Hong, *In the Shadow of the Moons*, 133.

8. Hong, *In the Shadow of the Moons*, 25.

9. Ibid.

10. Durst, *To Bigotry, No Sanction,* 64.

11. Hong, *In the Shadow of the Moons,* 24.

12. Barker, *The Making of a Moonie,* 42. See Walter Martin, *The Kingdom of the Cults,* ed. Hank Hanegraaff (Minneapolis: Bethany House, 1999), 354.

13. Hong, *In the Shadow of the Moons,* 25.

14. Barker, *The Making of a Moonie,* 42.

15. Hong, *In the Shadow of the Moons,* 26.

16. Orville Swenson, *The Perilous Path of Cultism* (Caronport, Saskatchewan, Canada: Briercrest Books, 1987), 220. See also Irvine Robertson, *What the Cults Believe* (Chicago: Moody Press, 1983), 75.

17. See James Beverley, "The Unification Church," in *Evangelizing the Cults,* ed. Ronald Enroth (Ann Arbor, MI: Servant, 1990), 75.

18. Josh McDowell and Don Stewart, *Understanding the Cults* (San Bernardino, CA: Here's Life, 1989), 99.

19. See Carroll Stoner and Jo Anne Parke, *All God's Children: The Cult Experience—Salvation or Slavery?* (Radnor, PA: Chilton, 1977), 154–55.

20. Barker, *The Making of a Moonie,* 2. See George A. Mather and Larry A. Nichols, *Dictionary of Cults, Sects, Religions and the Occult* (Grand Rapids: Zondervan, 1993), 282.

21. Ron Enroth, *Lure of the Cults and New Religions* (Downers Grove, IL: InterVarsity Press, 1987), 107.

22. J. Isamu Yamamoto, *Unification Church* (Grand Rapids: Zondervan, 1995), 17.

23. Kenneth Boa, *Cults, World Religions, and You* (Wheaton, IL: Victor Books, 1979), 173.

24. According to Barker, *The Making of a Moonie,* 115.

25. See Enroth, *Lure of the Cults and New Religions,* 18.

26. Ron Enroth, *Youth, Brainwashing and the Extremist Cults* (Grand Rapids: Zondervan, 1977), 110.

27. Boa, *Cults, World Religions, and You,* 174.

28. See Enroth, *The Lure of the Cults and New Religions,* 105.

29. Yamamoto, *Unification Church,* 13.

30. "Moon Runs Fronts in U.S.," *Spotlight,* 18 February 1991, 12. See also Swenson, *The Perilous Path of Cultism,* 85–86; Bob Waldrep, "Moonstruck: Unification Church in America," *The Watchman Expositor* 13, no. 5 (1996); "Moon Survey," *Statement DM 180,* Christian Research Institute, P.O. Box 7000, Rancho Santa Margarita, CA 92688; Steve Hassan, "Moon Front Organizations," Resource Center for Freedom of Mind, see http://www.freedomofmind.com/groups/moonies/moonfronts.htm.

31. Ruth Tucker, *Another Gospel: Alternative Religions and the New Age Movement* (Grand Rapids: Zondervan, 1989), 22.

32. Barker, *The Making of a Moonie,* 13.

33. Abanes, *Cults, New Religious Movements, and Your Family,* 144.

34. Bryce A. Pettit, "Unification Theology and the Cross of Christ," *Contend for the Faith,* ed. Eric Pement (Chicago: Evangelical Ministries to New Religions, 1992), 163.

35. J. Isamu Yamamoto, "Unification Church," in *A Guide to Cults and New Religions* (Downers Grove, IL: InterVarsity Press, 1983), 157.

36. Yamamoto, *Unification Church,* 31–32; *Divine Principle,* 2d ed., trans. Won Pok Choi (Washington, DC: The Holy Spirit Association for the Unification of World Christianity, 1974), 173, 231, 232, 430.

37. *Divine Principle*, 519.

38. Hong, *In the Shadow of the Moons*, 136.

39. *Divine Principle*, 283.

40. Swenson, *The Perilous Path of Cultism*, 222.

41. Sun Myung Moon: cited in Martin, *The Kingdom of the Cults*, 364.

42. See *Divine Principle*, 217–18.

43. Yamamoto, *Unification Church*, 44.

44. Hong, *In the Shadow of the Moons*, 19–20.

45. Yamamoto, *Unification Church*, 22.

46. Hong, *In the Shadow of the Moons*, 4, 5.

47. Ibid., 20.

CHAPTER 10: THE BAHA'I FAITH

1. Walter Martin, *The Kingdom of the Cults*, ed. Hank Hanegraaff (Minneapolis: Bethany House, 1999), 323.

2. Ibid.

3. John Boykin, "The Baha'i Faith," in *A Guide to Cults and New Religions* (Downers Grove, IL: InterVarsity Press, 1983), 25.

4. Martin, *The Kingdom of the Cults*, 323.

5. *The Baha'is: A Profile of the Baha'i Faith and Its Worldwide Community* (Oakham, Leicestershire: Baha'i Publishing Trust of the United Kingdom, 1994), 7.

6. See William S. Hatcher and J. Douglas Martin, *The Baha'i Faith: The Emerging Global Religion* (San Francisco: Harper & Row, 1984), 62–63. See also John Ankerberg and John Weldon, *Encyclopedia of Cults and New Religions* (Eugene, OR: Harvest House, 1999), 8.

7. Orville Swenson, *The Perilous Path of Cultism* (Caronport, Saskatchewan, Canada: Briercrest Books, 1987), 149.

8. J. E. Esslemont, *Baha'u'llah and the New Era: An Introduction to the Baha'i Faith* (Wilmette, IL: Baha'i Publishing Trust, 1980), 71.

9. Shoghi Effendi, *The Faith of Baha'u'llah* (Wilmette, IL: Baha'i Publishing Trust, 1959), 7–8. See *Gleanings from the Writings of Baha'u'llah*, trans. Shoghi Effendi (Wilmette, IL: Baha'i Publishing Trust, 1969), 81, 95, 140, 214.

10. *Uniting the Human Family: The Baha'i Faith* (N.p.: Regional Baha'i Council of the Southern States, 1998), 5.

11. Ibid., 8.

12. See *Gleanings from the Writings of Baha'u'llah*, 78, 95, 217, 287.

13. Ibid., 217.

14. *The Baha'is: A Profile of the Baha'i Faith and Its Worldwide Community*, 6. See Esslemont, *Baha'u'llah and the New Era*, 106–7, 113, 117, 158, 188. Hatcher and Martin, *The Baha'i Faith*, 87–88. *Baha'i World Faith: Selected Writings of Baha'u'llah and Abdul-Baha* (Wilmette, IL: Baha'i Publishing Trust, 1956), 246, 255, 259.

15. See Hatcher and Martin, *The Baha'i Faith*, 1–5. *The Proclamation of Baha'u'llah to the Kings and Leaders of the World* (Haifa: Baha'i World Center, 1978), 163.

16. *The Proclamation of Baha'u'llah to the Kings and Leaders of the World*, 74–75, 248.

17. Richard N. Ostling, "Slow Death for Iran's Baha'is," *Time*, 20 February 1984, 76.

18. See *Selections from the Writings of the Bab*, trans. Habib Taherzadeh (Haifa: Baha'i World Center, 1978), 11–17, 47, 54–55, 139, 173–74.

19. Hatcher and Martin, *The Baha'i Faith*, 8.

20. Ernest Pickering, "The Ecumenical Cult—Baha'ism," *The Discerner*, October–December 1973, 12.

21. *The Baha'is: A Profile of the Baha'i Faith and Its Worldwide Community*, 18.

22. Ibid., 19; Hatcher and Martin, *The Baha'i Faith*, 18–19.

23. *The Baha'is: A Profile of the Baha'i Faith and Its Worldwide Community*, 19. See also Esslemont, *Baha'u'llah and the New Era*, 15, 17–18, 22, 24. *Gleanings from the Writings of Baha'u'llah*, 89, 146, 147.

24. *Uniting the Human Family*, 13. See *Baha'i World Faith: Selected Writings of Baha'u'llah and Abdul-Baha*, 219, 233, 238, 258.

25. Esslemont, *Baha'u'llah and the New Era*, 23–24.

26. *The Baha'is: A Profile of the Baha'i Faith and Its Worldwide Community*, 37.

27. Esslemont, *Baha'u'llah and the New Era*, 46–47. See also *Gleanings from the Writings of Baha'u'llah*, 55–56, 171.

28. George A. Mather and Larry A. Nichols, *Dictionary of Cults, Sects, Religions and the Occult* (Grand Rapids: Zondervan, 1993), 32.

29. Hatcher and Martin, *The Baha'i Faith*, 49.

30. Esslemont, *Baha'u'llah and the New Era*, 40.

31. Ibid., 51–70. See also Swenson, *The Perilous Path of Cultism*, 148.

32. Esslemont, *Baha'u'llah and the New Era*, 66, 68, 69, 130, 180–81, 261–62, 267–68; Swenson, *The Perilous Path of Cultism*, 149.

33. See *The Baha'is: A Profile of the Baha'i Faith and Its Worldwide Community*, 57.

34. Boykin, "The Baha'i Faith," 27. See also Hatcher and Martin, *The Baha'i Faith*, 59, 66. See also *Baha'i World Faith: Selected Writings of Baha'u'llah and Abdul-Baha*, 12, 41.

35. Hatcher and Martin, *The Baha'i Faith*, 71–72.

36. Ibid., 170.

37. Boykin, "The Baha'i Faith," 30. See Esslemont, *Baha'u'llah and the New Era*, 2, 5, 40, 117–18, 166–69, 172, 173–74.

38. *The Baha'is: A Profile of the Baha'i Faith and its Worldwide Community*, 75. See Abdul-Baha, *Foundations of World Unity* (Wilmette, IL: Baha'i Publishing Trust, 1945), 15.

39. Pickering, "The Ecumenical Cult—Baha'ism," 13. See also *The Divine Art of Living: Selections from the Baha'i Writings* (Wilmette, IL: Baha'i Publishing Trust, 1944), 13.

40. Shoghi Effendi, *World Order of Baha'u'llah*, 115. See also Esslemont, *Baha'u'llah and the New Era*, 122–31, 157.

41. *Uniting the Human Family*, 11. See also *The Baha'is: A Profile of the Baha'i Faith and its Worldwide Community*, 13.

42. Hatcher and Martin, *The Baha'i Faith*, 115–21.

43. Ankerberg and Weldon, *Encyclopedia of Cults and New Religions*, 12.

44. Baha'i World Faith web site.

45. Hatcher and Martin, *The Baha'i Faith*, 82–83. Baha'u'llah, *Epistle to the Son of the Wolf*, trans. Shoghi Effendi (Wilmette, IL: Baha'i Publishing Trust, 1988), v.

46. See *Gleanings from the Writings of Baha'u'llah*, 30, 47–50, 53, 54, 59, 70.

47. Hatcher and Martin, *The Baha'i Faith*, 124.

48. *Baha'i World Faith*, 20–28.

49. See Esslemont, *Baha'u'llah and the New Era*, 12, 84, 88, 91, 105, 109, 110, 116, 118, 125, 128, 171, 173, 175, 176.

50. Ankerberg and Weldon, *Encyclopedia of Cults and New Religions*, 66.

51. Hatcher and Martin, *The Baha'i Faith*, 74.

52. See *Gleanings from the Writings of Baha'u'llah*, 3, 151, 193, 220, 318.

53. Hatcher and Martin, *The Baha'i Faith*, 123.

54. Ankerberg and Weldon, *Encyclopedia of Cults and New Religions*, 19.

55. See *Selections from the Writings of the Bab*, 3–8, 18–19, 23, 49, 111–13, 125–26, 153.

56. *The Kitab-I-Iqan* (Wilmette, IL: Baha'i Publishing Trust, 1995), 98.

57. *The Baha'is: A Profile of the Baha'i Faith and its Worldwide Community*, 35.

58. Hatcher and Martin, *The Baha'i Faith*, 126.

59. Cited in Martin, *The Kingdom of the Cults*, 325.

60. Baha'i leader: cited in Martin, *The Kingdom of the Cults*, 325. See *Gleanings from the Writings of Baha'u'llah*, 51, 52, 62, 83. *Selections from the Writings of the Bab*, 60–61, 137.

61. *World Order*, Summer 1978, 39.

62. Boykin, "The Baha'i Faith," 31. See Hatcher and Martin, *The Baha'i Faith*, 1, 2, 5, 6, 24, 25, 81, 83, 97.

63. *World Order*, Winter 1966, 27.

64. Cf. *The Proclamation of Baha'u'llah to the Kings and Leaders of the World*, 11, 103.

65. Abdu'l-Baha, *Some Answered Questions*, 119–21: cited in Boykin, "The Baha'i Faith," 32.

66. Boykin, "The Baha'i Faith," 32.

67. Huschmand Sabet, *The Heavens Are Cleft Asunder* (Oxford: Ronald, 1975), 112.

68. Baha'i leader: cited in Martin, *The Kingdom of the Cults*, 327.

69. See *The Divine Art of Living: Selections from the Baha'i Writings*, 62ff. Esslemont, *Baha'u'llah and the New Era*, 146–49, 235. *The Proclamation of Baha'u'llah to the Kings and Leaders of the World*, 73.

70. Hatcher and Martin, *The Baha'i Faith*, 113.

71. Udo Schaefer, *The Light Shineth in Darkness* (Oxford: George Ronald, 1973), 100.

72. Peter Simple, *Baha'i Teachings, Light for All Regions* (Wilmette, IL: Baha'i, 1970), 21.

73. *The Baha'is: A Profile of the Baha'i Faith and Its Worldwide Community*, 35.

74. Esslemont, *Baha'u'llah and the New Era*, 190–91.

75. *The Baha'is: A Profile of the Baha'i Faith and Its Worldwide Community*, 35.

76. Ibid., 35.

77. Baha'i leader: cited in Martin, *The Kingdom of the Cults*, 327.

78. Hatcher and Martin, *The Baha'i Faith*, 104–5.

79. Francis Beckwith: cited in Ankerberg and Weldon, *Encyclopedia of Cults and New Religions*, 14.

80. Benjamin B. Warfield, *The Person and Work of Christ* (Philadelphia: Presbyterian & Reformed, 1950), 56.

81. John Eadie, *A Commentary on the Greek Text of the Epistle of Paul to the Colossians* (Grand Rapids: Baker, 1979), 51.

82. Norman Geisler, *Christian Apologetics* (Grand Rapids: Baker, 1976), 338.

83. Ankerberg and Weldon, *Encyclopedia of Cults and New Religions*, 8.

84. Boykin, "The Baha'i Faith," 34.

85. Ruth Tucker, *Another Gospel: Alternative Religions and the New Age Movement* (Grand Rapids: Zondervan, 1989), 293.

86. Ankerberg and Weldon, *Encyclopedia of Cults and New Religions*, 34.

CHAPTER 11: UNITARIAN UNIVERSALISM

1. John Sias, *100 Questions That Non-Members Ask about Unitarian Universalism* (Nashua, NH: Transition, 1999), 19. See also George Sheridan, "Unitarian Universalist," in *Beliefs of Other Kinds: A Guide to Interfaith Witness in the United States* (Atlanta: Baptist Home Mission Board, 1984), 60. See John Ankerberg and John Weldon, *Encyclopedia of Cults and New Religions* (Eugene, OR: Harvest House, 1999), 502.

2. See John A. Buehrens and Forrest Church, *A Chosen Faith: An Introduction to Unitarian Universalism* (Boston: Beacon, 1998), 76.

3. Alan Gomes, "Unitarian Universalism," in Walter Martin, *The Kingdom of the Cults*, ed. Hank Hanegraaff (Minneapolis: Bethany House, 1999), 635.

4. Ibid., 634.

5. Alan Gomes, "Tolerate This! Answering Unitarian Universalist Pluralism," *Journal of Christian Apologetics*, vol. 1, no. 2, 35.

6. Ankerberg and Weldon, *Encyclopedia of Cults and New Religions*, 503.

7. Alan Gomes, *Unitarian Universalism* (Grand Rapids: Zondervan, 1996), 9.

8. Sheridan, "Unitarian Universalist," 60. See also *The Unitarian Universalist Pocket Guide*, ed. John A. Buehrens (Boston: Skinner House, 1999), ix.

9. George Kimmich Beach, *Catechism with an Open Mind* (n.p., 1995), 34.

10. Sheridan, "Unitarian Universalist," 60.

11. Buehrens and Church, *A Chosen Faith*, 43.

12. George A. Mather and Larry A. Nichols, *Dictionary of Cults, Sects, Religions and the Occult* (Grand Rapids: Zondervan, 1993), 286.

13. Sias, *100 Questions That Non-Members Ask about Unitarian Universalism*, 15; Beach, *Catechism with an Open Mind*, 46; Buehrens and Church, *A Chosen Faith*, 43; David Robinson, *The Unitarians and the Universalists* (Westport, CN: Greenwood, 1985), 3–4, 61–62, 65, 105; Arthur W. Brown, *William Ellery Channing* (New York: Grosset & Dunlap, 1961), 53.

14. See Gomes, *Unitarian Universalism*; Buehrens and Church, *A Chosen Faith*; Sias, *100 Questions That Non-Members Ask about Unitarian Universalism*.

15. Michael Servetus, *On the Errors of the Trinity*: cited in Jack Mendelsohn, *Why I Am a Unitarian Universalist* (Boston: Beacon, 1969), 6.

16. See *The Unitarian Universalist Pocket Guide*, 59.

17. Beach, *Catechism with an Open Mind*, 70.

18. Gomes, "Unitarian Universalism," in Martin, *The Kingdom of the Cults*, 638.

19. See Buehrens and Church, *A Chosen Faith*, 214.

20. Philip Schaff, *History of the Christian Church* (Peabody, MA: Hendrickson, 1996); in PC Study Bible, BibleSoft Company.

21. See *The Unitarian Universalist Pocket Guide*, 61.

22. See ibid., 65. See also *Universalism in America*, ed. Ernest Cassara (Boston: Beacon, 1971), 4.

23. Buehrens and Church, *A Chosen Faith*, 28–29.

24. See Robinson, *The Unitarians and the Universalists*, 4, 14, 26, 29–33, 38, 83–86, 184, 228–30.

25. See Gomes, *Unitarian Universalism*, 14–15. See also James Luther Adams, *An Examined Faith: Social Context and Religious Commitment* (Boston: Beacon, 1991), 62, 65, 100, 103, 355, 357.

26. Kathleen Elgin, *The Unitarians* (New York: David McKay, 1971), 76.

27. See Buehrens and Church, *A Chosen Faith*, 186.

28. See *The Unitarian Universalist Pocket Guide*, 68.

29. See Sheridan, "Unitarian Universalist," 60.

30. See Robinson, *The Unitarians and the Universalists*, 5, 7, 71, 143–57, 170, 175, 307.

31. See Buehrens and Church, *A Chosen Faith*, 158; and Gomes, "Unitarian Universalism," in Martin, *The Kingdom of the Cults*, 641.

32. Elgin, *The Unitarians*, 76. See also Gomes, *Unitarian Universalism*, 18.

33. Sheridan, "Unitarian Universalist," 60.

34. *Universalism in America*, ed. Ernest Cassara (Boston: Beacon, 1971), 22.

35. Buehrens and Church, *A Chosen Faith*, xx.

36. See, e.g., ibid., 192.

37. Ibid., xxii.

38. "Letter to the Christians," 41: cited in Gomes, "Unitarian Universalism," in Martin, *The Kingdom of the Cults*, 645.

39. Sias, *100 Questions That Non-Members Ask about Unitarian Universalism*, 2. *The Unitarian Universalist Pocket Guide*, ix, 2. See also Ankerberg and Weldon, *Encyclopedia of Cults and New Religions*, 507; Buehrens and Church, *A Chosen Faith*, xxiii. Robinson, *The Unitarians and the Universalists*, 6–7, 17–18, 88, 177, 180.

40. Beach, *Catechism with an Open Mind*, 68.

41. Ibid., 69. See also Buehrens and Church, *A Chosen Faith*, xxii.

42. Philip Hewett, *The Unitarian Way* (Toronto: Canadian Unitarian Council, 1985), 89.

43. Karl M. Chworowsky and Gist Raible, "What Is a Unitarian Universalist?" in *Religions in America*, ed. Leo Rosten (New York: Simon & Schuster, 1975), 272.

44. *The Unitarian Universalist Pocket Guide*, 8.

45. Poll cited in Ankerberg and Weldon, *Encyclopedia of Cults and New Religions*, 503.

46. Marta Flanagan, "We Are Unitarian Universalists," UUA pamphlet, 1. See Buehrens and Church, *A Chosen Faith*, xxiii.

47. *The Unitarian Universalist Pocket Guide*, 4.

48. Beach, *Catechism with an Open Mind*, 72.

49. Sias, *100 Questions That Non-Members Ask about Unitarian Universalism*, 4. Elgin, *The Unitarians*, 82. Robinson, *The Unitarians and the Universalists*, 15, 32, 56.

50. Sias, *100 Questions That Non-Members Ask about Unitarian Universalism*, 4.

51. Ibid., 4.

52. Ankerberg and Weldon, *Encyclopedia of Cults and New Religions*, 509.

53. Buehrens and Church, *A Chosen Faith*, 127.

54. Sias, *100 Questions That Non-Members Ask about Unitarian Universalism*, 4.

55. See Robinson, *The Unitarians and the Universalists*, 14–15, 121–22, 150–51, 165, 177.

56. Sias, *100 Questions That Non-Members Ask about Unitarian Universalism*, 2.

57. Ibid., 3.

58. Robinson, *The Unitarians and the Universalists*, 29–31, 40. See also Gomes, *Unitarian Universalism*, 52–53.

59. Cited in Conrad Wright, *Three Prophets of Religious Liberalism: Channing, Emerson, Park* (Boston: Beacon, 1978), 62.

60. Sias, *100 Questions That Non-Members Ask about Unitarian Universalism*, 6. See also Elgin, *The Unitarians*, 80. Robinson, *The Unitarians and the Universalists*, 5, 29, 39, 41, 64–65, 105–6, 301.

61. Sias, *100 Questions That Non-Members Ask about Unitarian Universalism*, 4.

62. Ibid., *100 Questions That Non-Members Ask about Unitarian Universalism*, 6. See also Beach, *Catechism with an Open Mind*, 34.

63. Buehrens and Church, *A Chosen Faith*, 7.

64. Hewett, *The Unitarian Way*, 90: cited in Gomes, *Unitarian Universalism*, 58.

65. Sias, *100 Questions That Non-Members Ask about Unitarian Universalism*, 4. Elgin, *The Unitarians*, 80.

66. See, e.g., Beach, *Catechism with an Open Mind*, 60.

67. Sias, *100 Questions That Non-Members Ask about Unitarian Universalism*, 21.

68. John Van Shaik Jr.: cited in Ankerberg and Weldon, *Encyclopedia of Cults and New Religions*, 513. See also Robinson, *The Unitarians and the Universalists*, 66–72.

69. Wright, *Three Prophets of Religious Liberalism*, 99.

70. Sias, *100 Questions That Non-Members Ask about Unitarian Universalism*, 9–10.

71. G. Marshall, "Unitarian Universalists Believe," UUA pamphlet, 2. See also Buehrens and Church, *A Chosen Faith*, 45.

72. Marshall, "Unitarian Universalists Believe," 2.

73. See Robinson, *The Unitarians and the Universalists*, 3, 5, 10–11, 17, 50, 54–55, 123–25, 171–72.

74. Beach, *Catechism with an Open Mind*, 62. See also Elgin, *The Unitarians*, 81.

75. Buehrens and Church, *A Chosen Faith*, 15.

76. Sias, *100 Questions That Non-Members Ask about Unitarian Universalism*, 4. See also Robinson, *The Unitarians and the Universalists*, 20, 65, 66, 313.

77. Sias, *100 Questions That Non-Members Ask about Unitarian Universalism*, 9.

78. Cassara, *Universalism in America*, 17.

79. J. Mendelsohn, "Meet the Unitarian Universalists," UUA pamphlet, 1974.

80. Sias, *100 Questions That Non-Members Ask about Unitarian Universalism*, 9.

81. *The Unitarian Universalist Pocket Guide*, 5.

82. Sias, *100 Questions That Non-Members Ask about Unitarian Universalism*, 4.

83. Ankerberg and Weldon, *Encyclopedia of Cults and New Religions*, 503.

84. Ibid., 508.

85. Ibid., 517.

86. Gomes, *Unitarian Universalism*, 35–36.

87. Donald Wiseman: cited in Norman Geisler, *Christian Apologetics* (Grand Rapids: Baker, 1976), 322.

88. Nelson Glueck, *Rivers in the Desert* (Philadelphia: Jewish Publications, 1969), 31.

89. William F. Albright: cited in Josh McDowell, *Evidence That Demands a Verdict* (San Bernardino, CA: Campus Crusade for Christ, 1972), 68.

90. Norman Geisler and William Nix, *A General Introduction to the Bible* (Chicago: Moody Press, 1978), 28.

91. C. S. Lewis, *God in the Dock* (Grand Rapids: Eerdmans, 1972), 26.

92. Ibid., 26.

93. C. S. Lewis, *Mere Christianity* (New York: Macmillan, 1960), 40–41.

94. Gomes, *Unitarian Universalism*, 35.

CHAPTER 12: ONENESS PENTECOSTALISM

1. George A. Mather and Larry A. Nichols, *Dictionary of Cults, Sects, Religions and the Occult* (Grand Rapids: Zondervan, 1993), 213.

NOTES

2. Modalism surfaced early in church history. Sabellius, a major proponent of this modalistic view, was condemned in A.D. 263. Paul of Samosata, another advocate, was condemned in A.D. 269.

3. David K. Bernard, *The Oneness of God* (Hazelwood, MO: Word Aflame, 1983), 15.

4. See E. Calvin Beisner, *"Jesus Only" Churches* (Grand Rapids: Zondervan, 1998), 70. See also Mather and Nichols, *Dictionary of Cults, Sects, Religions and the Occult*, 214.

5. Mather and Nichols, *Dictionary of Cults, Sects, Religions and the Occult*, 214.

6. John Ankerberg and John Weldon, *Encyclopedia of Cults and New Religions* (Eugene, OR: Harvest House, 1999), 367.

7. Gregory Boyd, *Oneness Pentecostals and the Trinity* (Grand Rapids: Baker, 1992), 10.

8. Ankerberg and Weldon, *Encyclopedia of Cults and New Religions*, 369.

9. See Gordon Magee, *Is Jesus in the Godhead or Is the Godhead in Jesus?* (Hazelwood, MO: Word Aflame, 1988), 14.

10. Kenneth V. Reeves, *The Godhead* (St. Louis: Trio, 1999), 11.

11. Bernard, *The Oneness of God*, 66.

12. Reeves, *The Godhead*, 79, 85. See also Bernard, *The Oneness of God*, 56.

13. Magee, *Is Jesus in the Godhead or Is the Godhead in Jesus?* 15; Bernard, *The Oneness of God*, 67.

14. Bernard, *The Oneness of God*, 208.

15. Robert Graves, *The God of Two Testaments* (N.p.: Robert Graves and James Turner [privately published], 1977), 50–51; cf. Bernard, *The Oneness of God*, 207–11.

16. Magee, *Is Jesus in the Godhead or Is the Godhead in Jesus?* 23–24. See Boyd, *Oneness Pentecostals and the Trinity*, 29–30; Bernard, *The Oneness of God*, 69.

17. Bernard, *The Oneness of God*, 132.

18. Ibid., 128, 134.

19. Ibid., 136.

20. Robert Sabin, "The Man Jesus Christ," Oneness Ministries Handout: cited in Boyd, *Oneness Pentecostals and the Trinity*, 32.

21. Bernard, *The Oneness of God*, 98.

22. Reeves, *The Godhead*, 7

23. Ibid., 50.

24. Magee, *Is Jesus in the Godhead or Is the Godhead in Jesus?* 21.

25. Ibid.

26. C. G. Norris, *The Mighty God in Christ* (St. Paul: Apostolic Bible Institute, n.d.), 6.

27. Bernard, *The Oneness of God*, 103.

28. Ibid., 106.

29. Ibid., 127.

30. Magee, *Is Jesus in the Godhead or Is the Godhead in Jesus?* 25; Reeves, *The Godhead*, 69.

31. Magee, *Is Jesus in the Godhead or Is the Godhead in Jesus?* 31–32.

32. Boyd, *Oneness Pentecostals and the Trinity*, 35.

33. Bernard, *The Oneness of God*, 106.

34. Ibid., 117.

35. Ibid., 116.

36. Ibid., 182–83.

37. Magee, *Is Jesus in the Godhead or Is the Godhead in Jesus?* 42.

38. Bernard, *The Oneness of God*, 172.

39. Boyd, *Oneness Pentecostals and the Trinity*, 43.

40. Magee, *Is Jesus in the Godhead or Is the Godhead in Jesus!* 18–19.

41. Bernard, *The Oneness of God,* 177.

42. Magee, *Is Jesus in the Godhead or Is the Godhead in Jesus!* 19, 28, 33.

43. Boyd, *Oneness Pentecostals and the Trinity,* 44.

44. Bernard, *The Oneness of God,* 147.

45. Ibid., 282.

46. David Bernard, *Oneness and Trinity* (Hazelwood, MO: Word Aflame, 1990), 30, 33–34, 39–41.

47. Charles Clanton, Crawford Coon, and Paul Dugas, *Bible Doctrines: Foundation of the Church* (Hazelwood, MO: Word Aflame, 1984), 81.

48. Bernard, *The Oneness of God,* 138–39.

49. David Bernard, C. A. Brewer, and P. D. Buford, *Meet the United Pentecostal Church International* (Hazelwood, MO: Word Aflame, 1989), 50–51.

50. Ralph V. Reynolds, *Truth Shall Triumph: A Study of Pentecostal Doctrines* (Hazelwood, MO: Word Aflame, 1965), 8–9.

51. See John F. Walvoord, *Jesus Christ Our Lord* (Chicago: Moody Press, 1969), 22–25.

52. James Oliver Buswell, *A Systematic Theology of the Christian Religion* (Grand Rapids: Zondervan, 1979), 1:105.

53. Charles C. Ryrie, *Basic Theology* (Wheaton, IL: Victor Books, 1986), 248.

54. Gregory A. Boyd, "Sharing Your Faith with a Oneness Pentecostal," *Christian Research Journal,* Spring 1991, 7.

55. Albert Barnes, *Notes on the Old Testament Isaiah* (Grand Rapids: Baker, 1977), 193.

56. J. F. Stenning, *The Targum of Isaiah* (London: Oxford Press, 1949), 32.

57. Boyd, *Oneness Pentecostals and the Trinity,* 70.

58. Robert M. Bowman, *Why You Should Believe in the Trinity* (Grand Rapids: Baker, 1989), 43.

59. Ibid., 38.

60. Benjamin B. Warfield, *The Person and Work of Christ* (Philadelphia: Presbyterian & Reformed, 1950), 66.

61. Boyd, *Oneness Pentecostals and the Trinity,* 52.

62. Ibid., 145.

CHAPTER 13: FREEMASONRY

1. See John J. Robinson, *Born in Blood: The Lost Secrets of Freemasonry* (New York: M. Evans, 1989), 176–77. See also John Ankerberg and John Weldon, *The Secret Teachings of the Masonic Lodge* (Chicago: Moody Press, 1990), 25.

2. See George Mather and Larry Nichols, *Masonic Lodge* (Grand Rapids: Zondervan, 1995), 27.

3. Ankerberg and Weldon, *The Secret Teachings of the Masonic Lodge,* 49.

4. For a description of Masonic initiation ceremonies, see Robinson, *Born in Blood,* chs. 14–16.

5. See ibid., 178.

6. See Michael Baigent and Richard Leigh, *The Temple and the Lodge* (New York: Arcade, 1989), 126. See also William E. Hammond, *What Masonry Means* (New York: Macoy, 1952), 17ff.; and Henry Wilson Coil, *A Comprehensive View of Freemasonry* (Richmond, VA: Macoy, 1973), 5.

7. Baigent and Leigh, *The Temple and the Lodge,* 174; Robinson, *Born in Blood,* 179; Coil, *A Comprehensive View of Freemasonry,* 69, 76–85, 122–31; see Mather and Nichols, *Masonic Lodge,* 8.

8. See Robinson, *Born in Blood,* 181.

9. Coil, *A Comprehensive View of Freemasonry*, 378.

10. Ankerberg and Weldon, *The Secret Teachings of the Masonic Lodge*, 258.

11. Alphonse Cerza, *Let There Be Light: A Study in Anti-Masonry* (Silver Spring, MD: The Masonic Service Association, 1983), 1.

12. Coil, *A Comprehensive View of Freemasonry*, 134.

13. Albert Mackey, *The Manual of the Lodge* (New York: Clark Maynard, 1870), 20.

14. Mather and Nichols, *Masonic Lodge*, 11.

15. Ibid. See also Ron Carlson, *Fast Facts on False Teachings* (Eugene, OR: Harvest House, 1994), 75.

16. Cited in Mather and Nichols, *Masonic Lodge*, 11.

17. Robinson, *Born in Blood*, 253.

18. Mather and Nichols, *Masonic Lodge*, 15.

19. See Mather and Nichols for this section, *Masonic Lodge*, 15–25.

20. See Coil, *A Comprehensive View of Freemasonry*, 204–13.

21. Albert Mackey, *Encyclopedia of Freemasonry* (Chicago: Masonic History, 1946), 2:847.

22. Henry Wilson Coil, *Coil's Masonic Encyclopedia* (New York: Macoy, 1961), 158.

23. Ibid., 13.

24. *Liturgy of the Ancient and Accepted Scottish Rite of Freemasonry for the Southern Jurisdiction of the United States*, pt. 2 (Washington, DC: The Supreme Council, 1982), 198–99.

25. See Robinson, *Born in Blood*, 255.

26. *Little Masonic Library* (Richmond, VA: Macoy, 1977), 1:138.

27. Charles H. Lacquement, "Freemasonry and Organized Religions," *The Pennsylvania Freemason*, February 1989, 7.

28. Robinson, *Born in Blood*, 255.

29. Ibid., 256.

30. Norman Vincent Peale, "What Freemasonry Means to Me," *Scottish Rite Journal* (February 1993): 40: cited in Mather and Nichols, *Masonic Lodge*, 31.

31. Hammond, *What Masonry Means*, 99.

32. See ibid., 15.

33. Richard Thorn, *The Boy Who Cried Wolf: The Book that Breaks Masonic Silence* (New York: M. Evans, 1994), 22.

34. Robinson, *Born in Blood*, 255.

35. Coil, *Coil's Masonic Encyclopedia*, 520.

36. See Mackey, *Encyclopedia of Freemasonry*, 104.

37. Jim Tresner, "Conscience and the Class: Questions on Religion and Freemasonry," *The Northern Lights*, February 1993, 18: cited in Mather and Nichols, *Masonic Lodge*, 41.

38. Coil, *A Comprehensive View of Freemasonry*, 192.

39. Albert Mackey, *Mackey's Revised Encyclopedia of Freemasonry* (Richmond, VA: Macoy, 1966), 1:409–10.

40. J. W. Acker, *Strange Altars: A Scriptural Appraisal of the Lodge* (St. Louis: Concordia, 1959), 37.

41. Martin L. Wagner, *Freemasonry: An Interpretation* (Columbiana, OH: Missionary Service and Supply, n.d.), 338–39.

42. Jack Harris, *Freemasonry: The Invisible Cult in Our Midst* (Chattanooga: Global, 1983), 112.

43. See Ankerberg and Weldon, *The Secret Teachings of the Masonic Lodge*, 127.

44. H. L. Haywood, *The Great Teachings of Masonry* (Richmond, VA: Macoy, 1971), 138–39.

45. Grand Lodge of Texas, *Monitor of the Lodge* (N.p.: Grand Lodge of Texas, 1982), 19.

46. Harris, *Freemasonry*, 132.

47. *Mackey's Revised Encyclopedia of Freemasonry*, 1:269.

48. Haywood, *The Great Teachings of Masonry*, 138–39.

49. Cited in John Ankerberg, et al, *The Masonic Lodge: What Goes on Behind Closed Doors?* (Chattanooga: The John Ankerberg Evangelistic Association, 1986), 35.

50. Raymond Lee Allen, *Tennessee Craftsmen or Masonic Textbook* (Nashville: Tennessee Board of Custodians Members, 1963), 17.

51. A case in point is Thorn, *The Boy Who Cried Wolf*, 22.

52. Ibid.

53. Mather and Nichols, *Masonic Lodge*, 32.

54. Coil, *A Comprehensive View of Freemasonry*, 234.

55. Mather and Nichols, *Masonic Lodge*, 34–35. See also Ankerberg and Weldon, *The Secret Teachings of the Masonic Lodge*, 44–45.

56. See my book *The Complete Book of Bible Answers* (Eugene, OR: Harvest House, 1999).

57. E. K. Simpson and F. F. Bruce, *Commentary on the Epistles to the Ephesians and Colossians* (Grand Rapids: Eerdmans, 1975), 50.

58. See Ankerberg and Weldon, *The Secret Teachings of the Masonic Lodge*, 216–18.

CHAPTER 14: SATANISM

1. Craig Hawkins, "The Many Faces of Satanism," *Forward*, Fall 1986, 1.

2. See Richard Abanes, *Cults, New Religious Movements, and Your Family* (Wheaton, IL: Crossway Books, 1998), 51.

3. Bob Passantino and Gretchen Passantino, *Satanism* (Grand Rapids: Zondervan, 1995), 7.

4. Hawkins, "The Many Faces of Satanism," 1.

5. Larry Kahaner, *Cults That Kill: Probing the Underworld of Occult Crime* (New York: Warner Books, 1988), 70.

6. See Blanche Barton, *The Secret Life of a Satanist: The Authorized Biography of Anton LaVey* (Los Angeles: Ferel House, 1990), 205.

7. George A. Mather and Larry A. Nichols, *Dictionary of Cults, Sects, Religions and the Occult* (Grand Rapids: Zondervan, 1993), 244.

8. Abanes, *Cults, New Religious Movements, and Your Family*, 55.

9. Hawkins, "The Many Faces of Satanism," 2.

10. Arthur Lyons, *Satan Wants You* (New York: Mysterious Press, 1988), 9.

11. Kenneth Lanning, "Satanic, Occult, Ritualistic Crime: A Law Enforcement Perspective," FBI Academy, Quantico, VA, October 1989, 10.

12. Lyons, *Satan Wants You*, 11.

13. Abanes, *Cults, New Religious Movements, and Your Family*, 53.

14. Lyons, *Satan Wants You*, 10.

15. Jon Trott, "About the Devil's Business," *Cornerstone*, vol. 19, no. 93, 10.

16. Passantino and Passantino, *Satanism*, 10. See also Hawkins, "The Many Faces of Satanism," 1.

17. "Satanism," *Encyclopedia Britannica*, 1999–2000, electronic media.

18. Abanes, *Cults, New Religious Movements, and Your Family*, 51.

19. Mather and Nichols, *Dictionary of Cults, Sects, Religions and the Occult*, 242.

20. See Abanes, *Cults, New Religious Movements, and Your Family*, 57.

21. Robert Bowman, "Satanism and Satanic Ritual Abuse: A Basic Introduction," Atlanta Christian Apologetics Project web site: www.atlantaapologist.org.

22. See Kahaner, *Cults That Kill*, 58.

23. Passantino and Passantino, *Satanism*, 40–41.

24. Mather and Nichols, *Dictionary of Cults, Sects, Religions and the Occult*, 243.

25. Passantino and Passantino, *Satanism*, 41.

26. Cited by Kahaner, *Cults That Kill*, 65. See also Passantino and Passantino, *Satanism*, 42–43.

27. Barton, 74–75. See also Passantino and Passantino, *Satanism*, 42–43.

28. Neville Drury and Gregory Tillett, *The Occult Sourcebook* (London: Routledge and Kegan Paul, 1978), 77.

29. Drury and Tillett, 78. See also John C. Cooper, *The Black Mask: Satanism in America Today* (Old Tappan, NJ: Revell, 1990), 54.

30. Kahaner, *Cults That Kill*, 71. See also Josh McDowell and Don Stewart, *Understanding the Cults* (San Bernardin, CA: Here's Life, 1989), 239.

31. Anton LaVey, *The Satanic Bible* (New York: Avon Books, 1969), 25.

32. McDowell and Stewart, *Understanding the Cults*, 238. See also Cooper, *The Black Mask*, 38.

33. Mather and Nichols, *Dictionary of Cults, Sects, Religions and the Occult*, 244.

34. Abanes, *Cults, New Religious Movements, and Your Family*, 59.

35. See Hawkins, "The Many Faces of Satanism," 5.

36. See Kahaner, *Cults That Kill*, 54–55.

37. "Black Mass," *Encarta Encyclopedia 2000*, Microsoft Corporation, electronic media.

38. Mather and Nichols, *Dictionary of Cults, Sects, Religions and the Occult*, 247.

39. Anton LaVey; quoted in John Fritscher, "Straight from the Witch's Mouth," in Arthur C. Lehmann and James E. Meyers, eds., *Magic, Witchcraft, and Religion*, 4th ed. (Mountainview, CA: Mayfield, 1996), 389.

40. Anton LaVey, *Devil's Notebook* (Portland, OR.: Ferel House, 1992), 22.

41. Passantino and Passantino, *Satanism*, 64.

42. Ibid.

43. Burton H. Wolfe, *The Devil's Avenger* (New York: Pyramid Books, 1974), 35.

44. Hawkins, "The Many Faces of Satanism," 4.

45. Anton LaVey, *The Satanic Bible* (New York: Avon Books, 1969), 40.

46. LaVey: cited in Fritscher, "Straight from the Witch's Mouth," 389.

47. LaVey, *The Satanic Bible*, 30, 33.

48. McDowell and Stewart, *Understanding the Cults*, 238.

49. Mather and Nichols, *Dictionary of Cults, Sects, Religions and the Occult*, 244.

50. Passantino and Passantino, *Satanism*, 76.

51. Hawkins, "The Many Faces of Satanism," 5.

52. Passantino and Passantino, *Satanism*, 52.

53. Bowman, "Satanism and Satanic Ritual Abuse: A Basic Introduction."

54. See Passantino and Passantino, *Satanism*, 55.

55. Ibid., 56.

56. Daniel Goleman, "Study Finds No Proof of Cults That Abuse Kids in Satan's Name, *Orange County Register*, 31 October 1994, 18.

57. Abanes, *Cults, New Religious Movements, and Your Family*, 54.

58. Ibid., 54.

59. See, e.g., Norman Geisler and Ronald Brooks, *When Critics Ask* (Wheaton, IL: Victor Books, 1992). See also Ron Rhodes, *The Complete Book of Bible Answers* (Eugene, OR: Harvest House, 1999).

60. Thomas Ice and Robert Dean, *A Holy Rebellion* (Eugene, OR: Harvest House, 1990), 46.

61. Fred Dickason, *Angels, Elect and Evil* (Chicago: Moody Press, 1978), 122.

62. Henry Thiessen, *Lectures in Systematic Theology* (Grand Rapids: Eerdmans, 1981), 142.

63. Ibid., 142.

64. Charles C. Ryrie, *A Survey of Bible Doctrine* (Chicago: Moody Press, 1980), 94.

65. Charles C. Ryrie, *Basic Theology* (Wheaton, IL: Victor Books, 1986), 147.

66. Charles C. Ryrie, *Balancing the Christian Life* (Chicago: Moody Press, 1985), 124.

67. *See* Clinton E. Arnold, *Powers of Darkness: Principalities and Powers in Paul's Letters* (Downers Grove, IL: InterVarsity Press, 1992), ch. 7.

POSTSCRIPT

1. Socrates.

GLOSSARY

A Course in Miracles. New Age textbook written (via "automatic writing") by Helen Schucman. The "course" teaches that the solution to man's problem is a rediscovery of one's Christhood.

Age of Aquarius. Astrologers believe man's evolution goes through progressive cycles corresponding to the signs of the zodiac. Each of these lasts between 2,000 and 2,400 years. It is believed that man is now moving from the Piscean Age (the age of *intellectual* man) into the Aquarian Age (the age of *spiritual* man).

Agency. Mormon term that describes each human being's right to choose between good and evil. People progress toward godhood by making "wise use" of their agency in premortality, mortality, and postmortality.

Akashic Record. Occultists believe the physical earth is surrounded by an immense spiritual field known as *Akasha,* in which is impressed—like a celestial tape recording—every impulse of human thought, will, and emotion. Some New Age seers claim to have the ability to "read" the Akashic Record.

Analytic Mind. Scientology term referring to man's conscious and rational mind. It is the part of the mind that thinks, observes data, remembers that data, and resolves problems with data.

Animism. The belief that inanimate things possess souls or spirits.

Anointed Class. Refers to the 144,000 Jehovah's Witnesses with a heavenly destiny (see Rev. 7:4; 14:1–3).

Anthroposophy. Esoteric school of thought founded by Rudolf Steiner in 1912. The term literally means "wisdom of man," so chosen because it teaches that people possess the truth within.

Aquino, Michael. Satanist who founded the Temple of Set.

Atman. Hindu term referring to the individual soul.

Attunement. Sometimes referred to as at-one-ment, the term relates to the New Age belief that oneness with God can be attained by human beings.

Auditor. A minister or minister-in-training of the Church of Scientology. The auditor leads auditing sessions.

Avatar. One who "descends" into human form from above, never having gone through incarnation. Such a one is considered a manifestation of divinity and seeks to reveal divine truths especially important to a particular age.

Bab, The. Baha'i term used for Mizra Ali Muhammad, who represents the beginnings of the Baha'i Faith.

Baha'u'llah. Baha'i term used for Mirza Husayn Ali, the great prophet of whom "the Bab" spoke. Baha'u'llah literally means "the glory of God."

Baptism for the Dead. Mormon ritual in which one is baptized on behalf of a dead relative.

Barbour, Nelson. Adventist preacher who had a profound impact on the theology of Watchtower leader Charles Taze Russell.

Beth Sarim. Magnificent residence constructed in San Diego by the Jehovah's Witnesses for the Old Testament patriarchs, who were supposed to have been resurrected in 1925.

Bhakti Marga. Hindu term referring to a particular means of enlightenment (the way of devotion).

Bodhisattva. A being who has earned the right (by attaining perfection via many reincarnations) to enter into Nirvana or into illumination, but instead voluntarily turns back from that state in order to aid humanity to reach that same state. The Christ is said to be a Bodhisattva.

Book of Mormon. Primary Scripture of the Mormon church. It is said be God's uncorrupted revelation to humankind, the "fullness of the everlasting gospel."

Brahman. Hindu term referring to the Universal Soul.

Caste. A term applied to the social groups in India, which rank in a hierarchical order. The four primary castes—from highest to lowest—are: *Brahmins* (priests), *Ksatriyas* (warriors or rulers), *Vaisyas* (peasants), and *Sudras* (unskilled laborers).

Celestial Kingdom. The highest kingdom of glory, which is inhabited by faithful Mormons.

Channeling. New Age form of mediumship or Spiritism. The channeler voluntarily yields control of his or her capacities (both cognitive and perceptual) to a spiritual entity with the intent of receiving paranormal information.

Clear. Person who, according to Scientology, is now in control of his or her behavior instead of being controlled by engrams.

Collective Christ. New Age term referring to the whole of humanity as collectively indwelt by the Christ.

Compartmentalization. The process in which cults selectively ignore facts that obviously contradict their claims.

Cosmic Christ. New Age term referring to a divine universal spirit or a cosmic force.

Cosmic Consciousness. Refers to a spiritual and mystical perception that all in the universe is "one" (including oneness between God and man).

Cosmic Humanism. The New Age view that sees man as having virtually unlimited potential because of his inner divinity.

Crowley, Aleister. An occultist whose books are foundational to modern Satanism.

Daughters of the Eastern Star. Masonic order for girls, ages 14 to 20, whose fathers are Masons or whose mothers are members of the Eastern Star.

Day of Declaration. Some New Agers believe the Christ (as a single Avatar) will soon reveal himself on the "Day of Declaration" via worldwide television.

Deep Ecumenism. New Age term coined by Matthew Fox referring to a coming together of all persons of all religions at a mystical level.

Divine Principle. Primary scripture of the Unification Church, written by Reverend Moon.

Eddy, Mary Baker. Founder and leader of Christian Science up until the time of her death (1910).

E-Meter. A mechanical instrument (Electro-psychometer) used in Scientology auditing sessions to locate engrams in the reactive mind.

Endowment Ritual. Mormon ritual in which one is given a new name, learns secret handshakes, and is given protective sacred undergarments.

Engram. Scientology term referring to sensory impressions stored in the reactive mind that can cause various emotional and physical symptoms.

Entered Apprentice. First degree in Blue Lodge Freemasonry.

Esoteric Christianity. Mystical interpretation of Christianity that sees its "core truth" as identical to that of every other religion (that is, all is God, all is one, and man is God). This approach seeks hidden or inner meanings in Scripture.

Esoteric. A word used to describe knowledge that is possessed or understood by only a few.

Etheric Earth. Occultists believe an etheric earth exists behind the physical earth. It is thought to be made up of a fine energy substance from which is created the mold for every form that is manifested in the physical plane. All material forms in the physical universe find their ultimate source in this energy substance of the etheric realm.

Fellow Craft. Second degree in Blue Lodge Freemasonry.

Fillmore, Charles and Myrtle. Founders of the Unity School of Christianity.

First Presidency. A "collective trio" that leads the Mormon church. It is made up of the president of the church and a first and second counselor.

Four Position Foundation. Unification term referring to a husband and wife living in a loving relationship with God who then produce children. God, the two parents, and the child make up a Four Position Foundation.

Franz, Frederick. Fourth president of the Watchtower Society.

Great Invocation, The. New Age prayer distributed by Lucis Trust that has been translated into over 80 languages. The purpose of this prayer is to invoke the "second coming of the Christ."

Group Guru. New Age term referring to the whole of humanity as collectively indwelt by the Christ.

Guru. An enlightened master, even a godman, who is believed to be in his last of many thousands of reincarnations.

Holism. New Age term referring to all reality being organically one.

Holmes, Ernest. Founder of the Religious Science church.

Initiation. Occultists use this term in reference to the expansion or transformation of a person's consciousness. An "initiate" is one whose consciousness has been transformed so that it now perceives inner realities.

Inspired Version. Joseph Smith's edited version of the Bible. (He added to and subtracted from the King James Version.)

International Order of Job's Daughters. Masonic order for girls between the ages of 11 and 20, focusing heavily on moral and spiritual development.

International Order of Rainbow for Girls. Masonic order that prepares girls for eventual membership in the Eastern Star (another Masonic order).

Jabulon. A Masonic compound word for God derived from "Ja" (for Jehovah), joined with "Bel" or "Bul" (for Baal, the ancient Canaanite God), and "On" (for Osiris, the ancient Egyptian mystery god).

Jnana Marga. Hindu term referring to a particular means of enlightenment (the way of knowledge and meditation).

Karma Marga. Hindu term referring to a particular means of enlightenment (the way of action and ritual).

Karma. Refers to the "debt" a soul accumulates as a result of good or bad actions committed during one's life (or past lives). If one accumulates good karma, he or she will be reincarnated in a desirable state. If one accumulates bad karma, he or she will be reincarnated in a less desirable state.

Knorr, Nathan. Third president of the Watchtower Society.

Krishna. The "Supreme Personality of the Godhead," according to Hare Krishnas.

Krishnamurti, Jiddu. Indian man whom Annie Besant (who took over leadership of the Theosophical Society upon H. P. Blavatsky's death) promoted as being "Messianic Leader and Reincarnation of the World Teacher" (that is, the incarnation of the Christ for this age). After going along with Besant for a number of years, Krishnamurti eventually claimed it was all a big mistake.

LaVey, Anton. Satanist who founded the Church of Satan.

Law of Attraction. A mind science law that says that just as like attracts like, so our thoughts can attract the things they want or expect. Negative thoughts attract dismal circumstances; positive thoughts attract more desirable circumstances.

Maharishi Mahesh Yogi. Founder of Transcendental Meditation.

Maitreya. Some New Agers believe the "second coming of Christ" occurred in the early 1980s in the person of Maitreya. He is believed by some to be the leader of the "Spiritual Hierarchy of Masters."

Mass Incarnation. An incarnation of the Christ in all of humanity. Some New Age advocates say that this incarnation is presently taking place on a planetary scale.

Master Mason. Third degree in Blue Lodge Freemasonry.

Maya. Hindu term referring to mental illusion.

Medium. Refers to an occultist through whom disembodied spirits communicate.

MEST. Scientology term referring to matter, energy, space, and time. The physical universe.

Metaphysics. Branch of philosophy that focuses on the ultimate nature of reality.

Modalism. A view that understands the Father, Son, and Holy Spirit as modes of manifestation of the one God. This view denies the doctrine of the Trinity (three persons in one God).

Moksha. Hindu term referring to liberation from the continual cycle of rebirths.

Monism. Metaphysical theory that sees all of reality as a unified whole. Everything in the universe is seen as being composed of the same substance.

Moon, Reverend Sun Myung. Founder and leader of the Unification Church.

Moroni. Angel who appeared to Joseph Smith and informed him where the Book of Mormon gold plates were.

Mortality. A term used by Mormons in reference to the belief that following spirit existence in premortality, one takes on human flesh in order to undergo physical trials on earth.

New Age Seminars. Business seminars that typically teach attendees: (1) You are your own God; (2) You can create your own reality; and (3) You have unlimited potential.

New Thought. A term that surfaced as a way of describing the metaphysical groups that emerged from the philosophy of Phineas Parkhurst Quimby.

New World Translation. Jehovah's Witness translation that has "restored" the divine name *Jehovah* 237 times in the biblical text from Matthew to Revelation.

Notovitch, Nicholas. Primary proponent of the idea that Jesus went to India as a child. Influential among New Agers.

Order of DeMolay. Masonic order named after Jacques DeMolay.

Order of the Eastern Star. Masonic order open to women who are related to Masons.

Other Sheep. Jehovah's Witnesses who are not members of the Anointed Class. These look forward, not to a heavenly destiny, but to living eternally on an earthly paradise.

Overshadowing. New Age term referring to the occult means used by a "Master" to inhabit a human disciple's body. Some New Agers believe that Maitreya (the Christ) manifested himself through his disciple, Jesus, by overshadowing.

Panentheism. The view that all is in God and God is in all.

Postmortality. A term used by Mormons in reference to one's return to the spirit world following physical death.

Prabhupada. Founder of International Society for Krishna Consciousness (ISKCON) (Hare Krishnas).

Preclear. Scientology term referring to one who is not yet "clear" (of engrams).

Premortality. A term used by Mormons in reference to the idea that humans lived as spirits in a preexistent state before being born on earth.

Prince Hall Freemasonry. An all-black Masonic lodge founded by Prince Hall, a black man.

Quimby, Phineas Parkhurst. As the father of the mind sciences espoused the metaphysical idea that the source of physical healing lies in the mind. He was convinced that physical diseases were caused by wrong thinking or false beliefs. These false beliefs are allegedly remedied by "the Christ" (an impersonal mind-principle).

Reactive Mind. Scientology term referring to the place where painful memories are stored. It is said to be active below the level of consciousness.

Russell, Charles Taze. Founder and first president of the Jehovah's Witnesses.

Rutherford, Judge. Second president of the Watchtower Society.

Samsara. Hindu term referring to the continual cycle of death and rebirth. It literally means "to wander across."

Sankirtana. Krishna devotional method that involves chanting while dancing with the accompaniment of small brass hand-cymbals.

Science and Health with Key to the Scriptures. Primary Scriptures of the Christian Science church, written by Mary Baker Eddy.

Scientology. Religion founded by L. Ron Hubbard. An applied religious philosophy that focuses largely on removing engrams from one's reactive mind via auditing sessions.

Scottish Rite. Branch of Freemasonry one can pursue after completing the Blue Lodge. Confers 29 degrees.

Shriner. Masonic member of *Ancient Arabic Order of the Nobles of the Mystic Shrine.*

Smith, Joseph. Founder and first prophet of the Mormon church.

Spiritual Hierarchy of Masters. This is a group of formerly historical persons who have finished their earthly evolutions and voluntarily help lesser-evolved human beings to reach their level.

Sutras. Collections of aphorisms (or proverbs) that highlight the teachings of the Vedas and Upanishads (Indian scriptures).

Syncretism. The attempt to syncretize (combine or unify) different religious systems.

Telestial Kingdom. The third kingdom of glory (in Mormonism) where the great majority of people go. It is reserved for those who have been carnal and sinful throughout life.

Terrestrial Kingdom. The second kingdom of glory that is reserved for non-Mormons who live moral lives as well as for "less than valiant" Mormons.

Theosophy. Occult school of thought founded by H. P. Blavatsky. The term literally means "divine wisdom."

Thetan. Scientology term derived from the Greek letter *theta*, which Scientologists say is a symbol for thought or spirit. A *thetan* is said to be an immortal spirit.

Transmission Groups. Enlightened groups made up of "attuned" individuals who allegedly "transmit" spiritual energy to the minds of other people in order to raise the Christ consciousness of the planet.

Tritheism. Belief that the Father, Son, and Holy Spirit are distinct gods.

Unitarians. A theological movement that rose to prominence during the sixteenth-century reformation and spread from Europe to England and then on to America. They are called "Unitarians" because they deny the doctrine of the Trinity.

United Church of Religious Science. An offshoot of New Thought that espouses the idea that every person is a potential Christ. Jesus was merely a way-shower who embodied the impersonal Christ.

Unity School of Christianity. An offshoot of New Thought that espouses the idea that salvation is attained by "at-one-ment" with God—a reuniting of human consciousness with God consciousness. Jesus achieved such at-one-ment; all people can.

Universalists. Theological movement of individuals who believe in the salvation of all human beings and strongly oppose the doctrine of hell and eternal punishment.

Values Clarification. A New Age curriculum that teaches that values are not to be imposed from without (such as from Scripture or from parents) but must be subjectively discovered from within. The underlying assumption is that there are no absolute truths or values.

Vedas. The oldest and most sacred scriptures of Hinduism. (The word *veda* means "sacred knowledge.")

Word of Wisdom. Refers to the Mormon prohibition of coffee, tea, alcohol, or tobacco.

York Rite. Branch of Freemasonry named after York, England, the seat of the Ancient York Grand Lodge. One can join this after completing the Blue Lodge.

Young, Brigham. Senior Mormon apostle at the time of Joseph Smith's death. He quickly assumed leadership and became the second president and prophet of the Mormon church.

Zoroastrians. Followers of Zoroastrianism, a Persian religion founded by Zoroaster (c. 628 B.C.–c. 551 B.C.). Zoroastrianism is an ethical religion that espouses an ongoing struggle between two primal spirits: Ahura Mazda (the good spirit) and Angra Mainyu (the evil spirit). Mazda will ultimately triumph.

BIBLIOGRAPHY

CULTS IN GENERAL

Abanes, Richard. *Cults, New Religious Movements, and Your Family.* Wheaton, IL: Crossway Books, 1998.

Ankerberg, John, and John Weldon. *Cult Watch: What You Need to Know about Spiritual Deception.* Eugene, OR: Harvest House, 1991.

_____. *Encyclopedia of Cults and New Religions.* Eugene, OR: Harvest House, 1999.

Beliefs of Other Kinds: A Guide to Interfaith Witness in the United States. Atlanta: Baptist Home Mission Board, 1984.

Boa, Kenneth. *Cults, World Religions, and You.* Wheaton, IL: Victor Books, 1979.

The Compact Guide to World Religions. Edited by Dean C. Halverson. Minneapolis: Bethany House, 1996.

Contend for the Faith. Edited by Eric Pement. Chicago: Evangelical Ministries to New Religions, 1992.

Ellwood, Robert S. *Religions and Spiritual Groups in Modern America.* Englewood Cliffs, NJ: Prentice-Hall, 1973.

Enroth, Ronald. *A Guide to Cults and New Religions.* Downers Grove, IL: InterVarsity Press, 1983.

_____. *The Lure of the Cults.* Downers Grove, IL: InterVarsity Press, 1987.

Gerstner, John H. *The Theology of the Major Sects.* Grand Rapids: Baker, 1980.

Gomes, Alan. *Unmasking the Cults.* Zondervan Guide to Cults and Religious Movements. Grand Rapids: Zondervan, 1995.

Hoekema, Anthony A. *The Four Major Cults.* Grand Rapids: Eerdmans, 1978.

Martin, Paul. *Cult-Proofing Your Kids.* Grand Rapids: Zondervan, 1993.

Martin, Walter. *The Kingdom of the Cults.* Edited by Hank Hanegraaff. Minneapolis: Bethany House, 1999.

_____. *Martin Speaks Out on the Cults.* Ventura, CA: Regal Books, 1983.

_____. *The New Cults.* Ventura, CA: Regal Books, 1980.

_____. *The Rise of the Cults.* Ventura, CA: Regal Books, 1983.

Mather, George A., and Larry A. Nichols. *Dictionary of Cults, Sects, Religions and the Occult.* Grand Rapids: Zondervan, 1993.

McDowell, Josh, and Don Stewart. *Understanding the Cults.* San Bernardino, CA: Here's Life Publishers, 1983.

_____. *Handbook of Today's Religions.* San Bernardino: Here's Life Publishers, 1989.

Pement, Eric, ed. *Contend for the Faith: Collected Papers of the Rockford Conference on Discernment and Evangelism.* Chicago: Evangelical Ministries to New Religions, 1992.

Robertson, Irvine. *What the Cults Believe.* Chicago: Moody Press, 1983.

Saliba, John A. *Understanding New Religious Movements.* Grand Rapids: Eerdmans, 1995.

Sire, James. *Scripture Twisting.* Downers Grove, IL: InterVarsity Press, 1980.

Swenson, Orville. *The Perilous Path of Cultism.* Caronport, Saskatchewan, Canada: Briercrest Books, 1987.

Tucker, Ruth. *Another Gospel: Alternative Religions and the New Age Movement.* Grand Rapids: Zondervan, 1989.

THE BAHA'I FAITH

Abdul-Baha. *Foundations of World Unity.* Wilmette, IL: Baha'i Publishing Trust, 1945.

Baha'i World Faith: Selected Writings of Baha'u'llah and Abdul-Baha. Wilmette, IL: Baha'i Publishing Trust, 1956.

The Baha'is: A Profile of the Baha'i Faith and Its Worldwide Community. Oakham, Leicestershire: Baha'i Publishing Trust of the United Kingdom, 1994.

Baha'u'llah. *Epistle to the Son of the Wolf.* Translated by Shoghi Effendi. Wilmette, IL: Baha'i Publishing Trust, 1988.

Dahl, Arthur. *Baha'i: World Faith for Modern Man.* New York: Harper & Row, 1971.

The Divine Art of Living: Selections from the Baha'i Writings. Wilmette, IL: Baha'i Publishing Trust, 1944.

Effendi, Shoghi. *The Faith of Baha'u'llah.* Wilmette, IL: Baha'i Publishing Trust, 1959.

Esslemont, J. E. *Baha'u'llah and the New Era: An Introduction to the Baha'i Faith.* Wilmette, IL: Baha'i Publishing Trust, 1980.

Gleanings from the Writings of Baha'u'llah. Translated by Shoghi Effendi. Wilmette, IL: Baha'i Publishing Trust, 1969.

Hatcher, William S., and J. Douglas Martin. *The Baha'i Faith: The Emerging Global Religion.* San Francisco: Harper & Row, 1984.

The Proclamation of Baha'u'llah to the Kings and Leaders of the World. Haifa: Baha'i World Center, 1978.

Sabet, Huschmand. *The Heavens Are Cleft Asunder.* Oxford: George Ronald, 1975.

Schaefer, Udo. *The Light Shineth in Darkness.* Oxford: George Ronald, 1973.

Selections from the Writings of the Bab. Haifa: Baha'i World Center, 1978.

Simple, Peter. *Baha'i Teachings, Light for All Regions.* Wilmette, IL: Baha'i Publishing Trust, 1970.

Townshend, George. *Christ and Baha'u'llah.* London: George Ronald, 1957.

Uniting the Human Family: The Baha'i Faith. Regional Baha'i Council of the Southern States, 1998.

THE CHURCH OF JESUS CHRIST OF LATTER-DAY SAINTS

Benson, Ezra Taft. *The Teachings of Ezra Taft Benson.* Salt Lake City: Bookcraft, 1988.

Book of Mormon. Salt Lake City: The Church of Jesus Christ of Latter-day Saints, 1990.

Cannon, George Q. *Gospel Truth.* Salt Lake City: Deseret, 1987.

Cares, Mark J. *Speaking the Truth in Love to Mormons.* Milwaukee: Northwestern Publishing House, 1993.

Doctrine and Covenants. Salt Lake City: The Church of Jesus Christ of Latter-day Saints, 1990.

BIBLIOGRAPHY

Encyclopedia of Mormonism. Edited by Daniel H. Ludlow. New York: Macmillan, 1992.

Farkas, John R., and David A. Reed. *Mormonism: Changes, Contradictions, and Errors.* Grand Rapids: Baker, forthcoming.

Gorden, Kurt Van. *Mormonism.* Zondervan Guide to Cults and Religious Movements. Grand Rapids: Zondervan, 1995.

Gospel Principles. Salt Lake City: Church of Jesus Christ of Latter-day Saints, 1981.

Hinckley, Gordon B. *Truth Restored.* Salt Lake City: Corporation of the President of The Church of Jesus Christ of Latter-day Saints, 1979.

Hunter, Milton R. *The Gospel through the Ages.* Salt Lake City: Deseret, 1958.

Kimball, Spencer W. *The Miracle of Forgiveness.* Salt Lake City: Bookcraft, 1969.

_____. *Repentance Brings Forgiveness.* Salt Lake City: The Church of Jesus Christ of Latter-day Saints, 1984.

Martin, Walter. *The Maze of Mormonism.* Ventura, CA: Regal, 1978.

Matthews, Robert J. *A Sure Foundation.* Salt Lake City: Deseret, 1988.

McConkie, Bruce. *Mormon Doctrine.* 2d ed. Salt Lake City: Bookcraft, 1977.

McKay, David O. *Gospel Ideals.* Salt Lake City: Improvement Era, 1953.

McKeever, Bill, and Eric Johnson. *Questions to Ask Your Mormon Friend.* Minneapolis: Bethany House, 1994.

Ostling, Richard N., and Joan K. Ostling. *Mormon America: The Power and the Promise.* San Francisco: HarperSanFrancisco, 1999.

Petersen, Mark E. *As Translated Correctly.* Salt Lake City: Deseret, 1966.

Pratt, Orson. *The Seer.* Washington, DC: n.p., 1853–54.

Reed, David A., and John R. Farkas. *Mormons Answered Verse by Verse.* Grand Rapids: Baker, 1993.

Richards, LeGrand. *A Marvelous Work and a Wonder.* Salt Lake City: Deseret, 1958.

Smith, Joseph, Jr. *History of the Church of Jesus Christ of Latter-day Saints.* Salt Lake City: Deseret, 1973.

Smith, Joseph Fielding. *Doctrines of Salvation.* Salt Lake City: Bookcraft, 1975.

_____. *Man: His Origin and Destiny.* Salt Lake City: n.p., 1954.

_____. *The Way to Perfection.* Salt Lake City: Deseret, n.d.

Talmage, James E. *The Articles of Faith.* Salt Lake City: The Church of Jesus Christ of Latter-day Saints, 1982.

_____. *The Great Apostasy.* Salt Lake City: Deseret, 1975.

_____. *Joseph Smith—Seeker after Truth.* Salt Lake City: Deseret, 1951.

Tanner, Jerald, and Sandra Tanner. *The Changing World of Mormonism.* Chicago: Moody Press, 1981.

_____. *Major Problems of Mormonism.* Salt Lake City: Utah Lighthouse Ministry, 1989.

White, James. *Is the Mormon My Brother?* Minneapolis: Bethany House, 1997.

Widtsoe, John A. *Evidences and Reconciliations.* Salt Lake City: Bookcraft, 1987.

Young, Brigham. *Journal of Discourses.* London: Latter-day Saints' Book Depot, 1854–56.

HINDU-BASED CULTS

Ankerberg, John and John Weldon. *The Facts on Hinduism in America.* Eugene, OR: Harvest House, 1991.

Bloomfield, Harold H., Michael Peter Cain, Dennis T. Jaffe, and Robert B. Kory. *TM: Discovering Inner Energy and Overcoming Distress.* Boston: G. K. Hall, 1975.

Brooke, Tal. *Riders of the Cosmic Circuit.* Batavia, NY: Lion, 1986.

Daner, Francine. *The American Children of Krsna.* New York: Holt, Rinehart & Winston, 1976.

Dasgupta, Surendranath. *A History of Indian Philosophy.* 5 vols. Cambridge: Cambridge University Press, 1981.

Forem, Jack. *Transcendental Meditation: Maharishi Mahesh Yogi and the Science of Creative Intelligence.* New York: E. Dutton, 1973.

Hemingway, Patricia Drake. *The Transcendental Meditation Primer.* New York: David McKay, 1975.

Hopfe, Lewis M. *Religions of the World.* New York: Macmillan, 1991.

Hopkins, Thomas J. *The Religious Life of Man: The Hindu Religious Tradition.* Belmont, CA: Wadsworth, 1971.

Mangalwadi, Vishal. *The World of Gurus: A Critical Look at the Philosophies of India's Influential Gurus and Mystics.* Chicago: Cornerstone, 1992.

Noss, John B. *Man's Religions.* New York: Macmillan, 1974.

Prabhupada, A. C. Bhaktivedanta Swami. *Bhagavad-Gita: As It Is.* New York: Bhaktivedanta Book Trust, 1972.

Radhakrishnan, Sarvepalli, and Charles A. Moore, eds. *A Sourcebook in Indian Philosophy.* Princeton: Princeton University Press, 1957.

Russell, Peter. *TM: The Technique.* Boston: Routledge & Kegan Paul, 1976.

Yamamoto, J. Isamu. *Hinduism, TM & Hare Krishna.* Zondervan Guide to Cults and Religious Movements. Grand Rapids: Zondervan, 1996.

Yogananda, Paramahansa. *Autobiography of a Yogi.* Los Angeles: Self-Realization Fellowship, 1972.

Yogi. *Meditations of Maharishi Mahesh Yogi.* New York: Bantam, 1968.

Zaehner, R. C. *Hinduism.* London: Oxford University Press, 1966.

THE JEHOVAH'S WITNESSES

Aid to Bible Understanding. Brooklyn: Watchtower Bible and Tract Society, 1971.

Blood, Medicine, and the Law of God. Brooklyn: Watchtower Bible and Tract Society, 1961.

Bowman, Robert M. *Jehovah's Witnesses.* Zondervan Guide to Cults and Religious Movements. Grand Rapids: Zondervan, 1995.

_____. *Why You Should Believe in the Trinity.* Grand Rapids: Baker, 1989.

Chretien, Leonard, and Marjorie Chretien. *Witnesses of Jehovah.* Eugene, OR: Harvest House, 1988.

The Finished Mystery. Brooklyn: Watchtower Bible and Tract Society, 1917.

The Harp of God. Brooklyn: Watchtower Bible and Tract Society, 1921.

Jehovah's Witnesses and the Question of Blood. Brooklyn: Watchtower Bible and Tract Society, 1977.

Jehovah's Witnesses: The Organization Behind the Name. Brooklyn: Watchtower Bible and Tract Society, 1990.

Jehovah's Witnesses: Proclaimers of God's Kingdom. Brooklyn: Watchtower Bible and Tract Society, 1993.

"The Kingdom Is at Hand." Brooklyn: Watchtower Bible and Tract Society, 1944.

"Let God Be True." Brooklyn: Watchtower Bible and Tract Society, 1946.

"Let Your Name Be Sanctified." Brooklyn: Watchtower Bible and Tract Society, 1961.

Life Everlasting—In Freedom of the Sons of God. Brooklyn: Watchtower Bible and Tract Society, 1966.

Life—How Did It Get Here? Brooklyn: Watchtower Bible and Tract Society, 1985.

Magnani, Duane. *The Watchtower Files.* Minneapolis: Bethany House, 1985.

Making Your Family Life Happy. Brooklyn: Watchtower Bible and Tract Society, 1978.

Mankind's Search for God. Brooklyn: Watchtower Bible and Tract Society, 1990.

Man's Salvation Out of World Distress At Hand! Brooklyn: Watchtower Bible and Tract Society, 1975.

Martin, Walter, and Norman Klann. *Jehovah of the Watchtower.* Minneapolis: Bethany House, 1974.

The New World. Brooklyn: Watchtower Bible and Tract Society, 1942.

1980 Yearbook of Jehovah's Witnesses. Brooklyn: Watchtower Bible and Tract Society, 1980.

Paradise Restored to Mankind—By Theocracy. Brooklyn: Watchtower Bible and Tract Society, 1972.

Qualified to Be Ministers. Brooklyn: Watchtower Bible and Tract Society, 1955.

Reasoning from the Scriptures. Brooklyn: Watchtower Bible and Tract Society, 1989.

Reconciliation. Brooklyn: Watchtower Bible and Tract Society, 1928.

Reed, David A. *Blood on the Altar.* Amherst, NY: Prometheus Books, 1996.

_____. *How to Rescue Your Loved One from the Watchtower.* Grand Rapids: Baker, 1989.

_____. *Jehovah's Witness Literature.* Grand Rapids: Baker, 1993.

_____. *Jehovah's Witnesses Answered Verse by Verse.* Grand Rapids: Baker, 1992.

Rhodes, Ron. *Reasoning from the Scriptures with the Jehovah's Witnesses.* Eugene, OR: Harvest House, 1993.

Riches. Brooklyn: Watchtower Bible and Tract Society, 1936.

Should You Believe in the Trinity? Brooklyn: Watchtower Bible and Tract Society, 1989.

Studies in the Scriptures. Brooklyn: Watchtower Bible and Tract Society, 1897.

"Things in Which It Is Impossible for God to Lie." Brooklyn: Watchtower Bible and Tract Society, 1965.

You Can Live Forever in Paradise on Earth. Brooklyn: Watchtower Bible and Tract Society, 1982.

"Your Will Be Done on Earth." Brooklyn: Watchtower Bible and Tract Society, 1958.

MASONIC LODGE

Acker, J. W. *Strange Altars: A Scriptural Appraisal of the Lodge.* St. Louis: Concordia, 1959.

Allen, Raymond Lee. *Tennessee Craftsmen or Masonic Textbook.* Nashville: Tennessee Board of Custodians Members, 1963.

Ankerberg, John, and John Weldon. *The Secret Teachings of the Masonic Lodge.* Chicago: Moody Press, 1990.

Baigent, Michael, and Richard Leigh. *The Temple and the Lodge.* New York: Arcade, 1989.

Blanchard, J. *Scottish Rite Masonry Illustrated: The Complete Ritual of the Ancient and Accepted Scottish Rite.* Chicago: Charles T. Powner, 1979.

Cerza, Alphonse. *Let There Be Light: A Study in Anti-Masonry.* Silver Spring, MD: The Masonic Service Association, 1983.

Coil, Henry Wilson. *A Comprehensive View of Freemasonry.* Richmond, VA: Macoy, 1973.

Hammond, William E. *What Masonry Means.* New York: Macoy, 1952.

Harris, Jack. *Freemasonry: The Invisible Cult in Our Midst.* Chattanooga: Global, 1983.

Holy Bible (Temple Illustrated Edition). Nashville: Holman, 1968.

Liturgy of the Ancient and Accepted Scottish Rite of Freemasonry for the Southern Jurisdiction of the United States. Washington, DC: The Supreme Council, 1982.

Pike, Albert. *Morals and Dogma of the Ancient and Accepted Scottish Rite of Freemasonry*. Charleston, SC: The Supreme Council, 1906.

Robinson, John J. *Born in Blood: The Lost Secrets of Freemasonry*. New York: M. Evans, 1989.

Thorn, Richard. *The Boy Who Cried Wolf: The Book That Breaks Masonic Silence*. New York: M. Evans, 1994.

THE MIND SCIENCES

Armor, Reginald C. *Ernest Holmes, the Man*. Los Angeles: Science of Mind Publications, 1977.

Bach, Marcus. *The Story of Unity*. Englewood Cliffs, NJ: Prentice-Hall, 1962.

Cady, H. Emilie. *God a Present Help*. Lees Summit, MO: Unity Books, 1938.

_____. *Lessons in Truth*. Kansas City: Unity School of Christianity, 1941.

Cather, Willa, and Georgine Milmine. *The Life of Mary Baker G. Eddy and the History of Christian Science*. Lincoln: University of Nebraska Press, 1993.

Dresser, Horatio W. *A History of the New Thought Movement*. London: George G. Harrap, n.d.

Eddy, Mary Baker. *The First Church of Christ Scientist and Miscellany*. Boston: Trustees under the Will of Mary Baker G. Eddy, 1913.

_____. *Miscellaneous Writings*. Boston: Trustees under the Will of Mary Baker G. Eddy, 1896.

_____. *Rudimental Divine Science*. Boston: Trustees under the Will of Mary Baker G. Eddy, 1908.

_____. *Science and Health with Key to the Scriptures*. Boston: Trustees under the Will of Mary Baker G. Eddy, 1908.

_____. *Unity of Good*. Boston: Trustees under the Will of Mary Baker G. Eddy, 1908.

Ehrenborg, Todd. *Mind Sciences*. Zondervan Guide to Cults and Religious Movements. Grand Rapids: Zondervan, 1995.

Fillmore, Charles. *The Adventure Called Unity*. Unity Village, MO: Unity School of Christianity, n.d.

_____. *Christian Healing*. Unity Village, MO: Unity School of Christianity, 1954.

_____. *Jesus Christ Heals*. Lees Summit, MO: Unity School of Christianity, 1947.

_____. *The Metaphysical Dictionary*. Lees Summit, MO: Unity School of Christianity, 1962.

_____. *What Practical Christianity Stands For*. Lees Summit, MO: Unity School of Christianity, 1947.

Freeman, James D. *The Story of Unity*. Lees Summit, MO: Unity School of Christianity, 1954.

_____. *What Is Unity?* Lees Summit, MO: Unity School of Christianity, n.d.

Gottschalk, Stephen. *The Emergence of Christian Science in American Religious Life*. Berkeley: University of California Press, 1973.

Holmes, Ernest. *How to Use the Science of Mind*. New York: Dodd, Mead, 1950.

_____. *Keys to Wisdom*. Los Angeles: Science of Mind Publications, 1977.

_____. *The Philosophy of Jesus . . . for the World Today*. Los Angeles: Science of Mind Publications, n.d.

_____. *The Science of Mind*. New York: Dodd, Mead, 1938.

_____. *What Religious Science Teaches*. Los Angeles: Science of Mind Publications, 1975.

Holmes, Ernest, and Alberta Smith. *Questions and Answers on the Science of Mind*. New York: Dodd, Mead, 1953.

Holmes, Ernest, and Fenwicke Holmes. *The Voice Celestial.* Los Angeles: Science of Mind Publications, 1979.

Holmes, Fenwicke L. *Ernest Holmes: His Life and Times.* New York: Dodd, Mead, 1970.

Meyer, Louis E. *Reincarnation.* Unity Village, MO: Unity School of Christianity, 1976.

The Quimby Manuscripts. Edited by Horatio W. Dresser. New Hyde Park, NY: University Books, 1961.

Reid, James. *Ernest Holmes: The First Religious Scientist.* Los Angeles: Science of the Mind Publications, n.d.

Trine, Ralph Waldo. *In Tune with the Infinite.* New York: Thomas Y. Crowell, 1897.

Unity Statement of Faith. Lees Summit, MO: Unity School of Christianity, n.d.

Warch, William A. *The New Thought Christian.* Anaheim, CA: Christian Living, 1977.

THE NEW AGE MOVEMENT

Bailey, Alice. *The Externalisation of the Hierarchy.* New York: Lucis, 1957.

_____. *The Reappearance of the Christ.* New York: Lucis, 1948.

Ballard, G. W., and Donald Ballard. *Purpose of the Ascended Master's "I AM" Activity.* Chicago: Saint Germain Press, 1942.

Robert Basil. *Not Necessarily the New Age.* Buffalo: Prometheus, 1988.

Besant, Annie. *Esoteric Christianity.* Wheaton, IL: Theosophical Publishing House, 1970.

Blavatsky, H. P. *The Key to Theosophy.* Pasadena, CA: Theosophical University Press, 1972.

_____. *The Theosophical Glossary.* Los Angeles: The Theosophical Company, 1966.

Capra, Fritjof. *The Tao of Physics.* Boulder, CO: Shambhala, 1975.

_____. *The Turning Point.* New York: Simon & Schuster, 1982.

Chandler, Russell. *Understanding the New Age.* Dallas: Word, 1991.

Creme, Benjamin. *The Reappearance of the Christ and the Masters of Wisdom.* Los Angeles: Tara Center, 1980.

Dowling, Levi. *The Aquarian Gospel of Jesus the Christ.* Santa Monica: DeVorss., 1907.

Ferguson, Marilyn. *The Aquarian Conspiracy.* Los Angeles: J. P. Tarcher, 1980.

Fox, Matthew. *The Coming of the Cosmic Christ.* San Francisco: Harper & Row, 1989.

Gershon, David, and Gail Straub. *Empowerment: The Art of Creating Your Life as You Want It.* New York: Delta, 1989.

Groothuis, Douglas. *Unmasking the New Age.* Downers Grove, IL: InterVarsity Press, 1986.

Hanegraaff, Wouter J. *New Age Religion and Western Culture: Esotericism in the Mirror of Secular Thought.* Albany: State University of New York Press, 1998.

Karen Hoyt, ed. *The New Age Rage.* Old Tappan, NJ: Revell, 1987.

Keys, Donald. *Earth at Omega: Passage to Planetization.* Boston: Branden, 1982.

Klimo, Jon. *Channeling.* Los Angeles: Jeremy Tarcher, 1987.

Leadbeater, W. *A Textbook of Theosophy.* Adyar, Madras, India: Theosophical Publishing House, 1954.

Lipnack, Jessica, and Jeffrey Stamps. *Networking.* Garden City, NY: Doubleday, 1982.

MacLaine, Shirley. *Dancing in the Light.* New York: Bantam, 1985.

_____. *It's All in the Playing.* New York: Bantam, 1987.

Mangalwadi, Vishal. *When the New Age Gets Old.* Downers Grove, IL: InterVarsity Press, 1993.

Matrisciana, Caryl. *Gods of the New Age.* Eugene, OR: Harvest House, 1985.

Miller, Elliot. *A Crash Course on the New Age Movement.* Grand Rapids: Baker, 1989.

Muller, Robert. *New Genesis: Shaping a Global Spirituality.* New York: Doubleday, 1982.

Prophet, Elizabeth Clare. *The Lost Years of Jesus.* Livingston, MT: Summit University Press, 1987.

Rhodes, Ron. *The Counterfeit Christ of the New Age Movement.* Grand Rapids: Baker, 1990.

Ryerson, Kevin, and Stephanie Harolde. *Spirit Communication.* New York: Bantam, 1989.

Satin, Mark. *New Age Politics.* New York: Dell, 1978.

Simon, Sidney B., Leland W. Howe, and Howard Kirschenbaum. *Values Clarification.* New York: Hart, 1978.

Spangler, David. *Emergence: The Rebirth of the Sacred.* New York: Dell, 1984.

Starhawk, Miriam. *The Spiral Dance.* San Francisco: Harper & Row, 1979.

Steiner, Rudolf. *Knowledge of the Higher Worlds and Its Attainment.* Spring Valley, NY: Anthroposophic Press, 1947.

Talbot, Michael. *Mysticism and the New Physics.* New York: Bantam, 1982.

Thomas, I. D. E. *The Omega Conspiracy.* Oklahoma City: Hearthstone, 1986.

Thompson, William Irwin. *Passages about Earth.* New York: Harper Colophon Books, 1981.

Trevelyan, George. *Operation Redemption.* Walpole, NH: Stillpoint, 1981.

_____. *A Vision of the Aquarian Age.* Walpole, NH: Stillpoint, 1984.

Wilbur, Ken. *Up from Eden.* Boulder, CO: Shambhala, 1983.

Zukav, Gary. *The Dancing Wu Li Masters.* New York: Morrow, 1979.

ONENESS PENTECOSTALISM

Beisner, E. Calvin. *"Jesus Only" Churches.* Zondervan Guide to Cults and Religious Movements. Grand Rapids: Zondervan, 1998.

Bernard, David K. *In the Name of Jesus.* Hazelwood, MO: Word Aflame, 1992.

_____. *The Oneness of God.* Hazelwood, MO: Word Aflame, 1983.

Boyd, Gregory A. *Oneness Pentecostals and the Trinity.* Grand Rapids: Baker, 1992.

Clanton, Charles, Crawford Coon, and Paul Dugas. *Bible Doctrines: Foundation of the Church.* Hazelwood, MO: Word Aflame, 1984.

Graves, Robert Brent. *The God of Two Testaments.* N.p. 1977.

Magee, Gordon. *Is Jesus in the Godhead or Is the Godhead in Jesus?* Hazelwood, MO: Word Aflame, 1988.

Paterson, John. *God in Christ Jesus.* Hazelwood, MO: Word Aflame, 1966.

Reeves, Kenneth V. *The Godhead.* St. Louis: Trio, 1999.

Reynolds, Ralph V. *Truth Shall Triumph: A Study of Pentecostal Doctrines.* Hazelwood, MO: Word Aflame, 1965.

Rugger, Gary C. *Oneness, Trinity, Arian: Which Does Scripture Teach?* Bakersfield, CA: Sarah's Christian Books, 1988.

SATANISM

Barton, Blanche. *The Secret Life of a Satanist: The Authorized Biography of Anton LaVey.* Los Angeles: Feral House, 1990.

Carlson, Shawn, and Gerald Larue, eds. *Satanism in America.* El Cerrito, CA: Gaia, 1989.

Dickason, C. Fred. *Demon Possession and the Christian.* Westchester, IL: Crossway Books, 1987.

Drury, Neville, and Gregory Tillett. *The Occult Sourcebook.* London: Routledge and Kegan Paul, 1978.

Encyclopedia of Occultism and Parapsychology. Detroit: Gale Research, 1982.

Gross, Edward N. *Miracles, Demons, and Spiritual Warfare.* Grand Rapids: Baker, 1990.

Kahaner, Larry. *Cults That Kill: Probing the Underworld of Occult Crime*. New York: Warner Books, 1988.

Koch, Kurt. *Between Christ and Satan*. Grand Rapids: Kregel, 1962.

_____. *Satan's Devices*. Grand Rapids: Kregel, 1978.

LaVey, Anton Szandor. *The Satanic Bible*. New York: Avon, 1969.

_____. *The Satanic Rituals*. New York: Avon, 1972.

Lyons, Arthur. *Satan Wants You*. New York: Mysterious Press, 1988.

Moriarty, Anthony. *The Psychology of Adolescent Satanism*. Westport, CT: Praeger, 1992.

Parker, Russ. *Battling the Occult*. Downers Grove, IL: InterVarsity Press, 1990.

Passantino, Bob, and Gretchen Passantino. *Satanism*. Zondervan Guide to Cults and Religious Movements. Grand Rapids: Zondervan, 1996.

Russell, Jeffrey Burton. *The Devil: Perceptions of Evil from Antiquity to Primitive Christianity*. Ithaca, NY: Cornell University Press, 1977.

_____. *Mephistopheles: The Devil in the Modern World*. Ithaca, NY: Cornell University Press, 1986.

_____. *Satan: The Early Christian Tradition*. Ithaca, NY: Cornell University Press, 1981.

Wolfe, Burton H. *The Devil's Avenger*. New York: Pyramid, 1974.

SCIENTOLOGY

Corydon, Brent, and L. Ron Hubbard Jr. *L. Ron Hubbard: Messiah or Madman?* Secaucus, NJ: Lyle Stuart, 1987.

Hubbard, L. Ron. *The Creation of Human Ability*. Los Angeles: The Publications Organization Worldwide, 1968.

_____. *Dianetics: The Modern Science of Mental Health*. Los Angeles: Bridge Publications, 1992.

_____. *The Problems of Work*. Los Angeles: The Church of Scientology of California, 1977.

_____. *Science of Survival*. Los Angeles: American Hill Organization, 1974.

_____. *Scientology: The Fundamentals of Thought*. Los Angeles: The Church of Scientology of California, 1975.

_____. *Scientology: A New Slant on Life*. Los Angeles: The Church of Scientology of California, 1972.

_____. *What Is Scientology?* Los Angeles: Bridge Publications, 1992.

Malko, George. *Scientology: The Now Religion*. New York: Delacorte, 1970.

Scientology: Theology and Practice of a Contemporary Religion. Los Angeles: Bridge Publications, 1998.

Scientology: A World Religion Emerges in the Space Age. Church of Scientology Information Service, Department of Archives, 1974.

THE UNIFICATION CHURCH

Barker, Eileen. *The Making of a Moonie: Choice or Brainwashing?* Cambridge: Basil Blackwell, 1984.

Divine Principle. New York: The Holy Spirit Association for the Unification of World Christianity, 1973.

Durst, Mose. *To Bigotry, No Sanction*. Chicago: Regnery Gateway, 1984.

Hong, Nansook. *In the Shadow of the Moons: My Life in the Reverend Sun Myung Moon's Family*. Boston: Little, Brown, 1998.

Sontag, Frederic. *Sun Myung Moon and the Unification Church*. Nashville: Abingdon, 1977.

Stoner, Carroll, and Jo Anne Parke. *All God's Children: The Cult Experience—Salvation or Slavery?* Radnor, PA: Chilton, 1977.

Yamamoto, J. Isamu. *Unification Church.* Zondervan Guide to Cults and Religious Movements. Grand Rapids: Zondervan, 1995.

UNITARIAN UNIVERSALISM

Adams, James Luther. *An Examined Faith: Social Context and Religious Commitment.* Boston: Beacon, 1991.

Beach, George Kimmich. *Catechism with an Open Mind.* Boston: Skinner House, 1995.

Beliefs of Other Kinds: A Guide to Interfaith Witness in the United States. Atlanta: Baptist Home Mission Board, 1984.

Brown, Arthur W. *William Ellery Channing.* New York: Grosset & Dunlap, 1961.

Buehrens, John A., and Forrest Church. *A Chosen Faith: An Introduction to Unitarian Universalism.* Boston: Beacon, 1998.

Cassara, Ernest. *Universalism in America.* Boston: Beacon, 1971.

Elgin, Kathleen. *The Unitarians.* New York: David McKay, 1971.

Gomes, Alan. *Unitarian Universalism.* Zondervan Guide to Cults and Religious Movements. Grand Rapids: Zondervan, 1996.

Mendelsohn, Jack. *Why I Am a Unitarian Universalist.* Boston: Beacon, 1969.

Robinson, David. *The Unitarians and the Universalists.* Westport, CT: Greenwood, 1985.

Sias, John. *100 Questions that Non-Members Ask about Unitarian Universalism.* Nashua, NH: Transition, 1999.

The Unitarian Universalist Pocket Guide. Edited by John A. Buehrens. Boston: Skinner House, 1999.

Wakefield, Dan. *How Do We Know When It's God? A Spiritual Memoir.* Thorndike, MN: G. K. Hall, 1999.

Wright, Conrad. *Three Prophets of Religious Liberalism: Channing, Emerson, Park.* Boston: Beacon, 1978.

Scripture Index

SUBJECT INDEX

144,000, 91–92

A

Abanes, Richard, 157, 167, 300, 303, 309
aberration, Scientology, 159
Adam and Eve's fall, good thing, Mormon church, 64
Adams, Don, 86
Adams, John Quincy, 231
afterlife, conscious, contrary to Jehovah's Witnesses, 102
afterlife, two possible destinies, 75
agency, Mormonism, 66
Akashic Record, 24
Alley, Kirstie, 157
Amano, Yutaka, 149
America, religious landscape, 14
analytical mind, Scientology, 158–59
Ancient Arabic Order of the Nobles of the Mystic Shrine, 280
Ankerberg, John, 243
Anointed Class, Jehovah's Witnesses, 91
Anthony, Susan B., 231
anthropological argument for God's existence, 248
Anthroposophy, 136
Aquino, Michael, 299, 303
Arcane School, 137
Archer, Anne, 157
arguments for God's existence, 247–48
Asimov, Isaac, 42
astrology, 138
atman, Hinduism, 172
auditor, Scientology, 160
authoritarian leadership of cults, 31
automatic writing, 24

B

Bab, The, Baha'i Faith, 214
Back to Godhead, Hare Krishna, 179
Baha, Abdul, 213, 216, 218, 221

Baha'u'llah, 24, 26, 30, 214–16, 218–225, 228–29
Baha'i beliefs, 217–22
    compatibility with Christianity claimed, 219
    God unknowable, 219
    heaven and hell not literal, 222
    humans imperfect, not fallen, 221
    Jesus one of many manifestations, 220
    obedience to law critical, 221
    progressive revelation through manifestations of God, 217
Baha'i beliefs challenged, 223–29
    Baha'i Jesus, counterfeit Jesus, 225–28
    Bible does not predict Baha'u'llah, 224
    hollow claims of tolerance, 224
    it is a religion, 223
    uniting world religions futile, 223
Baha'i Faith, 212–29
    contrasted with Christianity, 223
    defined, 213
    emphasis on unity, 213
    grew out of Islam, 214
    history of, 214–17
    Mizra Ali Muhammad, 214
    spiritual assemblies, 216
Baha'u'llah, 215
Bailey, Alice, 137
Ballard, Guy and Edna, 137
Ballou, Hosea, 235
baptism for the dead, Mormonism, 66
baptism necessary, Oneness Pentecostalism, 261
Barbour, Nelson, 79
Barclay, William, 94
Barker, Eileen, 192, 196
Bateman, Merrill, 52
Beckwith, Frank, 223
Bell, Alexander Graham, 231
Benson, Ezra Taft, 58

lack of archaeological support for Book of
Mormon, 69
only two possible destinies in afterlife, 75
plagiarisms in Book of Mormon, 68
restored church claim, 67
Moroni, 54
Moyers, Bill, 48–49
Mozart, Wolfgang Amadeus, 277
Muhammad, Mizra Ali, 214
Muktananda, Swami, 170
Müller, F. Max, 149
Murray, John, 235

N

Nation of Islam, 22
neopaganism, 133–34
New Age in schools, 40, 48
New Age beliefs, 139–45
　Bible interpreted esoterically, 139
　God is all there is, 141
　Jesus attained Christhood, 141
　man is divine, 142
　many sources of revelation, 140
　salvation is enlightenment, 143
　second coming of Christ, 144
　sin is ignorance, 143
　spirit channeling, 140
New Age beliefs challenged, 145–52
　esotericism unreliable, 145
　Jesus didn't train under gurus, 149
　Jesus Himself will come again, 152
　man has a sin problem, 151
　man is not God, 150
　pantheism untenable, 148
　Spiritism condemned, 148
　world religions different, 147
New Age movement, 129–52
　growth of, 129–30
　not a cult, 130
　not merely Hinduism, 133
　spirituality, 133–34
　unity and diversity, 130
　worldview, 130
New Age movement, characteristics of, 131–33
　belief in coming utopia, 133
　deification of humanity, 132
　eclecticism, 131
　ecological orientation, 132
　monism, 131

networking, 132
not a conspiracy, 133
pantheism, 132
religious syncretism, 131
transformation, 132
New Age movement, roots of, 134–39
　ancient Gnosticism, 134
　counterculture of 1960s, 138
　inadequacy of secular humanism, 138
　influx of Eastern ideas, 139
　nineteenth-century Transcendentalism, 135
　revival of the occult, 135–38
New Age occultism, 135–38
　Anthroposophy, 136
　Arcane School, 137
　Astrology, 138
　I AM movement, 137
　Spiritism, 137
　Theosophical Society, 135
New Age school curriculum, 40
New Age seminars, 47
New Testament, warnings of false prophets, 19
New Thought movement, 105–7
New World Translation, 83, 94
Newton, Henry Ford, 278
Nichols, Larry, 288, 307
Nietzsche, Friedrich, 155
Nightingale, Florence, 231
Nixon, Richard, 193
Notovitch, Nicholas, 142

O

Oneness Pentecostalism, 253–75
　contrasted with Christianity, 263
　history, 253–55
　Oneness Pentecostalism beliefs, 255–62
　baptism necessary, 261
　Father and Son defined, 257
　holiness standard, 261
　Jesus is Father, Son, and Holy Spirit, 255
　salvation not easy, 260
　Son of God, 257–58
　speaking in tongues, 261
　Trinity false doctrine, 259
Oneness Pentecostalism beliefs challenged,
262–74

We want to hear from you. Please send your comments about this book to us in care of the address below. Thank you.

GRAND RAPIDS, MICHIGAN 49530

w w w . z o n d e r v a n . c o m